SELECTED WRITINGS
ON VISUAL ARTS AND CULTURE

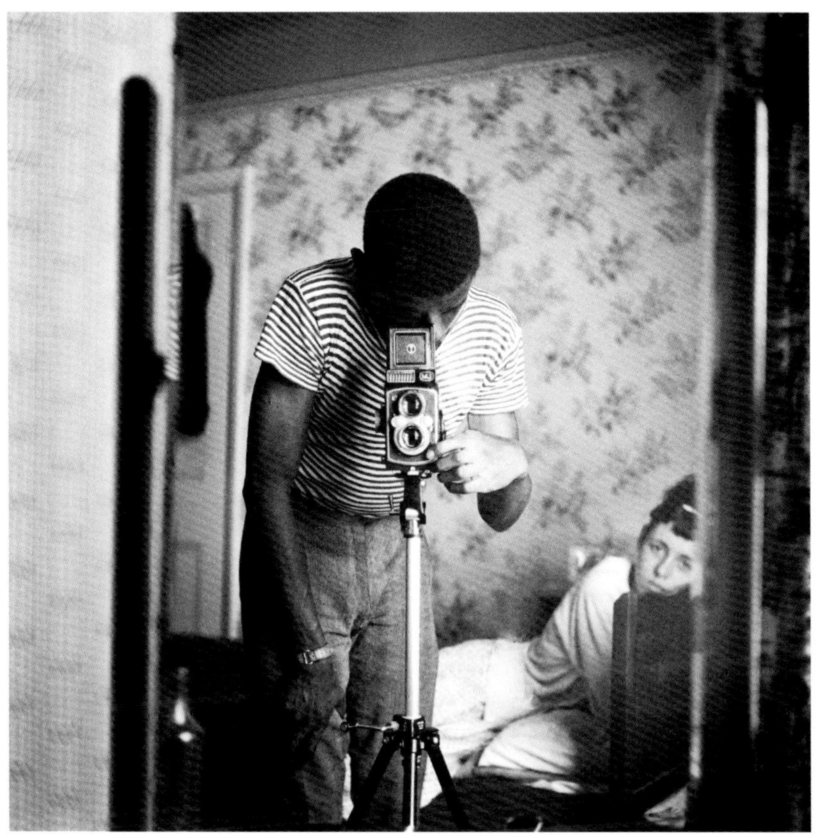

Armet Francis, *Self-portrait in Mirror*, 1964. © Armet Francis. All rights reserved,

SELECTED WRITINGS
ON VISUAL ARTS AND CULTURE

Detour to the Imaginary

Edited by **Gilane Tawadros**

Stuart Hall

DUKE UNIVERSITY PRESS | DURHAM AND LONDON | 2024

Library of Congress Cataloging-in-Publication Data

Names: Hall, Stuart, 1932–2014, author. | Tawadros, Gilane, editor. |
Hall, Stuart, 1932–2014. Works. Selections. 2016.

Title: Selected writings on visual arts and culture : detour to the
imaginary / Stuart Hall ; edited by Gilane Tawadros.

Description: Durham : Duke University Press, 2024. | Series:
Stuart Hall: Selected writings | Includes bibliographical references
and index.

Identifiers: LCCN 2023045063 (print)

LCCN 2023045064 (ebook)

ISBN 9781478030331 (paperback)

ISBN 9781478026105 (hardcover)

ISBN 9781478059332 (ebook)

Subjects: LCSH: Hall, Stuart, 1932–2014—Political and social views. |
Arts and society. | Art criticism. | Civilization, Western—20th century. |
Civilization, Modern—20th century. | BISAC: ART / Criticism &
Theory | SOCIAL SCIENCE / Black Studies (Global) | LCGFT: Essays. |
Lectures. | Reviews.

Classification: LCC NX180.S6 H35 2024 (print) | LCC NX180.S6
(ebook) | DDC 306.4/7—dc23/eng/20240316

LC record available at https://lccn.loc.gov/2023045063

LC ebook record available at https://lccn.loc.gov/2023045064

Supported by a Publications Grant from the Paul Mellon
Centre for Studies in British Art.

CONTENTS

ACKNOWLEDGMENTS

My warmest thanks to Catherine Hall for inviting me to edit this volume and for her immense support throughout the process. I am also deeply indebted to Bill Schwarz for his valuable editorial support and encouragement. I am very grateful to Ken Wissoker at Duke University Press for his warm engagement at every stage and to his team, who have been so helpful at different phases of the project. Given the subject of this anthology, it was critical to produce a richly illustrated book, which would not have been possible without the generous support of the Paul Mellon Centre and the Estate of Stuart Hall, as well as the very many artists who gave us permission to reproduce their works. Thanks are also due to Adjaye Associates, the Aga Khan Trust for Culture, Autograph, DACS, the Estate of Ronald Moody, Tate, and Victoria Miro Gallery. Homi Bhabha, Paul Gilroy, Sarat Maharaj, and Mark Sealy generously gave permission for their collaborative texts and conversations with Stuart to be included in the anthology. My special and heartfelt appreciation go to David A. Bailey, whose journey thinking-with/in the image with Stuart began many years before mine and whose photography, curatorial, and critical work laid the ground for Autograph, the Institute of International Visual Arts (INIVA), and much else. I miss Stuart hugely, but I feel privileged to have had the opportunity to work closely with him at INIVA for more than a decade and afterward to count him as a friend. I learned so much from him and am still learning.

Detour to the Imaginary:
Stuart Hall's Writings on the Visual Arts and Culture

Questions of Culture: "Absolutely Deadly Political Questions"

In 1994 Stuart Hall participated in the "Race Matters" conference at Princeton and delivered a paper that was subsequently published as the essay "Subjects in History: Making Diasporic Identities."[1] The essay acts as a prologue to this volume, which is the first publication to assemble a significant number of Stuart Hall's writings on the visual arts and culture. At the conference, Hall urged his audience to give up their commitment to the "politically pure" and embrace the fact that "cultural politics and questions of culture, of discourse and of metaphor are absolutely deadly political questions." To those wedded to the idea of political purity, he insisted that questions of culture were not secondary to questions of economic and political change but "*constitutive* of them" (my emphasis).

Hall's writings on politics, race, and media are familiar to readers, but less well-known are his writings on the visual arts and culture. Yet Hall's engagement with the visual arts can be traced back to his commentaries in the late 1950s in the journal *Universities and Left Review*. However, it was in the 1980s when his involvement with the visual arts, and in particular with a younger generation of black British artists, filmmakers, and thinkers, deepened, blossoming into a series of close collaborations and friendships. It was also manifest in his significant practical commitment to two

arts organizations that he chaired throughout the 1990s and the 2000s—
Autograph (Association of Black Photographers) and INIVA (Institute of
International Visual Arts).

This anthology brings together essays, lectures, reviews, catalog texts, and
conversations that provide an insight into why Hall immersed himself in
what he described as the "radically different" intellectual and aesthetic space
of the visual imaginary. The project with which he identified was one in
which diaspora artists, filmmakers, and thinkers in Britain sought to "challenge certain erasures and marginalizations inscribed in the visual field itself, to try to establish a certain 'presence' within the frame, to come 'into
the field of vision.'"[2]

The Turn to the Visual Arts

Why then are Stuart Hall's writings on the visual arts and culture so little
known among readers and scholars who are otherwise intimately familiar
with his other writings? As early as 1958, Hall made an impassioned defense
of Picasso and modern avant-garde art more generally ("a tradition of revolution, experiment, and change") in the face of the stultifying and regressive
conservatism of the Royal Academy of Arts at the time, embodied in the figure of Sir Charles Wheeler, then president of the Royal Academy, and in his
desire to uphold the "strictest standards of traditional teaching."[3] Yet Hall's
relationship to the visual arts continues to be viewed as a less significant,
post-academic activity that occupied the twilight years following his retirement as professor of sociology at the Open University in 1997. This volume
seeks to counter the view that Hall's involvement with the visual arts was peripheral to his other intellectual and political preoccupations and positions.
Hall's engagement with the visual was a critical part of his intellectual armor,
in many instances framing his insights into race and politics.

As the founding editor of the *New Left Review* (NLR) (formed from the
merger of *Universities and Left Review* and *The New Reasoner*, two journals
that emerged out of the political repercussions of Suez and Hungary in 1956),
Hall set out the agenda for the new journal in his introduction to the first
issue in 1960. The journal, said Hall, would embrace a broader conception
of politics, one that would include discussions of "the cinema or teen-age
culture," alongside traditional political and economic analyses, because the
former was "directly relevant to the imaginative resistances of people who
have to live within capitalism—the growing points of social discontent, the

projections of deeply-felt needs."[4] Hall's deep understanding of the work of the Italian Marxist Antonio Gramsci and what he describes as the "Copernican revolution in Marxist approaches to the state" that Gramsci initiated also sowed the seeds in his own thinking about the profound significance of culture and cultural formations to political discourse. Hall embraced in his work (and in his collaborative intellectual inquiries at the Centre for Contemporary Cultural Studies in Birmingham) the constitutive role that culture plays as the arena in which breaks and discontinuities with the status quo are played out, making it possible to "identify the turning points, when relations are qualitatively restructured and transformed—the moments of transition."[5]

Writing about the Partisan, a coffeehouse and center for the New Left in Soho established in 1958 by the young historian Raphael Samuel, a coeditor with Hall of the *Universities and Left Review* (*ULR*), Mike Berlin has recently drawn attention to the importance attached to the visual arts by the New Left, and he emphasizes its adoption of emerging forms and radical practices in graphics, typography, and illustration as well as painting and photography. The Italian graphic artist Germano Facetti was employed to design the covers of the *ULR* and *NLR*, and the publicity materials for the Partisan were produced by the acclaimed letterpress printer Desmond Jeffrey. The walls of the Partisan coffeehouse "were regularly decorated with paintings, prints and drawings by artists and a *ULR* Artists Group was formed by John Berger, Peter de Francia, Peter Peri and Michael Ayrton."[6] The photographer Roger Mayne, who documented working-class communities in North Kensington and London's emerging youth culture, also documented the young patrons of the Partisan and wrote for the *ULR* on the problems of realism in photojournalism.

The Partisan coffeehouse closed in 1963, and both Hall and Samuel moved on from the *New Left Review*. In the years that followed, Hall continued to write about the visual arts, particularly film and photography, and in the 1980s, he chaired the Commonwealth Photography Award, became a trustee of the Photographers' Gallery in London, and gave the keynote speech at the launch of Autograph (Association of Black Photographers) in 1988, later becoming chair of its board of trustees and chair of the board of INIVA (Institute of International Visual Arts), where I worked with Hall for more than a decade.

From the late 1970s, Hall began to see race as a prism through which to understand wider currents in British culture and society. In the 1980s, particularly, he came to recognize race and representation as a route through which to understand how race was constructed politically and culturally, and the ways in which a new generation of black artists and filmmakers were challenging these constructions and mapping new subjectivities and positions that held the potential for political and social change: "One of the most critical sites in this work is the intersection of racial, ethnic, gender and sexual difference; and in particular that of *the body* itself. The body is at one and the same time the 'container' of identity and subjectivity, the overdetermined point where differences collide, the epidermal surface on which racism etches its mark, and a ground of resistance from which alternative counter-narratives can be produced."[7] The problem of living with difference, argued Hall, was *the* problem of the twenty-first century: "If you are interested in a society which somehow learns, painfully, how to begin to learn to live with difference, to recognise the way it has constructed the other as the opposite of itself, you have to understand how the culture is working. In the arts things get said in ways in which they can't get said in any other domain."[8]

Hall's engagement with the visual arts, and more specifically with the black artists, thinkers, and organizations with which he became immersed, was his path to the revolutionary and experimental space of imagination where he identified the contours of a new conjuncture, a significant turning point in the discourse of race and nation that would give rise to profound insights about identity, difference, and globalization in the late twentieth century and early twenty-first century: "I'm interested in what people imagine, how they imagine, how they represent themselves, figurally, in the visual and literary field, how they position themselves in the narratives of self and society. And I am committed to the wider society having a greater access to these visions and dreams and nightmares and traumas and fears. So, the turn to the visual arts."[9]

Detour and Indirection

The subtitle of this book comes from a conversation between Stuart Hall and Bill Schwarz that took place at the Queen Elizabeth Hall in 2007 and that was subsequently published in *Soundings*. Asked by Schwarz whether, in this particular historical moment, the black visual arts in Britain represented a privileged way of looking at questions of race and diaspora, Hall explained: "If you want to learn more, or see how difference operates inside people's heads, you have to go to art, you have to go to culture—to where people imagine, where they fantasise, where they symbolise. You have to make the detour from the language of straight description to the language of the imaginary."[10]

The word *detour* draws from the lexicon of phrases and concepts from the Marxist philosopher Louis Althusser, which Hall deploys—"peppering so many of his writings and interviews," as Gregor McLennan notes in his introduction to Hall's writings on Marxism.[11] Here, however, the detour is not an Althusserian detour from experience and the concrete to abstraction but a movement away from the "language of straight description" to the more fluid and slippery "language of the imaginary." Hall was attracted to culture because, in his words, it constituted "the domain of indirection," which paradoxically provides direction: "As Shakespeare once said, 'By indirection find direction out.'" In order to enter the domain of culture, Hall argues, "we have to step back and go through the imaginary." Together with Shakespeare's "indirection," Hall uses the term *detour* to characterize his intentional rerouting away from the seeming "purity" of political and economic questions to the space of culture and the visual in order to *come back* with new insights and understandings regarding the "real" world of political and economic relations of power.

On different occasions, Hall sets out to distinguish between the space of the "real" and that of the "imaginary," locating the "mysterious place where art arises from experience, [which] is at the same time different from experience and reflects critically back on it." The world—real, historical, political—influences culture, but culture is not a mirror of the world. Looking back on black artistic practice in the 1980s in his essay "Assembling the 1980s: The Deluge—and After," Hall rejects a simplistic connection between politics and culture. Culture, he argues, doesn't exist in a vacuum, but politics cannot be understood outside of questions of representation:

> We are still not that far advanced in finding ways of thinking about the relationship between the [art]work and the world. We either make the connection too brutal and abrupt, destroying that necessary displacement in which the work of making art takes place. Or we protect the work from what Edward Said calls its necessary "worldliness," projecting it into either a pure political space where conviction—political will—is all, or into an inviolate aesthetic space, where only critics, curators, dealers, and connoisseurs are permitted to play. The problem is rather like that of thinking the relationship between the dream and its materials in waking life. We know there is a connection there. But we also know that the two continents cannot be lined up and their correspondences read off directly against one another.[12]

Race as a Prism

To understand how visual culture and the work of visual artists and film-makers operate as a critical part of Stuart Hall's intellectual tool kit, it is necessary to go back to the 1970s to consider how race and racial politics in Britain acted as the lens through which Hall was able to understand a profound shift in British politics at the end of the 1970s and early 1980s. In the 1970s, Hall was working as a professor at the Centre for Cultural Studies in Birmingham, where he and his colleagues carried out research into race, mugging, and the criminal justice system, which resulted in a book published in 1978 called *Policing the Crisis*. The book was produced in the context of a deepening political and social crisis in the 1970s in Britain and the rise of a new right-wing, free-market politics that was spearheaded by the Conservative politician Margaret Thatcher. The book is a forensic study into the different contributing factors that gave rise to the moral panic about mugging—crime statistics, media reporting, the courts, police attitudes toward young black men in Britain's cities—all of which contributed to this moral panic and provided the opportunity for the new Right in Britain to assert itself as the means by which order and authority could be restored.

It is important to emphasize that the deepening political and social crisis at that time was not all about race but that race *was* a recurring motif and that race and crime were at the center of what Thatcherism—Stuart Hall coined the phrase—could focus on as a way to try to roll back the social democratic consensus in Western Europe in the postwar period. By studying the rise of new Right politics and the increasing authoritarianism of the state through the lens of race, Hall was able to identify before many others how Margaret Thatcher's rise was not just a political victory for the new Right but—critically—that this marked a profound change in political culture as well as a shift to a new historical conjuncture. As Hall later wrote, Thatcherism was not simply a British manifestation; it was the beginning of globalization and a new stage in the global capitalist economy.

A Critical Decade

Six years before the "Race Matters" conference in Princeton, Hall had addressed the Black Film/British Cinema conference at the Institute of Contemporary Arts (ICA) in London, convened by Kobena Mercer, at which he drew attention to a profound shift in black cultural politics that signaled a wider transformation in the politics of race and nation in postwar Britain. The move from the relations of representation to the politics of representation itself, argued Hall, went beyond a simple strategy of reversal ("putting in place of the bad old essential white subject, the new essentially good black subject"), opening up "a continuous critical discourse about themes, about the forms of representation, the subjects of representation, above all, the regimes of representation" without guarantees. Critically, this involved a "recognition that 'black' is essentially a politically and culturally *constructed* category, which cannot be grounded in a set of fixed trans-cultural or transcendental racial categories and which therefore has no guarantees in Nature."[13] The shift away from an essentialist notion of blackness to an understanding that "black signifies a range of experiences" meant that the act of representation required more than the decentering of the subject but "actually exploring the kaleidoscopic conditions of blackness."[14]

Thinking about black British photography in the 1980s, Hall identified a struggle on two fronts: the first was the question of access to the means of representation ("the relationship of black photographers to the institutions, visibility and exclusion"), and the second was the question of what photographers did with the opportunities that came their way once the door had been opened. In the latter decades of his life, Hall was occupied in a sustained way with both questions: with the practical work of building new cultural institutions from the early 1990s onward—primarily Autograph and INIVA—that would provide access to black British artists and photographers, and, simultaneously, with the work of establishing "a wide, active dialogic community" that would be engaged in "interrogating, evaluating, reconstructing histories" and "putting back in place invisible discursive conditions which make new texts possible." This intellectual work, involving "scholarship, criticism and political and cultural interrogation," would be "part and parcel of a well-articulated theory and practice of black representation—doing it, writing about it, arguing about it, theorising it, writing its history and so on—it is all crucial work."[15]

In the 1980s Hall began to see in the struggle for representation by black artists, filmmakers, and writers questions that shaped the contours of the wider historical conjuncture: how was a generation of young, black British people primarily from Afro-Caribbean, African, and Asian backgrounds, who had been born and brought up in Britain, going to articulate their experiences and identities against the grain of fixed national and racial identifications? How were these "diasporic subjects" who were "the product of several histories, cultures, and narratives" and belonged to "several homes, most of them at least in part symbolic . . . to which there can be no return" going to construct new imaginaries which "cut across and interrupt the settled contours of race, *ethnos* and nation"?[16]

As Kobena Mercer points out, by turning his attention to the meaning of "black" as a subject position in the face of racial violence in all its forms, Hall identified the latent potency of a "transformational act of resignification" that could be the generative source of political rupture and social change.[17] Hall would later elaborate these questions in his important Du Bois Lectures at Harvard University in 1994. But it was in the late 1980s that he saw in the practice of black British artists and filmmakers a "new diasporic consciousness" that not only articulated unresolved conflicts and struggles in postwar British society but also gave rise to new ways of seeing and thinking differently, which offered up the possibility of social and political transformation.[18]

A Radically Different Intellectual and Aesthetic Space

A few years after the ICA Black Film/British Cinema conference in 1988, Stuart Hall became chair of Autograph (the Association of Black Photographers), and not long after, he became chair of INIVA (the Institute of International Visual Arts), two organizations with which he remained closely associated until the early 2000s and the establishment of Rivington Place, a new purpose-built building in East London designed by the architect David Adjaye to house both Autograph and INIVA (figs. I.1–I.3). In the intervening years, Hall's close friendships and collaborations with black artists, filmmakers, and curators, including David A. Bailey, Sonia Boyce, Mark Sealy, and myself, continued to grow, and key among those collaborations was the one with the artist Isaac Julien, which endured over a number of decades.

The first chapter of this book begins with a text Hall wrote for the publication *Isaac Julien: Riot*, an intellectual biography of the artist that was published in conjunction with an exhibition of Julien's *Ten Thousand Waves* at the Museum of Modern Art (MoMA) in New York in 2013–2014. In "Isaac Julien's Workshop," Hall recalls their thirty-year friendship, in which he was in conversation with Julien about his work and, occasionally, playing small walk-on roles in his films. Hall closes his essay by reflecting on the distinctive nature of the visual as a mode of thinking and the profound difference between the visual imaginary, as an aesthetic and intellectual thinking-and-making space, and Hall's own critical and analytical work. Just before his

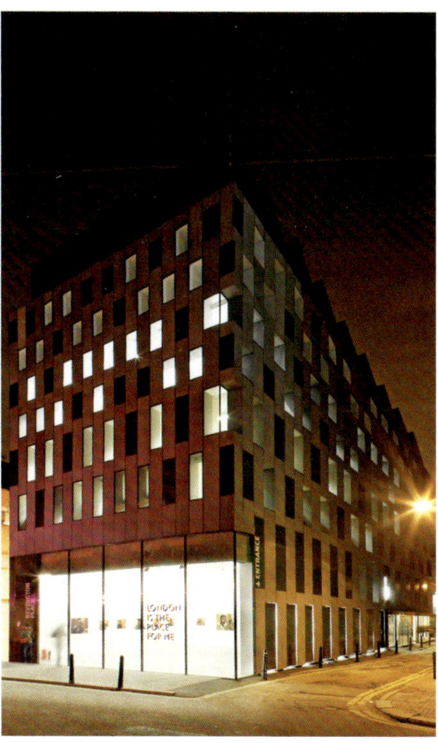

Figure I.1. Rivington Place, London, 2001. Exterior view. Courtesy of Adjaye Associates.

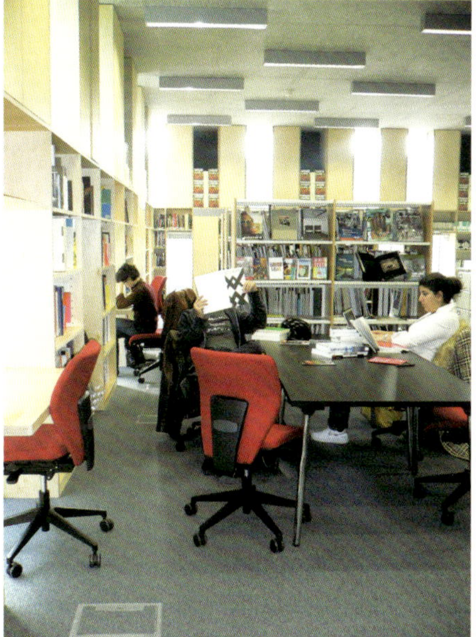

Figure I.2. Rivington Place, London, 2001. Stuart Hall Library at the Institute of International Visual Arts (INIVA). Courtesy of Adjaye Associates.

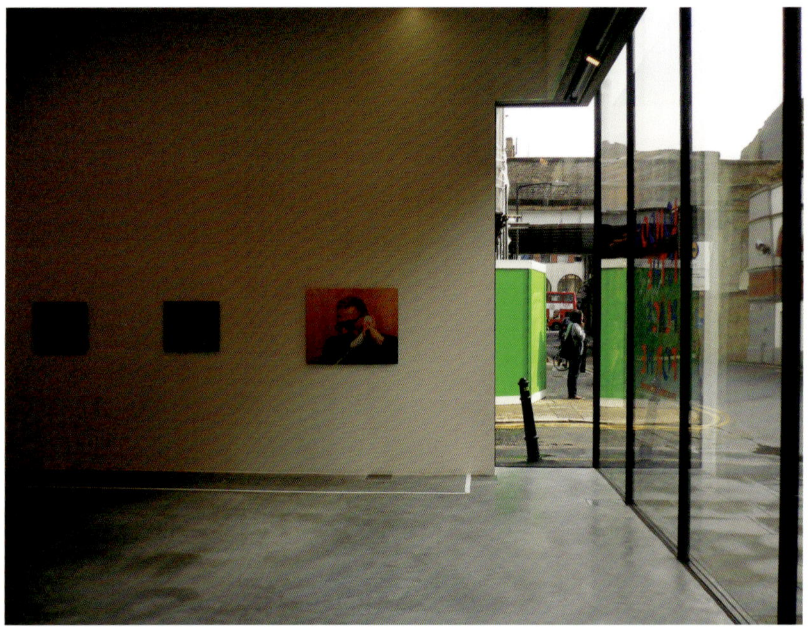

Figure I.3. Rivington Place, London, 2001. Main gallery space. Courtesy of Adjaye Associates.

death, both Stuart and his wife, the historian Catherine Hall, had been engaged in a series of conversations with Isaac Julien and his partner, Mark Nash, about a new work that Julien was researching on capitalism. The discussions revolved around "an effort to identify the distinctive characteristics of contemporary global capitalism," on the one hand, and on the other, "the problem of how to visualize an abstraction."[19] These conversations involved Stuart Hall more intimately than hitherto in Julien's creative and intellectual processes and the transformation of ideas into visual form:

> Confronted by another mode of thought made me acutely aware how radically different are the visual languages in which Isaac thinks and the critical, discursive, and analytic work I do. It made me reconsider, especially, the limits of the way I think. I think in a linear, sequential way, one idea provoking another. . . . Isaac is often thinking about the same problems, but his thought has entered a space or mode where ideas like mine, developing along what we may call a horizontal axis, immediately trigger or translate into an associative or analogical set of images, visual sequences, and narrative devices along a vertical axis, which obey a logic

of their own and are in no sense simply illustrative. This is the visual imaginary at work.[20]

Thinking-with/in the Image

Writing about a recent body of work by the artist Mitra Tabrizian that puts forward a pointed critique of the corporate world and its systems of representation (chapter 3, "The Way We Live Now"), Hall is at pains to emphasize that Tabrizian's works are not illustrations of ideas or concepts but are rather "visual concept-spaces" in which "ideas are worked through and 'realised' in a series of scenic tableaux, expanded and developed in another register—a kind of 'thinking-with/in the image.'"[21]

Stuart Hall's involvement with artists and art institutions brought him into the sphere of the visual, where he became intimately engaged with the process of "thinking-with/in the image," and this detour to the imaginary enabled him to circle back to pressing political questions: democracy, global capitalism, migration, diaspora, and difference. Throughout this volume, texts on individual artists and specific bodies of work are interweaved with reflections in which Hall steps back to survey pressing social and political issues, demonstrating his distinctive ability to combine multiple interpretative lenses, from the aesthetic to the institutional. As I witnessed at the board of trustees meetings that he chaired when I was director of INIVA, he moved effortlessly between practical conversations about the mechanics of institution building (finances, staffing, funders) and theoretical discussions about the organization's artistic and intellectual program.

In part I, "Thinking-with/in the Image," Hall's essay "Democracy, Globalization, and Difference," on the fate and future of democracy, is placed between texts in which he discusses specific bodies of work by the artists Isaac Julien and Mitra Tabrizian. Both artists were deploying visual language to interrogate contemporary global capitalism in very different ways: Julien through his films *Playtime* (2014) and *Kapital* (2013) and Tabrizian through her large photographic tableaux, such as *Silent Majority* (2001–2002) and *The Perfect Crime* (2003–2004). Hall's essay originated in a series of conferences, public debates, and film and video projects convened by Okwui Enwezor as part of the public inquiry that framed Documenta 11. As artistic director of this edition of the ambitious and extensive international contemporary art exhibition held in Kassel in Germany every five years, Enwezor programmed a series of five "Platforms," beginning in Vienna in

March 2001 and concluding in Kassel in September 2002. Hall participated in two of these platforms, which brought together interdisciplinary groups of artists, writers, theorists, philosophers, historians, activists, and others to radically rethink and enlarge the space of contemporary art. In his talk on Platform 1 ("Democracy Unrealized"), Hall maintained that democracy was "haunted by the ghost of its idea" and at the beginning of the twenty-first century faced "a radically new double demand," embodied in the presence of the stranger who staked a claim simultaneously for equality and social justice *and* for the recognition of difference. Julien and Tabrizian, in this perspective, are the "artist-strangers" interrogating democracy and calling out the "democratic deficit" *through* the visual.

The Creolizing Moment

Hall also contributed two papers to Documenta 11's Platform 3, held in St. Lucia in January 2002, which took as its overall title "*Créolité* and Creolization." Here we have been able to include only one of these papers, "*Créolité* and the Process of Creolization," which is in part III, "Fanon, Creolization, and Diaspora." Choosing between these two talks was not an easy decision. In the paper we present here, Hall explores the concepts of creole and creolization, recounting the time shortly after he arrived in Britain, when he immersed himself in the contending interpretations of the formation of post-enslaved cultures that had developed in Caribbean culture. He returned to "the African survival versus creolization debate" and began to fashion the analytic tools to "understand how the culture of Caribbean migrants in the new diaspora would evolve."[22] Hall described this as the "'creolizing' moment in Cultural Studies." It is difficult to overestimate how critical this "creolizing" turn was in shaping Hall's theoretical outlook, opening up critical insights about identity, diaspora and migration: "The perception arose that identity is not just 'being' but also 'becoming'—always continuing to emerge in response to different historical circumstances; formed in that place where vicissitudes of subjectivity (where the 'subject' as a subject-of-culture first emerges) is positioned by, and repositions itself in, the narratives and discourses of a culture and a history. This idea has been formative for my understanding of how the already 'creolized' migrants emerged as 'new subjects' under the new conditions of diaspora-formation."[23]

Hall's essay acts as the anchor for the two other texts in this part. The first, "The After-Life of Frantz Fanon," looks at the renewed interest of black artists in the Martiniquan psychiatrist and philosopher Frantz Fanon, in the context of the exhibition *Mirage: Enigmas of Race, Difference and Desire*, curated by David A. Bailey, which took place at the Institute of Contemporary Arts (ICA) in London in May 1995. The second, Hall's "Legacies of Anglo-Caribbean Culture: A Diasporic Perspective," first appeared in a major monograph on the nineteenth-century Jamaican artist Isaac Mendes Belisario in which Hall draws out the long *durée* by which diasporan artists today address slavery's afterlives. He goes on to map the work of several black British artists who undertook Belisario's diasporic journey in reverse, "returning to some of the thematic ground that his work occupied" and articulating the broken, decentered legacies of slavery, "ruptured by a turbulent history and the traumas of migration, and unsettled by the 'play' of nostalgia and desire that haunts every 'return,' real or symbolic."[24]

Diasporic Subjects

In the 1980s Stuart Hall began to write and speak about the visual arts with increasing regularity, addressing how these "new subjects" represented themselves through a variety of visual forms from photography and film, through to painting, installation, and sculpture. This anthology combines writings in a range of registers and voices, from the conversational to the academic. There are short-form writings on films—such as Isaac Julien's *Young Soul Rebels* (1991) and Julian Henriques's *Babymother* (1998)—which appeared in the British Film Institute's influential journal *Sight and Sound*. And alongside these I include his intervention "New Ethnicities," originally delivered at the seminal ICA conference, Black Film/British Cinema, and subsequently published in the ICA Documents series. All three of these texts appear in part II, "The New Politics of Representation," alongside his essay "Cultural Identity and Cinematic Representation," which was originally published in a volume on Caribbean cinema in which Hall characteristically strays away from talking about film per se to asking a question: who is the emergent new subject of "Caribbean cinema"? In seeking to answer this question, Hall concludes that cinema is not "a second-order mirror held up to reflect what already exists" but "a form of representation that is able to constitute us as new kinds of subjects and thereby enable us to discover who we are."

The anthology is organized thematically rather than chronologically to reflect the way in which Hall critically explores new territory in one essay and then returns, on later occasions, to similar terrain, honing and amplifying his arguments. A decade separates the essays "The Vertigo of Displacement: Shifts within Black Documentary Practices" (cowritten with David A. Bailey and published in "Critical Decade," a special edition of *Ten.8* devoted to black British photography), and "Preface to *Different*." These appear in part V, "Photography, Representation, and Black Identity."

The earliest text in this volume, "Reconstruction Work: Images of Post-war Black Settlement," was first published in 1984 in the photography journal *Ten.8*. Here, Hall returns to the "creolising moment," addressing the question of how his generation of West Indian migrants were captured through the prism of photography at the moment of their arrival in Britain. The essay works as a keynote for part VI, "Reconstruction Work: Histories, Archives, and Diaspora." It is followed by "The 'West Indian' Front Room," in which Hall deconstructs, object by object, the iconography of the Caribbean front room, reassembled as an installation by Michael McMillan, which Hall identifies as "a creative cultural act . . . of that doubly-inscribed, hybrid or creolised kind . . . a cumulative migrant space, the result of a movement between two places, two cultures." Moving from the intimacy of the archive of black vernacular culture to the blind spots of race in the official culture of the archive and the museum, the essays "Constituting an Archive" and "Whose Heritage? Unsettling 'The Heritage,' Reimagining the Post-nation" engage with the absences and elisions of the dominant institutions of the art world that have persistently ignored the black British presence, resisting its imprint on the construction of Britishness. Here is Stuart Hall at the coal face of institution building, moving between the aesthetic and institutional, the theoretical and the practical. Making artworks, creating new archives, curating exhibitions, writing new art histories, reimagining the museum: all these activities are part of the "critical work" required to unsettle and disturb the grain of official culture and established museum historiography.

In the essays "Modernity and Its Others: Three 'Moments' in the Post-war History of the Black Diaspora" (part VI) and "Assembling the 1980s: The Deluge—and After" (part IV, "Assembling the 1980s"), Hall takes on the mantle of the art historian, but eschewing the lofty, progressive logic of traditional art history in favor of a narrative of black diaspora visual arts in postwar Britain in which "the artwork itself appears as a constitutive element in the fabric of a wider world of ideas, movements, events, while at the same time offering us a privileged vantage point on that world."[25] In assembling the 1980s through the frame of postwar black visual arts in Britain, Hall was simultaneously mapping the journey leading to "a profound 'conjunctural shift'" in the late twentieth century, a significant rupture in the global order of things. This loosely assembled "movement" in black artistic practice was, Hall writes, "driven by the struggles of peoples, marginalized in relation to the world system, to resist exclusion, reverse the historical gaze, come into visibility, and open up a 'third space' . . . in cultural representation. It . . . belongs to that uneven, contradictory, and bitterly contested transformation of cultural life now in progress across the globe, which attempts to de-centre Western models and open a broader, more transcultural and 'translative' perspective on cultural practice and production."[26]

The Offshore, Postcolonial, Diasporic Imaginary

In recent years, museums in Europe and the United States have been seeking to redress the blind spots that relegated so many artists to the margins of the official histories of modernism. Challenging these omissions was key to the political project of INIVA, with which Hall was so energetically and intimately involved for more than a decade. Together with Autograph, it frequently provided the institutional context where he drew attention to the racist and colonial legacies that continued to frame the exclusionary outlook of contemporary art institutions (see part VII, "Museums, Modernity, and Difference"). "The history of modernism," wrote Hall, "has been written as a set of triumphal practices, located in the West. In reality the world is absolutely littered by modernities and by practising artists, who never regarded modernism as the secure possession of the West." Writing some years later in his memoir, *Familiar Stranger*, Hall made explicit the political imperative for contesting official narratives of modernism and modernity: "The idea of modernity has had to be recast, not as a pure disinterested fact but as an exercise in what Foucault, borrowing from Nietzsche, calls 'the will to power.'" By challenging the established accounts of modernism and modernity, it was possible to articulate alternative relations of power that did not relegate the global majority to the margins of history and knowledge.[27]

In the final part of the volume, "Dreaming in Afro," the selected essays return Hall to the subject of Africa, "not Africa recollected in nostalgia, or site of redemptive return," but Chris Ofili's reimagined Africa, "not remembered but dreamt in its translated 'Afro' idiom." Here, says Hall, "the imaginary at work is irredeemably 'off-shore', post-colonial, diasporic." In 2003 Hall was involved in two projects at the Venice Biennale: Chris Ofili's project with David Adjaye for the British Pavilion, for which Hall wrote the essay "Chris Ofili: Dreaming in

Afro," and my exhibition of African and African diaspora artists, *Fault Lines: Contemporary African Art and Shifting Landscapes*, to which he contributed the essay "Maps of Emergency: Fault Lines and Tectonic Plates," where, once again, he challenged simplistic conceptions of Africa as a uniform, undifferentiated and static geographical and historical space. He sought here to assess individual artworks in relation to how each "speaks out of a specific historical conjuncture, is engaged in a labour of remapping . . . [and is taking] a new sighting on Africa's present 'state(s) of emergency.'"

In the later chapters, Stuart Hall repeatedly locates visual art practice as one of the key sites of contention and resistance in late capitalism, where one kind of globalization, from above, is being contested "in an as yet unequal struggle" by another kind of globalization, from below. The "radically different" intellectual and aesthetic space of the imaginary became a crucial site for Hall's theoretical deconstruction of the logics of late capitalist globalization. In the work of at least two generations of black British artists and filmmakers with whom he was deeply engaged, Hall discerned the contours of an emergent historical and political conjuncture that reflected the struggle between two opposing forces, as yet unresolved, which would shape the "culture wars" of the new phase of globalization: "In the cultural field as in others, what counts is 'the balance of forces.' And those processes of resistance, though they do not add up to a single, solid 'block' but have a matrix and network character, do reflect themselves in the unexpected rise of new forms, in the proliferation of differences and the deployment of new artistic languages, as well as in the contestations which occur around lived popular culture. These are the 'culture wars' of the new globalisation and they are every bit as intense and distinctive as occurred in the first phase of globalisation."[28] Just as he had anticipated the political configuration that he christened "Thatcherism" through the prism of race, Stuart Hall anticipated the significance of the "culture wars" in late capitalism through the lens of black British artistic practice. The struggle remains as yet unresolved.

NOTES

1 See Wahneema Lubiano, ed., *The House That Race Built: Black Americans, U.S. Terrain* (New York: Pantheon, 1997), 289–300.

2 Stuart Hall, "Legacies of Anglo-Caribbean Culture," this volume.

3 Stuart Hall, "Big Sir and the Oranges and Lemons," *Universities and Left Review* 4 (Summer 1958): 79.

4 Stuart Hall, "Introducing *nlr*," *New Left Review* 1 (January–February 1960): 1–3.

5 Stuart Hall, "Popular Culture and the State," in *The Anthropology of the State: A Reader*, ed. Aradhana Sharma and Akhil Gupta (Oxford: Blackwell, 2006), 361.

6 Mike Berlin, *The Partisan Coffee House 1958–1963* (London: Four Corners Gallery, 2017), 14–15.

7 Stuart Hall and Mark Sealy, *Different* (London: Phaidon, 2001), 38.

8 Stuart Hall, "Living with Difference: Stuart Hall in Conversation with Bill Schwarz," *Soundings* 37 (2007): 153.

9 Hall, "Living with Difference," 154.

10 Hall, "Living with Difference," 152.

11 Gregor McLennan, "Editor's Introduction," in *Stuart Hall: Selected Writings on Marxism* (Durham, NC: Duke University Press, 2021), 3.

12 Stuart Hall, "Assembling the 1980s: The Deluge—and After," this volume.

13 Stuart Hall, "New Ethnicities," this volume.

14 David A. Bailey and Stuart Hall, "The Vertigo of Displacement: Shifts within Black Documentary Practices," this volume.

15 Bailey and Hall, "Vertigo of Displacement."

16 Stuart Hall, *The Fateful Triangle: Race, Ethnicity, Nation*, ed. Kobena Mercer (Cambridge, MA: Harvard University Press, 2017), 172.

17 Kobena Mercer, "Introduction," in *Fateful Triangle*, 18.

18 Mercer, "Introduction."

19 Stuart Hall, "Isaac Julien's Workshop," in *Isaac Julien: Riot* (New York: Museum of Modern Art, 2013), 226.

20 Hall, "Isaac Julien's Workshop," 229.

21 Stuart Hall, "New Ethnicities," this volume.

22 Stuart Hall, "Creolization, Diaspora, and Hybridity in the Context of Globalization," in *Créolité and Creolization: Documenta 11, Platform 3,* ed. Okwui Enwezor et al. (Ostfildem-Ruit: Hatje Cantz, 2003), 187–88.

23 Hall, "Creolization, Diaspora, and Hybridity," 188.

24 Stuart Hall, "Legacies of Anglo-Caribbean Culture: A Diasporic Perspective," this volume.

25 Hall, "Assembling the 1980s."

26 Hall, "Assembling the 1980s."

27 Stuart Hall, "Museums of Modern Art and the End of History," this volume; Stuart Hall, with Bill Schwarz, *Familiar Stranger* (London: Allen Lane, 2017), 124.

28 Hall, "Creolization, Diaspora, and Hybridity," 198.

Subjects in History: Making Diasporic Identities

I am the only participant from another part of the "black diaspora," and, as a consequence, what we in England know as the "burden of representation" lies particularly heavy on my shoulders. As a consequence of that burden, it seems to me incumbent in some ways to try to add to an ongoing discussion; my function, it seems to me, is partly to bring to bear on the discussion a perspective that adds a transnational, global, "diasporic dimension" to what is inevitably U.S. terrain. I'm going to do so, in part, by referring to a number of points that have already arisen in the debate simply to bring to bear on them some experiences, some similar and parallel lines of approach and political work elsewhere in the "black Atlantic."

I don't want to get into details, into particular aspects of ideological analysis, or cultural production, although I'm going to draw some examples from cultural production. Instead, I want to outline something more general; I want to express some views about the place of cultural politics in the present racial conjuncture, about how it is shifting and changing, and about the problems thrown up in our attempts to theorize and define adequate strategies for dealing with the place of cultural politics. That is what is required by the moment the conference itself addressed, and to do so I want to return to that conference's "electric opening," which I'll never forget, not to rerun the West-Steinberg conversation,[1] but partly to explain the reason for my own brief intervention in that debate in order to spell out the grounds on which I made it. To those of you who weren't there, I simply said, "Please remember that questions of culture are not superstructural to the problems of economic and political change; they are constitutive of them!"

What does it mean to take seriously, in our present conjuncture, the thought that cultural politics and questions of culture, of discourse, and of metaphor are absolutely deadly political questions? That is my purpose. I want to persuade you that that is so. And that we ought to sort of preach on this occasion, no, not only to give up the bad habits of smoking and drinking and whoring and gambling, but to give up certain forms of political essentialism and the way in which it makes you sleep well at night.

There are two basic reasons at this point why I wanted to suggest to you why questions of culture and representation, of cultural productions, and of aesthetics, politics, and power are of absolute centrality. There are many other reasons, but I can't deal with them now. I want to deal with two particular reasons because they are central to how we need to conceptualize the question of race itself. You see, if indeed, as we mouth the mantra, race is indeed a sociohistorical concept, not a transhistorical discourse grounded in biology, then it must function not through the truth of the "biological referent" but as a discursive logic. That is to say, as a logic in which, of course, the biological trace still functions even when it's silent, but now, not as the truth, but as the guarantor of the truth. That is a question of discursive power. Not a question of what is true but what is *made* to be true. Such is the way in which racial discourses operate. To use a familiar Foucault phrase, it is a "regime of truth." I want to insist that its logic is discursive in this sense, that racial discourses produce, mark and fix the infinite differences and diversities of human beings through a rigid binary coding. That logic establishes a chain of correspondences both between the physical and the cultural, between intellectual and cognitive characteristics; it gives legibility to a social system in which it operates; it allows us to decipher different signifiers from the racial fixing of the signifier "race"; and through that reading it organizes, regulates, and gives meaning to social practices through the distribution of symbolic and material resources between different groups and the establishment of racial hierarchy.

To say that is to say that race is a discourse, that it operates through the movement of the signifiers, and yet, at the same time, to say that the whole historical organization of human social practices through the binary coding of race is dependent on the meanings that it is able to give to the relationships of power and representation between human societies.

The second reason culture is absolutely central to our concerns, in my view, is that it constitutes the terrain for producing identity, for producing the constitution of social subjects. It is one of the social conditions of existence for setting subjects in place in historical relations, setting them in place, in position. They are unable to speak, or to act in one way or another, until they have been positioned by the work that culture does, and in that way, as subjects they function by taking up the discourses of the present and the past.

It is that taking up of positions that I call "identities." You see the consequence of turning the paradigm around that way: the political question (for there is always a political question, at any rate, in the way I pose the issue) is not "How do we effectively mobilize those identities which are already formed?" so that we could put them on the train and get them onto the stage at the right moment, in the right spot—an act the Left has historically been trying to do for about four hundred years—but something really quite different and much deeper.

How can we organize these huge, randomly varied, and diverse things we call human subjects into positions where they can recognize one another for long enough to act together, and thus to take up a position that one of these days they might live out and act through as an identity? Identity is at the end, not the beginning, of the paradigm. Identity is what is at stake in political organization. It isn't that the subjects are there and we just can't get to them. It is that they don't know yet that they are subjects of a possible discourse. And that always in every political struggle, since every political struggle is always open, it is possible either to win their identification or to lose it.

Indeed, for those of you who have been in politics for as long as I have, usually it is possible both to win and to lose it, and then to win it again and to lose it again, in an infinitely recurring struggle. That is the open-ended, contingent nature of political struggle, and just as a warning to intellectuals, there isn't any final theoretical solution, any grand deconstructive scheme which we can pull out of the air, which we can ensure will tell us that the subjects are going to stay like that, that the subjects are in place and the moment is going to come. And then the intellectuals can go home and get on with their business. It isn't like that. Remember: identifications, not identities. Once you've got identification you can decide which identities are working *this* week.

I speak of the process of identification, of feeling yourself through the contingent, antagonistic, and conflicting sentiments of which human beings are made up. Identification means that you are called in a certain way, interpolated in a certain way: "you, this time, in this space, for this purpose, by this barricade with these folks." That's what is at stake in political struggle. And you can't ahead of time either know that or know how to recognize that, or know how to imagine the collectivity that all those folks together might make. For how else would you know them? They weren't there before, or they weren't gathered together in the proper place. You can only come as you were, come together because somehow you can represent yourself and begin to share an imagined community of some kind with others which without representation and culture you could not express to anybody else.

The idea that somehow, out of some space, a politics of antiracism will arise without our giving thought as to how the subjects of it are to be formed is, to my mind, unintelligible. So then the questions that arise are, how and what kind? What are the natures of the cultural, social, and political identities that can and cannot be formed in these processes so as to conduct a political struggle, a cultural and social struggle that has the possibility of affecting something in the world? I want to insist that that is an open question, because I think at some level it remains more difficult than we think to take on the implications of what I've just been trying to say. Because when that rigid binary, racial logic is being used against us, we certainly know what's wrong with it. But when it seems to be working for us, we find that it's extremely difficult to give it up. We just can't let go of it in good moments, it makes us feel together; we can't imagine what a politics would be like if it wasn't there. How would you mobilize, what would you say to people, on what basis would you appeal to them, under what banner would you get them together? The whole thing begins to disintegrate, polarize, pluralize, get away from us, and we find ourselves confused by it. So, unfortunately, I think, people who know in their hearts that if you say race is not biological, that it is historical, cultural, and political, know you must follow the logic of that provision in terms of the alternative strategies you try to develop. Then, just at one minute to midnight, you're not beyond reaching for the final guarantee, and the whole biological fix actually slips back into place. Therefore, I want to explore what I think are the difficulties of what I'm going to call the end of the essentialized black subject, the end of an essentialist conception of the black experience.

One of the problems that confront a politics of this kind is that it affects some of our most central cultural and political concepts and images. Take the notion of tradition, for example. It is almost impossible to think of a cultural community as shared cultural meanings which exist over any period of time, which persist and have persisted over any period of time, which have managed to survive against all the odds, without thinking of the element of tradition that has enabled that community to hold together. Nevertheless, I think one of the implications of what I've just been saying is, indeed, that the question of tradition itself has to be conceptually rephrased.

Let me (walking dangerous waters, I know) talk about civil rights. Could one imagine the civil rights struggle of the sixties without the long traditions of black struggle that historically go back at least as far as the beginning of slavery? And yet, is there anybody here who wouldn't want to describe the civil rights movement as a movement that produced new black subjects? But new black subjects—now, what is that "new" then in the light of the tradition? Would it have happened without that tradition? Absolutely not. Where would traditions of struggle, where would the accumulated knowledge, where would the expectivity of human values that kept people going in dark days, where would that have come from if there hadn't been languages and historical traditions of one kind or another that sustained them across time? That sustained human beings in their lives of struggle across time—and yet the particular way that black people occupied that identity, lived that identity, and struggled around it, produced something which had never been seen before.

This is not the game you know, of trading "your victimage is bigger than mine," "my heroism is bigger than yours"—you don't have to say it's greater than what has happened before. That's not my argument; but my argument is that it was, and is, significantly different. And what was different about it was a particular reworking of that tradition under the force of the present conjuncture, not of a tradition which is simply a transmission belt that takes you from the past teleologically marching through to the future. A reworking that precisely delivers the much more complex idea that is a phrase you know well, "the changing same." That reworking transmits the capacity to be both the same and different, both located in a tradition and yet not constrained by it. Able to think freely on the basis of the particular ground. That reworking is almost musical and it has to be. What else is any successful blues, any successful jazz standard, or any gospel song but the given ground and the performance that translates it? But you couldn't listen to it if all there was was just the same damn thing once over again. It has to be that process of reworking the elements of a tradition, of taking forward what has been left, or engaging what is new, and of trying to put together a new kind of configuration. If you don't believe me because you think civil rights belongs to you, let me tell you that it didn't simply belong to you and it didn't simply produce some new black subjects here, it produced a lot of new black subjects elsewhere.

In the place where I came from in Jamaica, the conjuncture of the civil rights movement and the black consciousness movement of decolonization, the naming—the possibility at last to name the unspeakable fact of slavery and the imaginative, metaphorical connection with Africa—made Jamaica, where I was born, a black country for the first time in the 1960s. I don't mean it was the first time any black people were there. I mean black as a political category. I mean black as a culture. I mean black as a sociohistorical fact. It was the first time that I ever called myself that. I had called myself thousands of things before, but until that historical moment, it had been a word that I would never have applied to my own identity. So, if your own identities don't change, believe me, mine certainly have. They keep going on and on, and not only that, I most recognize them when other people say something different. In the sixties, after having been in England for ten years over that period when Afro-Caribbeans came to Britain for the first time, I went home and my mother said to me, "I hope they don't think you're one of those immigrants over there." I had never called myself an immigrant in all my life, and suddenly I said, "That's what I am." After all, I've gone to the people's place, I'm going to stay whether they like it or not, I intend to get a job if they're going to give me one. What am I but an immigrant? My life, far from the unfolding of this great identity I always knew about, this fabric endlessly unfolding but not changing toward some particular end, changes drastically, and when I get to the end, I can't say "There you are, you've always been like that, God help me, always been like that." No, the transformations have made me something different. Because historically, to say suddenly that you know we are black people, and to name the names, meant that the cultural terrain on which those names worked and struggled was thereby transformed. Cultural change is constitutive of political change and moral awareness of human consciousness.

And I want to say a word about political history as a way of passing on to another element and its complexity. In the 1970s, the signifier "black" was adopted as a political category of struggle, both by Afro-Caribbean migrants and by migrants from the Asian continent. People who manifestly were not, in any of the significant ways in which the term "race" had ever been used, the same race called themselves by the racial signifier. They said, "Since the British can't tell the difference between us, we must be the same." We might as well call one another by the same name. That's what identity is; it always has a constitutive outside. Those people didn't know about a "constitutive outside," but they knew one when they got it. Since they were manifestly not white, they were black. They called themselves black. They organized under that *political* roof.

It was a very important moment politically in Britain. It isn't the moment that we're in now. That significance has gone. It is partly dissolved into a variety of new, more ethnically specific signifiers. People now call themselves not only Asians, but Indians, Bangladeshis, Pakistanis, and indeed, South Indians. Things have moved into a new kind of ethnicized politics of difference. And that has presented certain profound difficulties of political organization when the signifier "black" has disappeared.

Still, I want to speak about this moment that I've just mentioned. What is this moment of the pluralization of cultural difference? Sometimes it is a racialized kind, sometimes an ethnicized kind—which is in my view increasingly characteristic of social antagonisms on a world scale. These antagonisms are a product of huge, planned, and unplanned world migrations—the greatest and most constitutive cultural fact of the late modern world, the planned and unplanned, forced and unforced movements of peoples, taking up hundreds of years later after that first forced migration of slavery with which modernity began. Here we are in late modernity, and what is happening is exactly the same kind of proliferation of movement as peoples. They are torn apart by poverty, by drought, by civil war, by the international arms trade, and they are moving, moving, moving from their settled homes to somewhere else.

Let me put that in cultural terms. They're moving like we have done before into the narratives, through which they will have to tell their history of migration, loss, displacement, redefining themselves, of home, of another home, of the question of where is home, of all of the images and metaphors of a perpetually unsettled people. That is the modern fact that is transforming this society; it is transforming Europe, Western European society. It is a world-historical fact of astonishing proportions and partly because it goes by different names—now refugees, now economic migrants, etc. And partly because it happens in this completely unplanned late-modern way, where people just calculate for themselves that the only thing to do is to buy a one-way plane ticket and get on a plane for paradise or, you know, the South Bronx, or wherever paradise is these days, in that way trying to resolve what is the global maldistribution of material and symbolic goods.

One of the consequences of that fact, within different national societies, has been to pluralize and complicate the terrain of social struggle. For what you find in each society is the integration of different forms of racialized and ethnicized difference, marked in different ways with very different and discrete histories. Nevertheless, it is part of the long history of the dialectics of "othering": these are all others of one kind or another, those that weren't othered through slavery were othered through colonialism or othered through imperialism. And some were othered through all three. Each of these people cling to the particular homes and identities that were formed through those histories. But what is most dramatic about them is that they are now convened in the very center of modernity, in the very "hotbed" of the modern, and what we find then as a consequence is that what the modern itself now means is precisely this conflict, this struggle, this complicated and differentiated line of struggle, between those who have had to move, and go on moving to survive, who have constantly been "the racialized other" of some system of supremacy, and on the other hand, the cultural nationalist racism that is the backlash against this multicultural drift, which is evolving in every society of the advanced, modern, Western industrial world.

I won't at this stage try to tell you what it means to us to see active fascism in the streets of London, to see the fascist right in alliance with a respectable center, to hear what we've heard before said about blacks, now said about North Africans, now said between peoples who call themselves European, who are hastily cobbling together in these societies that are hybridized and mongrelized to their roots. I couldn't find a "pure folk" anywhere. One would have to go into the museum to dig up the pure Bosnian-Serbian folk. Haul him out, mount him, etc.

Nevertheless, cobbling is a kind of defense against the modern world, a defense against living with difference, this retreat into the bunker of cultural and racist nationalism. I call it by that name, because although in its many respectable forms it doesn't recognize itself as such, this racism exists as a defense of "Englishness," of "Britishness," and of "Americanness." How could anybody object to Americans, or some Americans, defending a certain kind of "Americanness"? Who could argue against the possible claim that American children might not speak the "American language" first in American schools, and what is racist about that, what could possibly be racist about that?

I told a story recently in the Du Bois Lectures at Harvard, of a very close friend of Mrs Thatcher's, Lord Tebbit, who has devised a simple kind of handy test for deciding who culturally belongs to whom and who does not (call it "the Tebbit test"). It is a very simple one. It's a question of whether or not the migrant families cheer the Pakistanis and the West Indians when they come touring for cricket. You have only to go to the cricket match and pavilion, and look around when the West Indians get to six hundred or whatever it is, and the "black stands," the ones closest to the Oval, start to jump up and down, you know you can identify them. Because clearly their hearts cannot be in the right place. On the other hand, it is a very serious business indeed, this question of reconstructing a "little Englandism," reconstructing a little Americanism, through the struggles that are sometimes called "the culture wars."

Don't fool yourself that this is some superstructural, marginal question. At the center of this is the question of who can belong, who has access to the transmission belt through which Britishness, Englishness, is carried and can be inculcated. And who doesn't belong. And whether or not they have yet arrived at the moment when the lines are going to be drawn in blood and fire. Symbolic lines are being drawn, and what we know about culture is that once the symbolic difference exists, that is the line around which power coheres. Power uses difference as a way of marking off who does and who does not belong.

That is the shape of a new kind of cultural difference that impacts and sits atop another older kind: the politics of cultural difference. Today people sometimes say, "Of course, politics is a very confusing game, because there aren't those old stabilized identities around which we used to mobilize, and there aren't exactly those old kinds of struggles that we used to know how to fight." It is not, I warn you, because things are going through a little postmodern shake, and then they're going to settle down; then we're going to go back to the stabilized, well-organized, clearly demarcated frontiers of the past. We are in a new political conjuncture not without racism, not a conjuncture without difference; it is not a conjuncture without poverty and deprivation and marginalization on a world scale. But it is one in which the marking of difference, the careful and overlatticed marking of finely drawn distinction, can't be easily convened under a single political roof and fought in a simple battle. It is a much more differentiated, sophisticated, positional kind of struggle that has to be developed, to be conducted, if we are serious about refusing its human cost.

Sometimes the term "diaspora" is used as a way of conjuring up a kind of imagined community that would cut across the configurations of cultural nationalism. And I'm not only very much in favor of that, having contributed in some way to giving the term "liftoff." But let me warn you and warn myself that after all diaspora, too, has been the site of some of the most closed narratives of identity known to human beings. It is a word that has lodged there for a people who are not going to change, who sat on top of a sacred text and erected the barriers, and who then wanted to make the return exactly to the place where they came from. And who have gone back and sat on the head of all the other people who were there, too. If you open yourself to the politics of cultural difference, there is no safety in terminology. Words can always be transcoded against you, identity can turn against you, race can turn against you, difference can turn against you, diaspora can turn against you because that is the nature of the discursive.

I am trying to persuade you that the word is the medium in which power works. Don't clutch onto the word, but do clutch onto certain ideas about it. The diaspora is a place where traditions operate but are not closed, where the black experience is historically and culturally distinctive but is not the same as it was before. We are to move from one end of the diaspora to another and be ready to move from differently translated worlds, each with its own inflection, places where the law is almost certainly the law of syncretism, of taking in influences, of translating what has been given, of disarticulating and rearticulating, of creolization. And here I give my last injunction: to give up smoking and give up the idea, the commitment to the politically pure. The future belongs to the impure. The future belongs to those who are ready to take in a bit of the other, as well as being what they themselves are. After all, it is because their history and ours is so deeply and profoundly and inextricably intertwined that racism exists. For otherwise, how could they keep us apart?

NOTES

> This essay first appeared as "Subjects in History: Making Diasporic Identities," in *The House That Race Built*, ed. Wahneema Lubiano (New York: Vintage, 1998), 289–300.

1 During the discussion following on Steinberg's critique of Cornel West's ideas about the "underclass," and after a few additional criticisms leveled from the floor, I stood up to intervene in order to address what I saw as an unhelpful reduction of culture to the conditions of the economic.

PART I | THINKING-WITH/IN

THE IMAGE

CHAPTER 1

Isaac Julien's Workshop

Over the course of a friendship of more than thirty years, I have been in conversation with Isaac Julien about—and even occasionally played a small walk-on role in—the remarkable body of work that has precipitated his rise to international stature in the art world. This has involved listening, discussing, commenting on projects and scripts, sharing ideas, and the hilarious anecdotes that enliven a rich and valued friendship. But Isaac's social circles are extraordinarily wide, his interlocutors diverse, so I make no strong claims here. He reads and researches in depth. Projects evolve. He is astonishingly knowledgeable about contemporary cinema and has a deep but well-concealed—and often grossly underestimated—engagement with critical theory.

We first met in the heady days of Sankofa and its workshops. *Territories* (1984), which explored intersections among political, sexual, and racial domains, was resonant with issues that I and others were exploring, though I don't know of any direct influence. But I publicly defended *The Passion of Remembrance* (1986) when it was assailed as "too experimental" (code for "politically incorrect") by a distinguished but rather essentialist group of black intellectuals.

I was delighted when Isaac invited me to read a few lines in *Looking for Langston* (1989) (fig. 1.1), his exquisitely photographed and seductive rereading—"against the grain"—of Langston Hughes and the Harlem Renaissance, a work that I regard as the masterpiece of black art filmmaking of his generation. I remain a fan of his only feature film, *Young Soul Rebels*

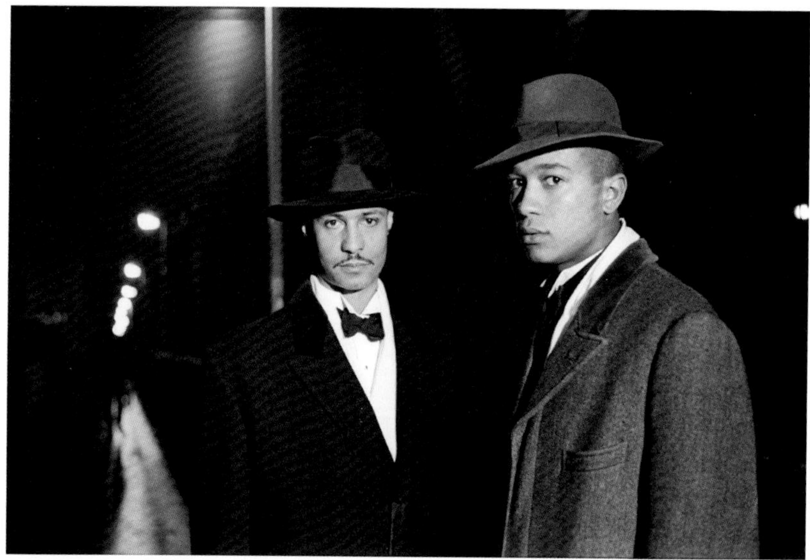

Figure 1.1. Isaac Julien, *I Love My Friend (Looking for Langston Vintage Series)*, 1989/2016. Ilford classic silver gelatin fine art paper mounted on aluminium and framed. 58 × 74.5 cm. © Isaac Julien, 2022. Courtesy of the artist.

(1991), celebrating the rise of black British soul music and its impact on the London of his youth.

I appeared briefly in *The Attendant* (1993) as the well-dressed but naïve visitor to the British Museum, gullibly taken in by the displays on the gallery walls but failing to grasp the operatic sexual tableaux unfolding behind them. Isaac promised to cast me next time as one of his beautiful, languorous, harnessed young "angels" from this other scene—a promise still to be fulfilled! Later I was involved in his brilliant reconstruction of Frantz Fanon, *Black Skin White Mask* (1996), in whose complex structure my conversation with Françoise Vergès forms one strand.

Isaac played a pivotal role in that significant moment in the black-diaspora arts when gay sexuality, masculinity, and race exploded into the same visual frame. We often discussed the problems of black media representation, and, later, the complicated issues involved in shooting a film about homophobia in Kingston, Jamaica (*The Darker Side of Black*, 1994). I enjoyed his mischievous accounts—accompanied with much feigned rolling of the eyes—of the vicissitudes involved in making his "lonesome cowboy" and Hockney-esque poolside idylls *The Long Road to Mazatlán* (1999) and *Vagabondia* (2000).

I was in Saint Lucia at a symposium on *"créolité"* in 2002, organized for the Documenta 11 exhibition, when Isaac was preparing to film the great Caribbean poet Derek Walcott for *Paradise Omeros*. I saw rushes from *True North* (2004)—unexpectedly, one of his most seductive films, with its startling blue-ice landscapes—whose central male figure (the first African-American to reach the North Pole) was played by the stunningly elegant, icily "cool" black actress Vanessa Myrie; and its match, *Fantôme Afrique* (2005), with its contrasting "hot" tropical reds and oranges. I greatly admired *Derek* (2008), Isaac's intimate, loving film about Derek Jarman, with its ready-made cottage set in the lunar-scrub landscape around Dungeness nuclear power station. And I closely followed the development of the magnificent nine-screen installation *Ten Thousand Waves* (2010), as it evolved from its origins in the tragedy of the Chinese-migrant cockle-pickers who drowned in Morecambe Bay in 2004 to the richly sumptuous, multidimensional evocation of the enigma that is modern China and the beautifully composed accompanying still photographs.

More recently, my wife, Catherine, and I have been in stimulating conversation with Isaac and his partner, Mark Nash, about his forthcoming project *Playtime* (figs. 1.2 and 1.3). The idea of an installation by Isaac on contemporary capitalism was intriguing, though no surprise to those not taken in by his personal style, which can be as non-intellectual as he chooses to make it. These exchanges have included, at one end, an effort to identify the distinctive characteristics of contemporary global capitalism, and at the other, the problem of how to visualize an abstraction.

We participated in a seminar at the Hayward Gallery, London, in 2012, when Isaac showed clips from films about capitalism and then conducted a long interview with David Harvey, the Marxist urban geographer and dialectical materialist, now engaged in an ambitious rereading of Karl Marx's work. I don't know how much of what I said on that occasion was relevant to Isaac's thinking about "choreographing capital." I was trying to express my sense that Harvey had opened up a rich vein of questions, some closely connected with Isaac's thinking (about, say, "capital cities"—all ambiguities intentional). Harvey is a sophisticated, articulate, and accessible expositor, but he tends in the end to retreat to the relative safety of the claim that (as he said in an answer to Paul Gilroy) the essential architecture of Marx's capital is still intact, and that whatever its shortcomings and gaps, Marx's grasp of "the fundamental laws of the capitalist mode of production" remains essentially correct.

I am not persuaded by this defense. Harvey thinks Marx's omissions do not touch the fundamentals. After all, he says, Marx could not anticipate

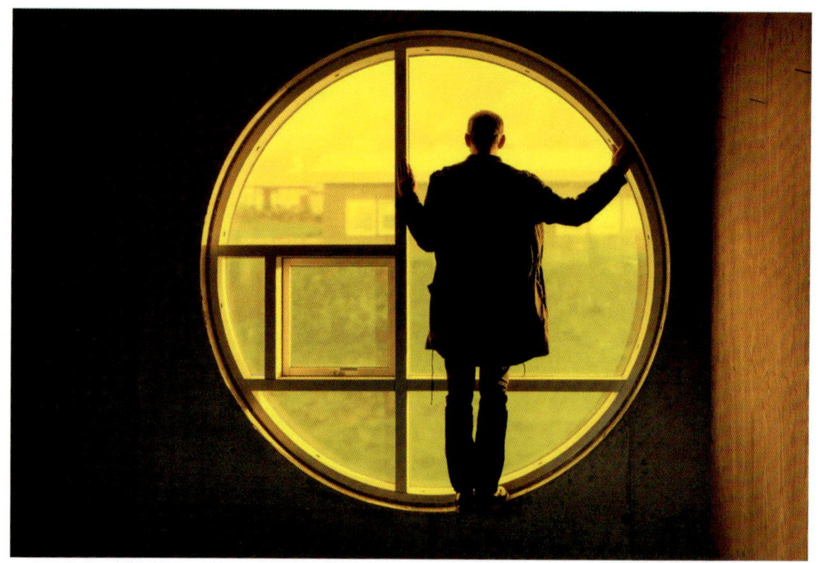

Figure 1.2. Isaac Julien, *Eclipse (Playtime)*, 2013. Endura Ultra photograph. 160 × 240 cm. © Isaac Julien, 2022. Courtesy of the artist.

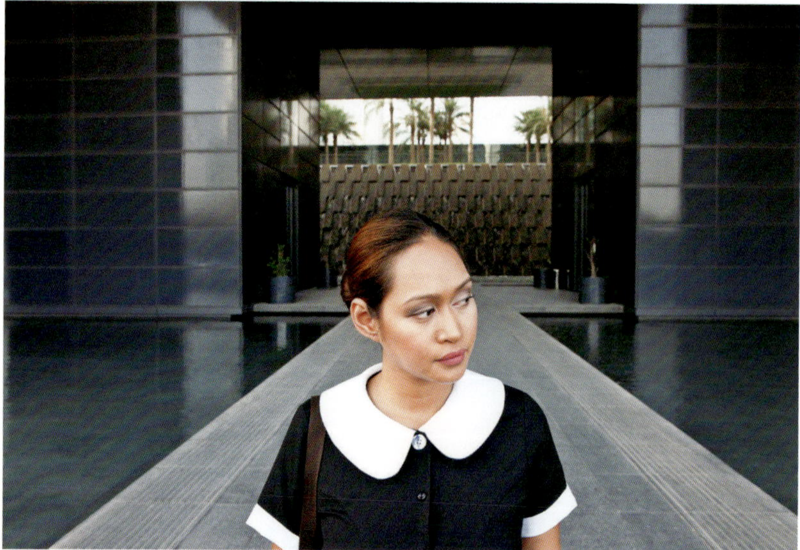

Figure 1.3. Isaac Julien, *Playtime*, 2013. Still with Mercedes Cabral as the House Worker. © Isaac Julien, 2022. Courtesy of the artist.

everything: he was a critic of political economy, not a prophet of universal truth. However, I think it is not a question of simply adding more elements (such as race, sexuality, or gender) to the paradigm—the problems flow from the heart of the analysis itself, and thus modify its claims. I had in mind the way racialization fragments the so-called "unity" of the working class; or the unexamined masculinist assumptions underlying the figure of "the worker"—the male breadwinner; or the absence of any conceptualization of the gendered nature of the *reproduction* of labor power, a process fundamental to capitalist accumulation but occurring far from "production," in familial and domestic sites where women and sexuality play a critical role. Marx passes over these in silence, and they have been sidelined in subsequent Marxist thought.

Harvey recognizes significant shifts within Marx's own thought—for example, between the "productionist" emphasis of *Capital* volume 1 and the (much neglected) "reproduction/consumption" focus of the maddeningly abstract but fascinating volume 2. When challenged, though, he defends the integrity of Marx's work: fundamentally, not much has changed. He argues that, despite dramatic shifts in class structure, an early-morning subway ride into Manhattan clearly demonstrates the continuing existence of a modern proletariat. The gap between rich and deprived residents and areas of the city are all immediately visible.

True. But what unifies that complex and diverse class formation, "the modern urban poor"? It now includes men and women, white and black, the long-term unemployed, the single-parent mother, people whose family relations have broken down, the vulnerable, the destitute, the marginalized, social misfits, dropouts, rough sleepers, the chronically ill or addicted, illegal immigrants, and asylum seekers without papers. Few of these could be described as exchanging their labor "productively" against capital. Is this a "proletariat" in the classic sense? Do they share a common class position or consciousness with today's technologically highly skilled workforce? Marx spoke of the "lumpen proletariat": what became of them? Expanded to include everyone but the wealthy one percent, the term "proletariat" loses its historical specificity.

I think the high point of the "proletariat" occurred in the years immediately following World War I—the moment of Britain's General Strike, the Turin factory occupations, the Scottish "Red Clyde" labor movement, Rosa Luxemburg, class war in Germany, social democratic Vienna, etc. Since then, we are in new territory. The reassuring use of familiar but increasingly inappropriate concepts occludes momentous shifts in class composition, when what is required is to confront them in all their radical complexity. In short, I wanted to put to Harvey that, in practice, he was already "revising" many of Marx's so-called "fundamental laws," and had gone much farther in his rethinking than he was prepared to acknowledge. I wanted to urge him to be more, not less, openly "revisionist."

Isaac is certainly fascinated by these debates, and they will find a place in *Playtime*. But I was uncertain as to how much he wanted to entangle his project in doctrinal debates from the past. However, this raised an important issue: in what phase of capitalist development was *Playtime* to be located? Catherine kept reminding him about the long continuities that connect present to past: for example, how modern forms of "unfree labor" (sexual exploitation, enforced prostitution, domestic servitude, the indebtedness to and enforced dependency of migrants and asylum seekers on their so-called "sponsors") in some ways parallel the older relation of New World "unfree" slavery and indenture to the "free labor" early industrializing system in Britain.

I urged Isaac to position the work firmly in what was most novel, different, and distinctive about global capitalism *today*: still perhaps generically governed by Marx's "fundamental laws" but now relentlessly global and transnational, driven by finance capital and the search for short-term profits, embedded in institutions, processes, structures, relationships, and ideologies characteristic of the neoliberal, "market-society," free-enterprise version of capitalism that emerged in the 1980s. Complex modalities mark out this system as a new stage, and it is what gave us the "long boom," whose shaky, shady, and risk-addicted foundations were exposed by the financial crisis of 2007–8.

This "free-market" system has created yawning gaps worldwide between rich and poor, and between developed and developing societies. Along with staggering accumulations of corporate and personal wealth, it has produced greater unevenness of development and more multiplying interdependencies than ever seen before. It sponsored the wave of post-war global migration that contradictorily connects the offices of the global super-rich (themselves now transcontinental and ethnically diverse) and their migrant night cleaners. A pervasive, ruthlessly competitive and privatized "common sense" has penetrated popular consciousness, corrupted business practices and public life, and invaded and transformed every sphere of life—not least the global art market, with an ensuing impact on artists and their work that first attracted Isaac's attention.

We kept returning to historical specificity and "choreographing capital." What figures could be used to typify it? What about the speed at which global capital investment and financial markets now work, as compared with the early twentieth century, when the dynamic drive for expansion was most effectively visualized through frantic images of Wall Street's trading floor in full flow? Today, driven by financial capital and the relentless search for short-term profits, new markets, and resources, the exponential scale of global investment is sustained by the new digital technologies and space-time condensations, the proliferation of clever but dodgy derivative products, and other "scams" dominated by anonymous hedge funds and venture capitalists. As for typification: with Bertolt Brecht's top-hatted plutocrats, one knew where one was. But the present form of capitalism is best instantiated by twenty-something Harvard Business School graduates who, away from the hubbub and hand signals, watch their screens, refine their algorithms, program their computers, and run automated banking systems that make investment decisions affecting the lives of millions. Isaac understood that these shifts posed *formal* questions, involving new visual and narrative strategies, even a new cinematic language. Earlier attempts to picture capitalism have fed his thinking, but I would be surprised if the major influence was not related to form rather than content—perhaps a variant of the dialectical montage described in Sergei Eisenstein's famous notes on his unmade film about capital?

Isaac began drawing the gestation period not to a "conclusion" but toward its next stage. The project has radically changed shape: it is now not one project but a set of related, differently framed, and narrated pieces. Recently, the first draft treatment arrived. It represents a truly astonishing transformation from a discursive to a visual idiom. The long process of reflection has been transmuted, by a sort of alchemy, into a visual frame. Reading it was both familiar and strange. Traces of many of the themes that we discussed were evident, but the "treatment" itself was quite another thing.

Confronted by another mode of thought made me acutely aware how radically different are the visual languages in which Isaac thinks and the critical, discursive, and analytic work I do. It made me reconsider, especially, the limits of the way I think. I think in a linear, sequential way, one idea provoking another. (I am not speaking about a scientific logic here: my work is notoriously eclectic!) Isaac is often thinking about the same problems, but his thought has entered a space or mode where ideas like mine, developing along what we may call a horizontal axis, immediately trigger or translate into an associative or analogical set of images, visual sequences, and narrative devices along a vertical axis, which obey a logic of their own and are in no sense simply illustrative. This is the visual imaginary at work.

I know all about this theoretically, but I have only once or twice come so close to and been so intimately involved with this process of transformation. I feel enormously privileged to have had an opportunity to watch it happening in the "laboratory" of Isaac's visual imagination.

NOTE

This essay first appeared in *Isaac Julien: Riot* (New York: Museum of Modern Art, 2013), 222–31.

CHAPTER 2

Democracy, Globalization, and Difference

One is tempted to say of democracy what, according to an essay by Immanuel Wallerstein, Mahatma Gandhi said of Western civilization. "What do you think of Western civilization, Mr Gandhi?" someone asked him. To which he replied, "It would be a good idea." The organizers of Documenta 11 were wise to recognize that, in relation to the conditions of existence of artistic practice today, few topics are more significant than the fate and future of democracy. Art today is increasingly "democratic" in a loose sense: more people, from wider conditions of life, are able to practice it, and its subject matter has been radically democratized—whatever invisible symbolic frame the artist is able to weave around a subject makes it count as "a work of art." On the other hand, the "art world" remains a highly exclusive "club," its discourse precious and rarified and more than ever penetrated through and through by money and the market. Documenta 11 calls for a timely inventory of democracy's present vicissitudes. For an inventory of its possibilities is difficult to undertake without immediately encountering its opposite—democracy's *impossibility*. At the end I may try, briefly, to say why this *impossibility* may be democracy's saving grace. But before we make this redemptive move, let me stare its down-side in the face.

I understand its impossibility in two senses, one practical, one more conceptual. The meaning of the word *democracy* is now so proliferated, so loaded down with ideological freight, so indeterminate where it stands at the nexus on different, often mutually exclusive paradigms—liberal democracy, participatory democracy, popular democracy—that it is virtually useless. So unstable that it often cannot sustain meaningful dialogue, so that it is questionable whether it is any longer "good to think with." Increasingly emptied of real content, as the gap between real and ideal widens, it is progressively weighed down by the plentitude of its unfulfilled promises. It is simultaneously too empty and too full. It can only be used in its radically deconstructed form. It is, to coin a phrase, under deep *erasure*.

The second aspect relates to this gap between real and ideal. The discourse of democracy is, to use the language of spectrality, haunted by the ghost of its ideal. The problem is that the gap between any actually existing system of democracy and its status as a universal regulative idea is read teleologically. So that each manifestly inadequate historical example is seen as another stage in the inevitable onward march toward its full realization—a moment of Hegelian reconciliation between democracy's "real" and democracy's "reason." To the contrary, I want to argue that this "lack" is not contingent but constitutive of the democratic idea, which can only function as what Ernesto Laclau calls "a horizon"—without specific, transhistorical content: a necessarily empty signifier. According to Laclau, a horizon is that "which establishes, at one and the same time, the limits and the terrain of constitution of any possible object—and that, as a result, makes impossible any 'beyond.'"[1] I will return to this idea at the end.

The spirit animating democracy through its many actual forms is that legitimate government must rest on the incorporation and the active consent and participation of all, and this "all" implies a radical equality between the totality of its subjects, carrying with it the promise of the levelling of power. When in the historical world has such a system been constructed in any way but across its manifest *lack*? Athenian democracy—small enough to give the appearance of transparency—existed in a tiny circle of light supported by the invisibility of forced labor and surrounded by the immense darkness of the barbarian other. The Lockean ideal enshrined in the American Constitution was the privilege of propertied men, not the poor, women, the enslaved or indigenous people. The "freedom" of this exclusion was recently once again vividly demonstrated in the US Electoral College, which legitimated the passage of the presidency to the candidate who had lost the popular vote. The Declaration of the Rights of Man and the Citizen, an inspirational democratic document worldwide, could not ensure that the Assembly would recognize the inalienable rights to freedom of black Haitian slaves—the "Black

Jacobins" who, paradoxically, had been inspired precisely by the Abbé Reynal, the *philosophes*, and *liberté, égalité, fraternité*. The popular democracies, in a Brechtian move, elected the Party in place of the People. In Western democracies, the long struggle to reform and expand the franchise inched forward to assimilate a wider and wider tranche of adult men, but fiercely resisted the enfranchisement of women and could not universalize democracy's ideal even to its own poor and powerless citizens. In T. H. Marshall's historicist reading of citizenship, the progressive movement—first, equality before the law, then the franchise, then the "amelioration of class" through the welfare state—comes to a shuddering halt before the frontier of giving socioeconomic rights any deep content: a threshold the international doctrine of human rights found impossible to encompass.[2]

This should not be taken as meaning that the subject of democracy is no longer worth pursuing. It remains a powerful idea animating radical demands everywhere, and a critical idea to bring to bear against and to lever open the actually existing structures of power: though, probably, more in its adjectival sense—the "democratization of social life"—than in its substantive form. These days, when I hear "democracy" I am pretty certain that I am already launched on the treacherous seas of some deep and complex ideological manoeuvre. This does not mean that it has some already given historical content toward which it is always "tending" which one day will be completed in its already known forms. Nor does it mean that its efficacy is limited to the West, though we may have to radically rethink the conditions of existence it may require to become strategically operative in societies where the other conditions of existence in which it has become embedded in the West are not present. Ideas are not limited to their place of origin, though we should expect their radical transformation as they begin to "travel": increasingly so, as cultures cease to be autonomous, self-sustaining, enclosed entities, writing the scripts of their members from birth to death and entering the cosmopolitan condition where ideas, images, as well as forms of life flow across boundaries and begin to indigenize—a topic to which I will also return.

Nevertheless, despite this more qualified optimistic note, the limited inventory I want to offer as a way of starting this investigation is less about democracy's potential, "unrealized" possibilities, and more about its actually existing realization in the contemporary setting. And here my argument is that in recent years, the balance in what we may call the relations of democratic forces has decisively swung against the democratic tide. The gap I referred to earlier between the stuttering incompleteness of its forms of empirical realization and its onward march as transhistorical ideal has been hegemonized. The ideas circulating within democracy's wider frame have been condensed into "liberal democracy," and liberal democracy reduced to the system that now prevails in the Western developed "democratic capitalist" world. This form of democracy is said to have reached such a close approximation to its ideal that it is, for all practice purposes, complete. It may require tinkering here and here, and the sort of regular motor maintenance check to make sure the engine is running smoothly. But generally, in its sublating movement of supercession, the system is close to the complete "exhaustion" of its potential through its "realization"; bringing us, as Francis Fukuyama has argued, at last, face to face with "The End of History," in the sense that there are no great political conceptions of freedom and equality to come, no profound ideological work remaining to be done, no new political goals that are not already within our empirical grasp. Liberal democratic Man is The Last (natural) Man. This is the quasi-Hegelian conflation that underpins Fukuyama's vision of liberal democracy as "the only coherent political aspiration that spans different regions and cultures around the globe."[3]

Fukuyama explicitly connects this completion of the liberal democratic dream *within* the West to its new, *global* mission. The link is secured by the fact that, as Fukuyama puts it, "A liberal revolution in economic thinking has [everywhere] sometimes preceded, sometimes followed, the move toward political freedom around the globe."[4] In short, as Derrida notes acerbically, "The alliance of liberal democracy and of the free market"—their absolute and ultimate interdependence—is "the good news of this later quarter century."[5] It is this couplet that has made liberal democracy the political advance guard of the tremendous avalanche of neoliberal orthodoxy now sweeping the post–Cold War world with evangelical zeal. Fukuyama does not altogether deny liberal democracy's "dark side," nor that, here and there, the system may need a little light renovation. But these are assigned to the side of the contingent— "the empirical flow of events in the second half of the century."[6] Their accumulation in no way refutes, qualifies, or undermines the ideal, which remains "perfect"—the only coherent global aspiration to freedom. What Derrida calls "the telos of a progress that [has] the form of an ideal finality."[7]

Of course, the interchangeability of liberal democratic conceptions of political freedom and market freedom is not new. The conjunction of two, mutually qualifying terms—*liberal* and *democracy*—already marks the site of this fateful convergence. But in more reformist times, each was supposed to qualify and in some way limit the other. "Liberal" recognized that the market remained the best "impartial" allocator of economic resources, and one could go only so far in interfering with its "logic": that capital accumulation provided the economic basis of living standards and prosperity, and imposed its limits on how far economic power could be "democratized." Liberal also implied the full panoply of other liberal relations that constituted the conditions of existence of actually existing liberal democracy: individual autonomy; an abstract-equivalent notion of the citizen; a formal not a substantive conception of equality; a neutral, culture-blind state ("veiled in assumed ignorance," as they say); and representative government. But "democracy" promised the constitution of public political spaces in which private interests would be required to take account of a wider set of "public" interests. It recognized that government could not be conducted without acquiring the consent of its citizens; that institutions should somehow be "accountable" not only to their owners or governors but to wider social interests; that the power of capital and the inequalities of power, everywhere the inevitable consequence of capitalist market societies, should enter a trade-off against the power of one person–one vote. I am not suggesting that this ideal-typical picture—liberal democracy as the best of all possible shells for the development of market capitalism, Lenin might have said—ever prevailed in practice. But I am pointing out the room for struggle, contestation, and negotiation produced by the necessary interdependency but mutually limited effect of this heavily compromised formation. These are indeed the only spaces in which genuine social reforms have been won.

It is by taking this best-possible reading of liberal democracy and contrasting with it recent developments in three spheres that I constitute my provisional inventory. It is, then, something radically new—we are in a radically new conjuncture—when the two terms are positively advanced, not as an articulation, but as linked by an internal necessary within a single, self-sealing totality. From this perspective I want to discuss, first, the hollowing out of democracy at the very moment of its so-called apotheosis; second, the way the transnational diffusion and flow of power, in contemporary forms of Western-dominated economic, financial, and cultural globalization, short-circuits and undermines even the limited countervailing powers won in the nation-state era; and third, how the emergence of "difference" in every sphere of life subverts and undermines the basic but unspoken assumption of cultural and social homogeneity that underwrites optimal definitions of liberal democracy, piercing the very heart of the concept.

Pluralization and fragmentation of the social and political field are well-advanced features of late modern Western societies. This does not mean that

there are no centers of power nor that the great inequalities of power, resources, and privilege that used to pass under the general category of "class"
have ceased to exist. In most Western societies, the inequality gap between
the haves and the have-nots has widened significantly even in the most recent
period of sustained economic growth. This is now a constitutive feature of
Western "success," and has occurred, of course, in tandem with a parallel trend
on the global stage. But the complexities of modern technology, the special-
ization of labor markets, the advanced character of the division of labor, the
expansion of "the political" multiplying the sites of antagonism and diffusing
the centers where the operative decisions that affect our lives are taken, are not
only, to different degrees in different developed societies, the fate of "late modernity" but have deep consequences for the "settled" forms of citizenship and
democratic participation arrived at by the middle of the twentieth century.
The pluralization of social antagonism and the production of new subjects
have, we would argue, positive potential for the struggles to widen political
participation and for the deepening of democratic life. But their immediate
effect is dislocating: the loss of effectivity and distinctiveness by the old ideologies that articulated different social interests and hegemonized the ideological field, and the waning or ossification of the political parties that were the
principal articulating points of mediation and contestation between popular
consent in a representative system and the system of governmentality.

Though by no means concluded, I would argue that not the deepening
of democratic contestation but the *hollowing out* of liberal democracy has
been its principal tendency. In the absence of more developed political ideologies, populism, the market, and different versions of nationalism provide, in principle, articulating grounds. Populism—the use of "the people"
as an empty signifier to conflate into a single "big tent" interests that are
different and antagonistic—is, of course, especially attractive because it simultaneously replicates *and* supplants the more democratic alternative it
replaces. The people and the popular are such near-cousins, such seductive
synonyms, that the sleight of hand involved is hardly perceptible. The second articulating principle is the way market freedom now condenses metonymically every kind of freedom. Why bother with the difficult process of
articulating alliances, constructing subjects, and winning political representation when, in our detotalized individuality, we can instantly participate
through immediate consumption, or even by a mouse click, in the big "free"
bazaar of life? One tiny indicator of the growing "marketization" of social
life in Britain, which must here be my main source of examples, is the way

the specification of professions, knowledge, expertise, and role is dissolved by the acid of equivalence of "the consumer." We no longer have teachers and students, doctors and patients, social workers and clients, local administrators and citizens, but the all-encompassing *consumer*. Britain's Labour prime minister, Tony Blair, confronting the crisis in public education—a "democratic" issue if ever there was one—declared all public-sector workers, including teachers, to be "the forces of conservatism," then, in a more positive vein, encouraged them to boost their confidence by thinking of themselves as "social entrepreneurs" and to acquire something of the status currently enjoyed by "businessmen." This is a tell-tale symptom of that larger movement which has brought about the collapse of the very idea of "the public," the cynicism which greets the idea that economic ministers making judgments about "competition" should take a wider "public interest" into account, and of course the remorseless drive to "privatization."

The evidence of what we call the short-circuiting of democratic contestation and accountability is overwhelming: the centralization of executive power, even within the so-called parliamentary system, coupled with the erosion of local government and local democracy; the managerialist style of governance, with the country run like a private corporation with the prime minister as its CEO and elections as occasional meetings of an emasculated body of shareholders; the expansion of an entrepreneurial style of governance, where government functions and departments are increasingly "outsourced" or converted into agencies, with no clear line of accountability, and public servants are recommended to entrepreneurialize their practice and "take ownership" of policy.

Critics who question whether the neoliberal revolution inspired by Mrs Thatcher in Britain had real practical effects on the governance of the country rarely take account of the role played by American-style management ideology as "the vanishing mediator" in the relay between ideology and practice. Then there is the "mediatization" of politics which, in the present era, has reached a new intensity. I refer to the massive manipulation of public opinion and consent by the swollen echelon of political public relations and focus-group polling; the way special-interest lobbying outweighs the cumbersome practices of public argument; the consistent adaptation of policy to the agendas of the media, which become a more authentic ventriloquizing "voice" for "the people" than the people themselves; and, in the UK certainly, the obsessive use of "spin," which some regard as a mere surface affliction, but which, in the context of the Third Way—determined to square every circle and triangulate every social interest—is profoundly endemic to the system. Finally, there is the drift of liberal, democratic politics to the "radical center," a vacuous concept in itself as even Third Way supporters themselves can see, with its Third Way commitment to a politics "beyond left and right," a politics, as Chantal Mouffe has argued, without antagonism, without enemies—that is to say, a politics without politics: politics as a management technology. Despite various strategies of social amelioration and redistribution by stealth, my government is remorselessly opposed, ideologically, to redistribution *as an idea*—and hence cannot provide a range of deprived and dispossessed groups more generally with an articulating theme or construct a constituency for it.

All of this is, to a very real extent, the consequence internally of the new liberal orthodoxy as a so-called public philosophy and the advance of transnational global techno- and financial capitalism. It is underpinned by the profound belief that neoliberal forms of globalization are "inevitable": like Fate, they can only be obeyed. The role of government is, therefore, to help create the conditions for private capital to prosper, to pursue at home those privatizing and deregulative strategies calculated to make the nation more competitive in the global environment, to ease the path of transnational capital and, most particularly, to educate and tutor its citizens to adapt to the new cold climate, to adapt to the logic of market forces, by removing the "disincentives" posed by universal forms of welfare; to encourage the two-thirds who *are* prospering to make private provision for life's vicissitudes—birth, parenting, education, health insurance, insurance against redundancy in "flexible" labor markets, retirement, care in old age, and death—and to drive down to its lowest level the threshold of the "residuum," who must be rigorously means-tested to receive aid and are invited, US-style, as rapidly as possible, to wean themselves from the infantilism of "welfare dependency." I know that the UK's favoring of the American model of what Michael Walzer calls Liberalism 1 over the more European social-market model, while of course wanting to "play its full part in Europe"—the Third Way always wants to have its cake *and* eat it—may distort my perspective. Things may not yet be so bad in your neck of the woods, but I am sure this is a nightmare coming your way.

I want to say less, because more is known and more already said, about the impact on liberal democracy as "the only coherent conception of political freedom around the globe" of what the Documenta 11 briefing calls "the neoliberal globalist onslaught" and the forces of transnational global capitalism. I focus on one aspect—some consequences for democracy unrealized.

One can see why a Western-driven globalization prefers to operate where liberal democracies have been established. Foreign investment, the transnational movement of finance capital, technology, and corporate base work best where there is stability of sociopolitical conditions, and where governments that are required to collaborate and be complicit with global penetration have the legitimacy of popular consent. Dictatorships are notoriously unstable; human rights abuses by authoritarian regimes give the international corporations that are taking competitive advantage of divergent labor market conditions a bad name and can stimulate international mobilization. New technologies, labor patterns, cultural models work best where there is a sympathetic basic value orientation toward change, innovation, and modernity: they work best where societies have political systems whose orientation, modes of operation, and basic values are symbiotic with Western ones. Modern mass production and mass marketing on a global scale require indigenization: the local settings must be ones in which the logic of market forces has been socially embedded and culturally internalized. Where non-liberal democratic forms of popular mobilization occur—ultra-nationalist, theocratic, ethnic, racial, or charismatic—they tend to be anti-Western, anti-modernity, and opposed to globalization's free play. In the drive to transform society in Eastern Europe, liberal democracy and the market have been indivisibly linked, dismantling both authoritarian forms of politics and state-oriented economics. In the developing world, the neo-liberal tide requires the dismantling of barriers and regulative checks once considered protectively essential to the project of nation-building that characterized the first phase of the post independence and postcolonial projects.

Increasingly, the transnational exercise of economic and cultural power is beyond the reach of democratic systems limited by the nation-state and has effectively escaped democratic regulation at the global level. How can relatively weak and hard-pressed new nations bargain, with any semblance of equality, with the overdeveloped Western powers, the bases from within which transnational global capitalism operates? How can developing nations, whose futures depend on acquiring the technology and "know-how" of the New Economy and finding a niche in increasingly free-trade, unregulated financial, commodity, service, media, and cultural markets, find the space to work out some balanced solution between "tradition" and "modernity" in their respective cultures, in the face of the homogenizing cultural assault? I am not so cynical to believe that all international organizations are merely a convenient cover for the free play of American imperializing interests. I know that some developing countries have tried to use what muscle they have in these global forums to win some advantages for the poorer peoples of the earth. But, far from constituting an embryonic transnational regulatory system, they have been dominated by Western interests and the engines driving through a particular version of globalization—deregulating and dismantling the barriers and inhibitions to technological and cultural penetration, imposing structural adjustment programs that intervene directly in the balance of social forces, insisting on free-trade terms that expose fragile markets, using advanced technologies and the Western patent system to destroy local enterprise and social-service provision, for instance, making subsistence farmers totally dependent for seed on Western agrobusiness and blocking the distribution of cheaper generic drugs to poor peoples devastated by HIV and other diseases and chronic infections.

I want to comment on only one aspect of this scenario. Liberal democracy took root in and remains embedded within what David Held calls "a fixed and bounded territorial conception of political community"[8]—the nation-state. Of course, as we have all learned from Immanuel Wallerstein, capitalism as a world-system benefited from the extraordinary interdependence and complicated tensions between the growing international capitalist market and the nation-states, and the trend toward national autonomy and the trend toward globalization are *both* rooted in modernity. Liberal democracy took advantage of this tension to win space and reforms within the political arena of particular nation-states which could not at that stage be generalized across the world-system. Until very recently, it has been within nation-states that the struggles to expand the sphere of representation have been conducted, and the nation-state, not primarily international law, that has been the guarantor of civic and citizens rights. It is rarely recalled that Article 3 of the Declaration of the Rights of Man and the Citizen (1789) reads, "The principle of all sovereignty lies essentially in *the nation*; no group, no individual may have any authority that does not expressly proceed from it."

However, as power increasingly flows "across, around, and over territorial boundaries," "the neat correspondence between national territory, sovereignty, political space, and the democratic political community" is disrupted.[9] It is not (yet) the case that the powerful nation-states are disappearing. It is hard to see any strengthening of the international regulatory system which does not have nation-states as key players in the process of reform. However, their "reach" has been curtailed, their capacity to insulate themselves from the cold winds of global forces and influences is greatly diminished, their capacity to sustain sovereign national economies, polities, cultures uncontaminated by global power is profoundly transformed. In addition, they are busy reorienting themselves, their political structures and economic goals, toward success within a wider globalizing horizon. Even within the serious limits of liberal democracy, this is the source of a growing "democratic deficit" on a world scale.

Here I want only to note a troubling ambivalence, which brings us to our last main area. In his recent overview of the logic of globalization, Fredric Jameson notes that although "nation-states today remain the only concrete terrain and framework for political struggle," any temptation to secede from the global system in order to protect oneself from its worst effects seems to provide a counterpoint "where a nationalist politics might rear its head."[10] In fact, as we have hinted, the many varieties of nationalism, racism, xenophobia, and fundamentalism that have re-emerged center stage to global politics are often, in part (though I would argue not exclusively) responses to—reactions against, even—the pressure of a modernizing globalization. Many are the symptoms of a failed nationalist project in hostile international circumstances or of a failed modernization. Many are not all entirely antimodernity but instead, Janus-like, mix past and future in highly unstable amalgamations—combining a search for mythic origins in an invented tradition with a ruthless competition to secure nation-state status in the global power stakes at the very moment when the star of the nation-state is waning. This is the case with Balkan nationalisms and, for example, in the way modernism and traditionalism are combined in the current claims of the Hindu fundamentalists in India. But this would be to suggest that every form of resistance which has to make use of the nation-state space is by definition backward and reactionary—which is to suggest that it has a universally fixed political content, itself a form of "fundamentalism." Also, it implies the binary contrast between "them," who are still prey to irrational and antimodern impulses, and "us," who are thoroughly "modern." I cannot hope to resolve the complex issues of strategies of resistance here. I have only to say that when, during the Asian crisis, President Mahatia of Malaysia suspended all currency exchanges, or if the president of South Africa were now to consciously break international drug-patent law in the name of national survival, these are "nationalist" reprises I can live with. And to note, on the other hand, in the advanced democracies the resistance to a more cosmopolitan outlook—to the increasingly mixed character of our populations and more culturally diverse claims on citizenship—that frequently takes the form of a profoundly "fundamentalist" reaction, an attempt to demonize the strangers in our midst, to close the doors of the culture and to climb back into an embattled and defensive little nationalism, with its clear racist, xenophobic, and culturally differential supplements. This is now evident everywhere in Europe, and is the underlying source of that gut-Europhobia that now afflicts the British soul.

Globalization is not directly responsible for what the Documenta 11 briefing calls "the large-scale displacements and immigration that today are reshaping the face of once stable societies" and the "widened horizon of notions of citizenship" this has produced. But it is one of globalization's unintended consequences, in a larger sense. Post-war, it begins with the movements of national independence and wars of national liberation that triggered decolonization; and has been greatly intensified by the unofficial opening up of borders and boundaries due to a host of factors: globalization itself and the push and pull of economic opportunities; poverty, immiseration, unemployment, and structural underdevelopment; political and military coups, tribal and ethnic conflicts, civil wars; natural disasters or environmental catastrophes like drought, floods, erosion, global warming, and climate and ecological change; more recently "ethnic cleansing," racism, and xenophobia; and across all that, the unsponsored movement of peoples in search of better times.

I want to consider briefly two ideal-typical responses to the demands for, on the one hand, equality, social justice, and inclusion, and on the other hand for inclusion and the recognition of difference. The first response is essentially *assimilationist*. This can be practiced in weaker and stronger forms, with a tolerant acceptance that the process will take time or the aggressive insistence that foreigners and strangers must either conform to the majority culture and embrace the universal liberal values of modernity or "go back home." But either way, the idea that national identity is not fixed eternally in the myths of historical time but is always a moving feast, constantly being historically redefined, or the recognition that the presence of multicultural differences obliges a society to expand, transform, and enlarge the boundaries and definitions of citizenship and the national community, are strongly resisted. Mr Hague, the leader of the Conservative opposition in the UK, recently described a Britain that is strongly integrated into Europe, hospitable and open to foreigners, welcoming to refugees and asylum seekers, and willing to renegotiate the boundaries of national belonging as fast becoming a "foreign country," alienated from itself. A profound assimilationism is the foundation stone of the revival of nationalist and racist movements and sentiment in Europe, providing the silent legitimation for widespread, if less vocal, forms of national exclusionism, racism, and cultural differentialism, which are more popular today than politicians are willing to acknowledge. The second response is what its enemies call *multiculturalism*, though we know in fact that this is a highly contested term and that there are many varieties which conceive difference in more open, inclusive, and interdependent ways. I am referring to the strongly pluralist conception of difference we find in some versions of "multiculturalism," which not only acknowledge the world significance of different cultural and religious traditions and recognize the strength of religious, cultural, linguistic, and other differences, but regard these as making "cultures" into organic, indivisible "wholes," which saturate entire communities, subordinating individuals to communally sanctioned forms of life exclusively on the basis of their membership within, as it were, a hierarchically arranged pecking order.

One sees here two extreme cases of the struggle between universalism and particularism which has a special salience for the debate about liberal democracy as a global project. The values of liberalism have historically been aligned with those of "modernity." As such, though they were deeply embedded in particular cultures and historical circumstances, they have been represented as the sign of universality itself and, in that form, used to insist on assimilation, "trumping" all cultural particularisms. The surmounting of the particularist threshold is often represented as liberal democracy's principal achievement and it is on that basis that it is seen as the necessary precondition for global modernization. From this perspective, all those who resist its universal appeal are represented as permanently mired in tradition and particularity. Thus the world struggle for liberal democracy assumes the form of a sacred struggle between the universalism of the West as the new global orthodoxy and the particularism of the rest.

But as Ernesto Laclau has cogently argued in *Emancipation(s)* and elsewhere, a logic of pure difference is only a viable strategy where an identity wants nothing from, and is not constitutively related to, any other identity. This is logically difficult to sustain, since all identity is constituted with reference to a lack—to that other which is not the same, from which "sameness" must differentiate itself. One cannot, as Laclau says, affirm an identity without also affirming the wider context which establishes the ground of its difference, or without the constitutive role of power which effects the exclusion that at any point marks off the sameness of an identity from the difference of its others. This of course entails a very particular conception of difference:

not the binary of fixed difference that treats ethnicities or cultures as integral "wholes," but what Derrida calls the "logic of *différance*"—"the playing movement that 'produces' . . . these differences, these effects of difference," the weave of differences that refuse to separate into fixed binary oppositions, where "every concept [or meaning] is inscribed in a chain . . . within which it refers to the other, to other concepts, by means of the systematic play of differences."[11] Identity can only be conceived through difference—present, as it were, only differentially, through its absence. As Laclau puts it, "all differential identity will be constitutively split; it will be the crossing point between the logic of difference and the logic of equivalence."[12] It is difficult to claim equal rights if one is only different from other groups and does not also share something with them which is the basis for the expansion of the claim. A pure logic of equivalence is the abolition of all difference. A "pure logic of difference" can be the basis only of a system of social apartheid and ethnic cleansing. To avoid this, the right to difference "has to be asserted within the global community—that is within a space in which that particular group has to coexist with other groups," which could not be possible "without some shared universal values, without a sense of belonging to a community larger than each of the particular groups in question."[13] If this is not to restore a universalism of the liberal variety, which zooms down from outer space and trumps every particular, it can only be by the recognition of the necessity of living with difference; by continually expanding *the opening to the other*—a reaching from within the particular toward some wider horizon, without the consolidation of some final closure. Universalization in this open sense "condemns all identity to an unavoidable hybridization, but hybridization does not necessarily mean decline through the loss of identity; it can also mean empowering existing identities through the opening of new possibilities."[14] We are dealing with an indeterminate notion of identity and what Chantal Mouffe has called an "agonistic" conception of democracy.

Laclau has argued that, for a minority group to affirm only the identity that it has at that moment, is to confirm its permanent marginalization: "If, on the other hand, it struggles to change its location within the community and to break with its situation of marginalization, it has to engage in a plurality of political initiatives" which not only expands the political field of contestation radically, but transforms that identity itself, taking it "beyond the limits defined by its present identity."[15] If the spheres of antagonism and democratic contestation are widened and multiplied, "universalism as a horizon is expanded at the same time as its necessary attachment to a particular content is broken."[16] That is why—though I cannot replicate the complexities of Laclau's argument here—he insists that democracy as a horizon has no specific or fixed content, since its content and field will change as it is expanded with each attempt to generalize or "universalize" it to wider spheres of application. Like the universal, it is "an always receding horizon resulting from the expansion of an indefinite chain of equivalent demands."[17] Since its role is to bring about this agonistic mediation between particularity and universalism, "there is no content that is a priori destined to fill it and it is open to the most diverse articulations. But this means that the 'good' articulation, the one that would finally suture the link between universal task and concrete historical forces, will never be found and that all partial victory will always take place against a background of an ultimate unsurpassable impossibility."[18] This is democracy's status as what Laclau calls "an empty signifier."

Democracy in either its liberal or more radical varieties has traditionally counterposed equality to difference, and political theory has been fixated by the impassable barrier between them. What the new situation seems to require is the development of a new articulation, a new political logic. The presence of the stranger presents democracy with this radically new double demand: for equality and social justice *and* for the recognition of difference, neither existing in a pure state, both qualifying and modifying the other in a ceaseless struggle. Far from marking the apotheosis of democracy itself, this eruption of difference at its center points to the depth of the transformations democracy—the promise of freedom and equality—has yet undergone and the struggles to come.

I am aware that I have altogether neglected to address how these considerations bear on the issues that most preoccupy Documenta 11. I want to do so but only in a concluding footnote. I have spent the recent months working on the text for a selection of photographic images produced by forty contemporary photographers from the margins of the West. They are part of a dynamic creative drive that emerged in the mid-1980s from outside the cultural and artistic mainstream, fuelled by the demand to bring their objective conditions and subjective experiences into the frame, to give the invisible visibility and to open a "third space" in cultural representation. This work, which is intensely varied, does not explicitly address political questions, but is preoccupied with its own "differences" and was driven by what was called at the time "the search for identity." What is quite extraordinary about this work is that it is *not* the product of what one might call "identity politics": it is about, and at the same time subverts, identity. It recognizes that we all come from somewhere, speak from some place, are multiply positioned and in that sense "located." But in its many different ways, it refuses to be rendered motionless by place, origin, race, color, or ethnicity. It knows that identity is always constructed within, not outside, representation and uses the symbolic space of the image to explore, construct, and at the same time go beyond identity. It is in some radical sense post-identity without being beyond the reach of its effects. It arises at the overdetermined space where different differences overlap and intersect. It is preoccupied with staging the self only in a way that is "open to the other." It represents a new kind of "vernacular cosmopolitanism." It eschews—thank goodness—any reference to political theory. But within its own symbolic time and space, it anticipates what Julia Kristeva calls the recognition of the fact that we are always "strangers to ourselves."

NOTES

This essay first appeared in *Democracy Unrealized: Documenta 11, Platform 1*, ed. Okwui Enwezor et al. (Ostfildern-Ruit: Hatje Cantz, 2001), 21–36.

1   Ernesto Laclau, *Emancipation(s)* (London: Verso, 1996), 102.
2   See T. H. Marshall, *Citizenship and Social Class* (London: Pluto, 1991 [1950]).
3   Francis Fukuyama, *The End of History and the Last Man* (London: Penguin, 1992), xiii.
4   Fukuyama, *End of History*, xiii.
5   Jacques Derrida, *Specters of Marx: The State of the Debt, the Work of Mourning, and the New International*, trans. Peggy Kamuf (New York: Routledge, 1993).
6   Derrida, *Specters of Marx*, 70.
7   Derrida, *Specters of Marx*, 57.
8   David Held and Anthony McGrew, with David Goldblatt and Jonathan Perraton, *Global Transformations: Politics, Economics, and Culture* (Cambridge: Polity, 1999).
9   Held and McGrew, *Global Transformations*.
10 Fredric Jameson, "Globalization and Political Strategy," *New Left Review* 4 (July/August 2000): 64.
11 Jacques Derrida, *Margins of Philosophy*, trans. Alan Bass (Chicago: University of Chicago Press, 1982), 11.
12 Laclau, *Emancipation(s)*, 53.
13 Laclau, *Emancipation(s)*, 32.
14 Laclau, *Emancipation(s)*, 65.
15 Laclau, *Emancipation(s)*, 49.
16 Laclau, *Emancipation(s)*, 34.
17 Laclau, *Emancipation(s)*, 34.
18 Laclau, *Emancipation(s)*, 63.

CHAPTER 3

The Way We Live Now

An appreciation of what is radically novel and innovative in Mitra Tabrizian's most recent work must begin with an understanding of what her previous work had already accomplished, for the latter provides the creative platform on which the new work stands. Powered by her deep involvement in the debates in the 1980s and 1990s around subjectivity and ideology, psychoanalysis and feminism, gender, race and sexuality, and informed by the explorations in photographic practice and the image which her earlier projects represented, Mitra Tabrizian has now vigorously mobilized and resumed all the "lessons" of that whole body of work in order to address radically new subject matter and to attempt a challenging project—a critique of the everyday life of contemporary corporate post-modernity and its "systems" of representation.

Tabrizian's involvement at the cutting edge of theoretical argument, which makes her work highly distinctive, is no external "add-on" to her visual practice. These arguments and ideas are integral to, and have been fully absorbed into, her creative practice. Freud on the narcissistic and fetishistic roots of "scopophilia"—the pleasure in looking; Lacan on "the mirror phase"; Laura Mulvey on the gendering of "the look," in *College of Fashion*; Foucault on the constitution and regulation of "the subject," in *Governmentality*, on the construction of the feminine through the codes and the "world" of advertising; Catherine Clement, Isabelle de Courtivron, Julia Kristeva, Joan Riviere on "woman as masquerade"—in the *femme fatale*/film noir "sequences" in *Correct Distance*; Homi Bhabha on fetishism and disavowal in the racial stereotype; Derrida on *différance*, women and the black man as "Other," in the narrative sequences of *The Blues*; Foucault, again, on the panoptic gaze of power, in that compelling, single, stereoscopic image of Khomeni's Islamic cultural revolution and Iranian women staged as part of the spectacle of power, in *Surveillance*. This original body of work represents a deep and sustained engagement with ideas—with the contemporary social and political world re-viewed *through* the subjective optic and what we may call a post-structuralist visual imaginary. The images function here not as "illustrations" or supports of already constituted concepts but as "visual concept-spaces" in which ideas are worked through and "realized" in a series of scenic tableaux or *mise-en-scène*, expanded and developed in another register—a kind of "thinking with/in the image." Lyotard and Baudrillard's ambivalent and doom-laden prophecies about the disappearance of meaning in a world of simulation provide the conceptual poles around which much of the new work circles.

This is a good example of how "the conceptual" functions for Tabrizian's work: as stimulus and challenge rather than as a constraining box. The question of whether Baudrillard is "right" or not is not what is at issue here. This is a different kind of "work." One can use the decline of mass politics and political participation, neutralizing of criticism, the weakness of popular resistance and the ebbing of the tide of democratic politics in the so-called "new world order" without swallowing whole the strategic exaggerations of Baudrillard's *Silent Majority*. One can explore visually the radical insight that the modern global economy is also, and necessarily, an "economy of signs," and that the boundaries between "the real" and the "hyper-real" are blurring, in a media-saturated age, without falling hook, line and sinker for the proposition that reality has been wholly subsumed into "the sign." One can appreciate the way contemporary politics has been thoroughly "mediatized," and the logic of the simulacrum substituting for the "worldliness" of the world, without subscribing to the risible—and ultimately irresponsible—idea that the Gulf War was nothing but a media event.

On the other hand, Baudrillard's argument that when the logic of the basic axioms of the systems which increasingly govern the postmodern, corporate, "global" economy are pushed to their extreme limits, they go into reverse gear "with unpredictable and chaotic results," beautifully encapsulates the effect on us spectators of those uncanny "mishappenings" in the scenarios of, say, *Beyond the Limits*. The high gloss, elegant couture, glamorous settings, the hi-tech gleam, the signs everywhere of refined consumerism, money and corporate style, draw us in. This is the familiar world of exclusive advertising, corporate promotions, PR and marketing, where commodity speaks to commodity. Are these images, we wonder, not in danger of falling into the trap of what the critics call "the fallacy of imitative form"—becoming, in effect, instances of the very thing they are critiquing? In fact, the spectatorial "distances" are, as always in Tabrizian's work, superbly calculated and judged. Only a tiny, often almost unnoticeable, detail here and there—the size and position of the sheep (nature as pure simulation), the bloody human organ being transmitted "down the line" in a glass jar by the executives (the all-encompassing power and "neutrality" of modern technology), or the hole in the head of the father lunching with his sons (the fine line between suicide and early retirement)—alerts us to the point where the otherwise self-confirming, self-sustaining one-dimensional "logic" of late capitalism has gone into serious default mode. Something here has not so much "gone wrong" as "gone only too right!" A world without affect, an emotionally hollow, "indifferent" universe, which, lacking any critical distance on itself, subjective inside or constitutive outside, has gone beyond its limits. "The crime becomes perfect when no-one notices."

In her catalogue essay, "Veils, Masks and Mirrors" for Mitra Tabrizian's earlier book, aptly entitled *Correct Distance* (Cornerhouse, 1990), the feminist art critic Griselda Pollock made two observations which still provide significant points of departure for more recent work. She noted that Mitra Tabrizian's images are all "contrived fictive spaces," adding that they "allow the spectators a distance from dominant forms of voyeurism and exhibitionism," as found in a variety of contemporary visual codes and discourses. Pollock also observed that Tabrizian's photographs "are never simply pictures of something. . . . They are as often practices *on* photography as practices *within* it." These insights provide a useful prism through which to approach the new work.

The images which comprise the projects in this book are indeed "fictive visual spaces." There is evidence everywhere of a photographic practice inscribed by "the cinematic." (Tabrizian is, of course, in other manifestations, a fine filmmaker.) They are exquisitely "staged"—triumphs of *mise-en-scène*. But they are also, in another, more psychoanalytic sense, "scenes" in which the unconscious forces of fantasy and desire, violence and difference, obeying an alternative "logic" or "dream-work" of their own, emerge into the surface of the image and freely play. These images operate as beautifully condensed narratives. Often—in *Lost Time* and *The Perfect Crime*, as in *The Blues* and *Correct Distance*, her "film noir"—the "story-lines" are sustained elliptically across "sequences"—like stills from a series of as yet unmade films. In

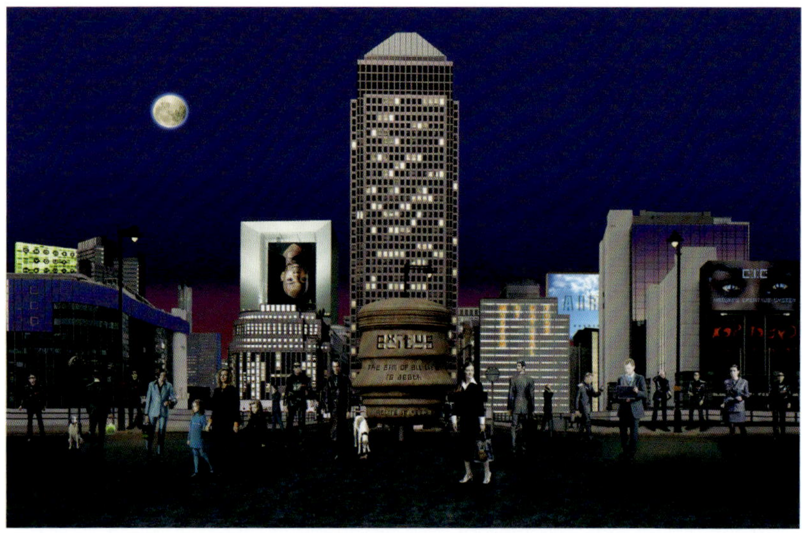

Figure 3.1. Mitra Tabrizian, *Minimal Utopia*, 1999. Lambda print. 72 × 120 cm. © Mitra Tabrizian. All rights reserved, DACS/Artimage 2022.

others—*Minimal Utopia* or *Silent Majority* (figs. 3.1 and 3.2)—the narrative is fused into a single image.

Some reference their cinematic equivalents directly—for example, the deliberate Takeshi Kitano-Tarantino-Reservoir Dogs echoes and references in the implied narrative of *The Perfect Crime* (fig. 3.3). The menacing violence of the gang fight to come, with its dramatic registration in black and white, is perfectly "staged": the "freeze-frame" positions the four black hoods, "going to meet the man," posed against an urban dead-end, in *End Zone*; the stereoscopic framing of the five, black-suited, white-faced executive criminals, waiting to "close the deal," in front of the black car with its white-walled tyres and gleaming body, in *Lost Station*. However, far from merely mimicking the cinematic discourse of the contemporary crime film, or mounting a moral critique of its violence, Tabrizian unravels and re-works its "logic" from the inside.

Un-framing the images from the *Pulp Fiction*–like locations and re-staging them, as she says, "within wider contexts of racial and sexual violence," allows the frames to become charged by deeper, more unconscious currents, permitting these powerful and eloquent contemporary images to signify "otherwise." The racial and sexual edge, so thoroughly disavowed in Tarantino's cynical, cartoon-eye universe, is restored. In *End Zone*, the degraded

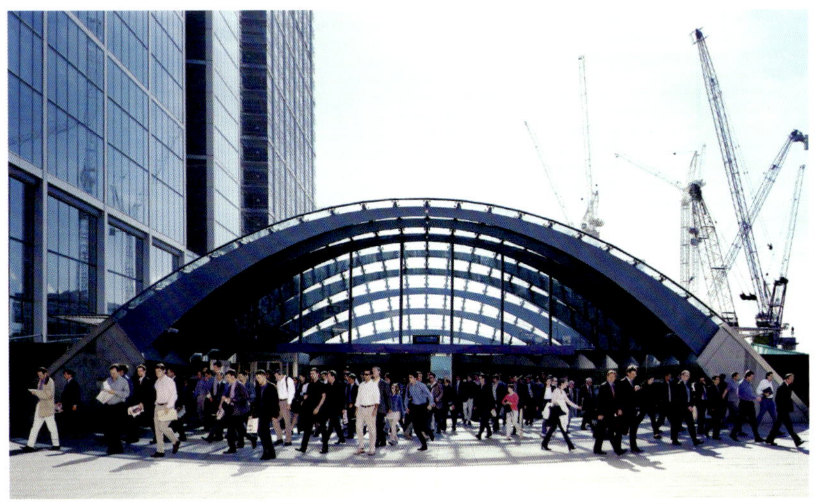

Figure 3.2. Mitra Tabrizian, *Silent Majority*, 2001–2002. Light Jet Type C print. 48 × 84 cm. © Mitra Tabrizian. All rights reserved, DACS/Artimage 2022.

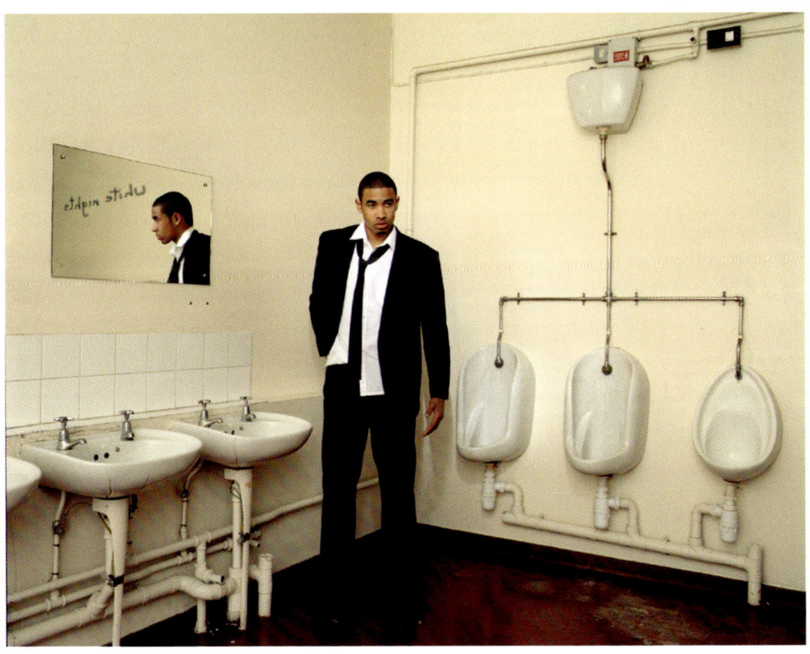

Figure 3.3. Mitra Tabrizian, *The Perfect Crime (White Nights)*, with Andy Golding, 2003–2004. Kodak Type C print. 48 × 60 cm. © Mitra Tabrizian. All rights reserved, DACS/Artimage 2022.

urban setting becomes a silent "actor" or subject of the sequence in its own right. The "look" from the bearded passer-by on the sidewalk, at the four black "suits," deconstructs them, repositioning them closer to the "doubling" discourse of *The Blues*, where vulnerability and aggression are held unresolved (in the knight's expression, in the hang of his body); and difference, which cannot be denied, nevertheless refuses to divide into its staged opposites. The fact that "the crime" has "gone missing" from the frame allows its meanings and resonances to expand, hovering ambivalently between the criminal and the corporate. The deeper, implied narrative in the visual text—with its punning titles incorporated as "clues," often in reverse mirror-shot—opens up the very ambiguities around race and difference, masculinity and violence, fear and vulnerability, which the discourse of the contemporary crime thriller film is deliberately designed to close down. "Who is the victim here, who is the victimiser?"

This ambivalence comes together, and is eloquently captured, in the most beautifully constructed "still" of the sequence *White K/nights* [*sic*]. The moving figure of the black "knight" is both hunter and hunted. His corporate gear is both styled, and in disarray. In the stolen privacy of the lavatory, his hard, masculine "front," like his tie and shirt, have become "undone." His "look," like that of the black figure looking at his white "double" in a mirrored reverse (in *Lost Frontier*, in *The Blues*), hangs, unresolved, between fear and violence. He seems trapped between the soiled white tile of the wash-basins and the grey-white enamel of the urinals, with his inner fears, like the squalid undergrowth of pipes, like entrails, brutally exposed. Here we can see Tabrizian, mobilizing all the resources of distance, staging and the economy of looking to draw the spectator into a disturbed and disturbing space, in that contemporary border-land between cinematic fantasy, racial identification and urban nightmare.

Minimal Utopia, on the other hand, takes us into the domain of sci-fi and the eerie dreamland of the city as futuristic urban dystopia. Here everything is pastiche, everything a simulacrum or dead double of itself. The constructed scene contains many people, but no single living thing. Even the grass beneath their feet is lab-produced astro-turf. Everyone is "power dressed," even the children. Their eyes and faces are empty, without expression. They are "dummies/dumbies." The dog belonging to the man in the elegant leather coat is sniffing one of their hands. A scene of total solitariness, without connection. Not a single path or eye-line crosses that of another. Everything is shrouded in an artificial lunar half-light, neither night nor day. Blue sky, only briefly glimpsed, is a screen projection on the side of a glass skyscraper of an ad selling shares in Air. The armed, private security cops who police the space are all mutants. Over everything, blankly surveying the scene, from two advertising screens, are the only two black faces present: the black boy, head and shoulders, hanging upside down; and the piercing electric-blue "eyes" and arched eyebrows of the person with the velvet-soft brown face. The latter offers us that rarest and most paradoxical of commodities—Nature's Creative System. This is an image of the new "global city," centre of financial flows, share options and the "futures" market, hub of the "new economy," the fully privatised, policed and gated city, the corporate utopia, where nobody is alive but everybody is "on line" and depression is kept at bay by the free availability of Frozac.

Who lives here? Mitra Tabrizian, who has "lovingly" constructed this scene before photographing it, has used it to stage a possible future already complicit in "the way we live now." She insists that we are already almost there. It must be read in conjunction with its alter ego, *Silent Majority*, another of her striking stereoscopic single images, of the morning crowd, hurrying out of the underground station, which yawns behind them like the mouth to Hades, and scurrying to work in the great glass business canyon of Canary Wharf to the left. This is the "crowd," the silent majority, that is absent from the clean, half-lit dead corporate spaces of *Minimal Utopia*. Where the figures in *Minimal Utopia* are lifeless and without movement, the working crowd in *Silent Majority* is full of "movement." Well dressed in a casual way, well-fed, they are neither your oppressed urban office-proletariat nor "the crowd that flowed over London Bridge . . . up the hill and down King William Street" in T. S. Eliot's *Waste Land*. But they are represented as wholly without political agency. Quite how this is communicated is something of a mystery. It has something to do with the way the great metal arc of modern brutalist urban architecture, which encloses them decisively into the bottom half of the frame, breaks the frame in two, cutting the crowd off from the light, air and open sky in the top half of the frame.

It is sometimes asked whether the political as a source of creativity in the visual arts is dead in the age of silent majorities, urban dystopias and postmodern closure. Few seem to have the ambition any longer even to try. Allan Sekula's series on life aboard the enormous, ocean-going tankers which are the lifeline of the global oil trade is one of the few attempts successfully to find a metaphor, outside the language of the documentary image, for the new deregulated global consumerist economy which has emerged since the 1970s.

In this context, Mitra Tabrizian's new work is a bold, ambitious, innovative, singular and courageous attempt to break the silence about the directions in which the contemporary postmodern corporate world is going and to find a new language, informed by the exploration in visual practice and theoretical argument of the last two decades, in which a wide-ranging, visually challenging critique of contemporary life can be mounted. For this alone, her new volume commands critical attention.

NOTE

This essay first appeared in Mitra Tabrizian, *Beyond the Limits* (Gottingen: Steidl, 2004), 1–6.

PART II

PART II · THE NEW POLITICS OF REPRESENTATION

Black Film/British Cinema

CHAPTER 4

New Ethnicities

I have centred my remarks on an attempt to identify and characterise a significant shift that has been going on (and is still going on) in black cultural politics. This shift is not definitive, in the sense that there are two clearly discernible phases—one in the past which is now over and the new one which is beginning—which we can neatly counterpose to one another. Rather, they are two phases of the same movement, which constantly overlap and interweave. Both are framed by the same historical conjuncture and both are rooted in the politics of antiracism and the postwar black experience in Britain. Nevertheless, I think we can identify two different "moments" and that the difference between them is significant.

It is difficult to characterise these precisely, but I would say that the first moment was grounded in a particular political and cultural analysis. Politically, this is the moment when the term "black" was coined as a way of referencing the common experience of racism and marginalization in Britain and came to provide the organizing category of a new politics of resistance, amongst groups and communities with, in fact, very different histories, traditions and ethnic identities. In this moment, politically speaking, "the black experience," as a singular and unifying framework based on the building up of identity across ethnic and cultural difference between the different communities, became "hegemonic" over other ethnic/racial identities—though the latter did not, of course, disappear. Culturally, this analysis formulated itself in terms of a critique of the way blacks were positioned as the unspoken and invisible "other" of predominantly white aesthetic and cultural discourses.

This analysis was predicated on the marginalisation of the black experience in British culture; not fortuitously occurring at the margins, but placed, positioned at the margins, as the consequence of a set of quite specific political and cultural practices which regulated, governed and "normalized" the representational and discursive spaces of English society. These formed the conditions of existence of a cultural politics designed to challenge, resist and, where possible, to transform the dominant regimes of representation—first in music and style, later in literary, visual and cinematic forms. In these spaces blacks have typically been the objects, but rarely the subjects, of the practices of representation. The struggle to come into representation was predicated on a critique of the degree of fetishisation, objectification and negative figuration which are so much a feature of the representation of the black subject. There was a concern not simply with the absence or marginality of the black experience but with its simplification and its stereotypical character.

The cultural politics and strategies which developed around this critique had many facets, but its two principal objects were: first the question of *access* to the rights to representation by black artists and black cultural workers themselves. Secondly, the contestation of the marginality, the stereotypical quality and the fetishised nature of images of blacks, by the counter-position of a "positive" black imagery. These strategies were principally addressed to changing what I would call the "relations of representation."

I have a distinct sense that in the recent period we are entering a new phase. But we need to be absolutely clear what we mean by a "new" phase because, as soon as you talk of a new phase, people instantly imagine that what is entailed is the *substitution* of one kind of politics for another. I am quite distinctly not talking about a shift in those terms. Politics does not necessarily proceed by way of a set of oppositions and reversals of this kind, though some groups and individuals are anxious to "stage" the question in this way. The original critique of the predominant relations of race and representation and the politics which have developed around it have not disappeared and cannot possibly disappear while the conditions which gave rise to it—cultural racism in its Dewesbury form—not only persists but positively flourishes under Thatcherism.[1] There is no sense in which a new phase in black cultural politics could replace the earlier one. Nevertheless, it is true that as the struggle moves forward and assumes new forms, it does to some degree *displace*, reorganise and reposition the different cultural strategies in relation to one another. If this can be conceived in terms of the "burden of representation," I would put the point in this form: that black artists and cultural workers now have to struggle, not on one, but on *two* fronts. The problem is, how to characterize this shift—if indeed, we agree that such a shift has taken or is taking place—and if the language of binary oppositions and substitutions will no longer suffice. The characterization that I would offer is tentative, proposed in the context of this essay mainly to try and clarify some of the issues involved, rather than to preempt them.

This shift is best thought of in terms of change from a struggle over the relations of representation to a politics of representation itself. It would be useful to separate out such a "politics of representation" into its different elements. We all now use the word "representation," but, as we know, it is an extremely slippery customer. It can be used, on the one hand, simply as another way of talking about how one imagines a reality that exists "outside" the means by which things are represented: a conception grounded in a mimetic theory of representation. On the other hand the term can also stand for a very radical displacement of that unproblematic notion of the concept of representation. My own view is that events, relations, structures do have conditions of existence and real effects, outside the sphere of the discursive; but that only within the discursive, and subject to its specific conditions, limits and modalities, do they have or can they be constructed within meaning. Thus, while not wanting to expand the territorial claims of the discursive infinitely, how things are represented and the "machineries" and regimes of representation in a culture do play a *constitutive* and not merely a reflexive, after-the-event role. This gives questions of culture and ideology, and the scenarios of representation—subjectivity, identity, politics—a formative, not merely an expressive, place in the constitution of social and political life. I think it is the move towards this second sense of representation which is taking place and which is transforming the politics of representation in black culture.

This is a complex issue. First, it is the effect of a theoretical encounter between black cultural politics and the discourses of a Eurocentric, largely white, critical cultural theory which, in recent years, has focussed so much analysis of the politics of representation. This is always an extremely difficult, if not dangerous, encounter. (I think particularly of black people encountering the discourses of poststructuralism, postmodernism, psychoanalysis and feminism.) Secondly, it marks what I can only call "the end of innocence," or the end of the innocent notion of the essential black subject. Here again, the end of the essential black subject is something which people are increasingly debating, but they may not have fully reckoned with its political consequences. What is at issue here is the recognition of the extraordinary diversity of subjective positions, social experiences and cultural identities which compose the category "black"; that is, the recognition that "black" is essentially a politically and culturally *constructed* category, which cannot be grounded in a set of fixed transcultural or transcendental racial categories and which therefore has no guarantees in Nature. What this brings into play is the recognition of the immense diversity and differentiation of the historical and cultural experience of black subjects. This inevitably entails a weakening or fading of the notion that "race" or some composite notion of race around the term "black" will either guarantee the effectivity of any cultural practice or determine in any final sense its aesthetic value.

We should put this as plainly as possible. Films are not necessarily good because black people make them. They are not necessarily "right-on" by virtue of the fact that they deal with the black experience. Once you enter the politics of the end of the essential black subject you are plunged headlong into the maelstrom of a continuously contingent, unguaranteed political argument and debate: a critical politics, a politics of criticism. You can no longer conduct black politics through the strategy of a simple set of reversals, putting in the place of the bad old essential white subject, the new essentially good black subject. Now, that formulation may seem to threaten the collapse of an entire political world. Alternatively, it may be greeted with extraordinary relief at the passing away of what at one time seemed to be a necessary fiction: namely, either that all black people are good or indeed that all black people are *the same*. After all, it is one of the predicates of racism that "you can't tell the difference because they all took the same." This does not make it any easier to conceive of how a politics can be constructed which works with and through difference, which is able to build those forms of solidarity and identification which make common struggle and resistance possible but without suppressing the real heterogeneity of interests and identities, and which can effectively draw the political boundary lines without which political contestation is impossible, without fixing those boundaries for eternity. It entails the movement in black politics, from what Gramsci called the "war of manoeuvre" to the "war of position"—the struggle around positionalities. But the difficulty of conceptualizing such a politics (and the temptation to slip into a sort of endlessly sliding discursive liberal-pluralism) does not absolve us of the task of developing such a politics.

The end of the essential black subject also entails a recognition that the central issues of race always appear historically in articulation, in a formation, with other categories and divisions and are constantly crossed and recrossed by the categories of class, gender and ethnicity. (I make a distinction here between race and ethnicity to which I shall return.) To me, films like *Territories, Passion of Remembrance, My Beautiful Laundrette* and *Sammy and Rosie Get Laid*, for example, make it perfectly clear that this shift has been engaged; and that the question of the black subject cannot be represented without reference to the dimensions of class, gender, sexuality and ethnicity.

Difference and Contestation

A further consequence of this politics of representation is the slow recognition of the deep ambivalence of identification and desire. We think about identification usually as a simple process, structured around fixed "selves" which we either are or are not. The play of identity and difference which constructs racism is powered not only by the positioning of blacks as the inferior species but also, and at the same time, by an inexpressible envy and desire; and this is something the recognition of which fundamentally *displaces* many of our hitherto stable political categories, since it implies a process of identification and otherness which is more complex than we had hitherto imagined.

Racism, of course, operates by constructing impassable symbolic boundaries between racially constituted categories, and its typically binary system of representation constantly marks and attempts to fix and naturalize the difference between belongingness and otherness. Along this frontier there arises what Gayatri Spivak calls the "epistemic violence" of the discourses of the Other—of imperialism, the colonized, orientalism, the exotic, the primitive, the anthropological and the folklore.[2] Consequently the discourse of antiracism had often been founded on a strategy of reversal and inversion, turning the "Manichean aesthetic" of colonial discourse upside down. However, as Fanon constantly reminded us, the epistemic violence is both outside and inside, and operates by a process of splitting on both sides of the division—in here as well as out here. That is why it is a question, not only of "black-skin, white-skin," but of *black skin, white masks*—the internalisation of the self-as-other. Just as masculinity always constructs femininity as double—simultaneously Madonna and Whore—so racism constructs the black subject: noble savage and violent avenger. And in the doubling, fear and desire double for one another and play across the structure of otherness, complicating its politics.

Recently I've read several articles about the photographic text of Robert Mapplethorpe—especially his inscription of the nude, black male—all written by black critics or cultural practitioners.[3] These essays properly begin by identifying in Mapplethorpe's work the tropes of fetishisation, the fragmentation of the black image and its objectification, as the forms of their appropriation within the white, gay gaze. But, as I read, I know that something else is going on as well in both the production and the reading of those texts. The continuous circling around Mapplethorpe's work is not exhausted by being able to place him as the white fetishistic gay photographer; and this is because it is also marked by the surreptitious return of desire—that deep ambivalence of identification which makes the categories in which we have previously thought and argued about black cultural politics and the black cultural text extremely problematic. This brings to the surface the unwelcome fact that a great deal of black politics, constructed, addressed and developed directly in relation to questions of race and ethnicity, has been predicated on the assumption that the categories of gender and sexuality would stay the same and remain fixed and secured. What the new politics of representation does is to put that into question, crossing the questions of racism irrevocably with questions of sexuality. That is what is so disturbing, finally, to many of our settled political habits about *Passion of Remembrance.* This double fracturing entails a different kind of politics because, as we know, black radical politics has frequently been stabilised around particular conceptions of black masculinity, which are only now being put into question by black women and black gay men. At certain points, black politics has also been underpinned by a deep absence or more typically an evasive silence with reference to class.

Another element inscribed in the new politics of representation has to do with the question of ethnicity. I am familiar with all the dangers of "ethnicity" as a concept and have written myself about the fact that ethnicity, in the form of a culturally constructed sense of Englishness and a particularly closed, exclusive and regressive form of English national identity, is one of the core characteristics of British racism today.[4] I am also well aware that the politics of antiracism has often constructed itself in terms of a contestation of "multi-ethnicity" or "multi-culturalism." On the other hand, as the politics of representation around the black subject shifts, I think we will begin to see a renewed contestation over the meaning of the term "ethnicity" itself.

If the black subject and black experience are not stabilised by Nature or by some other essential guarantee, then it must be the case that they are constructed historically, culturally, politically—and the concept which refers to this is "ethnicity." The term "ethnicity" acknowledges the place of history, language and culture in the construction of subjectivity and identity, as well as the fact that all discourse is placed, positioned, situated, and all knowledge is contextual. Representation is possible only because enunciation is always produced within codes which have a history, a position within the discursive formations of a particular space and time. The displacement of the "centred" discourses of the West entails putting in question its universalist character and its transcendental claims to speak for everyone, while being itself everywhere and nowhere. The fact that this grounding of ethnicity in difference was deployed, in the discourse of racism, as a means of disavowing the realities of racism and repression does not mean that we can permit the term to be permanently colonized. That appropriation will have to be contested, the term disarticulated from its position in the discourse of "multi-culturalism" and transcoded, just as we previously had to recuperate the term "black," from its place in a system of negative equivalences. The new politics of representation therefore also sets in motion an ideological contestation around the term "ethnicity." But in order to pursue that movement further, we will have to retheorise the concept of difference.

It seems to me that, in the various practices and discourses of black cultural production, we are beginning to see constructions of just such a new conception of ethnicity: a new cultural politics which engages rather than suppresses *difference* and which depends, in part, on the cultural construction of new ethnic identities. Difference, like representation, is also a slippery, and therefore contested concept. There is the "difference" which makes a radical and unbridgeable separation: and there is a "difference" which is positional, conditional and conjunctural, closer to Derrida's notion of *différance,* though if we are concerned to maintain a politics it cannot be defined exclusively in terms of an infinite sliding of the signifier. We still have a great deal of work to do to *decouple* ethnicity, as it functions in the dominant discourse, from its equivalence with nationalism, imperialism, racism and the state, which are the points of attachment around which a distinctive British or, more accurately, English ethnicity have been constructed. Nevertheless, I think such a project is not only possible but necessary. Indeed, this decoupling of ethnicity from the violence of the state is implicit in some of the new forms of cultural practice that are going on in films like *Passion* and

Handsworth Songs. We are beginning to think about how to represent a non-coercive and a more diverse conception of ethnicity, to set against the embattled, hegemonic conception of "Englishness" which, under Thatcherism, stabilizes so much of the dominant political and cultural discourses, and which, because it is hegemonic, does not represent itself as an ethnicity at all.

This marks a real shift in the point of contestation, since it is no longer only between antiracism and multiculturalism but *inside* the notion of ethnicity itself. What is involved is the splitting of the notion of ethnicity between, on the one hand, the dominant notion which connects it to nation and "race" and, on the other hand, what I think is the beginning of a positive conception of the ethnicity of the margins, of the periphery. That is to say, a recognition that we all speak from a particular place, out of a particular history, out of a particular experience, a particular culture, without being contained by that position as "ethnic artists" or film-makers. We are all, in that sense, *ethnically* located and our ethnic identities are crucial to our subjective sense of who we are. But this is also a recognition that this is not an ethnicity which is doomed to survive, as Englishness was, only by marginalising, dispossessing, displacing and forgetting other ethnicities. This precisely is the politics of ethnicity predicated on difference and diversity.

The final point which I think is entailed in this new politics of representation has to do with an awareness of the black experience as a *diaspora* experience, and the consequences which this carries for the process of unsettling, recombination, hybridisation and "cut-and-mix"—in short, the process of cultural *diaspora-isation* (to coin an ugly term) which it implies. In the case of the young black British films and film-makers under discussion, the diaspora experience is certainly profoundly fed and nourished by, for example, the emergence of Third World cinema; by the African experience; the connection with Afro-Caribbean experience; and the deep inheritance of complex systems of representation and aesthetic traditions from Asian and African culture. But, in spite of these rich cultural "roots," the new cultural politics is operating on new and quite distinct ground—specifically, contestation over what it means to be "British." The relation of this cultural politics to the past, to its different "roots," is profound, but complex. It cannot be simple or unmediated. It is (as a film like *Dreaming Rivers* reminds us) (fig. 4.1) complexly mediated and transformed by memory, fantasy and desire. Or, as even an explicitly political film like *Handsworth Songs* (figs. 4.2 and 4.3) clearly suggests, the relation is inter-textual—mediated through a variety of other "texts." There can, therefore, be no simple "return" or "recovery" of the

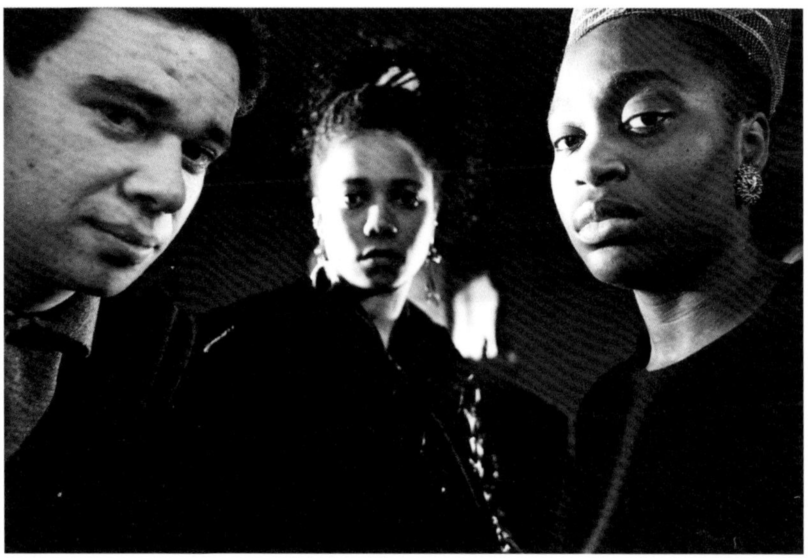

Figure 4.1. Martina Attille, dir., *Dreaming Rivers*, 1988. Production still: Corinne Skinner-Carter as Ms T (center). Film written and directed by Martina Attille for Sankofa Film & Video. Photo: Christine Parry. © Martina Attille. All rights reserved, DACS/Artimage 2022.

ancestral past which is not re-experienced through the categories of the present: no base for creative enunciation in a simple reproduction of traditional forms which are not transformed by the technologies and the identities of the present. This is something that was signalled as early as a film like *Blacks Britannica* and as recently as Paul Gilroy's important book *There Ain't No Black in the Union Jack*.[5] Fifteen years ago we didn't care, or at least I didn't care, whether there was any black in the Union Jack. Now not only do we care, we must.

This last point suggests that we are also approaching what I would call the end of a certain critical innocence in black cultural politics. And here, it might be appropriate to refer, glancingly, to the debate between Salman Rushdie and myself in *The Guardian* some months ago.[6] The debate was not about whether *Handsworth Songs* or *The Passion of Remembrance* were great films or not, because, in the light of what I have said, once you enter this particular problematic, the question of what good films are, which parts of them are good and why, is open to the politics of criticism. Once you abandon essential categories, there is no place to go apart from the politics

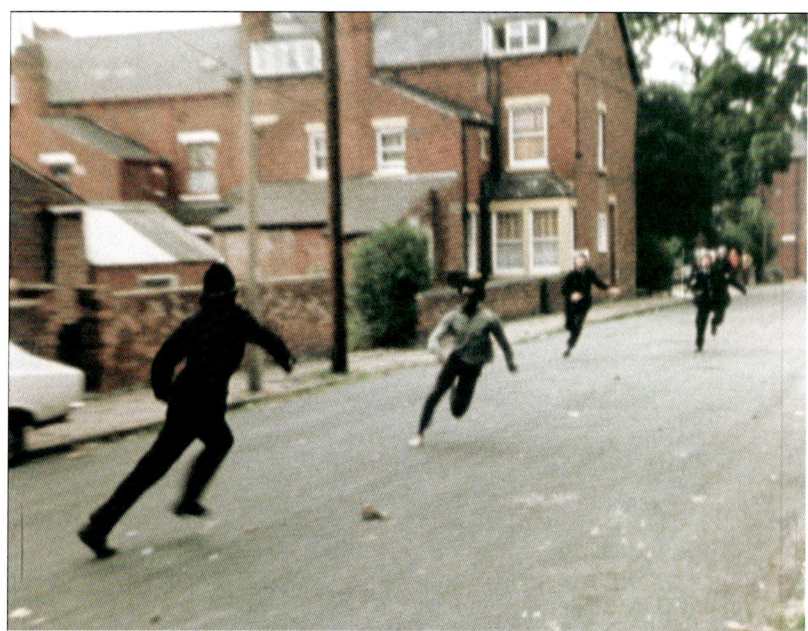

Figure 4.2. John Akomfrah, dir., *Handsworth Songs*, 1987. Single-channel 16mm color film transferred to video. 58 minutes, 33 seconds, with sound. © Smoking Dog Films. All rights reserved, DACS/Artimage 2022. Courtesy of Lisson Gallery.

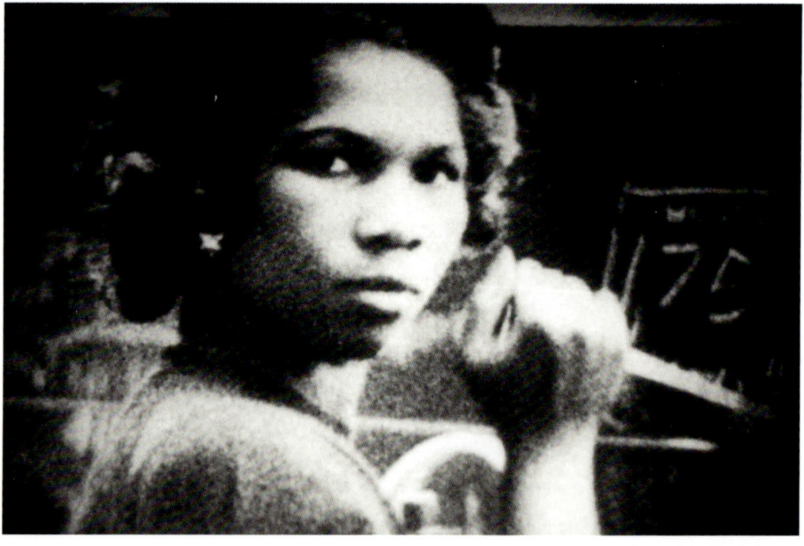

Figure 4.3. John Akomfrah, dir., *Handsworth Songs*, 1987. Single-channel 16mm color film transferred to video. 58 minutes, 33 seconds, with sound. © Smoking Dog Films. All rights reserved, DACS/Artimage 2022. Courtesy of Lisson Gallery.

of criticism and to enter the politics of criticism in black culture is to grow up, to leave the age of critical innocence.

It was not Salman Rushdie's particular judgement that I was contesting, so much as the mode in which he addressed them. He seemed to me to be addressing the films as if from the stable, well-established critical criteria of a *Guardian* reviewer. I was trying, perhaps unsuccessfully, to say that I thought this an inadequate basis for a political criticism and one which overlooked precisely the signs of innovation, and the constraints, under which these film-makers were operating. It is difficult to define what an alternative mode of address would be. I certainly didn't want Salman Rushdie to say he thought the films were good because they were black. But I also didn't want him to say that he thought they weren't good because "we creative artists all know what good films are," since I no longer believe we can resolve the questions of aesthetic value by the use of these transcendental, canonical cultural categories. I think there *is* another position, one which locates itself *inside* a continuous struggle and politics around black representation, but which then is able to open up a continuous critical discourse about themes, about the forms of representation, the subjects of representation, above all, the regimes of representation. I thought it was important, at that point, to intervene to try and get that mode of critical address right, in relation to the new black film-making. It is extremely tricky, as I know, because as it happens, in intervening, I got the mode of address wrong too! I failed to communicate the fact that, in relation to his *Guardian* article, I thought Salman was hopelessly wrong about *Handsworth Songs*, which does not in any way diminish my judgement about the stature of *Midnight's Children*. I regret that I couldn't get it right, exactly, because the politics of criticism has to be able to get both things right.

Such a politics of criticism has to be able to say (just to give one example) why *My Beautiful Laundrette* is one of the most riveting and important films produced by a black writer in recent years and precisely for the reason that made it so controversial: its refusal to represent the black experience in Britain as monolithic, self-contained, sexually stabilised and always "right-on"—in a word, always and only "positive," or what Hanif Kureishi has called "cheering fictions":

> the writer as public relations officer, as hired liar. If there is to be a serious attempt to understand Britain today, with its mix of races and colours, its hysteria and despair, then, writing about it has to be complex. It can't

apologise or idealise. It can't sentimentalise and it can't represent only one group as having a monopoly on virtue.[7]

Laundrette is important particularly in terms of its control, of knowing what it is doing, as the text crosses those frontiers between gender, race, ethnicity, sexuality and class. *Sammy and Rosie* is also a bold and adventurous film, though in some ways less coherent, not so sure of where it is going, overdriven by an almost uncontrollable, cool anger. One needs to be able to offer that as a critical judgement and to argue it through, to have one's mind changed, without undermining one's essential commitment to the project of the politics of black representation.

NOTES

This essay first appeared in *Black Film, British Cinema*, ICA Document 7, ed. Kobena Mercer (London: Institute of Contemporary Arts, 1988), 27–31.

1   The Yorkshire town of Dewesbury became the focus of national attention when white parents withdrew their children from a local school with predominantly Asian pupils, on the grounds that "English" culture was no longer taught on the curriculum. The contestation of multicultural education from the Right also underpinned the controversies around Bradford headmaster Ray Honeyford. See Paul Gordon, "The New Right, Race and Education," *Race and Class* 29, no. 3 (Winter 1987): 95–103.

2   Gayatri C. Spivak, *In Other Worlds: Essays in Cultural Politics* (London: Methuen, 1987).

3   See Kobena Mercer, "Imaging the Black Man's Sex," in *Photography/Politics: Two*, ed. Patricia Holland, Jo Spence, and Simon Watney (London: Comedia, 1987); and David A. Bailey, ed., "Black Experiences," *Ten.8* 22 (1986).

4   Stuart Hall, "Racism and Reaction," in *Five Views on Multi-racial Britain* (London: Commission for Racial Equality, 1978).

5   Paul Gilroy, *There Ain't No Black in the Union Jack: The Cultural Politics of Race and Nation* (London: Hutchinson, 1988).

6   Salman Rushdie, "*Songs* Doesn't Know the Score," *Guardian*, 12 January 1987; Stuart Hall, "Songs of *Handsworth* Praise," *Guardian*, 15 January 1987.

7   Hanif Kureishi, "Dirty Washing," *Time Out*, 14–20 November 1985.

CHAPTER 5

Threatening Pleasures:
A Conversation between Homi Bhabha,
Paul Gilroy, and Stuart Hall

PAUL GILROY: I'd like to begin with the way that *Young Soul Rebels* (figs. 5.1 and 5.2) focuses our attention on 1977. It is a very particular moment, where certain political and cultural forces coalesce. The film draws attention to their coming together in a way that is very different from more orthodox periodizations of recent political history—for example, the way in which 1968 and 1979 tend to stand out as significant changes of direction and momentum.

The film makes bold claims for 1977 and the social and political movements that emerged amid punk, the Jubilee, Rock Against Racism and the popular anti-fascist politics of the period. It suggests that these constructed the mentality of a specific political generation that developed through struggles in which questions of "race" are prominent and that the developing of an anti-fascist movement placed the tensions between class, "race" and sexuality very much to the fore.

STUART HALL: *Young Soul Rebels* represents an important break with a certain conventional reading of the politics of the 1970s. The film honours the moment of Rock Against Racism and the Anti-Nazi League—one of the high points of the anti-racist struggles of the 1970s and one of the few times when the sectarian politics of the Socialist Workers' Party were transcended by the pressure to make contact with wider social forces. But the film re-reads that moment through several other registers: sexual politics, the gay movement, the musical subculture, and so on. It was

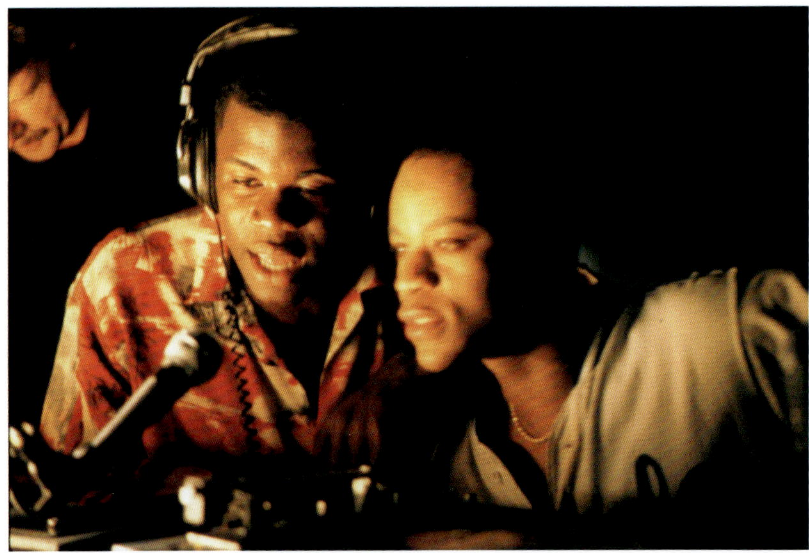

Figure 5.1. Isaac Julien, dir., *Young Soul Rebels*, 1991. Still with Mo Sesay as Caz (left) and Valentine Nonyela as Chris (right). © Isaac Julien, 2022. Courtesy of the artist.

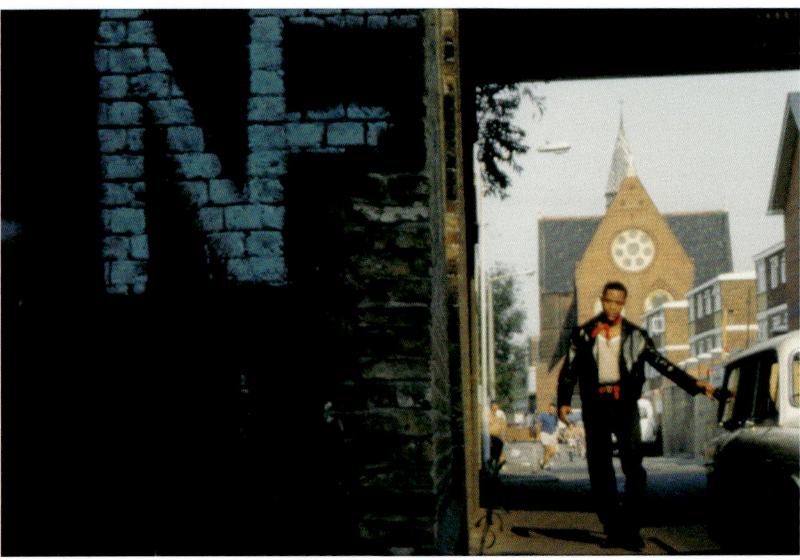

Figure 5.2. Isaac Julien, dir., *Young Soul Rebels*, 1991. Still with Valentine Nonyela as Chris. © Isaac Julien, 2022. Courtesy of the artist.

these broader cultural dimensions to that struggle which accounted for its popular depth and hence its effectivity in stemming the rising tide of skinhead fascism.

HOMI BHABHA: I think it's a departure from all those traditions of political film-making in which the representation of racism is located within issues of class, empire, demands for social equality of the "bourgeois" benevolence of the Harry Belafonte "B" movie. In *Young Soul Rebels*, it is sexuality—largely homoerotic or homophobic—that is the site on which questions of race, social location and community are staged. Pleasure, desire, eroticism and fantasy make cultural identification and political commitment ambivalent, complex affairs.

Though the film represents 1977, it provides a very 1990s reflection of why the left of the seventies found it so difficult to become the political vanguard for issues of race—namely that they repeatedly failed to link race and class in a way that was culturally effective. We see in this film that the sense of a political community among black youth was culturally complex. Politics was not simply the opposition to "bourgeois capitalist" values: it was the opening up of a range of identifications—music, style, sexual pleasure, friendship—that break out of the "black and white" polarities of political opposition.

PAUL GILROY: Obviously a concern with the forms of community and identification that stem from a specific locality is part of the way film seeks to answer the claims of patriotism and national identity. The relationship to fascism may not be so clear these days, but that popular politics around national belonging is still alive. The film contributes to the ongoing struggles.

But the kinds of community that the film appeals to are not fixed solely through notions of place. They operate across the airwaves, through the active use of music. This is a community established through what is dismissively talked about as "consumption," through desire and a kind of play around the body. These themes come together nicely in the concluding sequence in that tentative process of learning to dance in step with one another.

STUART HALL: I'm sure Paul is right. There are a number of imagined communities at work in the film. But locality is certainly one of the important ones. The handling of North-East London is both subtle and complex. A powerful claim is staked for both the *indigenous* and the contested relation of blacks to the local community. As the film represents it, it isn't a question of blacks as outsiders looking in or as naturalized insiders. *Young Soul Rebels* shows the relationship of blacks to the community in all its complexity of different overlapping networks, different alignments and the antagonisms or frontier effects which these create.

After all, Caz and Chris and the white skinheads who taunt them went to the same school and belong to the same housing estate. And some of these frontier effects cut through the black community itself, breaking up any notion of homogeneity or essentialism: for example, between Caz and the other black brothers in the garage about being gay and going out with the white Billibudd; or between the black brothers and Chris about being "half-caste"—a theme which unfortunately tended to get lost in the film.

HOMI BHABHA: Yes, the film produces a creative redefinition of "local space." The 1977 Silver Jubilee was so much about the celebration of local community, with all those "little Englands" decked out in red, white and blue bunting. The film turns this on its head and shows that there exists a range of cultural localities that conflict or coexist with each other. That's what makes a transient, transitional youth culture such an excellent choice for a film about sexuality and ethnicity—it doesn't allow either of those identities to become fixed.

PAUL GILROY: If we emphasize that too strongly we could get into this thing of saying, is it a realist film? Because the detail is so strong I think we can almost slip into seeing the film in those terms.

HOMI BHABHA: No, no way is it realist or documentary. This is suggestively expressed in the use of colour in the film: in the continual play of red-white-blue in all sorts of transformed situations that completely change the codes those colours stand for. *Young Soul Rebels* is about the way a community rewrites a more general history from its own perspective: it makes the past relive in the present. If you compare it to *Absolute Beginners* you see how that film turned Soho and the 1950s into a kind of nostalgic kitsch—a revival, not a rethinking.

PAUL GILROY: I want to change tack here and ask what you think about the film's central image of evil. I found the murderer a great disappointment: his motives, contradictions and inner life are unexplored. I like the way the murder acts as a means to test out different interpretations—the various standpoints within the film seek to fix the meaning of the event differently: one as a racial attack, as an expression of the inner ambivalence in some version of fascist sexuality, "an NF job."

But in the end these clashing interpretations are resolved so neatly through Ken. It is so conventional, that evil would be fixed in the person of a predatory, styleless, shambling, white male isolate (his anorak gives him away). It's almost a joke on the genre conventions that specify a certain type of dislocated, sexually confused killer.

STUART HALL: The white villain—the isolate—is also juxtaposed to the skinheads, who serve as a sort of chorus. The complexity of their position is acknowledged, but never developed.

PAUL GILROY: It isn't gone into very deeply, but let's not underestimate the radical note sounded by the intimacy between the skinheads and the blacks. Locality, community and masculinity connect Chris and Caz with the skinhead trio. The kind of playful banter they share is very subversive of a moralistic, anti-fascist, anti-racist discourse that gets challenged in the film in lots of ways, especially through the question of sexuality. The way these boys speak to each other undermines that moralistic approach, and with it the notion that this British fascism, if that's what it really is, is something external, something grafted on to working-class experience that doesn't belong there. There is real complexity in that.

HOMI BHABHA: "Evil" Ken, too, moves through the narrative in a complex way, I believe. Ken is both insider and outsider, he is both visible and invisible—that's why the "thriller" element turns on him. He is the rather "bent" supplier of stolen equipment, the wheeler-dealer who is also playing hide and seek with his own sexual ambivalence; his repressed homosexuality turns into a kind of racial hatred and compulsive, unspeakable attraction. Ken seems to be another attempt to say something against the easily recognizable antagonisms.

STUART HALL: I don't agree. To me, Ken occupies a more continuous space in the film. But although some of the ambivalences do work, I agree with Paul that he was left in the end as a figure of disembodied evil, and rather unexplored. The skinheads are on the edge of the action rather than part of it; not commenting on the action, so much as threatening to. So they are deliberately flatly drawn, consciously two-dimensional, necessarily performing "to type." I didn't think they needed to be any more developed.

PAUL GILROY: The shortcomings of Ken's characterization can, I think, be read as one consequence of the unsatisfactory way the thriller genre has been negotiated. Quite what that tells us about the difficult translation that black and other independent film-makers will have to make if they move into the overground is harder to determine. It may be that the debates and skills around the politics of representation in those artistic communities are not the ones necessary to make convincing commercial cinema. The film is not a thriller. It borrows from the thriller and mixes those borrowings with a range of other populist devices to orchestrate its gestures towards the box office.

STUART HALL: I think we sometimes underestimate what is implied in the movement from avant-garde film-making, like Isaac's previous film, *Looking for Langston,* to apparently more simple popular forms. The narrative drive in the thriller need not be straightforward, as *The Big Sleep* and other films show, but it's not an engine you can turn on and off at will. Obviously, Isaac was using the thriller form to explore a number of other rich themes. So you could ask, does "who killed whom" *matter*? The answer seems to be that it does, as *film noir* clearly shows.

I raise the question because more and more black film-makers are about to make the transition from the art house documentary to the mainstream, and doing so will often involve negotiating popular forms. I don't advocate capitulating to the genres, but I do recommend submitting to their imperatives rather more than *Young Soul Rebels* does most of the time.

HOMI BHABHA: You're right, as a detective thriller, the film is rather weak. But the *mise-en-scène* of the murder—the pick-up in the park—makes a good point about the thrill, the danger and the location of gay sexuality. There is another thriller convention that is cleverly used—the subtle exchange of looks, gazes, signs that might reveal some clue. Only in this film that exchange is also the code that expresses the erotic sexuality— the way a subculture creates symbols of affiliation through signs that are connective and yet at the same time always open to interpretation. This use of thriller conventions clued into gay gazes—so that characters and audiences are always looking for signs rather than being presented with "themes" or plots—perhaps this is an interesting mixture of genres in the film. Remember Isaac's penchant for making his audience "look for" things—*Looking for Langston*!

STUART HALL: The multi-layered structure means that it is impossible to align the film smoothly with the expectations of its potential audiences. Seeing *Young Soul Rebels* at a special NFT screening may lead us to underestimate how transgressive a film it is. Even at the preview, a section of the sympathetic black audience hissed the homosexual love scenes. I can imagine a young white audience, that loves the music, doing the same—perhaps from the opposite viewpoint. Like *My Beautiful Laundrette*, this is a subversive film even for the audiences to which it is primarily addressed, because it both helps to construct—and at the same time unsettles—the "black experience."

This is especially the case with the handling of sexuality and the erotic. The sexual scenes are powerful precisely because they are not there just to shock: this is not simply another "gay film." The love scene between Caz and Billibudd, especially the first half as they undress one another, is one of the most powerful scenes of its kind that I've seen on the screen. It powerfully constructs homoerotic desire: I doubt whether any heterosexual man could look at that scene, responding to the way fantasy and desire are at one and the same time controlled and evoked, and still say he didn't understand the nature of homoerotic desire. The intimacy of the camera, the fluidity of its movements as it passes backwards and forwards between the two men, its pacing matching the tempo of the unfolding of desire, the harsh colours disturbing the symmetry of the black/white bodies of the lovers. . . . The investment in that scene—in the acting, the staging and the shooting—is enormously powerful.

HOMI BHABHA: Here I must speak up for something of that same energy in the heterosexual scene.

STUART HALL: I thought the heterosexual love scene between Chris and Tracy lacked that powerful investment, and that presents a problem. The film has a four-part structure: at its centre is not a hero or a couple, but two friends, plus the two "external" figures the two men are related to. However, this four-part structure requires that no one figure or couple becomes the center. It needs to fire on both barrels at the same time, if you'll forgive the metaphor, to prevent the identification from becoming simplified. So the uneven investment in the film, in terms, for example, of the weighting of the two love scenes, throws it off balance.

HOME BHABHA: I have real problems with the way the film ends. There was, I thought, a brave attempt throughout to ask difficult questions about what we understand by community: at several crucial moments allegiance and identity are threatened, only for the bond to be strengthened. A sense of community around ethnicity may be threatened by a character's sexual preference for a white partner, so the conflict between ethnicity and sexual desire has to be discussed before solidarity can be re-affirmed. Community has to be created and negotiated; it isn't just there because you are black or gay.

The tension is well maintained partly through the use of music—the ghetto-blaster, the disc-jockey's rap—as a means of identification for youth subculture and as a means of establishing the public visibility necessary to the creation of a social bond. Don't forget that the ghetto-blaster and the tape it contains provide the vital clue to the thriller narrative.

This tension is lost in the rather sentimental end, where after the soul rebels emerge through the spectacular baptismal fire at the gig, they go home, clean their records and dance in happy coupledom—even if the couples are plural: gay, straight and across colour lines.

PAUL GILROY: Yes, I agree that the ending is a bit sentimental, though there is a genuine problem that the final frames seek to address. First, how do we represent a pluralized and open version of the black subject? And second, once we've found a way to summon it up, how do we bring it into the constellation of emergent identities which the anti-racist, polysexual, democratic aspirations of the film ask us to imagine?

It seems that we aren't going to capitulate to the sentiment of the place, region or locality. We aren't going to anchor these new possibilities in the idea of a national community or its various surrogates. We have seen all that getting constructed and deconstructed through the allegories of Empire, through anti-fascism, in relation to sexuality and also in the relationship between Caz and Chris and the skinheads who taunt them in their comings and goings. We don't accept the idealized and mystified black community offered by the barber's shop. We don't yet dare to fix that utopia on to the "mixed race" family. So how do we symbolize it? What order of representation is big enough to get it across?

The fictive kinship of the group at the end seems to me to be a promising attempt to find that symbol. I like the fact that this untidy collection of individuals discovers some fragile intimacy in that moment. I think it is an appropriate note with which to conclude.

STUART HALL: It depends on how you read the end. It worked for me as a sort of "coda"—almost as a moment out of time. I thought of it as related to the imagined construction of what Clause 28 calls a "pretended family relationship." What is going on between them at the end isn't sexual. We see a lot of sexuality in the film—it's intensely, compellingly erotic—but this is not. And it's not the solidarity of the political movement or of the musical subculture either. It is another kind of "civil space," private/public, private but not personal, public but not communal. Another "imagined community." It seemed to me to refer to the whole of the rest of the film, but not to be an attempt to conclude it. It's not the representation of an "imagined community" so much as the construction of it.

I felt this in the way the different bodies get drawn into the dance. Slowly everyone gets drawn in—each dancing together but differently. Specifically, it refuses coupling. It is like the emergence of a new kind of "family." I especially like the way Billibudd, the white boy, dances: a kind of tentativeness at first, as if he's learning to dance, learning to match his steps and rhythm to theirs. It has the tentativeness of emergence for me, a kind of utopian emergence.

NOTE

This discussion first appeared in *Sight and Sound*, n.s. 1, no. 4 (August 1991): 17–19.

CHAPTER 6

A Rage in Harlesden

Despite the much-acclaimed British cinema renaissance, black British films are still rarer than gold dust. *Babymother* (figs. 6.1–6.3), the new "reggae-musical" from Formation Films, courtesy of Channel Four Films, the Arts Council and sundry foreign backers, will be one of the first of the new cinematic wave to test the treacherous waters of British film distribution. Directed by Julian Henriques, former *Arena* and BBC arts-documentary producer, and produced by Parminder Vir, herself a successful television-documentary producer and his partner in Formation Films, *Babymother* is grounded in the vibrant black scene of dancehall—the latest musical sound (and look) to capture the imagination of Britain's urban black youth. Shot on location in Harlesden, one of London's black inner suburbs, using largely non-professional actors, it is a much expanded and transformed version of an idea first tried out by Henriques in a 1992 Channel 4 docudrama-with-music, *We the Ragamuffin*.

Babymother is the story of Anita (Anjela Lauren Smith), a young black woman who has two children for babyfather Byron (Wil Johnson), an ambitious reggae singer. Anita is determined—along with her two rude-girl friends Sharon (Caroline Chikazie) and Yvette (Jocelyn Esien)—to become a D-J, make a successful recording and be the toast of the local dancehall scene. However, life as a babymother on a Harlesden housing estate is a difficult base from which to launch this project, and Anita is having trouble with both the babyfather (who is more dedicated to his singing career than

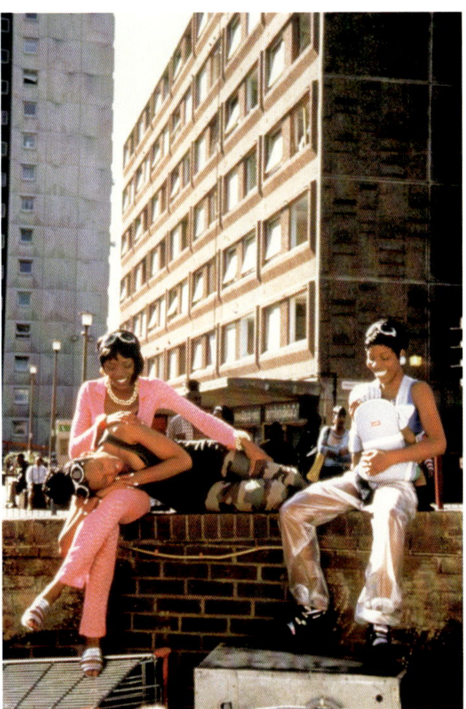

Figure 6.1. Production still from *Babymother* (Julian Henriques, dir., 1998). Photo credit: Colin Patterson. Courtesy of Julian Henriques.

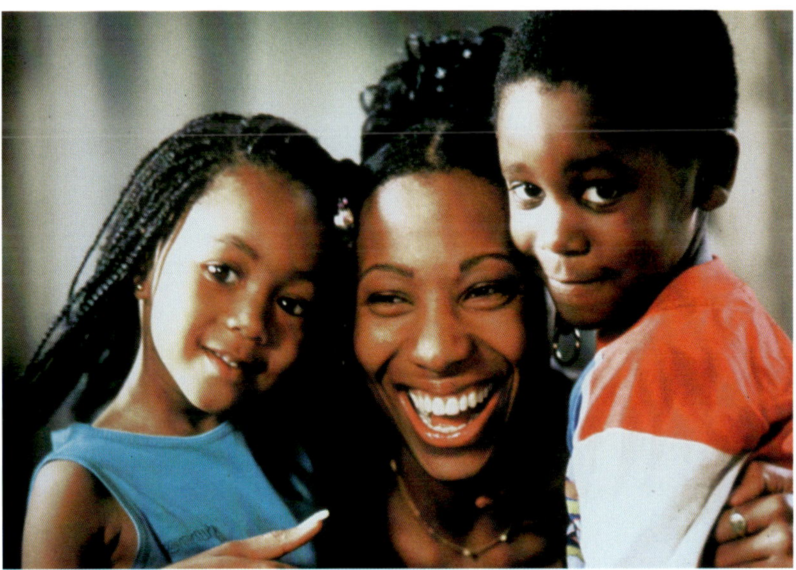

Figure 6.2. Production still from *Babymother* (Julian Henriques, dir., 1998). Photo credit: Colin Patterson. Courtesy of Julian Henriques.

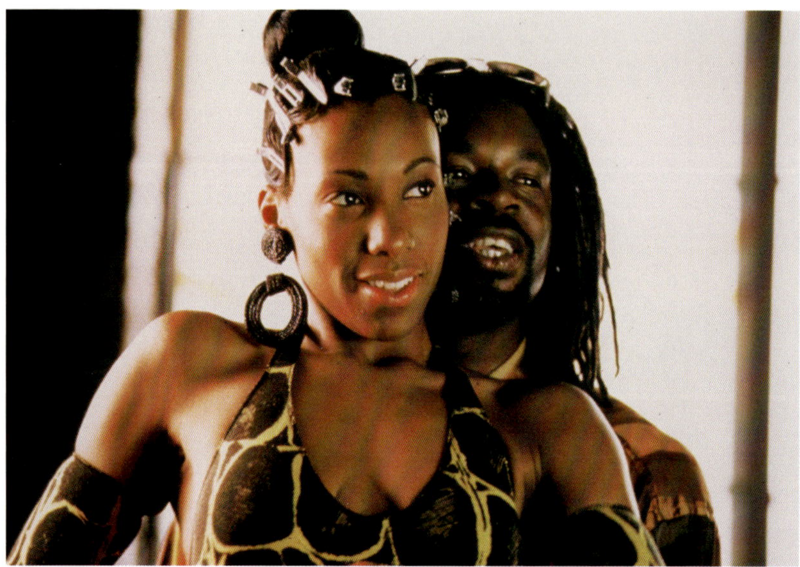

Figure 6.3. Production still from *Babymother* (Julian Henriques, dir., 1998). Photo credit: Colin Patterson. Courtesy of Julian Henriques.

to his paternal duties) and her mother and sister (who disapprove of her ragga style, attitude and ambitions), not to mention raising the money for the demo-tape session. The vicissitudes which accompany her struggles to survive, and her group's ultimate success in a competition with Byron, provide the film's main narrative drive.

This storyline, however, is merely the thin scaffold for the elements that really give *Babymother* its vitality and raw energy, which have everything to do with the dancehall scene. It is not the first film to be based on dancehall—but the low-budget, tape-to-film Hi-8 *Dancehall Queen* (shot by Don Letts and Rick Elgood for Chris Blackwell of Island Records fame), which commanded Jamaican screens without a break for six months, still languishes without a commercial release in Britain. Dancehall has been loosely appropriated into Britain's black inner suburbs from Jamaica's burgeoning club scene. The music derives by way of a series of sliding transfers from "roots" reggae, through hip-hop to D-J music and US-influenced gangsta rap: rhythms with which black youth has been beguiling the hearts and souls of white "wannabes" (that is, "want-to-be *blacks*") in the urban club scene for some time. The violent imagery, sexually explicit (often homophobic) lyrics and dance movements which characterized the so-called "slackness" style of the dominant male ragga singers (such as Buju Banton) have been translated into the stunningly glamorous, recklessly minimalist fashion outfits, incredible hairstyle constructions and erotic body-moves of their followers, the ragga girls. Indeed, the women's display/performances in dancehall—*to* or *at* or *for* their "men"?—have rapidly become its scandalous, spectacular centrepiece. The girls' taking of center stage, putting their new-found independence (or, not to mince words, "pussy-power") into the music and their bodies fully on the line—which is at the narrative heart of *Babymother*—represents the capture and overrunning of the last bastion of the male-dominated reggae scene. As the song puts it, "No need no ring 'pon we finger to be a man's wife / The loving wha' we have man want that for life / We live in the gym, non-stop exercise / And the body wha' we have make man stand up and rise." So much for patriarchal power.

Almost everything to do with dancehall itself in *Babymother* is first rate. The recording-studio sequences and dancehall scenes—especially the final showdown between Byron and Anita—are beautifully shot and exciting to watch, transmitting an authentic feel of the cultural vibes. The music—ranging from slow reggae to ferocious rap put-downs like "I Don't Care" and featuring some of the finest current black British performers (including Carroll Thompson and Cinderella)—is of consistently high quality.

But the other aspects of Anita's story—the love entanglements, the difficult relationships with her mother and sister and the scenes shot around Harlesden—are more problematic. Here the narrative tends to become cluttered, with too many dramatic turns that remain under-motivated. Designed to lend emotional depth to the portrait of Anita's life and social context to the story, these scenes feel as if they have been conceived and directed in a different register, owing more to well-made, social-realist British television drama than to the exuberant stylizations of the musical. The portrait of Harlesden remains sketchy and generalized, while the emotional scenes test the range of these engaging but inexperienced actors. There is a real question about the relationship between the everyday lives and the stylish dancehall performances of these rude boys and girls—whether, "in reality," these different facets belong together or are a Saturday night/Monday morning thing—but the tensions of this aspect of dancehall subculture are not convincingly explored, so the film's different registers appear as a lack of stylistic integration.

This is compounded by the fact that *Babymother* is described as a "reggae-musical." One expects the term musical to be used loosely here: that this will be a film about the music scene, which will provide the narrative excuse for a great deal of musical performance. But audiences may be surprised to find that the film also works to the conventions of the musical genre, with characters in everyday-life settings bursting into song—or rather, works in this way some of the time. Two scenes towards the beginning—where Byron woos his way back into Anita's affections and she, in song (and body), "responds"; and when he tries to win her by serenading from the bonnet of his convertible and the girls on the balcony send him packing in a musical "reply"—are strictly non-naturalistic in form. However, unaccountably, the genre conventions then disappear, the rest being conceived and shot in a broadly stylized naturalism.

This may be the result of revisions in the editing room or a change of heart as the production progressed, but the effect is to make the film's address to the audience difficult to read. Knowing references to other films and genres are all the rage these days, in the spirit of postmodern quotation, but this reflexivity works only if the shifts are self-consciously undertaken and clearly marked. It's difficult in *Babymother*'s case to see what introducing such references and then abandoning them is supposed to achieve.

All this suggests *Babymother* is unsure what kind of film it aims to be—as was Isaac Julien's *Young Soul Rebels* (1991), a film about black soul music, sexual politics and growing up black and male in London, a political thriller and a *film noir* rolled into one. It's as if black film-makers have so few chances to make films they are seduced into trying to realize all the movies they have in their heads in one go, in case they never get another shot at it. What looks like a failure of stylistic integration in *Babymother* may be the effect of trying to make a serious film about black popular life and a musical entertainment extravaganza within the same cinematic vehicle. It may also be a function of grafting on to a commercially risk venture a sure-fire popularity and box-office appeal, offering its audiences something on screen they can identify with.

This should not affect our overall assessment of *Babymother*'s achievement. New British cinema has not so far produced a successful film of any quality based on the music industry—its forays into youth culture have studiously avoided that culture's most exuberant aspects and primary domain: everything to do with the music scene. This is where black British youth culture—stylish, self-confident, aspirational, entrepreneurial and replete with attitude—has been making its indelible mark on British popular culture, transforming street fashion, dance and sexuality-as-public-spectacle in its wake. Having succeeded in introducing the black male body into contemporary media iconography, it intends to make a series of body-moves on the carefully constructed limits of the current "babe" style. Those wishing to know what the new "multicultural London" is really like should stroll down Harlesden High Street on a Friday afternoon, as the black boutiques close and the dancehall venues and Jungle-music clubs prepare to come to life, and listen to the white "rude boys" with their imitation locks talking a broad Estuary-Trench Town *patois*, and measure the length of the women's, as it were, skirts.

Babymother's audiences will be invited—perhaps for the first time—to look inside the engine of popular creativity, in all its raw excess, which is being tentatively invoked in more sober terms in New Labour's relentlessly empty hype about New Britain. This is a bit of New Britain little dreamed of by Norman Tebbit, or, one suspects, Tony Blair (though Peter Mandelson may have encountered it!). This film is wired directly into the motor of assertive energy which is powering so-called multicultural Britain, to whose rhythm London is increasingly swinging. Indeed, dancehall represents the thin, shapely, aggressively stylized and eroticized black body of Hot Britain struggling to get out from inside the sleeker, fatter, complacent corporate figure of Cool Britannia.

Cultural critics—in Harlesden, Kingston and on Brooklyn's Atlantic Avenue (for this is a black diasporic phenomenon, as Isaac Julien's 1994 television documentary *The Darker Side of Black* clearly shows)—are already at work trying to unravel what *Babymother* has to tell us about the current state of play in the gender wars. For dancehall represents one form of the cultural emancipation of young black women: the film's rude girls breaking out from being forever bossed about by the rude boys in the unthinkingly masculinist world of reggae culture. It transmits the sight and sound of an explosive declaration of independence—though the position of the rude girl who is also a babymother (implying the continuing importance but conspicuously absent presence of the babyfather) reminds us of the persistent ambiguities on which this independence is predicated. In dancehall women can simulate the wilder aspects of copulation in their dance movements on stage as explicitly and aggressively as any man, but they remain, as *Babymother* shows, emotionally centred on the absent male and are on display *for the men* (as well as, perhaps, for one another). Their sexual lives, their squabbles and jealousies, still revolve around the male figures to whom the performances appear to be primarily addressed.

These complex issues are well-represented within the film through Anita's tender moments alone with her children, the scenes of them with their father, when he's at home (which avoid the usual sentimentality), and the film's theme song itself, which underlines the message: "Babymother! Be a Mother to Your Child!" But they cannot be fully explored within the limits of its entertainment conventions. In that sense, *Babymother* marks another episode in second-wave feminism's long, incomplete march. It reminds us that popular culture, despite its elements of celebration and resistance, is also and always an ambiguous and contradictory space. Among other issues, *Babymother* poses the question of just how, and by what complicated shifts, the liberation of women is connected to girl power. And, as an added bonus in an engaging black British extravaganza, Anita, Sharon and Yvette make the Spice Girls look like convent fifth-formers at a Sunday afternoon tea party.

NOTE

This essay first appeared in *Sight and Sound*, n.s. 8, no. 9 (September 1998): 24–26.

CHAPTER 7

Cultural Identity and Cinematic Representation

Both the new "Caribbean Cinema," which has now joined the company of the other "Third Cinemas," and the emerging cinemas of Afro-Caribbean Blacks in the "diasporas" of the West put the issue of cultural identity in question. Who is the emergent, new subject of the cinema? From where does it speak? The practices of representation always implicate the positions from which we speak or write—the positions of *enunciation*. What recent theories of enunciation suggest is that, though we speak, so to say "in our own name," of ourselves and from our own experience, nevertheless, who speaks and the subject who is spoken of are never exactly in the same place. Identity is not as transparent or unproblematic as we think. Perhaps, instead of thinking of identity as an already accomplished historical fact, which the new cinematic discourses then represent, we should think, instead, of identity as a "production," which is never complete, always in process, and always constituted within, not outside, representation. But this view problematizes the very authority and authenticity to which the term "cultural identity" lays claim.

In this paper, then, I seek to open a dialogue, an investigation, on the subject of cultural identity and cinematic representation. The "I" who writes here must also be thought of as, itself, "enunciated." We all write and speak from a particular place and time, from a history and culture which is specific. What we say is always "in context," *positioned*. I was born into and spent my childhood and adolescence in a lower-middle-class family in Jamaica. I have lived all my adult life in England, in the shadow of the Black diaspora—"in the belly of the beast." I write against the background of a lifetime's work in cultural studies. If the paper seems preoccupied with the diaspora experience and its narratives of displacement, it is worth remembering that all discourse is "placed," and the heart has its reasons.

There are at least two different ways of thinking about "cultural identity." The first position defines "cultural identity" in terms of the idea of one, shared culture, a sort of collective "one true self," hiding inside the many other, more superficial or artificially imposed "selves," which people with a shared history and ancestry hold in common. Within the terms of this definition, our cultural identities reflect the common historical experiences and shared cultural codes which provide us, as "one people," with stable, unchanging and continuous frames of reference and meaning, beneath the shifting divisions and vicissitudes of our actual history. This "oneness," underlying all the other, more superficial differences, is the truth, the essence, of "Caribbeanness." It is this identity which a Caribbean cinema must discover, excavate, bring to light, and express through a cinematic representation.

Such a conception of cultural or national identity played a critical role in all the postcolonial struggles which have so profoundly reshaped our world. It lay at the center of the vision of the poets of "Negritude," like Aimé Césaire and Léopold Senghor, and of the Pan-African political project, earlier in the century. It continues to be a very powerful and creative force in emergent forms of representation amongst hitherto marginalized peoples. In postcolonial societies, the rediscovery of this identity is often the object of what Frantz Fanon once called a "passionate research . . . directed by the secret hope of discovering beyond the misery of today, beyond self-contempt, resignation and abjuration, some very beautiful and splendid era whose existence rehabilitates us both in regard to ourselves and in regard to others." New forms of cultural practice in these societies address themselves to this project for the very good reason that, as Fanon puts it, in the recent past, "Colonisation is not satisfied merely with holding a people in its grip and emptying the native's brain of all form and content. By a kind of perverted logic, it turns to the past of the oppressed people, and distorts, disfigures and destroys it."[1]

The question which Fanon's observation poses is what is the nature of this "profound research" which drives the new forms of visual and cinematic representation? Is it only a matter of unearthing that which the colonial experience buried and overlaid, bringing to light the hidden continuities it suppressed? Or is a quite different practice entailed—not the rediscovery but

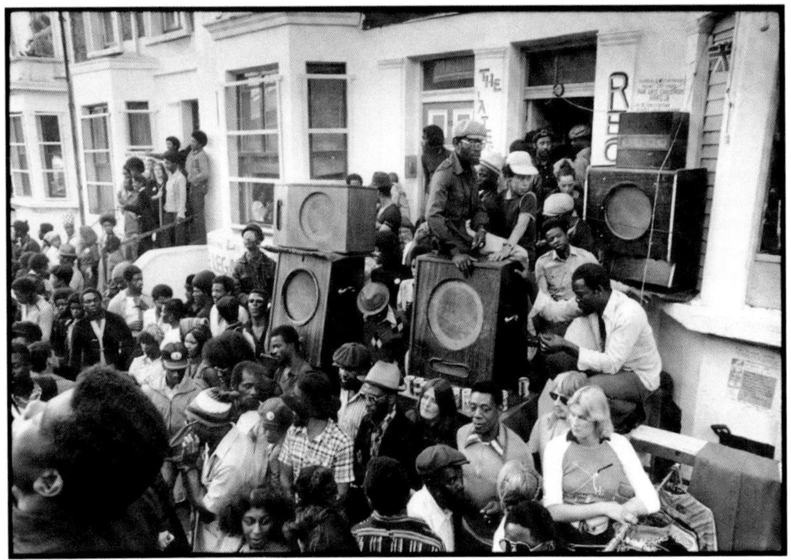

Figure 7.1. Armet Francis, *Sound System at Notting Hill Carnival*, 1969. © Armet Francis. All rights reserved, DACS/Artimage 2022.

the *production* of identity? Not an identity grounded in the archaeology but in the *re-telling* of the past?

We cannot and should not, for a moment, underestimate or neglect the importance of the act of imaginative rediscovery. "Hidden histories" have played a critical role in the emergence of some of the most important social movements of our time. The photographic work of a visual artist like Armet Francis (figs. 7.1 and 7.2), a Jamaican-born photographer who has lived in Britain since the age of eight, is a testimony to the continuing creative power of this conception of identity within the practices of representation. His photographs of the peoples of the Black Triangle, taken in Africa, the Caribbean, the U.S. and the U.K., attempt to reconstruct in visual terms "the underlying unity of the black people whom colonisation and slavery distributed across the African diaspora." His text is an imaginary reunification.

Crucially, his images find a way of imposing an imaginary coherence on the experience of dispersal and fragmentation, which is the history of all enforced diasporas. He does this by representing or "figuring" Africa as the mother of these different civilizations. His Triangle is, after all, "centered" in Africa. Africa is the name of the missing term, the great aporia, which

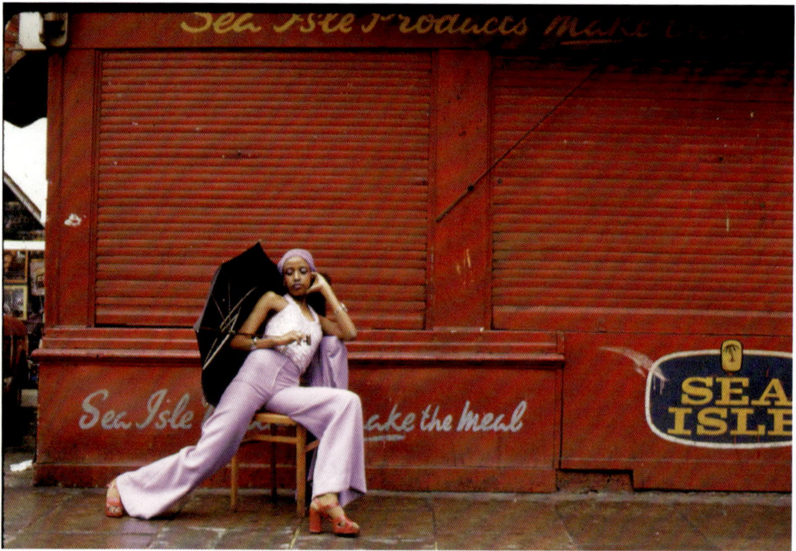

Figure 7.2. Armet Francis, *Fashion Shoot Brixton Market*, 1973. © Armet Francis. All rights reserved, DACS/Artimage 2022.

lies at the center of our cultural identity and gives it a meaning which, until recently, it lacked. No one who looks at these textual images now, in the light of the history of transportation, slavery, and migration, can fail to understand how the rift of separation, the "loss of identity," which has been integral to the Caribbean experience, only begins to be healed when these forgotten connections are once more set in place. Such texts restore an imaginary fullness or plenitude, to set against the broken rubric of our past. They are resources of resistance and identity, with which to confront the fragmented and pathological ways in which that experience has been reconstructed within the dominant regimes of cinematic and visual representation of the West.

There is, however, a related but different view of cultural identity, which qualifies, even if it does not replace, the first. This second position recognizes that, as well as the many points of similarity, there are also critical points of deep and significant *difference* which constitute "what we really are": or rather—since history has intervened—"what we have become." We cannot speak for very long, with any exactness, about "one experience, one identity," without acknowledging its other side—the differences and discontinuities which constitute, precisely, the Caribbean's "uniqueness." Cultural identity, in this second sense, is a matter of "becoming" as well as of "being." It belongs to the future as much as to the past. It is not something which already exists, transcending place, time, history, and culture. Cultural identities come from somewhere, have histories. But, like everything which is historical, they undergo constant transformation. Far from being eternally fixed in some essentialized past, they are subject to the continuous "play" of history, culture, and power. Far from being grounded in a mere "recovery" of the past, which is waiting to be found and which, when found, will secure our sense of ourselves into eternity, identities are the names we give to the different ways we are positioned by, and position ourselves within, the narratives of the past.

It is only from this second position that we can properly understand the truly traumatic character of "the colonial experience." The way we have been positioned and subject-ed in the dominant regimes of representation was a critical exercise of cultural power and normalization, precisely because they were not superficial. They had the power to make us see and experience ourselves as "Other." Every regime of representation is a regime of power formed, as Foucault reminds us, by the fatal couplet, "power/knowledge." And this kind of knowledge is internal, not external. It is one thing to place some person or set of peoples as the Other of a dominant discourse. It is quite another thing to subject them to that "knowledge," not only as a matter of imposed will and domination, by the power of inner compulsion and subjective conformation to the norm. That is the lesson—the sombre of majesty—of Fanon's insight into the colonizing experience in *Black Skin, White Masks.*

This expropriation of cultural identity cripples and deforms. If its silences are not resisted, they produce, in Fanon's vivid phrase, "individuals without an anchor, without horizon, colourless, stateless, rootless—a race of angels."[2] Nevertheless, it also changes our conception of what "cultural identity" is. In this perspective, cultural identity is not a fixed essence at all, lying unchanged outside history and culture. It is not some universal and transcendental spirit inside us on which history has made no fundamental mark. It is not once-and-for-all. It is not a fixed origin to which we can make some final and absolute Return. Of course, it is not a mere phantasm, either. It is *something*—not a mere trick of the imagination. It has its histories—and histories have their real, material, and symbolic effects. The past continues to speak to us. But this is no longer a simple, factual "past," since our relation to it is, like the child's relation to the mother, always-already "after the break." It is always constructed through memory, fantasy, narrative, and myth. Cultural identities are the points of identification, the unstable points of identification or suture, which are made within the discourses of history and culture. Not an essence but a *positioning*. Hence, there is always a politics of position, which has no absolute guarantee in an unproblematic, transcendental "law of history."

This second view of cultural history is much less familiar and unsettling. But it is worth spending a few moments tracing its formations. We might think of Caribbean identities as "framed" by two axes or vectors, simultaneously operative: the vector of similarity and continuity, the vector of difference and rupture. The one gives us some grounding in, some continuity with, the past. The second reminds us that what we share is precisely the experience of a profound discontinuity. The peoples dragged into slavery by the triangular Atlantic trade came predominantly from Africa—though when that supply ended, it was temporarily refreshed by indentured labor from the Asian subcontinent. This neglected fact explains why, when you visit Guyana or Trinidad, you suddenly see, symbolically inscribed in the faces of their peoples, the paradoxical "truth" of Christopher Columbus's mistake: you *can* find "Asia" by sailing west, if you know where to look! The great majority of the slaves were from Africa—already figured in the European imaginary, as the "Dark Continent." But they were also from different countries, tribal communities, villages, languages, and gods. African religion, which has been so formative in Caribbean spiritual life, is precisely *different* from Christian monotheism in having, not one, but a proliferation of gods. These gods live on, in an underground existence, in the pantheon of Black Saints which people the hybridized religious universe of Latin American Catholicism. The paradox is that it was the uprooting of slavery and transportation and the insertion into the plantation economy (as well as the symbolic economy) of the Western world that "unified" these peoples across their differences, in the same moment as it cut them off from direct access to that past.

Difference, therefore, persists—in and alongside continuity. And this is so, not only for the past but in the present. To return to the Caribbean after any long absence is to experience again the shock of "doubleness," of similarity and difference. As a Jamaican returning for the First Caribbean Film Festival (Images Caraïbes, June 1988) I "recognized" Martinique instantly, though I was seeing it for the first time. I also saw at once how different Martinique is from, say, Jamaica: and this is no mere difference of topography or climate. It is also a profound difference of culture and history. And the difference *matters*. It positions Martiniquans and Jamaicans as *both* the same *and* different. Moreover, the boundaries of difference are continually repositioned in relation to different points of reference. Vis-à-vis the developed West, we are very much "the same." We belong to the marginal, the underdeveloped, the periphery, the "other." We are at the outer edge, the "rim," of the metropolitan world— always "South" to someone else's *El Norte.*

At the same time, we do not stand in the same relation of "otherness" to the metropolitan centers. Each has negotiated its economic, political, and cultural dependency differently. And this "difference," whether we like it or not, is already inscribed in our cultural identities. In turn, it is this negotiation of identity which makes us, vis-à-vis other Latin American people, with a very similar history, different: Caribbeans—*les Antilliennes*—"islanders" to their mainland.

How, then, to describe this play of "difference" within identity? The common history—transportation, slavery, colonization—has been profoundly formative. It was also, metaphorically as well as literally, a translation. The inscription of difference is also specific and critical. I use the word "play" because the double meaning of the metaphor is important. It suggests, on the one hand, the instability, the permanent unsettlement, the lack of any final resolution. On the other hand, it reminds us that the place where this "doubleness" is most powerfully to be heard is "playing" within the varieties of Caribbean musics. This cultural "play" could not be represented, cinematically, as a simple binary opposition—"past/present," "them/us." Its complexity exceeds this binary structure of representation. At different places, times, in relation to different questions, the boundaries are re-sited. They become, not only what they have, at times, certainly been—mutually excluding categories but also, what they sometimes are—differential points along a sliding scale.

One trivial example is the way Martinique both *is* and *is not* "French." Superficially, Fort-de-France is a much richer, more "fashionable" place than Kingston—which is not only visibly poorer, but itself at a point of transition between being "in fashion" in an Anglo-African and Afro-American way—for those who can afford to be in any sort of fashion at all. Yet, what is distinctively "Martiniquais" can only be described in terms of that special and peculiar supplement which the Black and mulatto skin adds to the "refinement" and sophistication of a Parisian-derived *haute couture*: that is, a sophistication which, because it is Black, is always transgressive.

To capture this sense of difference which is not pure "otherness," we need to deploy the play on words of a theorist like Jacques Derrida. Derrida uses the anomalous "a" in his way of writing "difference"—*différance*—as a marker which sets up a disturbance in our settled understanding or translation of the concept. It sets the word in motion to new meanings without obscuring the trace of its earlier meanings. His sense of *différance*, as Christopher Norris puts it, thus "remains suspended between the two French verbs 'to differ' and 'to defer' (postpone), both of which contribute to its textual force but neither of which can fully capture its meaning. Language depends on difference, as Saussure showed . . . the structure of distinctive proposition which makes up its basic economy. Where Derrida breaks new ground . . . is in the extent to which 'differ' shades into 'defer' . . . the idea that meaning is always deferred, perhaps to the point of an endless supplementarity, by the play of significa-tion."[3] This second sense of difference challenges the fixed binaries which sta-bilize meaning and representation and shows how meaning is never finished or completed in this way but keeps on moving to encompass other, additional, or supplementary meanings, which, as Norris puts it elsewhere, "disturb the classical economy of language and representation." Without relations of dif-ference, no representation could occur. But what is then constituted within representation is always open to being deferred, staggered, serialized.

Where, then, does identity come into this infinite postponement of mean-ing? Derrida does not help us as much as he might here—and this is precisely where, in my view, he has permitted his profound theoretical insight to be reappropriated into a celebration of formal "playfulness," which evacuates it of its political meaning. For if signification depends upon the endless reposi-tioning of its differential terms, meaning, in any specific instance, depends on the contingent and arbitrary stop—the necessary and temporary "break" in the infinite semiosis of language. This does not detract from the original in-sight. It only threatens to do so if we mistake this "cut" of identity—this *posi-tioning*, which makes meaning possible—as a natural and permanent, rather than an arbitrary and contingent "ending." Whereas, I understand every such position as "strategic," and arbitrary, in the sense that there is no permanent equivalence between the particular sentence we close and its true meaning, as such. Meaning continues to unfold, so to speak, beyond the arbitrary closure which makes it, at any moment, possible. It is always either over-, or under-determined. There is always something "left over."

It is possible, with this conception of "difference," to rethink the posi-tionings and re-positionings of Caribbean cultural identities in relation to at least three "presences," to borrow Aimé Césaire's and Léopold Seng-hor's metaphor: *présence africaine*, *présence européenne*, and the third, most ambiguous, presence of all—the sliding term, *présence americaine*. I mean America, here, not in its first world sense, the big cousin to the North whose "rim" we occupy, but in the second, broader sense: America, the Newfound Land, the "New World," the *Terra Incognita*.

"*Présence africaine*" is the site of the repressed. Apparently silenced beyond memory by the power of the new cultures of slavery, it was, in fact, present everywhere: in the everyday life and customs of the slave quarters, in the languages and patois of the plantations, in names and words, often disconnected from their taxonomies, in the secret syntactical structures through which other languages were spoken, in the stories and tales told to children, in religious practices and beliefs, in the spiritual life, the arts, crafts, musics, and rhythms of slave and post-emancipation society. Africa, the signified which could not be represented, remained the unspoken, unspeakable "presence" in Caribbean culture. It is "hiding" behind every verbal inflection, every narrative twist of Caribbean cultural life. It is the secret code with which every Western text was "re-read." *This* was—is—the "Africa" that "is still alive and well in the diaspora."

When I was growing up as a child in Kingston, I was surrounded by the signs, music, and rhythms of this Africa of the diaspora, which only existed as a result of a long and discontinuous series of transformations. But, although almost everyone around me was some shade of brown or black (Africa "speaks"!), I never once heard a single person refer to themselves or to others as, in some way, or as having been at some time in the past "African." It was in the early 1970s that this Afro-Caribbean identity became historically available to the great majority of Jamaican people, at home and abroad. In this historic moment, the great majority of Jamaicans discovered themselves to be "black"—just as they discovered themselves to be the sons and daughters of "slavery."

This profound cultural discovery, however, was not, and could not, be made directly, without "mediation." It could only be made through the impact on popular life of the postcolonial revolution, the civil rights struggles, the culture of Rastafarianism, and the music of reggae—the metaphors, the figures, or signifiers of a new construction of "Jamaican-ness." This is a "new" Africa, as we might say, necessarily, "deferred"—as a spiritual, cultural and political metaphor.

It is the presence/absence of the "otherness" of Africa, in this form, which made it also the privileged signifier of new conceptions of Caribbean identity. Everyone in the Caribbean, of whatever ethnic background, must sooner or later come to terms with this African presence. Black, brown, mulatto, white—all must look "*présence africaine*" in the face, speak its name.

But whether it is, in this sense, an *origin* of our identities, unchanged by four hundred years of displacement, dismemberment, transportation, to which we could in any final or literal sense return, is more open to doubt. The original "Africa" is no longer there. It too has been transformed. History is, in that sense, irreversible. We must not collude with the West which, precisely, "normalizes" and appropriates Africa by freezing it into some timeless zone of the "primitive, unchanging past." Africa must at last be reckoned with by Caribbean people. But it cannot in any simple sense be merely recovered. It belongs, irrevocably, for us, to what Edward Said once called an "imaginative geography and history," which helps "the mind to intensify its own sense of itself by dramatizing the difference between what is close to it and what is far away."[4] Our belongingness to it constitutes what Benedict Anderson calls "an imagined community." To *this* "Africa," which is a necessary part of the Caribbean imaginary, we can't literally go home again.

The character of this displaced "homeward" journey—its length and complexity—comes across vividly, not yet in the Caribbean cinemas but in other texts. Tony Sewell's text and documentary archival photographs, *Garvey's Children: The Legacy of Marcus Garvey*, tell the story of a "return" to an African identity for Caribbean people which went, necessarily, by the long route—through London and the United States. It "ends," not in Ethiopia but with the Garvey statue in front of the St. Anne Parish Library in Jamaica, with the music of Burning Spear and Bob Marley's "Redemption Song." This is our "long journey" home. Derek Bishton's remarkably courageous and visual and written text, *Black Heart Man*—the story of a *white* photographer "on the trail of the promised land"—starts in England and goes through Shashamene, the place in Ethiopia to which many Jamaican people have found their way on their search for the Promised Land and the story of slavery, but it ends in Pinnacle, Jamaica, where the first Rastafarian settlement was established, and "beyond"—among the dispossessed of twentieth-century Kingston and the streets of Handsworth, where Bishton's voyage of discovery first began. This symbolic journey is necessary for us all—and necessarily circular.

This is the Africa we must return to but "by another route": what Africa has *become* in the New World, what we have made of "Africa." "Africa"—as we re-tell it through politics, memory and desire.

What of the second, troubling, term in the identity equation—the European presence? For many of us, this is a matter not of too little but of too much. Where Africa was a case of the unspoken, Europe was a case of that which is endlessly speaking—and endlessly speaking *us*. The European presence thus interrupts the innocence of the whole discourse of "difference" in the Caribbean by introducing the question of power. "Europe" belongs irrevocably to the question of power, to the lines of force and consent, to the pole of the *dominant* in Caribbean culture. In terms of colonialism, under-development, poverty, and the racism of color, the European presence is that which, in visual representation, has positioned us within its dominant regimes of representation: the colonial discourse; the literatures of adventure and exploitation; the romance of the exotic; the ethnographic and travelling eye; the tropical languages of tourism, travel brochure and Hollywood; and the violence, pornographic languages, of *ganja* and urban violence.

The error is not to conceptualize this "presence" in terms of power but to locate that power as wholly external to us—an extrinsic force, whose influence can be thrown off like the serpent that sheds its skin. What Frantz Fanon reminds us, in *Black Skin, White Masks*, is how its power is inside as well as outside: "the movements, the attitudes, the glances of the other fixed me there, in the sense in which a chemical solution is fixed by a dye. I was indignant; I demanded an explanation. Nothing happened. I burst apart. Now the fragments have been put together again by another self."[5] This "look," from—so to speak—the place of the Other, fixes us, not only in its violence, hostility, and aggression, but in the ambivalence of its desire. This brings us face to face, not simply with the dominating European presence as the site or "scene" of integration where those other presences which it had actively disaggregated were recomposed, reframed, put together in a new way, but as the site of a profound splitting and doubling: what Homi Bhabha has called "the ambivalent identifications of the racist world" . . . the "'otherness' of the self inscribed in the perverse palimpsest of colonial identity."[6]

The dialogue of power and resistance, of refusal and recognition, with and against "*présence européenne*" is almost as complex as the so-called "dialogue" with Africa. In terms of popular cultural life, it is nowhere to be found in its pure, pristine state. It is always already fused, syncretized, with other cultural elements. It is always-already creolized. Not "lost" beyond the Middle Passage, but ever-present, the harmonics in our musics to the ground-bass of Africa, traversing and intersecting our lives at every point. How can we stage this dialogue so that, finally, we can place it, without terror, rather than being forever placed by it? Can we ever recognize its irreversible influence, whilst resisting its imperializing eye? The enigma is impossible, so far, to resolve. It requires the most complex of cultural strategies. Think, for example, of the dialogue of every Caribbean filmmaker, one way or another, with the dominant cinemas of the "West"—of European and American filmmaking. Who could describe this tense and tortured dialogue as a "one way trip"?

I think of the third, "New World" presence, not so much in terms of power, as of ground, place, territory. It is the juncture-point where the other cultural tributaries met, the "empty" land (the European colonizers emptied it) where strangers from every other part of the globe met. None of the people who now occupy the islands—black, brown, white, African, European, American, Spanish, French, East Indian, Chinese, Portuguese, Jew, Dutch—originally "belonged" there. It is the space where the creolizations and assimilations and syncretisms were negotiated. The New World is the third term—the primal scene where the fateful/fatal encounter was staged between Africa and the West. It has to be understood as the place of displacements: of the original pre-Columbian inhabitants, the Arawaks, permanently displaced from their homelands; of peoples displaced in different ways from Africa, Asia, and Europe; the displacements of slavery, colonization, and conquest. It stands for the endless ways in which the Caribbean people have been destined to "migrate"; it is the signifier of migration itself—of travelling, voyaging, and return as fate, as destiny, of the Antillean as the prototype of the modern or postmodern New World nomad, continually moving between center and periphery. This preoccupation with movement and migration Caribbean cinema shares with many other "Third Cinemas," but it is one of our defining themes and is destined to cross the narrative of every film script or cinematic image. *Présence americaine* also has its silences, its suppressions. Peter Hulme, in his essay on "Islands of Enchantment,"[7] reminds us that the word "Jamaica" is the Hispanic form of the indigenous Arawak name of the island—"land of wood and water"—which Columbus's renaming ("Santiago") never replaced. The Arawak presence remains a ghostly one, visible in the islands mainly in their museums and archaeological sites, part of the barely knowable or usable "past." It is not represented in the emblem of the Jamaican National Heritage Trust, for example, which chose, instead, the figure of Diego Pimienta, "an African who fought for his Spanish masters against the English invasion of the island in 1655"—a deferred, metonymic, sly and sliding representation of Jamaican identity if ever there was one! Peter Hulme recounts the story of how Prime Minister Edward Seaga tried to alter the Jamaican coat of arms, which consists of two Arawak figures holding a shield with five pineapples surmounted by an alligator. "Can the crushed and extinct Arawaks represent the dauntless character of Jamaicans? Does the low-slung, near-extinct crocodile, a cold-blooded reptile, symbolize the warm, soaring spirit of Jamaicans?," Prime Minister Seaga asked, rhetorically.[8] There can be few political statements which so eloquently testify to the complexities entailed in the process of trying to represent a diverse peoples with a diverse history through a single, hegemonic "identity." Fortunately, Mr Seaga's invitation to the Jamaican people, who are overwhelmingly of African descent, to start their "remembering" by first "forgetting" something else got the comeuppance it so richly deserved.

Thus I think of the New World presence—America, *Terra Incognita*—as itself the beginning of diaspora, of diversity, of difference: as what makes Afro-Caribbean people already the people of a diaspora. I use this term here metaphorically, not literally. I do not mean those scattered tribes whose identity can only be secured in relation to some sacred homeland to which they must at all costs return, even if it means pushing other peoples into the sea. This is the old, the imperializing, the hegemonizing, form of "ethnicity." We have seen the fate of people of Palestine at the hands of this backward-looking conception of diaspora—and the complicity of the West with it. The diaspora experience, as I intend it here, is defined not by essence or purity, but by the recognition of a necessary heterogeneity, diversity; by a conception of "identity" which lives with and through, not despite, difference; by *hybridity*. Diaspora identities are those which are constantly producing and reproducing themselves anew, through transformation and difference. One can only think here of what is uniquely—essentially—Caribbean: precisely the mixes of color, pigmentation, physiognomic type; the "blends" of tastes that is Caribbean cuisine; the aesthetics of the "cross-overs," of "cut-and-mix," to borrow Dick Hebdige's telling phrase, which is the heart and soul of Black music.

Young Black cultural practitioners and critics in Britain are increasingly coming to acknowledge and explore in their works this "diaspora aesthetic": "Across a whole range of cultural forms there is a 'syncretic' dynamic which critically appropriates elements from the master-codes of the dominant culture and 'creolises' them, disarticulating given signs and re-articulating their symbolic meaning. The subversive force of this hybridising tendency is most apparent at the level of language itself where creoles, patois, and black English decentre, destabilise and carnivalize the linguistic domination of 'English'—the nation-language of master-discourse—through strategic inflections, reaccentuations and other performative moves in semantic, syntactic and lexical codes."[9]

It is because this "New World" is constituted for us as place, a narrative of displacement, that it gives rise so profoundly to a certain imaginary plenitude, recreating the endless desire to return to "lost origins," to be one again with the mother, to go back to the beginning. Who can ever forget, when once seen rising up out of the blue-green Caribbean, those islands of enchantment? And yet, this "return to the beginning" is like the Imaginary in Lacan—it can never be fulfilled or requited and hence is the beginning of the symbolic, of representation, the infinitely renewable source of desire, memory, myth, search, discovery—in short, the reservoir of our cinematic narratives.

I have been trying, in a series of metaphors, to put in place a different sense of our relationship to the past and thus a different way of thinking about cultural identity, which might begin to constitute new points of recognition in the discourses of the emerging Caribbean cinema. I have been trying to speak of identity as constituted, not outside but within representation, and, hence, of cinema not as second-order mirror held up to reflect what already exists but as that form of representation which is also able to constitute us as new kinds of subjects and thereby enable us to discover who we are. Communities, Benedict Anderson argues in *Imagined Communities*, are to be distinguished not by their falsity/genuineness but by the style in which they are imagined. This is the vocation of a modern Caribbean cinema; by allowing us to see and recognize different parts and histories of ourselves, to construct those points of identification, those positionalities we call "a cultural identity."

"We must not therefore be content," Fanon warns us, "with delving into the past of a people in order to find coherent elements which will counteract colonialism's attempts to falsify and harm. . . . A national culture is not a folklore nor an abstract populism that believes it can discover a people's true nature. . . . A national culture is the whole body of efforts made by a people in the sphere of thought to describe, justify, and praise the actions through which that people has created itself and keeps itself in existence."[10]

NOTES

    This essay first appeared in *Exiles: Essays on Caribbean Cinema*, ed. Mbye Cham (London: Africa World Press, 1992), 220–36.

1 Frantz Fanon, *Wretched of the Earth*, trans. Constance Farrington (New York: Grove, 1963), 170.

2 Fanon, *Wretched of the Earth*, 176.

3 Christopher Norris, *Deconstruction: Theory and Practice* (London: Methuen, 1982), 32.

4 Edward Said, *Orientalism* (New York: Random House, 1979), 55.

5 Frantz Fanon, *Black Skin, White Masks*, trans. Charles Lam Markmann (London: Pluto, 1986 [1952]), 109.

6 Homi Bhabha, "Remembering Fanon," foreword to Fanon, *Black Skin, White Masks*, xv.

7 Peter Hulme, "Islands of Enchantment," *New Formations* 3 (1987).

8 *Jamaica Hansard* 9 (1983–84): 363. Quoted in Hulme.

9 Kobena Mercer, "Diaspora Culture and the Dialogic Imagination: The Aesthetics of Black Independent Film in Britain," in *Black Frames: Critical Perspectives on Black Independent Cinema*, ed. Mbye B. Cham and Claire Andrade-Watkins (Cambridge, MA: MIT Press, 1988), 57.

10 Fanon, *Wretched of the Earth*, 188.

FANON, CREOLIZATION, AND DIASPORA

The After-Life of Frantz Fanon:
Why Fanon? Why Now? Why *Black Skin, White Masks*?

Why Fanon? Why, after so many years of relative neglect, is his name once again beginning to excite such intense intellectual debate and controversy? Why is this happening at this particular moment, at this conjuncture? And why is it around the text *Black Skin, White Masks* that the renewed "search for Fanon" is being conducted?[1] This essay addresses these questions as they were posed in the context of the ICA's *Mirage: Enigmas of Race, Difference and Desire*, a programme of film, installation, performance and visual art works by contemporary black artists who acknowledge some debt of influence, usually indirect, to Fanon's work (figs. 8.1 and 8.2). It is written in the spirit of the title of the conference which took place during the season: "Working with Fanon."

Why, of the many figures whose emblematic presence could have triggered off such a profusion of discursive and figural production, does the incitation turn out to be Frantz Fanon? Though at one time his name would have been widely known and recognised—usually as the signifier of a certain brand of incendiary Third World–ism—he is now virtually unknown, even amongst those young, practising, black writers and artists whose work appears, unwittingly, to betray the "trace" of his presence. Of course, events do not obey any singular, unfolding, teleology of causality or time. But I cannot help feeling that the re-call of Fanon, now, in this moment, here, in this way, has something of the overdetermined "return of the repressed" about it—a timeliness constituted from many directions at once, as well as a certain "un-timeliness."

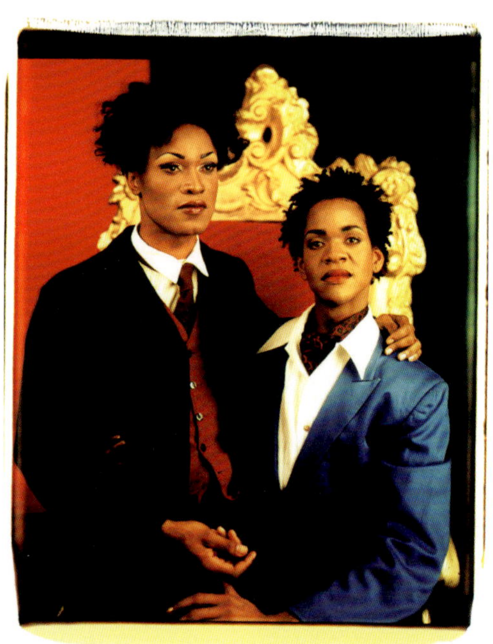

Figure 8.1. Lyle Ashton Harris, *Sisterhood* (in collaboration with Iké Udé), 1994. Duraflex print. 60 × 48 in. © Lyle Ashton Harris. Courtesy of the artist.

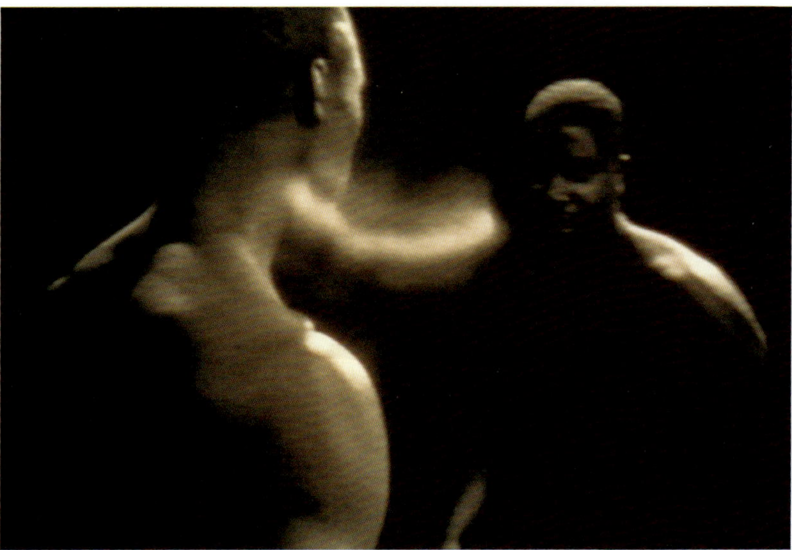

Figure 8.2. Steve McQueen, *Bear*, 1993. 16mm black-and-white film transferred to video, continuous projection, projection fills entire wall. 10 minutes, 35 seconds, no sound. © Steve McQueen. Courtesy of the artist, Thomas Dane Gallery, and Marian Goodman Gallery.

Rather than trying to recapture the "true" Fanon, we must try to engage the after-life of Frantz Fanon—that which Jacques Derrida would call, following his recent essay on Marx, his "spectral effect" (was *that* the *Mirage* of the title?) in ways that do not simply restore the past in a cycle of the eternal return, but which will bring the enigma of Fanon, as Benjamin said of history, flashing up before us at a moment of danger.[2] "The colonial man who writes for his people" that is, of course, colonial man and woman, an elision in Fanon which is as characteristic as it is un-timely, "ought to *use* the past with the intention of opening up the future," Fanon observed; "an invitation to an action and a basis of hope."[3] What action, what hope is proposed to us here? And why, of all his writings, is the subject of these aspirations *Black Skin, White Masks*?

For many years it was the essay on national liberation movements in *The Wretched of the Earth*, with its invitation to the violent, self-cleansing, self-remaking anticolonial struggle, which constituted, for many, the "invitation to an action"—and for others, the nightmare spectre of black barbarism stalking the streets. "They want to take our place" is the fantasy which best seems to describe the latter response—which is how Fanon himself described the white colonial settler's "paranoid fantasy of primordial dispossession" when confronted by the black man.[4] This contest over "which text of Fanon's?" as a way of trying to annex his political legacy after the event is far from concluded. In his sceptical but accomplished *tour d'horizon* of recent writing on Fanon, "Critical Fanonism," Henry Louis Gates, who is basically sympathetic to much in the postcolonial and poststructuralist enterprise, nevertheless takes some delight in exposing how varied, even internally contradictory, the recent "readings" of Fanon as a global theorist have been.[5] On the other hand, in an essay entitled "The Appropriation of Fanon," which savages the whole "revisionist" expropriation of Fanon, Cedric Robinson argues that to privilege *Black Skin, White Masks* over *The Wretched of the Earth* is a motivated political strategy which, perversely, reads Fanon backwards from his "immersion in the revolutionary consciousness of the Algerian peasantry" to the "petit-bourgeois stink" of the former text.[6]

It cannot be just by pure chance that it is *Black Skin, White Masks*, with its psychoanalytically inspired exploration of the unconscious mechanisms of racism and colonialism, its attention to the role of projective fantasy, its opening up of the dislocated subjective complexity of the "deceptively obvious 'fact of blackness'" and its attention to the dialectic of identity, otherness and desire, which provides the privileged ground of Fanon's "return" and of the contestation over him. Kobena Mercer, in his introductory essay to the *Mirage* catalogue, "Busy in the Ruins of Wretched Phantasia," reminds us—as if we are likely to forget—that, because every reading is also a re-reading, it is bound to be political. He offers us one condition of existence for Fanon's untimely "return": "Whereas earlier generations privileged the Marxist themes of Fanon's later work . . . at the height of the optimism of the postwar social movements, the fading fortunes of the independent left during the 1980s provided the backdrop to renewed interest in *Black Skin, White Masks*, Fanon's first and most explicitly psychoanalytic text." Although there is much to this argument, it is worth recalling how, both during his lifetime and since, almost as much rhetorical energy has gone into proving how far "Fanonism" deviated from anything like a classical Marxism. The struggle to colonise Fanon's work has been an ongoing process from the moment of his death, and the identification of Fanon's writing in terms of its "Marxist themes" in the '60s and '70s was, itself, already the product of a re-reading. As another contributory factor, Mercer cites the many-layered, discursive structure of *Black Skin, White Masks*, "whose authorial eye constantly oscillates between multiple points of view," and whose voice, we should add, draws on multiple registers, "autobiographical, clinical, sociological, poetical, philosophical, political."[7] I will come back to the dubious proposition of some final symptomatic breaks between Fanon's early and late work, as well as to the question of how we are to re-read the multivocality of *Black Skin, White Masks*.

The view, boldly stated by Fanon in his introduction to *Black Skin, White Masks*—that "only a psychoanalytic interpretation of the black problem can lay bare the anomalies of affect that are responsible for the structure of the complex" that is racism and colonialism—is what constitutes the novelty of this text.[8] But it also makes absurd the claim that "Fanon was a political activist rather than a theorist," which those who would recuperate Fanon to some earlier, more "revolutionary" manifestation find so seductive. Incidentally, the idea that it is only "politics," and not also "theory," which is at issue in these contentious readings and re-readings of Fanon is, of course, something that it suits the recuperators to have us believe, but it is not a proposition which can be seriously sustained. The problem is that Fanon's 1952 text anticipates poststructuralism in a startling way, even if the addition of the phrase "effective disalienation of the black man entails immediate recognition of social and economic realities" inflects his anachronistically prescient observation in an unexpected direction. The dependency complex, he says, "is the outcome of a double process, primarily economic . . . subsequently the internalization—or, better, the epidermalization—of this inferiority."[9] A wonderful word, *epidermalization*: literally, the inscription of race on the skin. This armature of "race" provides the black subject with that which elsewhere Fanon calls an alternative "corporeal schema." But, as he always insists, this schema is cultural and discursive, not genetic or physiological: "Below the corporeal schema I had sketched a historico-racial schema . . . woven . . . out of a thousand details, anecdotes, stories."[10]

Another deep source of the contemporary appeal of *Black Skin, White Masks* is the association it establishes between racism and what has come to be called the scopic drive—the eroticisation of the pleasure in looking and the primary place given in Fanon's text to the "look" from the place of the "Other."[11] It is the exercise of power through the dialectic of the "look"—race in the field of vision, to paraphrase Jacqueline Rose[12]—which *fixes* the Negro from the outside (Fanon's word, which I will use in this context) by the fantasmatic binary of absolute difference: "sealed into that crushing objecthood";[13] "overdetermined from without."[14] Not only is Fanon's Negro caught, transfixed, emptied and exploded in the fetishistic and stereotypical dialectics of the "look" from the place of the Other; but he/she *becomes*—has no other self than—this *self-as-Othered*. This is the black man *as* his [*sic*] alienated self-image; or as Homi Bhabha puts it, "not Self and Other but the 'Otherness' of the Self inscribed in the perverse palimpsest of colonial identity." It is this "bizarre figure of desire" which, as Bhabha rightly observes, "compels Fanon to put the psychoanalytic question to the historic condition of colonial man."[15]

There can be little doubt that, as Gates suggested, "Fanon's current fascination for us has something to do with the convergence of the problematic of colonialism with that of subject-formation."[16] This bringing to bear of the poststructuralist and psychoanalytic engines of contemporary theory on the primordial—and primordially resistant—structure of racism and the historic colonial relation excites in us a disjunctive frisson of stimulation and pleasure which is only, in part, cognitive (the *jouissance* of theory having long been underestimated). Nevertheless, the familiarity of these concepts, now, may lead us to underestimate the novelty and originality of Fanon's insights at the time of writing. The grain of his text runs incontrovertibly towards the recognition that an account of racism which has no purchase on the inner landscape and the unconscious mechanisms of its effects is, at best, only half the story. The simplistic counterposing of *Black Skin, White Masks* to *The Wretched of the Earth*, with the implication that, in the passage from one to the other Fanon somehow "graduated" from childish petit-bourgeois things to greater "maturity," does not explain why *The Wretched of the Earth* ends, in the chapter on "Colonial War and Mental Disorders," with a series of psychiatric case studies, presented in a language which clearly echoes the paradigm first sketched in *Black Skin, White Masks*. "Because it is a systematic negation of the other person and a furious determination to deny the other person all attributes of humanity, colonialism forces the people it dominates to ask themselves the question constantly: 'In reality, who am I?'" Fanon adds, pointedly, "Perhaps these notes on psychiatry will be found ill-timed and singularly out of place in such a book; but we can do nothing about that."[17] Nuff said.

In *Black Skin, White Masks*, this fixing of the Negro by the fantasmatic binaries of fear and desire which have governed the representation of the black figure in colonial discourse and which, Fanon argues, lie at the heart of the psychic reality of racism, is profoundly and mordantly explored. Indeed, the operation is unmasked in such a penetrating way that, in effect, we are tempted to read Fanon's text as more simple and straightforward than it is. Since the text so remorselessly returns to the binary oppositions *black/white, coloniser/colonised*, I wonder how many of his readers unconsciously slip into reading him as if binaries are the exclusive focus of his tale? As if the real title of his book was "Black Skin, White Skin"? Ignoring the fact that, though his subject is, of course, framed throughout by the dichotomous and manichean structure of racism as a binary system of representation and power, it is the split or divided self, the two sides within the *same* figure—the colonial Negro—which centrally preoccupies him.

The central figure of the book is the colonial Negro, especially the Antillean, who is obliged, in the scenarios of the colonial relation, to have a relationship to self, to give a performance of self, which is scripted by the coloniser, producing in him the internally divided condition of "absolute depersonalization."[18] The mechanisms of this substitution are very precisely described. The bodily or corporeal schema, which Fanon says is "a definitive structuring of self and the world," necessary to any sense of self because it "creates a real dialectic between my body and the world," is fragmented and shattered.[19] Such a scopic *gestalt*, which Jacques Lacan, for example, suggested is of great formative importance for the constitution of the subject, cannot be formed.[20] In its place, Fanon suggests, there arises the "historico-racial schema," which *weaves him* "out of a thousand details, anecdotes, stories"—"battered down by tom-toms, cannibalism, intellectual deficiency, fetishism, racial defects, slave ships, and above all: 'Sho' good eatin.'"[21] "Now the fragments have been put together again by another self."[22]

There are, Fanon insists, "two camps: the white and the black."[23] But, he adds, "Overnight, the Negro has been given two frames of reference within which he has to place himself. . . . For not only must the black man be black; he must be black in relation to the white man."[24] The problem which preoccupies Fanon, then, is not the *existence* of the white man in colonialism, but the fact that the black man can only exist in relation to himself through the alienating presence of the white "Other." As Homi Bhabha correctly observes, this is "not a neat division" but "a doubling, dissembling image of being in at least two places at once."[25] The subject to which Fanon addresses himself is historically specific. It is not racism as a general phenomenon but racism in the colonial relation which he dissects. His task was to unpack its inner landscapes—and to consider the conditions for the production of a new kind of subject and the decolonisation of the mind as the necessary subjective conditions for the decolonisation of the world: "I propose nothing short of the liberation of the man of color *from himself.*"[26] It is the opening up of this radical aperture at the centre of Fanon's text which constitutes its novelty, its originality, its "timeliness."

Today, the question for us is how to read, how to interpret, the problem he posed, the answers which his text proposes, and the invitation to action and to hope which it prefigured.

One response has been to occupy the structure of Fanon's argument, turning the mechanisms which he identifies against themselves. This takes the question of "the look" seriously, goes to the heart of the representational process itself, which Fanon—against the objectivist grain of the history of the analysis of racism—gave so central and constitutive a role. By the practices of trans-coding and re-signing, he attempted to contest, to disturb, to unsettle, and to re-inscribe the look "other-wise." Of course, for those who believe that history is a "process without a subject," this attempt to constitute forms of subjectivity and representation in some different register from that of the colonial relation may appear to be of little serious consequence: mere scribbling in the margins. Perhaps the short history of postcolonial Algeria, in which that so-called objective entity, "the Algerian peasantry," has been powerfully inscribed in several different and contradictory positions in the postindependence narratives, from "revolutionary vanguard" to "faithful multitude," may make them pause for thought. For those who take these questions of representation and subjectivity as *constitutive* of the politics of decolonisation, especially amongst the young cultural practitioners and visual artists of the African diaspora, Fanon's work has had an enormous, unpredicted and unpredictable influence in recent years—evidence of which is to be seen everywhere in the work exhibited, screened and performed in *Mirage*. The principal counterstrategy here has been to bring to the surface—into representation—that which has sustained the regimes of representation unacknowledged: to subvert the structures of "othering" in language and representation, image, sound and discourse, and thus to turn the mechanisms of fixed racial signification against themselves, in order to begin to constitute new subjectivities, new positions of enunciation and identification, without which the most "revolutionary" moments of national liberation quickly slide into their postcolonial reverse gear (Algeria being one of the most troubling and heart-wrenching instances).

From this practice of resignification—this new politics of the black signifier—has flowed both the amazing volume, but more significantly, the astonishing formal diversity, of much recent black art work. Again and again, this practice has taken the form of working *on the black body itself*: driving the suppressed violence of racism so deep into itself that it reveals the transgressive lineage of the suppressed desire on which it feeds; putting together what we may think of as new "corporeal schemas"; that which Fanon himself describes as having been fixed "as a chemical solution is fixed by a dye," dismembered "fragments . . . put together again by another self." Often, this process consists of the artist taking his or her own body as the "canvas," light-sensitive "frame" or "screen," so that the work of translation and re-appropriation is literally a kind of "re-writing of the self on the body," a re-epidermalisation, an *auto-graphy*.[27] Elsewhere, I have called this reworking of the abjected black body through desire the production of a new "black narcissus."[28]

The field of visual representation is foregrounded here because of the constitutive role of "the look" as a site of power-knowledge, of the sexualisation of the gaze, and its fantasmatic fetishisation of the body and the skin as signifiers of racial difference. However, the body in Fanon's text is both a privileged and an ambivalent site of strategic intervention. "O my body, make of me always a man who questions!"[29] In the "epidermalization" of the racial look, Fanon tells us, exclusion and abjection are imprinted on the body through the functioning of these signifiers as an objective taxonomy—a "taxidermy"—of radicalised difference; a specular matrix of intelligibility.

To that which W. E. B. Du Bois once referred in terms of "hair, skin and bone,"[30] after Fanon, we would have to add genitals.[31] We know that the fetishistic and stereotypical excess required to secure these markers of racial difference in a stable equivalence with the black body, far from being genetically secured, is a "form of intelligibility" which racism shares with other regimes of difference and othering with which it has many features in common—especially, of course, gender and sexuality.[32] It is therefore sometimes tempting to believe that these are indeed the "evidence" rather than the *markers* of difference. We mis-take their function as signifiers for their biological fact and thus read "race" as the product of a genetic or biological schema rather than as a *discursive regime.*

Many visual practices influenced by poststructuralist and psychoanalytic ideas seem to have managed to evade a foundational materialism, only to allow "the body" to make a surreptitious return as a sort of "token" of the material, a terminal signifier, which brings the discursive slide, the infinite semiosis of meaning around "race," to an abrupt halt. Sometimes, even in Foucault, who has taught us so much about its contingency (and even more in the Foucauldeans), "the body" seems to be invoked in the place where once stood those great transcendental signifiers, God, His Majesty and The Economy: becoming the last refuge, the *objet petit a*, of a misplaced materiality.

It is important that this work of returning to the enigmatic site of "the black body" in the representation of radicalised difference should not be mistaken for a return to a dehistoricised, transcendental, biologically fixed, essentialised conception of racial identity. The binary "Manicheism delirium [*sic*]" of racialised discourse to which Fanon so effectively draws attention is not given by nature.[33] It involves an arbitrary discursive operation, a suturing. Arbitrary, because "race" is a sliding signifier with equivalencies outside discourse that cannot be fixed. "Racism's very rigidity . . . is the clue to its complexity. Its capacity to punctuate the universe into two great opposite masks . . . the complexes of feelings and attitudes . . . that are always refusing to be so neatly stabilised and fixed. . . . All that symbolic and narrative energy . . . is directed to securing us 'over here' and them 'over there,' to fix each in its appointed species place."[34] "Race" is not a genetic but a social category. Racism is not a biological but a discursive regime. The so-called bodily insignia—black skin, thick lips, curly hair, penises "as big as cathedrals" and the rest—which appear to function as foundational are not only constituted through and through in fantasy, but are really signifying elements in the discourse of racism. Even in racist discourses, where the evidence of racial difference appears to be figured so *obviously* on the surface of the body, so plain for all to see ("Look! A Negro! . . . Mama, see the Negro! I'm frightened!"),[35] they are capable of carrying their negative connotations *only* because they function, in fact, as the signifiers of a deeper code—the genetic—*which cannot be seen* but which, it is believed, has the power of a science to fix and stabilise racial difference. It is not the status of racist discourse as "scientific" but the fact that its elements function *discursively* which enables it to have "real effects." They can only carry meaning because they signify, through a process of displacement, further along the chain of equivalencies—*metonymically* (black skin—big penis—small brain—poor and backward—it's all in the genes—end the poverty programme—send them home!). That is, because their arrangement within a discursive chain enables physiological signs to function as signifiers, to stand for and be "read" further up the chain; socially, psychically, cognitively, politically, culturally, civilisationally . . . (for an elaboration of the discursive character of racism, see my essay "Race—the Sliding Signifier").[36]

Fanon certainly knew that, in the system of radicalised exclusion and abjection sustained by the look from the place of the Other, the bodily schema is constituted, not given, and culturally and historically shaped ("Below . . . I had sketched a historico-racial schema").[37] Thus, any notion that the return to the site of the body represents a recovery of some essential ground or foundation that will restore the essential black subject is not only mistaken but has taken a message from Fanon's work which he explicitly precludes. These are indeed, to paraphrase Judith Butler, "bodies that matter": they count, not because they can produce the truth, but because they signify within what Judith Butler in another context calls the regulatory norm, the regulative "ideal" of the racial matrix. How could the black body function foundationally when, as Fanon shows, it is so manifestly constructed in narrative ("there were legends, stories, history, and above all, historicity"), through desire, in fantasy, through the exorbitant play of "lack" and "excess"? This is surely the lesson we should take from Fanon's long and uneasy dialogue with the Negritude movement.

This body of visual work, then, assumes that "the look" can be subverted, displaced, resisted. But can it be refused, destroyed, abandoned? Can the split—black skin/white masks—which threatens to destroy the black subject from within be healed? Is the subject not *inevitably* a site of splitting? And if so, what then is the status of the "universal, unified subject," beyond Negritude, towards which Fanon is gesturing in that highly resonant but ambiguous formulation at the close of his text: "The Negro is not. Any more than the white man"?[38]

Homi K. Bhabha's foreword to the 1986 edition of *Black Skin, White Masks* has become the *locus classicus* of many aspects of this debate, reminding us that "Remembering Fanon," as his text is called, remains a difficult and inevitably contested practice. In "Critical Fanonism," Henry Louis Gates, borrowing a phrase from Benita Parry, critiques Bhabha's reading for its "premature post-structuralism."[39] Both writers mean his attempt to produce Fanon as a sort of Lacanian *avant la lettre*, as if Fanon would have taken Lacan's position on the split in the subject, and treated "the Other" as the necessary source of division which arises in all so-called unified identities, and not "as a fixed phenomenological point opposed to the self."[40] Has Bhabha, then, been fishing around in that black box—Fanon's text—for all the world like a magician or a conjurer, drawing forth at the appropriate moment, to everyone's astonishment, the figure of the proverbial Lacanian rabbit?

In fact his critics, in their haste, do not always acknowledge how clearly Bhabha marks out the points in his text at which his interpretation departs from and goes beyond his Fanonian brief: "In his more analytic mode Fanon can impede the exploration of these ambivalent, uncertain questions of colonial desire. . . . At times Fanon attempts too close a correspondence between the *mise-en-scène* of unconscious fantasy and the phantoms of racist fear and hate that stalk the colonial scene";[41] "Fanon's sociodiagnostic psychiatry tends to explain away the ambivalent turns and returns of the subject of colonial desire";[42] "Fanon must sometimes be reminded that the disavowal of the Other always exacerbates the 'edge' of identification, reveals that dangerous place where identity and aggressivity are twinned."[43] Bhabha acknowledges that, again and again, Fanon falls back too hastily onto Sartrean and Hegelian ground, is too driven by the demand for "more insurgent answers, more immediate identifications," too hungry for an "existential humanism." Bhabha's real argument is, I believe, more complex. It is that Fanon constantly and implicitly poses issues and raises questions in ways which cannot be adequately addressed within the conceptual framework into which he seeks often to resolve them; and that a more satisfactory and complex "logic" is often implicitly threaded through the interstices of his text, which he does not always follow through but which we can discover by reading him "against the grain." In short, Bhabha produces a *symptomatic* reading of Fanon's text. The question for us, then, is whether we should limit such a "symptomatic reading." With what authority, but more significantly, with what effects, do we actively appropriate Fanon's work against the textual grain?

We should be clear that what is entailed here is not a matter of restoring the "true meaning" of the text or of fixing it once and for all in that fantasmagorical territory known as "what Fanon really meant." But it may be also important, in an archaeological or genealogical sense, to retrace the turns he actually took, to grasp the matrix of intelligibility within which he came to say what he did (and not say what he was unable to) and to confront its implications. For these conceptual moves and shifts had, for him then and for us now, real political consequences.

Let us put it simplistically. I think it is impossible to read *Black Skin, White Masks* without acknowledging that it is also—and not just by chance—the product of at least three interrelated but unfinished dialogues, to which Fanon kept returning throughout his life and work. First, there is Fanon's dialogue with traditional French colonial psychiatry (a much more elaborated formation than anything comparable in British colonialism, about which Françoise Vergès writes with great insight) and, within that, with psychoanalysis, Freud and the French Freudians. For, if this text is "where Lacan makes his interruption into colonial discourse theory," as Gates asserts, it is also where Fanon "reads" Lacan in the light of his own preoccupations.[44] In the long footnote on the "mirror phase," it is Fanon's *appropriation* of Lacan which strikes us most vividly.[45] First, the "Other" in this transaction is *raced*: "The real Other for the white man is and will continue to be the black man. And conversely." It is difficult not to agree that he writes here as if "the real Other" is indeed "a fixed phenomenological point." Secondly, the split in the subject which the "mirror phase" engenders, and which, for Lacan, is a *general* mechanism of misrecognition which provides the conditions of existence of all identification, is relocated by Fanon *in the specificities of the colonial relation*: "In the Antilles, perception always occurs at the level of the imaginary. . . . For the Antillean the mirror hallucination is always neutral [i.e., colourless]."

This divergence is critical. On the one hand, it reminds us, as a startling discovery, how racially neutral, how strikingly *un-raced*, Lacan's discourse is, and how rarely this unmarked whiteness of his language has received comment. On the other hand, it clearly marks Fanon's distance from the logic of Lacan's position. For Lacan, as Bhabha remarks, "identity is never an *a priori* nor a finished product; it is only ever the problematic process of access to an image of totality."[46] To this we might necessarily add that, for Lacan, identity also operates "at the level of the imaginary." Fanon follows Lacan in substituting the psychoanalytic concept of "identification" for the Hegelian concept of "recognition." This is a procedure which marks their common lineage in the French reception of Hegel, via the highly influential post-Heideggerean reading of *The Phenomenology* provided by Kojève.[47] But, for Fanon, the blockage which detotalises the Hegelian "recognition" of the One by the Other in the exchange of the *racialised* look, arises from the historically specific, specular structure of racism, not from the general mechanism of self-identification. The political implications of this deviation are highly significant. For the whole thrust of Bhabha's text—accepting a politics of subversion which lives with ambivalence, without trying to transcend or sublate it (*Aufhebung*)—is the *political* consequence of a Lacanian theoretical position, where ambivalence is a necessary part of the script, whereas Fanon's theoretical position— that this radicalisation of the "mirror stage" is a "pathological" condition, forced on the black subject by colonialism—has the political question of *how to end this alienation* inscribed in it. Fanon cannot, politically, "live with this ambivalence," since it is the ambivalence that is killing him!

So, is the mechanism of misrecognition which, according to Lacan, is the condition for the formation of subjectivity in the dialectics of desire "from the place of the Other" (implying a permanent "lack" of fullness for the self) part of a *general ontology*, or is it historically specific to the colonial relation? Fanon's answer, at least, seems clear. "There is of course the moment of 'being for others' of which Hegel speaks, but every ontology is made unattainable in a colonized and civilized society. . . . Ontology . . . does not permit us to understand the being of the black man. For not only must the black man be black; he must be black in relation to the white man. Some critics remind us that this proposition has a converse. I say this is false."[48]

In fact, the strategy of Fanon's text is to engage with certain positions which have been advanced as part of a general ontology, and then to show how this fails to operate or to explain the specific predicament of the black colonial subject. What we have to confront, then, is not some mere textual or theoretical squabble between the different ways in which the Lacanian "look from the place of the Other" is inscribed in Fanon's text and Bhabha's re-reading of it, which we can resolve by some brutal and arbitrary act of political judgement. It is a much deeper, more serious, more politically and theoretically resonant problem than that. It points to the as yet deeply unresolved question in so-called "postcolonial studies" as to how to reconcile— or at least hold in a proper balance—in its paradigm of explanation and reading, *both* Fanon's spectacular demonstration of the power of the racial binary to *fix*, and Bhabha's equally important and theoretically productive argument that all binary systems of power are nevertheless, *at the same time*, often if not always, troubled and subverted by ambivalence and disavowal. Our dilemma is how to *think together* the overwhelming power of the binary, which persists despite everything in all racially inflected systems of power and representation (and certainly survives their endless theoretical deconstruction); *and simultaneously* the ambivalences, the openings, the slippages which the suturing of racial discourse can never totally close up. In my view, this is inadequately resolved by subscribing to *either* position on its own. We remain between "Bhabha's moment of discursive ambivalence and Fanon's moment of fixity."[49]

Where did Fanon get this version of the dialectic of desire and recognition which, in a sense, he grafts on to Lacan? How did he get so deep into the Lacanian "look," and yet so profoundly misconstrue it? These are important questions, not least because it is precisely their double register—the absence of a final resolution between them—which constitutes the excitement of Fanon's work for so many contemporary black visual artists. This question brings us to the second overlapping but unconcluded dialogue, which Homi Bhabha's account tends to underplay for obvious reasons: the dialogue of Fanon with Sartre, or, more accurately, through Sartre to the ghost of Hegel, especially the master/slave dialectic outlined in *The Phenomenology*. The master/slave trope governs a great deal of Fanon's thinking in *Black Skin, White Masks*, as it did much of French intellectual thought at this time. It was in reference to the master/slave trope that Lacan said "at every turn, I take my bearings" and it is this metaphor which opens the dialogue of otherness and desire in Fanon's text: man can be for himself only when he is a "being-for-the-Other."[50] It speaks especially to Fanon's concerns, not only because of its historical relevance in the master/slave form (elsewhere, it had been translated as bondsman/serf), but also because of the centrality which Hegel's account gives to the "life-and-death struggle" which is the final phase of the slave's struggle for recognition. For Fanon, it is the fundamental inequality, the lack of all reciprocity inscribed in the positions of master and slave, when read in the colonial relation, which opens the necessity for the slave's struggle to the death—a theme which comes to dominate Fanon's later work.

However, here again, Fanon explicitly marks his difference from a general Hegelian ontology.[51] At the foundation of the Hegelian dialectic, he argues, "Man is human only to the extent to which he tries to impose his existence on another man in order to be recognized by him."[52] There must be "an absolute reciprocity . . . *'they recognize themselves as mutually recognizing each other.'*"[53] When this is resisted, it awakens the "desire for recognition" and it is this which makes the slave willing to undertake a savage struggle, even to the death, since it is "solely by risking life that freedom is obtained."[54] However, for Fanon, the Negro "slave" has never struggled to the death with the master, or staked his life. He has been *given* freedom, which is, in reality, nothing but the freedom to "assume the attitude of the master," to sit at his table. "Let's be nice to niggers."[55] Once again, then, the colonial relation has interposed a specificity which *deflects* the Hegelian master/slave dialectic (just as, earlier, it inflected the Lacanian "mirror phase") in a new direction.

In Hegel, Fanon argues, the master imposes a "slavish work" on the slave. But in turning from the master towards work, the slave "raises himself above his own given nature," creating himself objectively—"voluntarily and consciously, or, better, actively or freely."[56] However, Fanon says, in the colonial relation, the master does *not* want recognition, only work. And the slave does not abandon the master, but turns *to* him, abandoning the object. The Negro is therefore less independent in the struggle for recognition than the Hegelian slave, because he "wants to be like the Master." He is denied recognition, *and constructs his own being-for-himself through that denial.*

There is, however, another twist. The description of the look in the chapter titled "The Fact of Blackness" not only appropriates the Hegelian trope for Fanon's own purpose. It has also been further refracted through the existential universe of Sartre's re-reading of Hegel in *Being and Nothingness*. In Sartre, the "look from the place of the Other" is more appropriative and possessive than the narcissistic form it assumes in Lacan. It steals the self from its in-itself. It empties the subject, a metaphor which seems only a whisper away from Lacan's "lack" but is in fact light-years away, lodged as it is in a Sartrean universe of existential scarcity. As Sartre wrote in *Being and Nothingness*, "If we start with the first revelation of the Other as a look, we must recognize that we experience our inapprehensible being-for-others in the form of a possession. I am possessed by the Other. The Other's look fashions my body in its nakedness. . . . By virtue of consciousness the Other is for me simultaneously the one who has stolen my body from me and the one who causes there to be a being which is my being."[57]

I believe we can see the complex "trace" of the master/slave trope in a number of unexpected places in Fanon's text. I have noted the pervasive masculinist focus of *Black Skin, White Masks*. It is the question of the black *man's* desire—"What does the black man want?"—which, as Kobena Mercer points out, triggers the text. The chapters "The Woman of Color and the White Man" and "The Man of Color and the White Woman" which deal with the white woman's so-called pathological desire to sleep with black men, and with the neurotic meaning, as Fanon interprets it, of the black man's desire for white women, though containing some important insights into the way projective sexual fantasies become racialised as they become gendered and racialised fantasies become "genitalised" (rather than simply "sexualised"), are nevertheless extremely problematic. The absence of any proper discussion of how the general dialectics of the racialised look applies, and how it may be differentiated between black men and women, is even more troubling. The way Fanon deals with the black woman when she unexpectedly surfaces in his text registers as shocking, but not unsurprising: "Those who grant our conclusions on the psychosexuality of the white woman may ask what we have to say about the woman of colour. I know nothing about her."[58]

Equally troubling are the passages on homosexuality. It is in the context of the passage in which Fanon both acknowledges and disavows that there is any homosexuality in Martinique that he makes the astonishing remark about the "absence of the Oedipus complex in the Antilles."[59] The debate as to whether the Oedipus complex is culturally relative is a long-running saga. There may well be cultures where it can be shown to take another form or even not exist at all (although, far from freeing us from some Eurocentric tyranny, this usually throws us back to an essentialist biological notion of how sexual difference is constituted). But I am afraid the Caribbean is the *least* promising scenario in which to try to prove the absence of the Oedipal drama. With its son-fixated mothers and mother-fixated sons, its complex paternities common to all slave societies of "real" black fathers and "symbolic" white ones, along with its deeply troubled, assertively heterosexual and often homophobic black masculinities, the Caribbean "lives out" the loss of social power by substituting an aggressively phallocentred "black manhood." The absence of women and the mother in Fanon's text leads one to wonder whether, figuratively, he didn't *replace* the triadic structure of the Oedipal scenario with the binary coupling of the master/slave trope. This ambiguous "primal scene" was beautifully transposed during *Mirage* into a different, more complex and less homophobic register in *Bear*, Steve McQueen's 1993 film of two black men locked in a playful wrestle.

Do all these Hegelian and Sartrean convolutions matter? There are some critics who believe that the status of Fanon as a black hero and icon is damaged by the suggestion that he might have learned anything or—worse— actually been in dialogue with the themes of European philosophy. This kind of essentialism is worse than useless if we are to think seriously about Fanon. It reveals how little such critics understand Fanon's deep implication in French culture and philosophy as a result of his French colonial upbringing, formation and education in Martinique: how much of the tortured thinking-through of the complicities of the colonial relation which was part of the impulse behind *Black Skin, White Masks* was autobiographical in inspiration. These critics forget that Fanon, like many other bright young colonial intellectuals, went to study in France; became locked in a deep internal argument with the various currents of thought which he found there; and went to North Africa as a salaried member of the French colonial psychiatric service.[60] They do not understand that, in Martinique, for many intellectuals, to be anticolonial and opposed to the old white indigenous plantocracy was to be *for* French Republican ideology, with its rallying cry of liberty, equality and fraternity. Fanon may have travelled far from all that, but it is not clear that he ever left it all behind. The career of someone like his compatriot Aimé Césaire is incomprehensible without understanding the complexity of the relations which constituted French colonialism for black intellectuals in the Antilles.

The Hegelian-Sartrean convolutions matter in another respect. It is only in the light of Hegel's "life-and-death struggle" that we can understand the shadow of death which lengthens over Fanon's later work: that which he called "the savage struggle" and "the convolutions of death" is that which opens up the "possibility of the impossibility." It is death, Hegel's "absolute lord," that makes possible the restoration of the black man's self-constituting activity, "in-itself-for-itself."[61] This can be seen in Fanon's commitment-to-the-death to the Algerian struggle as well as *The Wretched of the Earth*, with its in-the-shadow-of-death urgency (it was written when Fanon already knew he was dying of leukemia) and its invocation of the necessity of violence in the revolutionary struggle for freedom.

This brings us to the third dialogue, which is Fanon's debate with Negritude, or the idea of black culture as a positive source of identification, and the question of cultural nationalism and race as an autonomous force. Fanon returns to this subject matter in *Black Skin, White Masks* in relation to Césaire, but more significantly in relation to Sartre's famous "Black Orpheus" preface to Senghor's *Présence Africaine* anthology of African writing. The underlying issue had to do with Fanon's complex relation, on the one hand, to Sartre's "humanist universalism," which saw Negritude as a necessary transitional stage of consciousness, and on the other hand Fanon's unresolved oscillations in relation to nationalism. He was critical of nationalism as the privileged form of Third World struggle; yet he was a passionate supporter of the national cultural movement in the wider revolutionary struggle in Africa. This made Fanon, in Neil Lazarus's terms, not a "nationalist" but a *nationalitarian*.[62] The question touches an issue of continuing controversy in postcolonial Africa and elsewhere which is probably more significant now in the wake of the crisis of the postindependence state than it was for Fanon at the time of writing, an issue whose surface was barely scratched by the ICA conference's focus on *Black Skin, White Masks*.

It was in relation to the Negritude question (which is far too convoluted to attempt to disentangle here) that Fanon wrote some of his most vitriolic phrases on the "illusion of black culture"—and where, incidentally, one can find one of his most ambiguous and startling uses of the word "mirage," which was the title of the ICA's project: "With his eyes on Africa, the West Indian . . . discovered himself to be a transplanted son of slaves; he felt the vibration of Africa in the depth of his body and aspired only to one thing: to plunge into the great 'black hole.' It thus seems that the West Indian, after the great white error, is now living in the great black mirage."[63] This was by no means his last or most definitive comment on the issue, but it is a pretty decisive one—and deeply paradoxical, as is so much of Fanon in relation to any simple cultural-nationalist appropriation of his legacy. The passages of severe criticism levelled at Césaire and Negritude in *Black Skin, White Masks* are countered elsewhere by a more sympathetic treatment. The supreme confidence with which Sartre "placed" Senghor's collection as "transitional" in relation to a universal humanism did not rest easily in Fanon's mind. He never resolved the tensions between these two claims.

I find myself in agreement, on this point at least, with Benita Parry's recent insistence on Fanon's "persistent instabilities," on the unresolved arguments and the incomplete oscillations which make *Black Skin, White Masks* fundamentally an *open* text, and hence a text we are obliged to go on working *on*, working *with*.[64] In particular, I am pulled back to Fanon's many voices as the sign of the multivocality of the dialogue going on in his head, which came to no settled conclusions. Parry proposes that *Black Skin, White Masks* is Fanon's "learning process," a kind of journey of self-education and self-transformation without the solace of an arrival.

I agree, then, with the reasons which Homi K. Bhabha advances for the importance of *Black Skin, White Masks* at this conjuncture. He characterises Fanon's text as a "jagged testimony of colonial dislocations" which in the end "refuses the ambition of any total theory of colonial oppression." In my reading of the text, Fanon *is* more consistently drawn to "the question of political oppression" in a specifically colonial historical context as "the violation of a human 'essence'" than Bhabha suggests. This refrain is textually insistent, central to his evolving political vision, less a "lapse into . . . a lament in his more existential moment" than Bhabha allows. But I also agree with Bhabha about Fanon's insistence on exploring the question "What does the black man want?" to its depths. This question, as enigmatic and unconsciously charged as Freud's "What does woman want?," nevertheless pushes us to that dangerous point, beyond the limit, where "cultural alienation bears down on the ambivalence of psychic identification."[65] This is a place many "right-on" critics are determined to avoid. Fanon's insistence on thinking this dangerous moment in terms of fantasy and the desire-for-the-Other transforms our notion of politics and of political demands. The question is, what are we to do with the "uncertain dark" which Bhabha suggests is always the accompaniment to the emergence of truly radical thought?

Does "working with Fanon" require that we undertake a symptomatic re-reading of *Black Skin, White Masks*, re-sighting through the aporias in his text a conceptual scheme which is somehow struggling towards enunciation; a "going beyond" of the text to that absent-presence which it implicates but cannot name? Or should we acknowledge that he did not name it because, though uncannily closer to it in more ways than many of his followers and subsequent critics have understood, he is also more distant? Racism is never, for Fanon, simply something which the Other does to Us. His thinking about it, though finally unresolved, is shaped by an appropriation of some ideas that significantly depart from and in some respects explicitly contradict the place from which we tend to read him today. This requires us to live with a much more radically incomplete Fanon; a Fanon who is somehow more "Other" to us than we would like him, who is bound to unsettle us from whichever direction we read him. This also requires us to engage with the uncomfortable truth that just as "truly radical thought never dawns without casting an uncertain dark," so there is no "life" without its after-life.

NOTES

This essay first appeared in *The Fact of Blackness: Frantz Fanon and Visual Representation*, ed. Alan Read (London: Institute of Contemporary Arts; Seattle: Bay Press, 1996), 12–37.

1 Frantz Fanon, *Black Skin, White Masks*, trans. Charles Lam Markmann (London: Pluto, 1986).

2 Walter Benjamin, "Thesis on the Philosophy of History," in *Illuminations*, trans. Hannah Arendt (London: Fontana, 1973), 247.

3 Frantz Fanon, *The Wretched of the Earth* (New York: Grove, 1966), 69.

4 Homi Bhabha, "Foreword: Remembering Fanon," in Fanon, *Black Skin, White Masks*, xv.

5 Henry Louis Gates, "Critical Fanonism," *Critical Inquiry* 17, no. 3 (Spring 1991): 457–70.

6 Cedric Robinson, "The Appropriation of Frantz Fanon," *Race and Class* 35, no. 1 (July/September 1993): 79–91.

7 Kobena Mercer, "Busy in the Ruins of Wretched Phantasia," in *Mirage: Enigmas of Race, Difference and Desire* (London: ICA/INIVA, 1995), 14–55.

8 Fanon, *Black Skin, White Masks*, 12.

9 Fanon, *Black Skin, White Masks*, 13.

10 Fanon, *Black Skin, White Masks*, 111.

11 Sigmund Freud, *On Sexuality*, Pelican Freud Library, vol. 7 (Harmondsworth, UK: Penguin, 1977).

12 Jacqueline Rose, *Sexuality in the Field of Vision* (London: Verso, 1986).

13 Fanon, *Black Skin, White Masks*, 109.

14 Fanon, *Black Skin, White Masks*, 116.

15 Bhabha, "Remembering Fanon," xiv.

16 Gates, "Critical Fanonism," 458.

17 Fanon, *Wretched of the Earth*, 203.

18 Frantz Fanon, *Towards the African Revolution* (Harmondsworth: Penguin, 1970), 63.

19 Fanon, *Black Skin, White Masks*, 111.

20 See Jacques Lacan, *Four Fundamental Concepts of Psychoanalysis* (London: Hogarth, 1977).

21 Fanon, *Black Skin, White Masks*, 112.

22 Fanon, *Black Skin, White Masks*, 109.

23 Fanon, *Black Skin, White Masks*, 10.

24 Fanon, *Black Skin, White Masks*, 110.

25 Bhabha, "Remembering Fanon," xvi.

26 Fanon, *Black Skin, White Masks*, 10 (emphasis added).

27 Fanon, *Black Skin, White Masks*, 109.

28 Stuart Hall, "Race—the Sliding Signifier," in *The Fateful Triangle: Race, Ethnicity, Nation*, ed. Kobena Mercer (Cambridge, MA: Harvard University Press, 2017), 31–79.

29 Fanon, *Black Skin, White Masks*, 232.

30 W. E. B. Du Bois, "The Conservation of Races," in *Negro Social and Political Thought*, ed. Howard Brotz (New York: Basic, 1966).

31 Fanon quotes Michel Cournot as saying that "four Negroes with their penises exposed would fill a cathedral" (*Black Skin, White Masks*, 169).

32 Judith Butler, *Bodies That Matter: On the Discursive Limits of Sex* (London: Routledge, 1993).

33 Fanon, *Black Skin, White Masks*, 183.

34 Stuart Hall, "Race, Culture, and Communications," *Rethinking Marxism* 5, no. 1 (Spring 1992): 10–18.

35 Fanon, *Black Skin, White Masks*, 112.

36 Hall, "Race—the Sliding Signifier."

37 Fanon, *Black Skin, White Masks*, 111.

38 Fanon, *Black Skin, White Masks*, 231.

39 Gates, "Critical Fanonism"; Benita Parry, "Problems in Current Theories of Colonial Discourse," *Oxford Literary Review* 9, no. 1/2 (Winter 1987): 27–58.

40 This is rather in the way that Althusser and Balibar in *Reading Capital* used structural concepts to "re-read" Marx in his partially theorised state, to produce—hey, presto!—the fully structuralist Marx. See Louis Althusser and Étienne Balibar, *Reading Capital* (London: New Left Books, 1970).

41 Bhabha, "Remembering Fanon," xix.

42 Bhabha, "Remembering Fanon," xx.

43 Bhabha, "Remembering Fanon," xxii.

44 Gates, "Critical Fanonism."

45 Fanon, *Black Skin, White Masks*, 161.

46 Bhabha, "Remembering Fanon," xviii.

47 Alexandre Kojève, *Introduction to the Reading of Hegel* (New York: Basic, 1969).

48 Fanon, *Black Skin, White Masks*, 109–10.

49 B. Hall, "Reading the Mulatta," unpublished ms., University of York, 1995.

50 See J. Forrester, ed., *The Seminars of Jacques Lacan*, 1 (Cambridge: Cambridge University Press, 1988), 222.

51 Fanon, *Black Skin, White Masks*, 220n8.

52 Fanon, *Black Skin, White Masks*, 216.

53 Fanon, *Black Skin, White Masks*, 217.

54 Fanon, *Black Skin, White Masks*, 218.

55 Fanon, *Black Skin, White Masks*, 220.

56 Kojève, *Introduction to the Reading of Hegel*, 229.

57 Jean-Paul Sartre, *Being and Nothingness* (New York: Citadel, 1969).

58 Fanon, *Black Skin, White Masks*, 179–80.

59 Fanon, *Black Skin, White Masks*, 180n44.

60 Françoise Vergès, "Chains of Madness, Chains of Colonialism: Fanon and Freedom," in *The Fact of Blackness: Frantz Fanon and Visual Representation*, ed. Alan Read (Seattle: Bay Press, 1996).

61 Fanon, *Black Skin, White Masks*, 218.

62 Neil Lazarus, "Disavowing Decolonisation," *Research in African Literatures* 24, no. 4 (Winter 1987).

63 Frantz Fanon, *Towards the African Revolution* (Harmondsworth: Penguin, 1970).

64 Benita Parry, "Signs of the Times," *Third Text* 28/29 (Autumn/Winter 1994).

65 Bhabha, "Remembering Fanon," xi.

CHAPTER 9

Créolité and the Process of Creolization

I begin with two apologies. First, for the schematic nature of my presentation. I am trying to map together a number of different areas in order to pose some basic questions about the process of creolization. This inevitably means that I cannot go into the complexity and detail which each of them deserves. Second, an apology for obliging Derek Walcott to listen to yet another exercise in "cultural theory," which I know he thinks is a tremendous waste of time.

I want to think about the passage from Édouard Glissant quoted in the notes prepared by the Documenta 11 team for this Platform, to the effect that "the whole world is becoming creolized." What can such a statement mean, and what are its conceptual implications? I explore these questions in the context of the themes proposed in the notes: "Can the concept of *créolité* be applied to describe each process of cultural mixing, or is it peculiar to the French Caribbean? Does it constitute a genuine alternative to the entrenched paradigms that have dominated the study of postcolonial and postimperial identities?" Do "*créolité*" and "creolization" refer to the same phenomenon, or does "creolization" offer us a more general model or framework for cultural intermixing? Should "creolization" replace such terms as hybridity, *méttisage*, syncretism? In short, what is its general conceptual applicability?

Obviously, Glissant's remark that the whole world is becoming creolized is a metaphorical, or better, a metonymical, statement. That is to say, it depends on the extension or expansion of a specific concept to other historical situations, other historical moments, other kinds of society, other cultural configurations. This can be a dangerous exercise, because it means mapping a concept across a number of conceptual frontiers; and the question is, at the end of this process, what relationship does the expanded concept have to the original? Has it moved so far as to have destroyed all the richness and specificity present in its first, more concrete, application? This is certainly the critique of "creolization" offered today by some Caribbean scholars, who say that its ubiquitous application has eroded its strategic conceptual value. Of course, it is impossible not to generalize concepts in theoretical work. The issue is, what is the appropriate level of abstraction, and what is gained/ lost in the process of generalizing it? I have tried to be aware of these traps in the exercise undertaken below.

I will try to stage this argument over two sessions. In the first, I want to ask whether notions of "creole" and "*créolité*" can be expanded from their meanings and conditions of existence in the French Antilles to other parts of the Anglophone Caribbean. And in tomorrow's session, I want to follow this by locating the question of "creolization" in the wider processes of globalization. In general, I would describe my approach as a strategy of "conjectural theorization."

We need to clear the ground by drawing some distinctions between the different meanings of these terms. First, the term "creole" itself. Its most common usage is as a way of describing the vernacular form of language which has developed in the colonies and become the "native tongue" of the majority of its inhabitants, through the combining of elements of European (mainly French) and African languages. Though the term originally had as strong a connection with Spanish (*criollo*), it has acquired, historically, particular resonances for the French colonial world. In "Free and Forced Poetics," Glissant describes Creole as "an idiom based on a French-derived vocabulary and an original syntax mixing African structures with speech habits from the Sixteenth and Seventeenth Century Norman sailors."[1] In the French sugar colonies—including the French Antilles, French Guiana, and, as Françoise Vergès argues,[2] places like Réunion in the Pacific Ocean (an island with a history similar to the Antilles and, like the others, part of "*Les Veilles Colonies*" [the Old Colonies])—creole was long considered a debased, corrupted "patois" or "bad French" spoken by "the natives." It long retained this association with the "native" and the "abjected." This is, indeed, how Europeans for many years regarded all the vernacular ideolects of native speakers in the Caribbean. More recently, however, as part of a concerted struggle for recognition against a former imperializing hegemony, creole has come to be acknowledged as having many of the characteristics of a so-called proper language in its own right, as well as being powerfully expressive of local conditions—and thus, as the *créolité* theorists argue, capable of sustaining a distinctive "vernacular" literature of its own.

The term "creole" has also been used sociologically, to refer to an identifiable fraction of colonial society, and this terminology is more common in the French territories than in the Anglophone Caribbean. It is still widely used in this sense in Martinique, Guadeloupe, French Guiana, and Haiti, as it is in Réunion and indeed in some of the African Francophone countries. In a looser sense, "creole" has also been used to refer to the traditions of early French and Spanish settlers in the Gulf States of the US. It is worth noting that, in the Anglophone Caribbean islands, the term is much more common in St. Lucia and Dominica, where the French influences remain strong, than in, say, Jamaica, where it is rarely used, except in an academic—and often pejorative—sense (e.g., "creole nationalism"). Elsewhere, the two places where it is to be found are Guyana and Trinidad, where it has quite a different meaning. There, it signals the difference between those of "Indian" and "African" descent. Guyanese talk about "Indians or creoles," and by creoles they mean "blacks" (whatever their actual skin-color), descendants of Africans born in Guyana, whereas "Indians" refers to the indentured population from Asia. These examples suggest that "creole" remains a powerfully charged but also an exceedingly slippery signifier. It seems impossible to freeze this term in its meaning, or to give it any kind of fixed or precise racial referent.

Originally, creoles were, of course, white Europeans born in the colonies, or those Europeans who had lived so long in the colonial setting that they acquired many "native" characteristics and were thought by their European peers to have forgotten how to be "proper" Englishmen and Frenchmen. Shortly thereafter, the term came also be to applied to black slaves. The distinction in any eighteenth-century plantation document listing the slaves employed on an estate or owned by a particular slaveholder marked the distinction between "Africans" and "creoles"; and much hung on it in terms of how well "seasoned" to local conditions the slave was, how far already acclimatized to the harsh circumstances and rituals of plantation life. "Africans" were slaves who were born in Africa and transported to the colonies; "creoles" were slaves born in, and thus "native to," the island or territory. The essential distinction is between those from cultures imported from elsewhere and those rooted or grounded in the vernacular local space.

Originally, the term "creole" in the Caribbean context had both a white and a black referent. It was applied to both native-born white and black populations, and only subsequently did it acquire the more specific, contemporary meaning of "racial mixing"—or as the *Oxford English Dictionary* puts it, "the result of inter-cohabitation between the two 'races.'" It was never historically, and is not today, fully fixed *racially*. This is a critical point in the argument, because in recent times it has come primarily to signify, as the dictionary suggests, "a person of mixed European and African blood," with the emphasis on racial miscegenation. But its primary meaning has always been about cultural, social, and linguistic *mixing* rather than about racial *purity*. However, "creole" seems to have been subject to the same semantic slide or struggle for appropriation and transcoding as other related terms, like "hybridity." Some theorists, like Robert Young, have, until recently, insisted that the term "creole" refers to racial categories and cannot help being drawn back to its inscription in racial theory.[3] However, contemporary theoretical usage has in fact emphasized the hybridity of cultures rather than the impurity of breeding and miscegenation, attempting to dislodge the term from its biologized and racialized inscription.

In his book *The Development of Creole Society in Jamaica, 1770–1920*, Edward Kamau Brathwaite discusses the creolization process which, at the beginning of his argument, primarily relates to white settlers who had become adapted or indigenized, and is later extended to include native-born black slaves and their descendants.[4] Toward the end of the book, Brathwaite projects the process forward into the present. He discussed the possibilities that are open to blacks now (i.e. at the time of writing, the middle of the twentieth century), who could, if they chose, become part of a not yet completed creolization process. It is clear that, at this point in his career, Brathwaite saw creolization as a kind of continuum: a process involving, at different historical moments, different groups, always in combination, in a society which is the product of their entanglement. The argument is about their mutual implication in a process of "indigenization."

Writers like Édouard Glissant use the term "creole" in a broader sense, to describe the entanglement—or what he calls the "relation" between—different cultures forced into cohabitation in the colonial context. Creolization in this context refers to the processes of "cultural and linguistic mixing" which arise from the entanglement of different cultures in the same indigenous space or location, primarily in the context of slavery, colonization, and the plantation societies characteristic of the Caribbean and parts of Spanish America and Southeast Asia. In Glissant's terms, slavery, the plantation, and the tensions and struggles associated with them were necessary conditions for the emergence of creole. This process of cultural "transculturation" occurs in such a way as to produce, as it were, a "third space"—a "native" or indigenous vernacular space, marked by the fusion of cultural elements drawn from all originating cultures, but resulting in a configuration in which these elements, though never equal, can no longer be disaggregated or restored to their originary forms, since they no longer exist in a "pure" state but have been permanently "translated."

Mary Louise Pratt calls such sites of entanglement "contact zones"—"social spaces where disparate cultures meet, clash, and grapple with each other, often in highly asymmetrical relations of domination and subordination."[5] The qualification is critical. Contrary to simpler versions of the colonizer/colonized paradigm in its truncated binary form, this "grappling" process is always a two-way struggle as well as always reciprocal, and mutually constituting. The colonized refashions the colonizer to some degree, even as the former is forced to take the imprint of the latter's cultural hegemony. This does not mean that in creole societies cultural elements combine on the basis of equality. Creolization *always* entails inequality, hierarchization, issues of domination and subalterneity, mastery and servitude, control and resistance. Questions of *power*, as well as issues of *entanglement*, are always at stake. It is essential to keep these contradictory tendencies together, rather than singling out their celebratory aspects. As James Clifford persuasively argued, every "diaspora" carries profound costs.[6]

However, the vernacular or indigenous "ground" which emerges out of this collision of cultures is a distinctive space—the "colonial"—which makes a whole project of literary expression and creative cultural practices possible—"the good side," if you like, of creolization and the essence of the argument about *créolité*. But there is always also "the bad side": questions of cultural domination and hegemony, of appropriation and expropriation, conditions of subalterneity and enforced obligation, the sense of a brutal rupture with the past, of "the world which has been lost," and a regime founded on racism and institutionalized violence.

I would argue that the process of creolization in this sense is what defines the distinctiveness of Caribbean cultures: their "mixed" character, their creative vibrancy, their complex, troubled, unfinished relation to history, the prevalence in their narratives of the themes of voyaging, exile, and the unrequited trauma of violent expropriation and separation. These are all, also, in different ways, what I would call translated societies—subject to the "logic" of cultural translation. Translation always bears the traces of the original, but in such a way that the original is impossible to restore. Indeed, "translation" is suspicious of the language of the return to origins and originary roots as a narrative of culture. Its modalities are always more multiple—a "traveling" conception of culture, to borrow Clifford's term:[7] a narrative of movement, of "transformations," rather than of "roots" or return. Translation is an important way of thinking about creolization, because it always retains the trace of those elements which resist translation, which remain left-over, so to speak, in lack or excess, and which constantly then return to trouble any effort to achieve total cultural closure. No translation achieves total equivalence, without trace or remainder. This is the logic of *différance* in the Derridean sense: of a kind of difference which refuses to fall back into its binary elements, which cannot be fixed in terms of this or that pole, but remains unsettled along a spectrum, and which has what Derrida calls the "play of *différance*" as one of its consistent effects.

Heuristically, I have tried elsewhere to think of the process of creolization in the Caribbean in terms of three "presences": *présence africaine, présence européenne,* and *présence américaine.*[8] *Présence africaine* is the subterranean trace or voice of "Africa"—that "Africa" which is "alive and well in the diaspora." It refers to that submerged element which was rarely allowed to speak in its own voice. For centuries, it could only express itself by indirect means, through what Henry Louis Gates calls the strategies of "signifyin'":[9] by detour, evasion, mimicry, by subverting the cultural dominant from below, by appropriation, translation, and expropriation. Its subterranean rhythms have continued to surface—in surprising, often transformed, ways. As the West Indian novelist George Lamming put it, "Africa invades us like an invisible force."[10] This is the presence which has been, until quite recently, almost impossible to hear in the Caribbean *on its own terms.* The "rediscovery" of this voice—its return to the surface, in societies like Jamaica in the 1960s and '70s—constituted the basis of a cultural revolution, which made the place, self-consciously, for the first time, a "black society."

Présence africaine only sometimes appears as a set of literal "survivals." Its broader, more ubiquitous "presence" is in and through its many translated forms (i.e. creolized). And it is not always *africaine* in the geographical sense. There are other powerful "presences" which belong to the same pole of "the below," the excluded majorities, which are not African. Most significantly, there is the powerful presence of the East Indian communities, the survivors of that "second slavery" called indenture, which is central to the story of rural labor and identity in the Caribbean; as well as the Chinese and other minorities, who belong, for the purposes of this argument, to the experience of dispossession associated with *présence africaine*; though the relation between these minorities is also a deeply troubled one (the designation "African" being itself one of the principal sources of antagonism).

Présence européenne, by contrast, is the voice that speaks all the time, the one we can never not hear. It is the colonizing voice, which everywhere until recently confidently assumed its own ascendancy. Nevertheless, culturally speaking, it is no purer than *présence africaine*. Insofar as it has become "indigenized" within Caribbean society, and is not simply an external noise beamed *at* the "tropicalization" of having to exist alongside a set of very different cultural impulses in the intimacy of a very different, "undomesticated," native space. What is more, this *présence européenne* is also internally diverse. It derives from the influence of the French, British, Dutch, Portuguese, and Spanish empires, which struggled for ascendancy in the Caribbean, each of which inflects the way in which it combined with *présence africaine* across the region. Today, it "speaks" with a richly demotic American accent.

However, the crucial element that distinguishes creolization belongs with the third presence—*présence américaine*. I mean by this, not the region's big cousin to the North, which is a cultural, economic, military, and indeed imperial force of its own right in the Caribbean of yesterday and today. I am referring to an older concept—"America" as the New World—a sort of "primal scene" of the encounters between different worlds for which the Caribbean has historically provided the crucible. Early woodcuts, like Jan van der Straet's engraving of Amerigo Vespucci's arrival in the New World, *Europe Encounters America*, do indeed represent the encounter as the prelude to a rape: "America" signified here as a native woman, "surprised" in her hammock in the primeval forest by the Spanish male conquistadors. However, the colonizers—always men—have their feet firmly planted on *terra firma*, bearing aloft the insignias of power—the standard of Their Catholic Majesties of Spain surmounted by a cross. The primal scene, then, is a "scene" of violent expropriation and conquest as well as the "site" of a tabooed desire, where the scandal of "cultural miscegenation" between these worlds is staged. It occurs at a liminal distance from all the sites of origin. It represents the disruptive force of "the local"—the vernacular, the indigenous, the "native ground"—with which they are all required, in one way or another, to come to terms.

In most of the Caribbean islands, after the first century of conquest, all the social forces which created plantation societies came from "somewhere else." They did not "originally" belong. They were "conscripted," whether they wanted to be or not, to a process of indigenization. We must think of this emerging colonial space as constituting a distinctive "third space"—a space of unsettledness, of conquest, of forced exile, of unhomeliness. This aspect is often missing in our accounts of creolization; creolization as the process of "indigenization," which prevents any of the constitutive elements—either colonizing or colonized—from preserving their purity or authenticity; the critical interruption of hybridity, the rupture which breaks or interrupts the lines that connect the different *présences* to their originary pasts. This is the New World as the necessary site of *dis*-placement, of *diaspora*. Viewed as a potential space of intense and original creativity, this creole or diasporic third space is an example of what George Lamming has recently called "the premature global character of its [the Caribbean's] formation":[11] a symbolic anticipation, *avant la lettre*, of the very diasporic public sphere described by Okwui Enwezor, which—under the much-transformed circumstances of trans-national, transcultural, postcolonial, and global developments—Documenta 11 is trying to represent.

To define the distinctiveness of any one of these creolized societies in the Caribbean, all these different elements must be present. What differentiates one from another is the "logic" of their combination. The foregrounding of one element over another in the "set" is what defines Caribbean cultural par-ticularity. Think of the different ways in which "*présence africaine*" appears in, say, Haiti, Jamaica, Trinidad, and Cuba. It is as if the three "presences" form a sort of Lévi-Straussian combinatory which, without pushing the structuralist language too far, gives a "deep variant structure" to the culture. Run the combination one way, and—as it were—you get Cuba. Inflect the elements differently and you suddenly see Martinique, Jamaica, Dominica, Grenada. All three elements are always present in each; but they are never actively combined or dynamic within the culture in the same proportions. It is a question of accentuation. Cultural change is thus a matter of de- and re-accentuation within the combinatory. For example, the cultural revolu-tion of the 1960s and 1970s to which I earlier referred marked the decisive, dramatic, epochal shift of accent from the European to the African pole. This is to think the distinctiveness of Caribbean societies in terms of the way in which similarity and difference are, as it were, differently combined under the pressure of colonization, post-plantation and postcolonial society at the level of the deep structure of the culture. There is no perfect or com-pleted model of this process. Everything is a variant. Everything is still in transformation.

This "cultural model" gives us a different perspective on the thematics of *créolité*. The characteristics Glissant lists include multiplicity of sources; the acceptance of dissemination and the movement as against any idea of a closure or a teleological return to the beginning; a resistance to notions of cultural authenticity; a preference for the languages, the imagery, and the strategies of exile, displacement, of voyaging, migrations, and returns. For Glissant, it is marked by entanglement. But it would be strange to describe the thematics of Caribbean vernacular culture without also including the notions of trauma, rupture, and catastrophe: the violence of being torn from one's historic resting place, the brutal, abruptly truncated violence in which the different cultures were forced to coexist in the plantation system, the requirement to bend and incline to the unequal hegemony of the Other, the dehumanization, the loss of freedom. . . . So there are also, always, within *créolité*, the recurring tropes of transplantation and forced labor, of mastery and subordination, the subjugations of plantation life and the daily humiliations of the colony; as well as the whole range of survival strategies—mimicry, signifyin', vernacularization, substitution of one term by another, the underground, subversive, rhythmic "rereading" of an overground, dominant harmonics. . . . "Language," George Lamming recently reflected, "is a source of control. Language is also a source of invention."[12]

Créolité, in its narrower sense, must be understood as a specific discourse, arising from a certain critically self-conscious Francophone reading of, or a theoretical reflection on, the broader processes of creolization we have just described. It has been philosophically elaborated in the French Caribbean, where writers and literary theorists like Bernabé, Chamoiseau, and Confiant have reflected on what we might call the literary and artistic consequences of the creolization process.[13] The *créolité* theorists argue that creolization has produced, not the debased, hybrid, vulgar, vernacular culture incapable of sustaining great work of literature and art, but a potential new basis from which a popular creativity which is distinctive, original to the area itself, and better adapted to capture the realities of daily life in the post-colony, can be, and is being, produced. *Créolité* is thus, for them, the existential and expressive basis for cultural production—for writing, poetry, music, art. It has the status of a literary program or philosophical "manifesto," a call to arms for creative practitioners and intellectuals, almost an appendix to the project of national self-constitution. *Créolité* references the construction of a literary or artistic project out of the creolizing process. However, I would argue that it is the cultural processes of creolization which provide the necessary conditions of existence for the *créolité* program.

Since the conditions of creolization exist everywhere across the region, we would therefore expect to find aspects of *créolité* elsewhere in the Caribbean, even if called by another name. Heather Smyth has recently reminded us that the literary preoccupation in the Caribbean with creolization has produced several versions or models, including "Wilson Harris's study of syncretism; Édouard Glissant's *Antillanité*; the *créolité* of Jean Bernabé, Patrick Chamoiseau, and Raphaël Confiant; Antonia Benítez Rojo's *The Repeating Island*; and Edward Kamau Brathwaite's work on creolization."[14] Though few artists and intellectuals outside the French Caribbean call this phenomenon *créolité*, its underpinning conditions are certainly not limited to the French context. However, this fact may require us to modify the strict protocols of *créolité* which the Francophone intellectuals deploy. I want to give three brief examples.

First, there is the project of what has been called "nation language," very much associated with the work of the poet, historian, and critic Edward Kamau Brathwaite. We have already referred to Brathwaite's seminal historical work on creolization. An important milestone in this debate was Melville J. Herskovits' 1951 book *The Myth of the Negro Past*, the first major anthropological text which ran against the grain of orthodoxy—namely, that everything of the African past was destroyed in the Middle Passage— and began to talk seriously about African survivals. Extraordinarily important work has been done since then on African survivals in such areas as Caribbean religion, religious practices, and folklore; in music, musical form, and dance; in daily life, social customs, and rituals, as well as in language itself. Its effect has been to shift the balance toward the study of how "Africa" survived as a subterranean force in Caribbean culture. Brathwaite has made a critical contribution to this project.

In both his historical and critical writing and his poetic practice—a major body of work—Brathwaite has highlighted the need to challenge the hegemony of the language of the colonizer, which he calls a "prison language," and return to the inspiration of "nation language." "Nation language," he argues in *History of the Voice*, "is the submerged area of that dialect which is much more closely allied to the African aspect of experience in the Caribbean. It may be in English: but often it is an English which is like a howl, or a shout, or a machine-gun, or the wind or a wave. It is also like the blues. And sometimes it is English and African together."[15] In his poetic work Brathwaite has explored this subterranean vein, focusing on the force of oral tradition, the spoken rather than the written, "as much on sound as on song." His experimentation with sound, rhythm, and the structure of the poetic line has sought to destroy the tyranny of the pentameter and other classic English literary cadences, and to intrude the acoustic and the oral elements into poetry. He charts how, for younger poets, nation language has become "the classical norm": coming "out of the same experience as the music of contemporary popular song: using the same riddims [rhythms]; the same voice-spreads, syllable clusters, blue notes, *ostinado*, syncopation and pauses."[16]

Ostensibly, Brathwaite's practice seems to—and has been read as if it does—stem from and lead remorselessly back to an ancestral African source. His perspective is certainly "Afrocentric" rather than creolist in emphasis. But this may be to misread a necessary re-accentuation for a wholesale substitution. Although his argument begins with the significance of pre-transportation ancestral culture for the Caribbean, by the time Brathwaite gets to the end of his argument, he has to recognize that its "survival" in the Caribbean can only happen as a consequence of multiple *translations* in the New World itself, and their *reshapings* in the conditions of the plantation, the colony and the post-colony. They surface in the form of, not the repetition of, a set of traditional inherited forms, but in combination with other factors, and as a *continuum*. When he specifies "the ancestral," he includes not only Shango and Anansesem, and of course Kumina, but also "Spiritual (Aladura) Baptist services, ground-nations, yard-theatres, ring games, tea-meeting speeches etc."—typically Caribbean events and occasions. His concluding summary points, it seems, toward the creole as we have tried to define it here. "In the same way as we have come to accept the idea (and reality) of Caribbean speech as continuum; ancestral through creole to national and international forms, so we must be able to begin to recognize and accept the similarly remarkable range of literary expression within the Caribbean and throughout Plantation America. To confine our definition of literature to written texts, in a culture that remains ital in most of its people proceedings, is as limiting as its opposite: trying to define Caribbean literature as essentially orature—like eating avocado without its likkle salt."[17]

In my second example, I want to be impertinent enough to speak briefly about Derek Walcott's project in his presence. Walcott's project, if I may so describe it, is certainly not a Jamaican one, like Brathwaite's. Further, we know that they have in fact clashed publicly on the very question of the use and abuse of "nation language." Walcott's "project" belongs to St. Lucia, which is interestingly poised between different versions of the dominant colonizing presence, France and England, instead of, as in the Jamaican case, Spain and England. Whereas in Jamaica, the local languages were often described as "patois," St. Lucia has a fully formed, recognized, French-based creole. Walcott, however, has said that he has tried to write in creole, but the writing for which he is best known is not in creole or in patois, and he has actually spoken in important debates as to why that would seem to him an intolerable limitation. Indeed, one might say that the one aspect which most distinguishes this supremely important body of Caribbean work is its absolute mastery of the complexities of English—of English prosody, English rhythms, English writing, including not only contemporary practitioners, but the whole lineage of literature in the English language. So, at last we find a non-creolized Caribbean poet. Derek Walcott, we might say, gets the Nobel Prize for Literature for an outstanding literary performance, but not because he is a poet of creolization or a practitioner of *créolité*.

However, I want to suggest that, if you read the settings and situations, or look at the imagery, of Walcott's poetic work, lyric, epic, or narrative; or if you consider the structures of feeling at work in the text; if you look, above all, at the rhythms of the language, and the rhythmic structures, of the work; if you consider its imaginary universe; if you think of the ways the heightened diction dips into the rhythm and intonation of the spoken vernacular; or of the "spoken," conversational opening of his great epic poem *Omeros* itself; if one confines oneself to the first six or eight lines—you need to go no further than that, or if you think of the whole project of the poem— remapping the departures and returns of Caribbean history and the Antilles onto the Aegean and the *Odyssey*; you will see that Walcott's poetic practice constantly struggles to harness these rich poetic resources into the service of forging a distinctively Caribbean "voice" for a highly Caribbean imaginary. His poetic sentences move continuously in and out of the cadences, the stresses, and inflections, if not of the strictly syntactical form, of the vernacular. *Omeros*, despite its classical connotations, is not written in the pentameter, but deliberately departs from it, adopting—and adapting freely— instead, the *terza rima* from the model of Dante's *Divine Comedy*: Dante, a master in his own time of the vernacular, who is also, to our surprise, quoted admiringly by a very different kind of poet—Edward Kamau Brathwaite ("it all begins with Dante Alighieri . . ."). Musing on the question of language in the largest sense, Walcott has written, in his poem *A Far Cry from Africa*:

> I who have cursed
> The drunken officer of British rule, how choose
> Between this Africa and the English tongue I love?
> Betray them both, or give back what they give?
> How can I face such slaughter and be cool?
> How can I turn from Africa and live?

George Lamming, who quotes this passage in *The Pleasures of Exile*, is right to insist that this ambivalence is a major source of Walcott's creative energy. That ambivalence is also dead-center to the creolizing project. This, then, is not the performance of a "creole poet." But to say that Walcott's work exists or could have been produced outside of the context of a creolized culture seems to me untenable. *Omeros* is, without question, a great poem of the creolizing imaginary.

For my third example in this thought-experiment, I want to take the model of Rastafarianism. Here at last we find a cultural phenomenon which insists on tracing everything back to its ancestral African roots, and which does want to make the return journey. The return journey is not only, for Rastafarians, the essence of their spiritual and political "program"; their world view is predicated on the myth of the redemptive return. This is one of the most profound mythic structures of the New World. One cannot understand the culture of the plantation Americas—before and after Emancipation—without the redemptive promise of a return to the Promised Land: though it is translated as "Africa" and the release from the bondage of slavery in Babylon by Rastafarians, whereas it symbolized the escape from servitude and Freedom to the enslaved, who often found its promise in borrowed, translated, Christian language of the only book slaves were encouraged to read—The Bible. In fact, the one may well have been modelled on the other in the mythic imagination. Both have deployed this idea as a vehicle for expressing the resistance to bondage, "suffering," and the profound hope for Freedom and liberation. The same idea is at the center of Garveyism, which had a significant relationship to the emergence of Rastafarianism in the early years of the twentieth century. It constitutes a profound trope throughout the New World.

Rastafarianism in its many forms has had a massive impact on Anglophone culture in the Caribbean, above all in Jamaica, where it was the motor of the cultural revolution of the 1960s and 1970s to which I have referred.

So, here, you might think, is—at least—an example of a truly non-creolized alternative, a viable alternative cultural strategy. The Rastafarian version is predicated on a notion of "roots," whereas creolization deploys the logic of "routes." From within the imperative of the Rastafarian or an Afrocentric world view, creolization is a disaster, because it weakens by an intolerable "missing" or hybridity the purity of faith and "tribe," and the commitment to a redemptive return.

The essence of returning to Africa is condensed, for Rastafarians, in their belief in the divinity of Haile Selassie, the former ruler of Ethiopia and, at the time, emperor of the first independent black African state. Selassie is revered as Ja—the Lion of Judah, King of Kings. Selassie was an important symbolic figure for a Pan-African perspective, since he was the king of the only independent black society on the continent—Ethiopia. Of course, people of African descent in the Caribbean came from many places in Africa, especially on the west coast of the continent. The only place they didn't come from was Ethiopia! There are instructive stories about Rastafarians who in the 1970s did actually attempt to return to Ethiopia, and who had a hard time being either recognized or accepted by the Ethiopian people. This is not to deny that Ethiopia has an important symbolic function in Pan-Africanism and in the re-identification with Africa, and a significant religious impact on Jamaican society, especially in the form of a variety of Ethiopian and Coptic-based churches and sects. Many sacred African texts have been absorbed into the Rastafarian belief system. But *the* sacred book, their most sacred source of interpretation (or as they would put it, "reasoning"), is the Bible, originally introduced to Christianize the slaves by European missionaries, which the Rastafarians have wholly appropriated by the textual strategy of inversion—reading the Bible backwards, against the grain; translating it upside down; reading it according to an alternative code; translating it metaphorically from its meaning as the story of God's Chosen People (the Jews) to the story of the enslavement and the dreams of freedom of Ja's "chosen tribes," and their long servitude in the "Babylon" of slavery and colonialism.

Rastafarianism has had a profound impact on popular culture, especially through music. If you ask about reggae's sources, I think most Europeans, who love reggae music, think it derives from the rediscovery of an original African rhythm. Certainly, some aspects of reggae are based on the persistence into the present of submerged traditions of African drumming and other rhythmic patterns in Jamaican folk culture. But another aspect of reggae combines this with a whole range of other, more recent, musical and rhythmic influences.

Its worldwide interest, which imagined it as a triumph of the "folk" over modern commercialism, was sustained on the back of an incredible technological revolution. This was a "folk music" [*sic*] produced by small commercial companies in backyard fit-ups of the modern recording studio and mixing desk, augmented by the wonders of modern sound amplification through its sound systems, transported worldwide via the transistor set, the vinyl, and CD revolutions, and universally copied with the help of the latest recording devices by "rastas" and "rude boys" in Handsworth, Birmingham, or Atlantic Avenue, New York, living with their own, diasporic versions of "Babylon." So even this example, which looks at first sight as if it were grounded in an authentic African source and the return to origins, turns out, when examined more closely, to be another variant in the long and complex creolization repertoire.

I am fully aware of the synoptic and superficial level at which I have been obliged to approach this complex problem. My primary purpose here has been to open up the interrogative space around the question of the process of creolization. I am aware that, in stressing the common features of the way the process has unfolded in the Caribbean, I have tended to lose sight of what is specific to each of these variants: specific to place, to history, and especially to the forms of the culture itself. I have not dealt with the question of the creolizations of the Indian Ocean, which have many similarities; or of the African city, where there is colonization but no plantation society, and the economic exploitation of labor in a colonial context but no chattel slavery, but where, nevertheless, something like the same creative "third indigenous space" has emerged. Nor have I considered whether "creole" is an appropriate term to apply to the vibrant and hybrid black British cultural forms which have arisen in Britain in the wake of the post-war migrations. Without ignoring the specificities, which remain critical, my provisional conclusion is that there is something quite distinctive, throughout these and other colonial settings, where different cultures were brought together and forced to coexist under the brutal impact of colonization, slavery, and transportation, which produced a specific cultural model: and the heart of that model is the process of creolization. This is to be understood, not by going back to and disentangling mythic origins, but by analyzing the ways in which creolization is a historical and an ongoing process, and moreover the one which produced the Caribbean and Caribbean people as distinctively "modern," albeit modern in a peculiarly "colonial" or "postcolonial" way. Despite the humiliations and the suffering which slavery and colonization entailed, creolization remains the only basis in the present of creative practices and creative expression in the region. Whether creolization also provides the theoretical model for wider processes of cultural mixing in the contemporary, post-global world remains to be considered.

NOTES

This essay first appeared in *Créolité and Creolization: Documenta 11, Platform 3*, ed. Okwui Enwezor et al. (Ostfildem-Ruit: Hatje Cantz, 2003), 27–42.

1 Édouard Glissant, "Free and Forced Poetics," *Alcheringa* 2, no. 2 (1976): 9.

2 Françoise Vergès, *Monsters and Revolutionaries: Colonial Family Romance and Métissage* (Durham, NC: Duke University Press, 1999), 4.

3 Robert J. C. Young, *Colonial Desire: Hybridity in Theory, Culture and Race* (London: Routledge, 1994).

4 Edward Kamau Brathwaite, *The Development of Creole Society in Jamaica, 1770–1820* (Oxford: Clarendon, 1971).

5 Marie Louise Pratt, *Imperial Eyes: Travel Writing and Transculturation* (London: Routledge, 1992), 4.

6 James Clifford, "Diasporas," in *Routes: Travel and Translation in the Late Twentieth Century* (Cambridge, MA: Harvard University Press, 1977), 244–78.

7 James Clifford, "Traveling Cultures," in *Routes: Travel and Translation in the Late Twentieth Century* (Cambridge, MA: Harvard University Press, 1997), 17–46.

8 See Stuart Hall, "Cultural Identity and Diaspora," in *Identity: Community, Culture, Difference*, ed. Jonathan Rutherford (London: Lawrence and Wishart, 1990), 222–37.

9 See Henry Louis Gates, *The Signifying Monkey: A Theory of African-American Literary Criticism* (New York: Oxford University Press, 1988).

10 George Lamming, *The Pleasures of Exile* (London: Michael Joseph, 1960).

11 George Lamming, "The Sovereignty of the Imagination," interview by David Scott, *Small Axe* 6, no. 2 (September 2002): 124.

12 Lamming, "Sovereignty," 124.

13 See Jean Bernabé, Patrick Chamoiseau, and Raphaël Confiant, *Éloge de la Créolité* (Paris: Gallimard, 1989).

14 Heather Smyth, "'Roots beyond Roots': Heteroglossia and Feminist Creolization in *Myall* and *Crossing the Mangrove*," *Small Axe* 6, no. 2 (September 2002): 1.

15 Edward Kamau Brathwaite, *History of the Voice: The Development of Nation Language in Anglophone Caribbean Poetry* (London: New Beacon, 1984), 13.

16 Brathwaite, *History of the Voice*, 45.

17 Brathwaite, *History of the Voice*, 49.

CHAPTER 10

Legacies of Anglo-Caribbean Culture:
A Diasporic Perspective

In what sense could the gaze that Isaac Mendes Belisario brought to bear on his Jamaican subjects be described as "diasporic"?[1] Kobena Mercer has referred to "the critical process of dialogism" that defines a contemporary diasporic aesthetic—that "syncretic dynamic which critically appropriates elements from the master-codes of the dominant culture and *creolizes* them, disarticulating given signs and re-articulating their symbolic meaning otherwise."[2] Such performative moves require the destabilizing intervention of something "other"—for instance, in language, the subversive intrusion of creole, patois, and black urban vernacular on standard English. Not many such dramatic, transcoding moves are to be found in Belisario's work, though it would be wrong to presume that therefore the diasporic logic of translation had been suspended, since we are so often aware of the "something else" present in his work.

Mercer's diasporic aesthetic was a practice emerging among Black British filmmakers in the United Kingdom in the 1980s, but it had a long and complex antecedent history in the Caribbean itself. Aspects of African cultures did survive the violence of forced transportation and insertion into plantation slavery and colony life, but only in fragmented forms: obliged to "transculturate," practiced only when shielded from the masters' eyes, ventriloquized or hiding out inside translated versions of the dominant culture.[3] The colonial culture, though brazenly imposing itself everywhere, also quickly became hybridized. The barriers that race, wealth, power, hierarchy, authority, and ownership imposed between the slaving culture and the enslaved became permeated and subverted from below by the informal practices and illegal intimacies of plantation life. The Jamaican folk culture that emerged was thus the product of extensive creolization—the process of linguistic and cultural mixing that arises from what Édouard Glissant calls "the entanglement" of different cultures, obliged to cohabit in the same indigenous space in the context of slavery, colonization, and plantation societies—"often," as Mary Louise Pratt reminds us, "within radically asymmetrical relations of power."[4]

What became Jamaican folk culture was the product of a transculturation process between, as it were, three "presences." The *African presence* is the trace of that particular version of Africa that is "alive and well in the diaspora," rarely, until recently, allowed to express itself in its own voice, but deploying indirect, subterranean means—detour, evasion, mimicry, parody, appropriation, and translation: the carnivalizing strategies of what Henry Louis Gates calls "signifyin.'" The *European presence* is the colonizing voice that everywhere confidently assumed its own superiority and ascendancy, but that by long cohabitation became subverted and translated. The *New World presence* is the "primal scene" of indigenization—but also of conquest—that staged the violent encounters between these different worlds.[5] Caribbean cultures and cultural forms were, and continue to be, positional along this creolizing spectrum, inscribed in that weave of differences and similarities that Derrida called *différance*—the "playing movement that produces . . . these effects of difference," in which each element refers to other elements by means of the syntagmatic "play" of differences, but in which they refuse finally to separate into fixed binary oppositions, making their recovery in their original, pure forms impossible.[6]

Can Belisario's work be understood in terms of this logic of cultural translation? Jamaica had become diasporic well before the 1830s, if only because everyone there had come from somewhere else. As a Jew in a British slave colony, Belisario must have known something of that de-centeredness, that double-consciousness, which constitutes the ground of the diasporic. He belonged, in the older sense of "locally born," precisely to "creole society." Did he not also experience at some level, both "at home" in Jamaica, and when he went "home" [*sic*] to England, as well as after his return, that feeling of displacement that arises from negotiating between the homegrown and the colonial variants of the dominant culture?

Though classified in Jamaica with the white minority, he belonged in fact to the trading, merchant, professional, and artistic "middling" classes of urban colonial society, not to the plantocracy, whose wealth and power derived from the slave economy, or to the white accountants and overseers who managed it, or to the governing elite, with its military, administrative, and Westminster connections. Ethnically, he was not an unthinking, paid-up, Anglo-Saxon, Anglican settler-in-the-tropics, but a Sephardic Jew: a member of a minority (technically, a minority of a minority) whose acceptance into full citizenship within Jamaican society was of recent origin, and whose ambivalent relation to the governing classes certainly did not go unmarked or unremarked by them. He was closer to those more marginal, non-English, minorities—French refugees from Haiti, Spanish exiles from the Spanish-American wars of independence, Lebanese, Chinese, and other traders and merchants—who, for one reason or another, had pitched up in Kingston.

Kingston was indeed his milieu—a crowded, sprawling, brawling, turbulent, chaotic, racially-mixed, and socially-mobile tropical colonial seaport town, with a complex relationship to both the England it could desire and mimic but not reproduce, and the slave plantation economy, whose narrow racial hierarchies, brutal regimes, and coarse manners it depended on but did not precisely mirror. The wealthier colonists who aspired to metropolitan lifestyles and manners supported a thriving local theatrical and art scene that included many itinerant British artists, and to this urban elite Belisario belonged.

Like so many creole "sons," after an early Jamaican childhood, Belisario was sent to be educated in England and trained there as an artist before returning on the eve of abolition—though he had spent enough time in London's Spanish and Portuguese Bevis Marks Synagogue to produce a beautiful image of its interior. He seemed to have felt similarly "at home" in the picturesque landscape tradition in which he was trained, and with whose "Jamaican" representatives—George Robertson, Joseph Bartholomew Kidd, James Hakewill—he must have already been familiar. The eye he brought to the Jamaican plantation and countryside was deeply informed by its conventions. He travelled through rural Jamaica as a commissioned artist, his relationship to it mediated by his patrons amongst the governing elite and the wealthier merchants, including the governor, the Marquis of Sligo, and many Jews.

It is therefore difficult to argue that the gaze Belisario turned on his Jamaican subjects was not in some way "diasporic." He inhabited different worlds and moved between them—here and there. More significantly, he "looked" from more than one place, and that look was mediated through several frames (though we know very little about how he negotiated them in everyday life). Especially in the colonial context, there is no simple act of looking without the discursive apparatus through which things are seen. The first moment of the encounter with the New World was one of wonder—"All this is marvelous. The land is high and has many ranges of hills and mountains," Columbus wrote.[7] Thereafter, the New World was not so much "discovered" as endlessly "produced" as a readable, lookable text. This gaze is never innocent—a fantasy that disavows the conditions of "seeing"—and the subject of the gaze is never secure and self-sufficient outside the specular relations of looking that implicate the viewer, constituting him/her as a subject in the "mirror" of the look.

How, then, did Belisario manage to give such a generally composed, unruffled, settled view of colonial Jamaica at a moment of such tumultuous change and social upheaval? Did his sense of how he was positioned remain quite as untroubled as it appears from much of his work? How are we to explain the absence—the *erasure*—that lies at the center of his enterprise? The heart of the matter is the question of the African presence and the unspeakable institutional violence of a slave regime—the foundations on which the whole colonial edifice rested. This was not Belisario's subject, of course, but one cannot help asking, how could it not, in some way, be? The assured, topographical perspectives, the well-judged distances and scenic vistas of Belisario's splendid plantation paintings and watercolors testify to the confidence, the sureness of touch, the untroubled sweep of vision that his inhabitation of the picturesque tradition afforded him. However, they acquire another dimension in terms of what they render invisible. Black people—whether slaves or apprentices—are, of course, present in these paintings; but his view of them is distanced. They are "figures in"—supports to—"a scene," but they are not its real subject. They do not disturb or interrupt any slight-lines. In his views of Kelly's Pen, Kelly's Estate, and Cocoa Walks, the Marquis of Sligo's estates there they are, walking, working at various tasks, tending the cattle, sometimes—as in the man sitting at rest with his lunch pail—posed in pastoral stillness. They tend to be placed in close proximity to the domesticated space of the great estate houses, only rarely laboring in the cane fields.

The most striking feature is that of *scale*. The African figures are wholly subordinated in scale and consequently seem diminished in significance—in comparison with the breadth and beauty of the surrounding Jamaican landscape and the grandeur of the plantation houses—by the optics of scenic representation. The trees, by contrast, are not just tall and branching—they are stupendous, sublime, filling the great sky, dwarfing people and animals.

Was this a "view" already embedded in and overdetermined by the conventions of looking? They remind us that, in the picturesque, the scene's the thing.

There are, of course, the *Sketches of Character*—the street figures, hawkers, and traders in the manner of the "Cries" sketches of the London poor, and the black mummers, entertainers, and Jonkonnu figures dressed up in costumes or exaggerated versions of their masters' and mistresses' clothes. The former are seen with a well-observed, detached, benevolent gaze. They are not masked, but they seem to *wear*, rather than *be*, their "characters." We are aware of other frames—the dubious discourse about "the Negro character," the "othering" of the London poor by their illustrators—intruding on the local scene. Seeing them fully seems to depend on our being able to overlay them with the template of their English prototypes—the milkmaid, the chimneysweep—to appreciate the *frisson* of difference that their racialization brings to Belisario's treatment of them. The "Cries" convention threatens ultimately to overwhelm them.

The masked figures, street entertainers, and Jonkonnu masqueraders are a different matter. One cannot help speculating on what drew Belisario to these figures: whether simply their illustrative quality—part of the quaint curiosity of Kingston life—or something deeper and more troubling in their representational value. Did he feel troubled by their deeply ambivalent performativity—transitional figures at a historic moment of change? Did he grasp intuitively their representative significance as a peak of "high" creolization? Did he understand how intricately its double registers were being exploited—in what Mary Louise Pratt calls "the mirror dance of colonial meaning-making": at once publicly performed and brilliantly displaced, a way of "signifyin'" what could not otherwise be openly spoken or shown without calling down disapproval or punishment?[8]

Certainly, they have a lively vivacity: the big drum and jaunty hats—New Orleans–style—of the three members of the "Band of the Jaw-Bone"; the long red jackets, striped trousers, and delicately tripping feet of the dancing "House John-Canoe," with an entire house on his head—so precariously perched, so very like/so deeply "differenced" from the estate houses in Belisario's own plantation scenes; all of them secretly signifying at some level, and yet cleverly disguising, their connections with the tradition of "worn objects" found in the masked and ceremonial rituals of Ibo, Yoruba, and other West African cultures. The "French Set-Girls" in their full, ribboned crinolines dance a sort of *fandango* with umbrellas, swirling around the transposed figure of an English "Jack-in-the-Green" (what is he doing here?), his

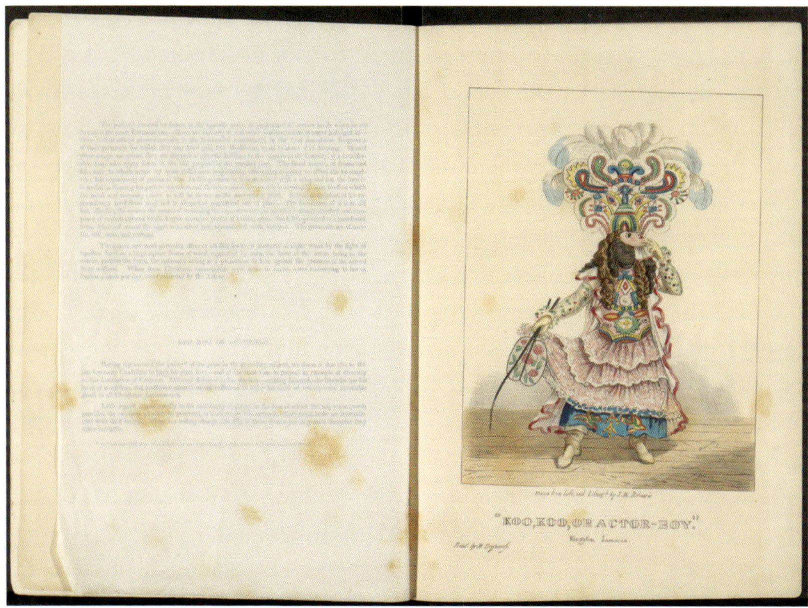

Figure 10.1. Isaac Mendes Belisario, *Koo-Koo, or Actor-Boy*, from *Sketches of Character, in Illustration of the Habits, Occupation, and Costume of the Negro Population in the Island of Jamaica*, 1837. Lithograph with watercolour. Yale Center for British Art, Paul Mellon Collection.

cloaked back broodingly positioned within the exuberant scene of creole revelry surrounding him. *Koo-Koo, or Actor-Boy* (fig. 10.1), with his flowing curls, richly brocaded, full-length tunic, and bowed slippers, stands out from the crowd—a striking presence. Paradoxically, masking has deepened rather than distanced his impact. He is caught here in mid-performance, sweeping aside, with a dramatic gesture, the masking fan, only to reveal—layer on layer—another level of deception, another blank face, whose shockingly intense *whiteness* now propels the eye sideways to the black faces of his audience—no innocent, "Smile Orange" folks, these—openly revelling in the "play" of the licenced spectacle. What is it that Belisario has caught here—mimicry or parody? Time out or slavery laughing back?

These lithographs of Jamaican street entertainers clearly have a connection to the rich subterranean tradition of "masquerade" that we find taking a variety of different forms across the region: from the stick-fighters and *baton-nieres* of Haiti and the stylized *capoeira* "warriors" of Bahia, to the elaborate world of costumed figures and the litany of folk "characters," where Catholic pre-Lenten carnival or European masked ball traditions met the West African masking ceremonies to produce the "playing mas" of the carnivals of Trinidad, Brazil, and other places. Belisario's figures keep their distance from the performances at the darker end of this spectrum, where the enslaved consciously parodied and laughed behind the backs of their hands at the excessive elegance and vulgar refinery in which their masters and mistresses paraded themselves. This found expression in, for example, the Carnival character of "Dame Lorraine," with her gown of colored scraps sewn on to burlap, her makeshift fans, stupendous hats and phenomenally expanded bosom; or the reprise of the violence of daily existence, such as the performances associated with Canboulay (Cannes Brulées), where the habit of driving the enslaved against their will with whips and horns to put out fires in the cane fields was riotously rehearsed. Canboulay resurfaced after emancipation as street processions with field workers, in a bitter and threatening parody, "playing" the driver, cracking the whip, the torch-lit marchers satirizing their own former enslavement by "disturbing the peace," bellowing songs of defiance, blowing horns, and wielding sticks.[9]

The doubling of registers, the complex symbolic reversals by which the terrors of servitude are simultaneously "normalized," rehearsed, and "replayed" as violent parodic masquerade, signifies a complexity of meaning-making that it would be difficult to infer from Belisario's entertainers. Here, the subversive element of the carnivalesque—the world turned upside down—and the mockery towards the master class of the "signifying monkey" tradition, which we know invested Jonkonnu ceremonies and frequently led to their proscription on the estates because of their subversive purpose and riotous consequences, seem somehow to have been effectively *contained*.

What one misses, then, is any more direct way of referencing the three hundred years of enslavement that formed the hidden infrastructure of Belisario's "scene"; the near-unrepresentable horrors of the transatlantic passage that brought African people to this strange, beautiful place; the regimes of violence, human degradation, and racialized abjection that were their normal conditions of existence.[10] For all their liveliness, what finally remains absent is the straight, unmasked, frontal look in the face, the black face filling the frame, the play of ordinary human emotion and feeling.

It would be more than a hundred years before a group of Caribbean artists undertook Belisario's diasporic journey in reverse and, under the very different circumstances of post-war mass migration, found themselves returning—

if only by reversal—to some of the thematic ground that his work occupied. Before and after World War II, a "first generation" of migrant Caribbean artists—Aubrey Williams, Frank Bowling, Donald Locke—who spearheaded the Black British diaspora of the post-war era, came "home" to Britain, alongside many writers and artists from the empire, on the eve of decolonization, with the intention, in an ironic reprise of the last leg of the triangular trade, of expropriating modernism and becoming modern artists.[11]

One of the earliest was the Jamaican sculptor Ronald Moody, who came to London to study in 1923, first exhibited wood-carvings in Paris in 1937, and spent fifty-three years as a practicing diasporic black artist in France and the United Kingdom. His magnificent figure of *John, the Baptist*, his powerful, beautifully finished heads and torsos of the Negro male—with what Veerle Poupeye rightly calls their "hieratic monumentality, frontal emphasis and silent inwardness"—paralleled in many ways the "Negro" sculpture of the Harlem Renaissance and the Jamaican "school" of sculpture and painting inspired by Edna Manley, the wife of Jamaican prime minister Norman Manley, and the sculptor of that iconic work of nationalist inspiration, *Negro Aroused* of 1935.[12] From that moment forward, a more indigenously grounded Jamaican art takes shape—its local scenes and landscapes more brilliantly "tropical" in comparison with Belisario's tastefully subdued palette (for example, Albert Huie or David Pottinger), or darker, heavier in line, more threatening and brooding (as in Karl Abrahams or Dunkley); its so-called "primitives" or "intuitives" [*sic*] (like Kapo, Leonard Daley, or Brother Everald Brown) much more directly in touch with the spiritual and spirit worlds of the African, Rastafarian, Revivalist, and Pentecostal religious traditions of Jamaican folk culture; and even its more cosmopolitan, avant-garde modern practitioners (David Boxer [fig. 10.2] and K. Khalfani Ra), adapting contemporary art practices and a "more universalized modernist framework" to rework national, slave, and postcolonial themes.[13]

Those who came to reflect on these developments from a diasporic place, this "first" generation, though strongly identified with the struggle for colonial independence, were cosmopolitan and universalist in outlook. The "second" generation of black British diaspora artists, who led an enormous explosion of artistic work in the eighties, were born and educated in Britain: children of the men and women of the *SS Windrush* whose arrival in 1948 signalled the formation of the post-war black British diaspora. The latter were more preoccupied with questions of race, racism and black identity, and later with issues of gender and sexuality, and were more culturally nationalist in outlook.[14] They

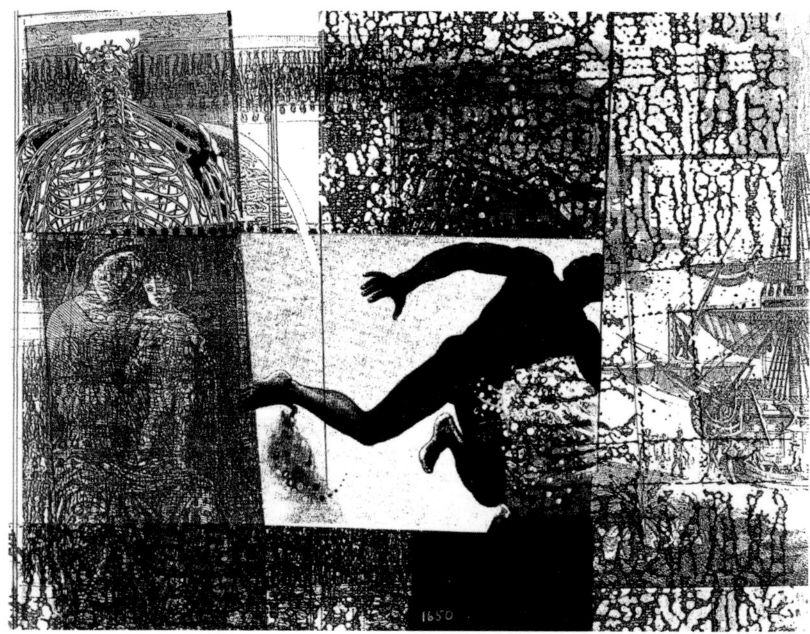

Figure 10.2. David Boxer, *The Black Books II 1612–1733*, page 1650, 2003. Digital collage on paper. 24 1/2 × 8 7/8 × 2 in. (62.23 × 22.543 × 5.08 cm). Museum purchase, made possible by Lynda Hartigan, Stephen S. Lash, Joan Vaughan Ingraham, Alex Ingraham, Samuel Ingraham, and Allie Blodgett, and gift of the artist, 2005. M27761.B. Courtesy of the Peabody Essex Museum, Salem, MA.

included Eddie Chambers (who, with Keith Piper, pioneered this "wave" with the radical "black art" group, the Pan-Afrikan Connection, in the early eighties and who recently curated an exciting show of younger, emerging Jamaican artists in Kingston), Sonia Boyce, Lubaina Himid, Maud Sulter, Claudette Johnson, Veronica Ryan, Marlene Smith, and Donald Rodney; photographers like Armet Francis, Vanley Burke, Joy Gregory, Ingrid Pollard, Maxine Walker, Roshini Kempadoo, Dave Lewis, David Bailey, Franklyn Rodgers, and Clement Cooper; and filmmakers like Isaac Julien, John Akomfrah, Menelik Shebbazz, Reece Auguiste, and Martine Attille. Many of these artists continue actively to practice today, alongside a younger, "third" generation, including Hew Locke, Yinka Shonibare, Faisal Abdu'Allah, and Chris Ofili, who are more actively engaged with contemporary art practice and the crossover into new media, but who are thematically still strongly connected with earlier preoccupations.[15]

It would be a mistake to try to discover unbroken lines of connection between the work of twentieth-century and contemporary black diaspora artists and the legacies of nineteenth-century Anglo-Caribbean art and culture associated with Belisario. A tumultuous and disruptive century of historical change—in effect the whole history of independent Jamaican art—intervenes between the two periods. In Belisario's lifetime, the diasporic lines of influence ran from metropolis to periphery. In this period, the lines of flow have been largely reversed, margin to center. This marks a critical shift, though it does not constitute a terminal break. The diasporic, whose "logic" persists in recuperating the past in the present, reworking and translating as it goes, does not—as I tried to say earlier—easily accommodate absolute beginnings, unilinear directions, or terminal closures. Quite contrary to its conventional meaning, which is organized around ideas of fixed origins, chosen peoples, sacred homelands, exclusive identities, and redemptive returns, the diasporic continues in fact to recombine, disseminate and proliferate. It works as much through reversals of vision, reading against the grain, or syntagmatically, by working further along the chain, as it does by evolutionary continuities or final endings. Some of the invisibilities of which we spoke in relation to Belisario's work came to constitute the very absent object against which much of the practice of more recent diasporic artists was directed. Their project was to challenge certain erasures and marginalizations inscribed in the visual field itself, to try to establish a certain "presence" within the frame, to come "into the field of vision." If there are "legacies," then, they are likely to be broken and de-centered ones, distended or condensed across time, space, and context, ruptured by a turbulent history and the traumas of migration, and unsettled by the "play" of nostalgia and desire that haunts every "return," real or symbolic.

The faces of the black women in Sonia Boyce's *Big Woman's Talk* of 1984 certainly seem like a different sort of subject, and unapologetically fill the frame. (She once said, "I drew my feet very big on patterned background. 'I'm here, you can't wish me away.'")[16] *Big Woman's Talk* tells a very "diasporic," if often neglected, story about the centrality of black women and their closeness within families in the struggle for survival in strange places. Boyce's 1986 companion piece to this work, *Lay Back, Keep Quiet and Think of What Made Britain So Great*, is, like some of Belisario's work, though in a completely different idiom, a meditation on colonialism, gender, and identity. The background to its four panels was originally a wallpaper design conceived as a tribute to fifty glorious years of Queen Victoria's reign, which, in a performative move, Sonia Boyce has appropriated and transformed. The first three panels retell the colonial conquests of the Cape Colony, India, and Australia—as Gilane Tawadros remarked, "[weaving] the colonial and imperial character of Britain's past . . . into the contours of the decorative wallpaper." In the fourth panel, however, the face and piercing eyes of a black woman (a self-portrait) look out boldly at us from the patterned background, bringing the historical "narrative" to a conclusion in an unexpected place. This image "affirms the status of identity as the sum total of the intersection of diverse but related histories and cultures."[17]

The "mark" of this summarizing panel, a black rose, is superimposed in the earlier three, replacing the red rose, symbol of Englishness, and stamping them with its difference. This rose motif is further reworked in her decoratively bold and much-reproduced crayon drawing, *She Ain't Holding Them Up, She's Holding On (Some English Rose)* of 1986 (fig. 10.3) with its richly ambivalent title and compositional structure. The artist herself is eloquently represented at the center of all these works, as Rasheed Araeen rightly observed, "not as a mirror but as a metaphor."[18]

In Joy Gregory's 1990 *Autoportrait* photo series (figs. 10.4a–10.4c), there is nothing else in the frame, nothing for the eye to see, nowhere else to look, except at the black woman "in the field of vision." Or rather parts of her—eyes, eyebrows, mouth, neck, ears, half-profile, hands-covering face—that Gregory allows us to see: for the deliberately distorted staging of these self-images, disrupting the "normal" distances of viewing, their isolation in space and fragmented shapes, also *breaks* the frame in a wider sense, refusing the wholeness of the tradition of Western portraiture and, in a counter-move, obliging us to see and look otherwise. As I argued elsewhere:

> Black self-portraiture in this historical moment has broken many of its links with the dominant western humanist celebration of self and has become more the staking of a claim, a wager. Here, the black self-image is, in a double sense, an exposure, a coming-out. The self is caught emerging . . . the experience of rupture, break, discontinuity, of loss and resistance to loss, of migration, upheaval, of the struggle to live within multiple locations and to sustain multiple strategies of resistance are allowed to invade the mythical inner wholeness of the self-image.[19]

Lubaina Himid was born in Tanzania but has lived and worked in Britain since the 1950s and began to exhibit alongside Afro-Caribbean artists in the 1980s. Slavery and servitude, colonialism and history, the degradation of

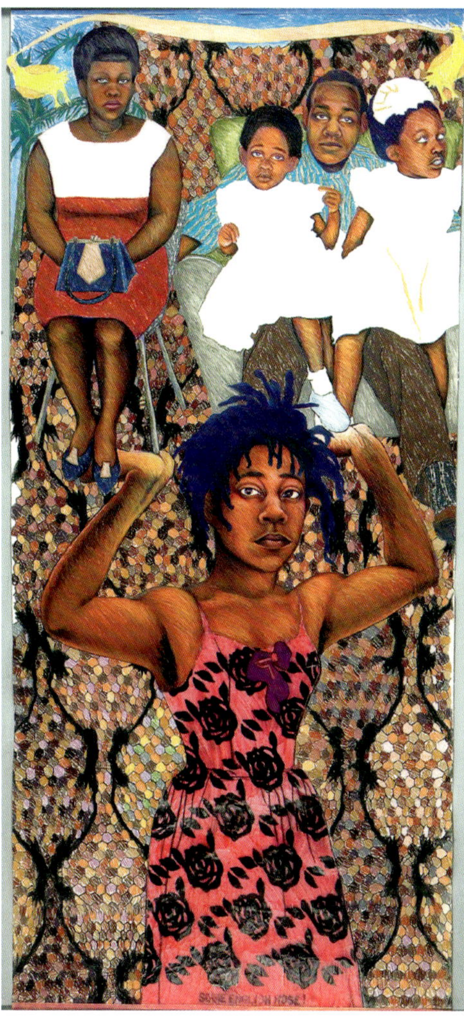

Figure 10.3. Sonia Boyce, *She Ain't Holding Them Up, She's Holding On (Some English Rose)*, 1986. Pastel and mixed media on paper. 227 × 113.5 cm. © Sonia Boyce. All rights reserved, DACS/Artimage 2022.

African people and the arrogance of white patriarchal power and wealth, and the subordination of women's experience and their creativity, have been constantly recurring themes in her work. She has been engaged over the years in a still unfinished sequence of small-scale, beautifully condensed, delicately sketched, and colored *Scenes from the Life of Toussaint L'Ouverture*, in which the personal and the heroic, the intimate and the political are perfectly fused.[20]

Lubaina Himid has also challenged and disrupted the "western" artistic tradition. In *A Fashionable Marriage* of 1986, she used drawing, painting, and cut-outs to transform Hogarth's famous *The Countess's Morning Levee* of

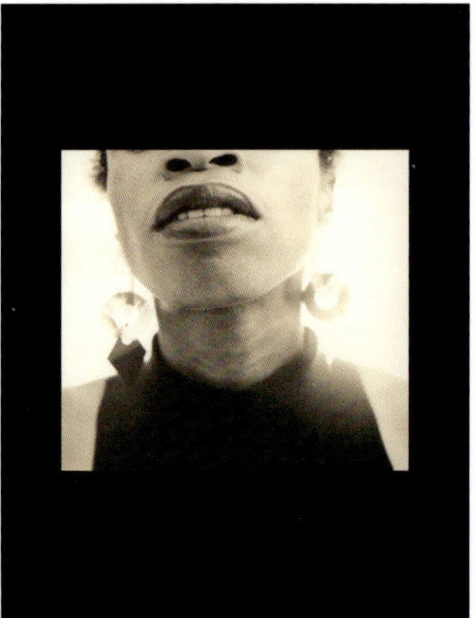

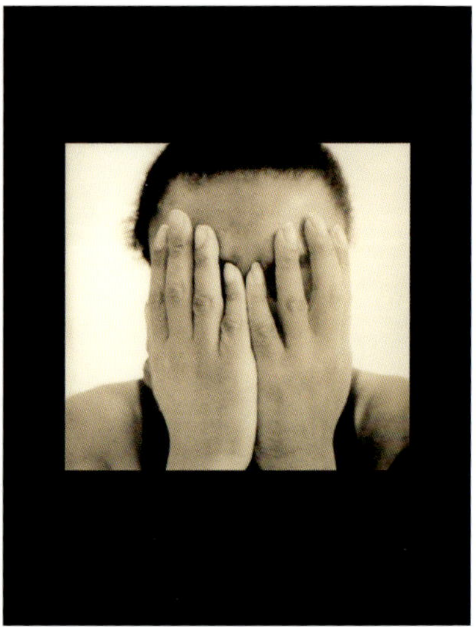

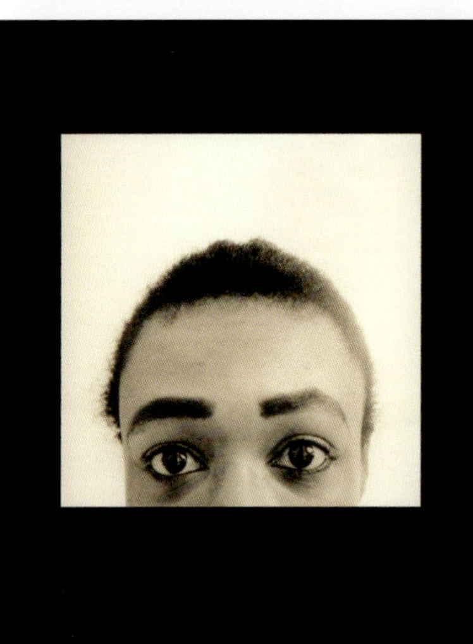

Figures 10.4a–10.4c. Joy Gregory, from the *Autoportrait* series, 1989–1990. Photographs, inkjet on paper. © Joy Gregory. All rights reserved, DACS/Artimage 2022. Courtesy of the artist and commissioned by Autograph, London.

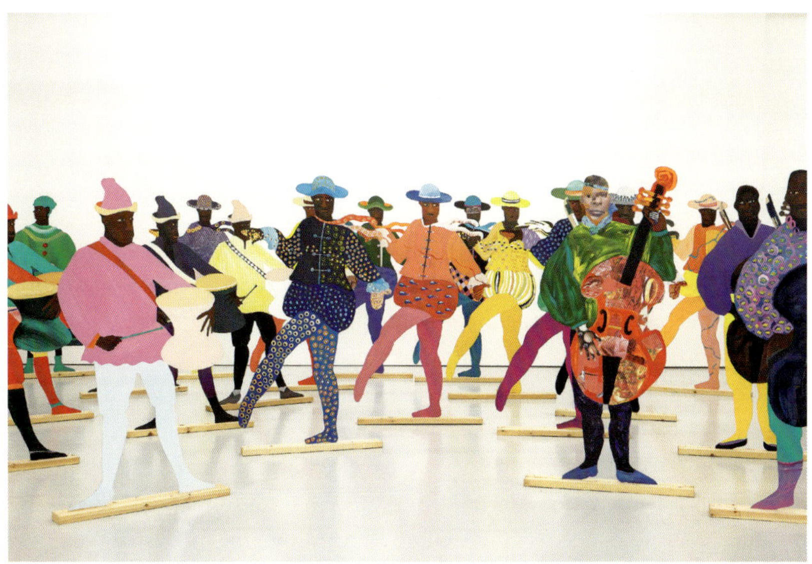

Figure 10.5. Lubaina Himid, *Naming the Money*, 2004. Installation view, Navigation Charts, Spike Island, Bristol, 2017. © Lubaina Himid. Image courtesy of the artist, Hollybush Gardens, London, and National Museums, Liverpool. © Spike Island, Bristol. Photo: Stuart Whipps.

1743 into a contemporary pastiche. In the striking 1984 installation *Freedom and Change*, she transformed Picasso's *Two Women Running on the Beach* into a woven, embroidered, and painted assemblage of two women in fluid motion, dark figures in brightly patterned shifts, running along a shoreline and urging on ahead of them four angular cut-out hunting dogs. Gilane Tawadros comments that "the particular place from which Himid's women assert their historical experience is the coastline, an ambivalent site which marks the frontier of slavery, colonialism, and migration but which also denotes the positivity of the diasporic experience."[21]

Himid's 2004 installation, *Naming the Money* (fig. 10.5), takes us directly back to Belisario. Originally planned as ten canvases, it proliferated into one hundred, half life-size, cut-out and freestanding painted portraits of African figures in various poses, exhibited with accompanying voice and music. In her letter to Lucy Wharton, the Hatton Gallery curator, about "her love affair with the painted portraits," she describes how the ones she did in the 1970s were of domestic objects and furniture.[22] In the 1980s, however, she saw painted figures of black slaves that had been given as gifts by the King of Spain to the King of France. She made six cut-out men with three-foot penises: "white men, funny, a bit aggressive and loved and loathed in equal measure," which triggered her move into the Black Art Movement.[23] Other cut-out installations followed including, in 1985, the much-reproduced *Carrot Piece*, in which a white man in pink tights riding a unicycle tempts, with a fishing rod baited with a carrot, a black man in African dress and carrying a drum. Of the cut-out form, Himid says they are "fabulous to make, ludicrous to store, audience friendly and critically challenging . . . real but like toys, un-judgmental friends, sturdy companions, mirrors and fantasy figures all in one."[24]

The American artist Alex Katz was once thought to have invented the form, but Himid discovered they were traditional to East Africa, "as memorial effigies from wood and plaster, decorated with pigment and cloth to honour dead elders," whose names were carved on the front.[25] This borrowing and fusion across boundaries, translation of traditions and trans-coding of sources to create something unique that transcends its parts, is the hybridizing, syncretizing, diasporic artistic imaginary at work.

Himid's painted "portraits" of black men and women immediately invoke Belisario's *Sketches of Character*. Like the *Sketches*, they are deliberately stylized. But, by comparison, liberated from their backgrounds and their "typicality," freestanding in space, her figures—doing, making, or playing things, walking or posing and dancing—are astonishingly lively and mobile in stance, posture, movement and attitude. They have lost all lingering sense of servitude or deference. In the artist's original installation, they seem to be moving and conversing among themselves, vividly convivial, in a vibrant scene—a fancy-dress party, a stage, a market . . .

Their extraordinarily intense colors—deep blues and greens, brilliant reds and yellows—intensify these effects. Color has transfused the cut-outs with a kind of life. As is generally the case in her work, Himid's use of color here deliberately breaks the literal representational connection in order to "free" her subjects into an imaginary space. Each figure wears an individual facial expression. Some are, of course, in masquerade or dressed up as courtiers or servants, others in African dress of brilliantly colored printed cloth, but the effect is not to disguise or distance them—they have not become generalized or anonymous. Rather, they seem to be coming into life before our eyes as "persons"—individualized, identified, named. Each figure is in two versions, each has two names—an African name and an English one given by a master or slave-owner, together with an individually composed short verse, which, in the installation, the figure "speaks": "My name is Masilo, They call me George . . ." or, "My name is Nilla, They call me Jenny. . . ." This double-naming process is fundamental to the conception of the piece. "Each cut out has a name . . ." read on an invoice attached to the back.[26] *Naming the Money* thus has a double reference, both to the European practice of dressing their African slaves like courtiers as a conspicuous adornment to their wealth and power, and to the way "house" slaves, who worked within the households in plantation slavery in the New World, were costumed by their masters and mistresses. It also explores how fundamental it was to the process of enslavement for the enslaved to lose their names and to have other identities imposed on them—and thus how important it would be to the process of survival for them both to recover an old name and to invent a new identity. This entailed constructing a different sort of connection between past and future than that which slavery implied, one in which the processes of costuming, masking, and mimicry we see in Belisario's Jonkonnu portraits, for example, were necessary detours.

Keith Piper was born into and grew up in the black British diaspora in the 1970s. "The aesthetics of peeling paint, rust and dereliction and the multi-layered look of fly-posters," typical of the decaying inner-city areas of the declining industrial Midlands, is palpable in the collaged, peeled, fraying, scarred, over-written surfaces and the crude juxtaposition of "thematically unrelated but politically charged" found images of his early work.[27] With the bold, graphic styles, aggressive attitudes, anti-racist themes, and strong slogans that he and Eddie Chambers pioneered, this highly politicized art belongs to a new Pan-African "moment" in the black arts in Britain. However, what Marcus Wood calls the near-unrepresentable worlds of the Middle Passage and slavery, an absent-presence in Belisario's work, have been recurring references and motifs in Piper's work; though—in a typically diasporic way—they often came to Piper's generation *mediated* through the racial politics of the embattled British inner cities and the Black Power and Black Art movements of the American Civil Rights struggles of the sixties. The tortured, enslaved, lynched, above all, crucified black body—mainly male, but as gender and feminism powerfully entered and inflected his work, female as well, and reminiscent of the "blackened" figure of Christ that is recurrent in Pan-African art and the syncretic religious movements of the Caribbean region—became one of Piper's most privileged iconic images.

Keith Piper's major work of the 1990s, the 1991 installation *A Ship Called Jesus* (fig. 10.6), explores the relationship between slavery and Christianity and, as Kobena Mercer puts it, "the various ways in which the fundamentalist

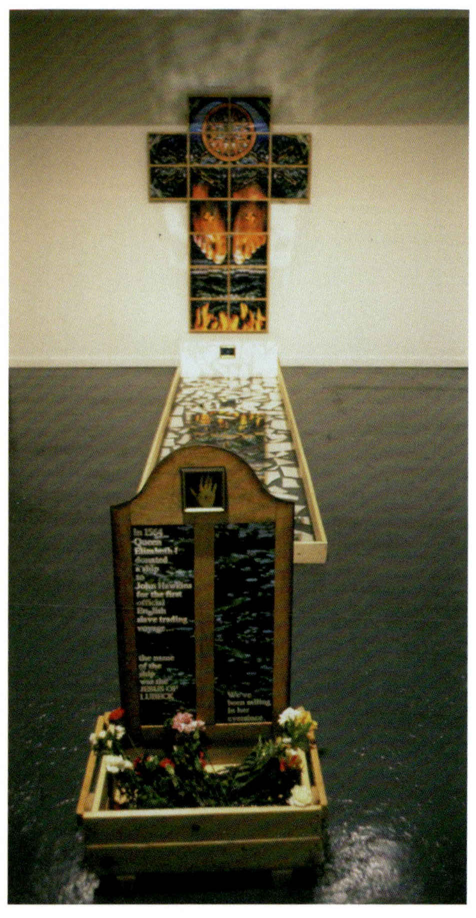

Figure 10.6. Keith Piper, *A Ghost of Christendom*, 1991. Computer montage on board. 6 × 4 ft. From the exhibition *A Ship Called Jesus*. First installation titled "The Ghosts of Christendom." Ikon Gallery, Birmingham, 1991. © Keith Piper. Courtesy of the artist.

desire for certainty . . . expresses a response to the unrepresentable experience of chaos, trauma and loss." Mercer sees the work as "the inscription of a desire to find new practices of freedom by asking what art can do to liberate subjectivity from the obligations of an identity tethered to the signifying chains of history."[28] The installation is named after the ship *The Jesus of Lubeck*, which Queen Elizabeth gave to Sir John Hawkins, the merchant-pirate who led slave-raiding ventures off the west coast of Africa.

This work consists of three sections. The first, "The Ghosts of Christendom"—a series of light-boxed, computer-produced images of historical figures, arranged like a stained-glass window—is a meditation on the unrequited memories of slavery and the Middle Passage. Close by is a crucifix-shaped box where two black feet, marked by the stigmata, emerge from a background of hands, chains, and fire. There is also a headstone and a grave—a sort of "ship"—made from broken mirrors. The second, "Rites of Passage," with its images projected across a pool of water, reflects on the history of the founding of the independent black churches that Piper sees as a positive outcome of transatlantic transportation's terrifying "rites of passage." The third, "The Fire Next Time," reflects on the ambiguous nature of this legacy—the temptations in all "fundamentalisms," whether religious or political, "to catch hold of frenetic change and to draw back and fix it to some past mythical point of stability and order. To literally stop history in its tracks."[29] This impressively multi-layered work—drawing in, reworking, and "relocating the remains" from many sources that are rich in historical memories, resonances, and associations about the Caribbean's violent and traumatic origins—is, in theme, treatment, and one can only say "structure of feeling," many worlds away from Belisario's though it may be the product of the same translational logic which is to be seen in his work, if only one knows how to look.

Roshini Kempadoo has made the diasporic journey in dramatic reverse. Born in Britain, she spent much of her childhood moving between England, Barbados, Trinidad, and Jamaica, including a long period in Guyana, before returning at eighteen to study in the United Kingdom. She now lives between England and her "second home" in Trinidad. She is a photographer-turned-digital artist, producing computer-enhanced images in quasi-narrative form. Her work explores the question of whether, "through the fragmentary, non-linear, multi-mediated, fictionalized reconstructions of the past" that the new digital technologies make possible, other narratives and new partial truths about the past can be made to emerge.[30] Much of her recent work focuses—as did Belisario's—on the plantation. *Ghosting* (figs. 10.7a and 10.7b) uses what we may call Trinidad's plantation-related archive—oral accounts, documents, photographs, maps—to critique the colonial period in the Caribbean, with the plantation system as its "key enterprise," and to rethink the process of dismantling and renegotiation, "marked by the abolition of slavery, the compensation of the landowners, the introduction of indentured migrant labor and the steady political and economic struggles for civil and human rights, independence and self-rule" that followed. How, this work asks, can the multimedia artwork, "with its hyper-textual digital aesthetic and interactive possibilities," be used as a way of reworking the land/space of the plantation? How can the plantation be seen as a site of absence and visibility?[31]

In a characteristically diasporic twist, Kempadoo's *Endless Prospects* used photographic and sound resources—landscapes, scenes of village life, and

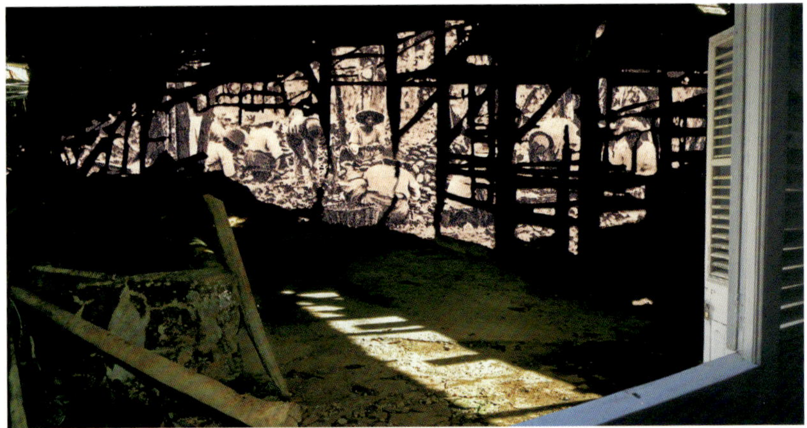

Figure 10.7a. Roshini Kempadoo, *Ghosting*, 2004. Project still, from a multimedia single-projection installation commissioned by the Leicester City Art Gallery and the Peepul Centre, Leicester. Collection of the artist. © Roshini Kempadoo, 2022.

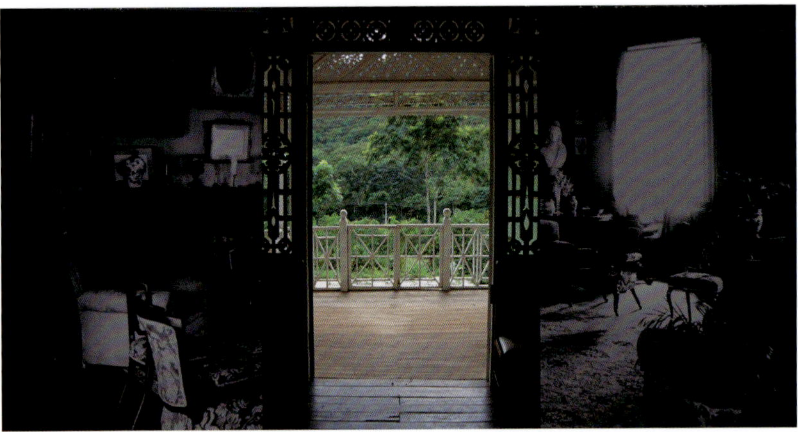

Figure 10.7b. Roshini Kempadoo, *Ghosting*, 2004. Project still, from a multimedia single-projection installation commissioned by the Leicester City Art Gallery and the Peepul Centre, Leicester. Collection of the artist. © Roshini Kempadoo, 2022.

interviews with residents from the areas around two plantation estates—to construct a site-specific installation in the Pitzhanger Gallery in London in 2004. This was originally the grand Pitzhanger Manor House owned by Sir John Soane, a powerful and ambitious Victorian architect, who built, among others, the Bank of England, Nos. 10, 11 and 12 Downing Street, and the elegant house that is now the Sir John Soane Museum. *Endless Prospects* introduced "the colonial," now as a constructed fictional or imaginary space, directly into the space of rule and governance in England at a moment of colonial expansionism. The latter is exemplified by what Kempadoo calls the voyeuristic landowners' or ruling-class "gaze" of "endless views, vistas, horizons, global and far-reaching prospects," with their specially constructed, mirror-enhanced interior perspectives and their exterior stereoscopic views, framed through windows and doorways.[32] This project, then, invites us to think again about the meaning and effects of the practices of scenic representation handled with such assurance in Belisario's Jamaican landscapes.

Kempadoo's recent work deconstructs the boundaries between "here" and "there" by persistently moving across and between the two poles of the "black Atlantic." *Sweetness and Light* of 1996 (figs. 10.7c and 10.7d) is a series of digitally produced images set in the grounds of English country house estates near Windsor on a wintry day. Images of black women, disturbed from an unquiet resting place far away, have begun, eerily, to appear to be "coming home" [*sic*] to this unfamiliar setting, haunting the proto-typically English landscape from which they have been banished by a pervasive amnesia. In one image in the series, the bodies of African women appear, like wraiths, standing between the columns of a colonnaded balustrade overlooking a wood. In another, two mustachioed Victorian sailors, one with his arm familiarly embracing a half-naked black woman, have uncannily emerged as if in a "scene" projected against the open half of a large, wooden estate gate. A third repeats the first, but this time— in a reprise that includes a reflection on the technologies of representation— the "illusion" is interrupted by the "modern," digitalized figure of the artist herself, who "breaks into the frame." Imaged in the posture of a waitress, she carries a tray on which stands a computer and monitor, which she holds up as a contrasting image against the balustrade with its black figures. This screen within a screen enables her to summon back from the past the "ethnographic" image of an Edwardian, colonial explorer-adventurer in his straw boater, hands casually in his pockets, standing in front of two rows of "native" [*sic*] women.

In this and other work referred to earlier, the diasporic imaginary seems to have come full circle. What was once a line of tasteful transmission from

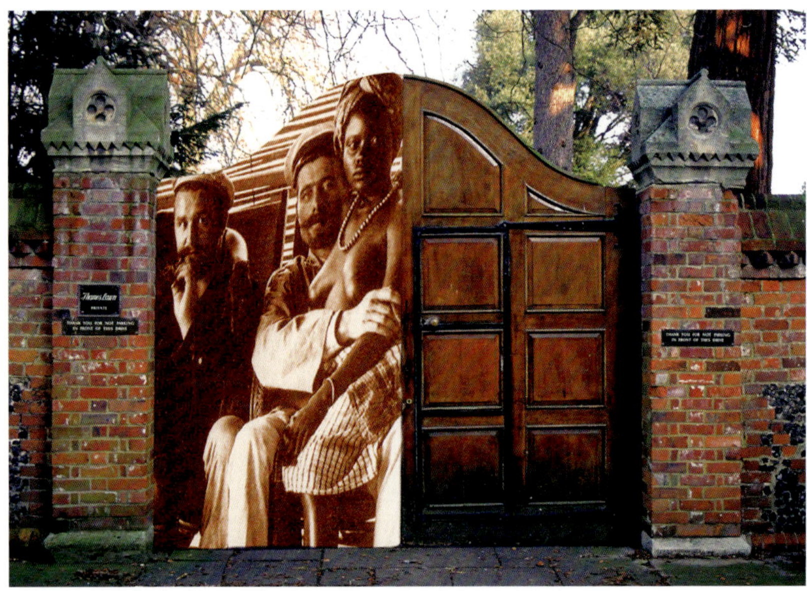

Figure 10.7c. Roshini Kempadoo, *Sweetness and Light: Great House People (no. 4)*, 1996. Lambda print; originally created for the internet exhibition *La Finca/The Homestead*, supported by Northwestern University, Evanston, IL, and Universidad Politécnica de Valencia, Spain. Collection of the artist. © Roshini Kempadoo, 2022.

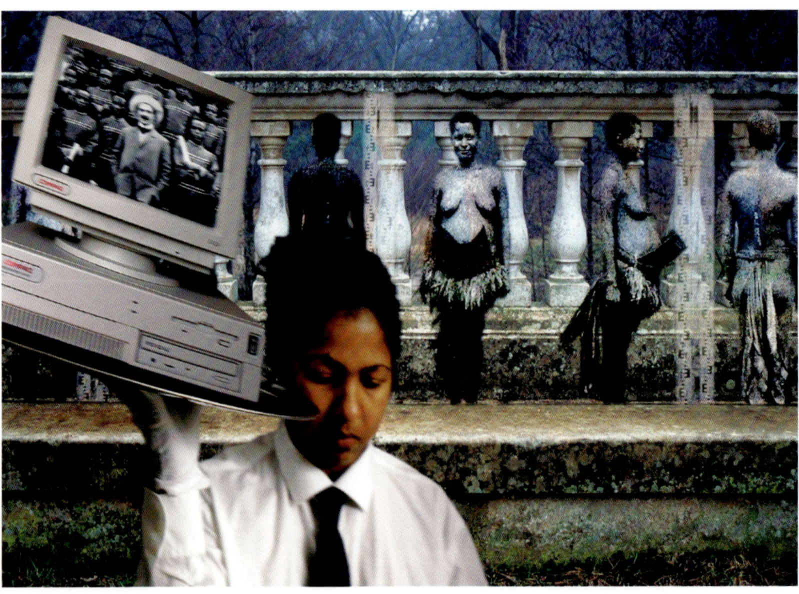

Figure 10.7d. Roshini Kempadoo, *Sweetness and Light: Great House People (no. 3)*, 1996. Lambda print; originally created for the internet exhibition *La Finca/The Homestead*, supported by Northwestern University, Evanston, IL, and Universidad Politécnica de Valencia, Spain. Collection of the artist. © Roshini Kempadoo, 2022.

center to periphery has become a critical response to questions of history, slavery, colonization, and power from what one might call "the place of the other." These works deliberately and disturbingly

> truncate the distance between colonizer and colonized, abridging the *cordon sanitaire* between "here" and "there," forcing the two realities (finally) to co-exist in the same space, to recognize their mutual implication . . . allow[ing] the long-disavowed "presence" of the world of plantation slavery to come into view, visually, inside the metropolis.[33]

NOTES

This essay first appeared in *Art and Emancipation in Jamaica: Isaac Mendes Belisario and His Worlds*, ed. Tim Barringer, Gillian Forrester, and Barbaro Martinez Ruiz (New Haven, CT: Yale University Press, 2007), 179–95.

1 Stuart Hall, "Thinking the Diaspora: Home-Thoughts from Abroad," *Small Axe* 3, no. 6 (1999): 1–18.

2 Kobena Mercer, *Welcome to the Jungle: New Positions in Black Cultural Studies* (London: Routledge, [1994]), 63.

3 On transculturation, see Fernando Ortiz, *Cuban Counterpoint: Tobacco and Sugar* (Durham, NC: Duke University Press, 1995 [1940]).

4 Stuart Hall, "Créolité and the Process of Creolization," in *Créolité and Creolization: Documenta 11, Platform 3*, ed. Okwui Enwezor et al. (Ostfindern-Ruit: Hatje Cantz, 2003), 27–41; Édouard Glissant, *Le discours Antillais* (Paris: Éditions du Seuil, 1981). Glissant discusses the creole counter-discourse at length. See also Mary Louise Pratt, *Imperial Eyes: Travel Writing and Transculturation* (New York: Routledge, 1992).

5 The "three presences" are more fully elaborated in Stuart Hall, "Cultural Identity and Diaspora," in *Identity: Community, Culture, Difference*, ed. Jonathan Rutherford (London: Lawrence and Wishart, 1990).

6 On this argument, see Jacques Derrida, "*Différance*," in *Margins of Philosophy* (Chicago: University of Chicago Press, 1982), especially 12–13, 17; and Jacques Derrida, *Positions*, trans. Alan Bass (Chicago: University of Chicago Press, 1981).

7 Christopher Columbus, "Letter on the First Voyage," in *The Four Voyages of Christopher Columbus*, ed. and trans. J. M. Cohen (London: Century Hutchinson, 1988), 116.

8 See Henry Louis Gates, *The Signifying Monkey: A Theory of Afro-American Literary Criticism* (Oxford: Oxford University Press, 1988).

9 Dylan Kerrigan, "Creatures of the Mas," *Caribbean Beat* 71 (January–February, 2005).

10 Marcus Wood, *Blind Memory: Visual Representations of Slavery in England and America, 1780–1865* (Manchester: Manchester University Press, 2000). Wood questions whether the Middle Passage and slavery are "representable."

11 Stuart Hall, "Black Diaspora Artists in Britain, Three Moments in Post-war History," *History Workshop Journal* 61 (Spring, 2006); and Rasheed Araeen, *The Other Story: Afro-Asian Artists in Post-war Britain* (London: South Bank Centre, 1989).

12 Veerle Poupeye, *Caribbean Art* (London: Thames and Hudson, 1998).

13 See Poupeye, *Caribbean Art*, especially chapter 2, "Modernism and Cultural Nationalism," and chapter 3, "Popular Religion, the Festival Arts and the Visionary."

14 See the account offered in Hall, "Black Diaspora Artists."

15 See David Bailey and Stuart Hall, eds., "Critical Decade: Black British Photography in the 80s," special issue, *Ten.8* 2, no. 3 (1992); Stuart Hall and Mark Sealy, *Different: Contemporary Photography and Black Identity* (London: Phaidon, 2001); Araeen, *Other Story*; David Bailey, Ian Baucom, and Sonia Boyce, eds., *Shades of Black: Assembling Black Artists in 1980s Britain* (Durham, NC: Duke University Press; London: Institute of International Visual Arts, 2005); and Gilane Tawadros, ed., *Changing States: Contemporary Art and Ideas in an Era of Globalisation* (London: Institute of International Visual Arts, 2004).

16 Araeen, *Other Story*, 101.

17 Gilane Tawadros, "Beyond the Boundary," in *Black British Cultural Studies*, ed. Houston A. Baker, Manthia Diawara, and Ruth Lindeborg (Chicago: University of Chicago Press, 1996), 263.

18 Araeen, *Other Story*, 102.

19 Hall and Sealy, *Different*, 58.

20 The latest sequence in this series was commissioned by the Institute of International Visual Arts as a seventieth birthday gift to the author.

21 Tawadros, "Beyond the Boundary," 243.

22 The letter was later published as Lubaina Himid, "Written on a Train from Preston to London," in *Naming the Money* (Newcastle: University of Newcastle, 2004), 9.

23 Himid, "Written on a Train," 9.

24 Himid, "Written on a Train," 10.

25 Himid, "Written on a Train," 10.

26 Himid, "Written on a Train," 6.

27 Kobena Mercer, "Witness at the Crossroads: An Artist's Journey in Post-colonial Space," in *Keith Piper: Relocating the Remains*, ed. David Chandler (London: Institute of International Visual Arts, 1997), 20, 21.

28 Mercer, "Witness at the Crossroads," 62.

29 Keith Piper, *A Ship Called Jesus* (Birmingham: Ikon Gallery, 1991), 21.

30 See Ashwani Sharma, "Passion for the Real: Violence and the (Post)-Colonial Sublime," in abstracts of papers for the Visible Evidence XI conference (Bristol: University of Bristol, 2003).

31 Roshini Kempadoo, "Ghosting: (In)visibility and Absence of Racialised Landscapes," in abstracts of papers for the Visible Evidence XI conference (Bristol: Bristol University, 2003).

32 Roshini Kempadoo, "Tracing the Image: Artist's Notes on Re-interpreting Trinidad Landscapes: Endless Prospects," in *Exposure* 38, no. 2 (2005): 3.

33 Hall and Sealy, *Different*, 77.

PART IV

ASSEMBLING THE 1980S

CHAPTER 11

Minimal Selves

A few adjectival thoughts only . . .

Thinking about my own sense of identity, I realize that it has always depended on the fact of being a *migrant*, on the *difference* from the rest of you. So one of the fascinating things about this discussion is to find myself centered at last. Now that, in the postmodern age, you all feel so dispersed, I become centered. What I've thought of as dispersed and fragmented comes, paradoxically, to be *the* representative modern experience! This is "coming home" with a vengeance! Most of it I much enjoy—welcome to migrant hood. It also makes me understand something about identity which has been puzzling me in the last three years.

I've been puzzled by the fact that young black people in London today are marginalized, fragmented, unenfranchised, disadvantaged and dispersed. And yet, they look as if they own the territory. Somehow, they too, in spite of everything, are centered, in place; without much material support, it's true, but nevertheless, they occupy a new kind of space at the centre. And I've wondered again and again: what it is about that long discovery-rediscovery of identity among blacks in this migrant situation, which allows them to lay a kind of claim to certain parts of the earth which aren't theirs, with quite that certainty? I do feel a sense of—dare I say—envy surrounding them. Envy is a very funny thing for the British to feel at this moment in time—to want to be black! Yet I feel some of you surreptitiously moving towards that marginal identity. I welcome you to that, too.

Now the question is: is this centering of marginality really *the* representative postmodern experience? I was given the title "the minimal self." I know the discourses which have theoretically produced that concept of "minimal self." But my experience now is that what the discourse of the postmodern has produced is not something new but a kind of recognition of where identity always was at. It is in that sense that I want to redefine the general feeling which more and more people seem to have about themselves—that they are all, in some way, *recently migrated*, if I can coin that phrase.

The classic questions which every migrant faces are twofold: "Why are you here?" and "When are you going back home?" No migrant ever knows the answer to the second question until asked. Only then does she or he know that really, in the deep sense, she/he's never going back. Migration is a one-way trip. There is no "home" to go back to. There never was. But "why are you here?" is also a really interesting question, which I've never been able to find a proper answer to either. I know the reasons one is supposed to give: "for education," "for the children's sake," "for a better life, more opportunities," "to enlarge the mind" etc. The truth is, I am here because it's where my family is not. I really came here to get away from my mother. Isn't that the universal story of life? One is where one is to try and get away from somewhere else. That was the story which I could never tell anybody about myself. So I had to find other stories, other fictions, which were more authentic or, at any rate, more acceptable, in place of the Big Story of the endless evasion of patriarchal family life. Who I am—the "real" me—was formed in relation to a whole set of other narratives. I was aware of the fact that identity is an invention from the very beginning, long before I understood any of this theoretically. Identity is formed at the unstable point where the "unspeakable" stories of subjectivity meet the narratives of history, of a culture. And since he/she is positioned in relation to cultured narratives which have been profoundly expropriated the colonized subject is always "somewhere else": doubly marginalized, displaced always *other* than where he or she is, or is able to speak from.

It wasn't a joke when I said that I migrated in order to get away from my family. I did. The problem, one discovers, is that since one's family is always already "in here," there is no way in which you can actually leave them. Of course, sooner or later, they recede in memory, or even in life. But these are not the "burials" that really matter. I wish they were still around, so that I didn't have to carry them around, locked up somewhere in my head, from which there is no migration. So from the first, in relation to them, and then to all the other symbolic "others," I certainly was always aware of the self as only constituted in that kind of absent-present contestation with something else, with some other "real me," which is and isn't there.

If you live, as I've lived, in Jamaica, in a lower-middle class family that was trying to be a middle-class Jamaican family trying to be an upper-middle class Jamaican family trying to be an English Victorian family . . . I mean the notion of displacement as a place of "identity" is a concept you learn to live with, long before you are able to spell it. Living with, living through difference. I remember the occasion when I returned to Jamaica on a visit sometime in the early 1960s, after the first wave of migration to England, my mother said to me: "Hope they don't think you are one of those immigrants over there!" And of course, at that point I knew for the first time I was an immigrant. Suddenly in relation to that narrative of migration, one version of the "real me" came into view. I said: "Of course, I'm an immigrant. What do you think I am?" And she said in that classic Jamaican middle-class way, "Well, I hope the people over there will shove all the immigrants off the long end of a short pier." (They've been shoving ever since.)

The trouble is that the instant one learns to be "an immigrant," one recognizes one can't be an immigrant any longer: it isn't a tenable place to be. I, then, went through the long, important, political education of discovering that I am "black." Constituting oneself as "black" is another recognition of self through difference: certain clear polarities and extremities against which one tries to define oneself. We constantly underestimate the importance, to certain crucial political things that have happened in the world, of this ability of people to constitute themselves, psychically, in the black identity. It has long been thought that this is really a simple process: a recognition—a resolution of irresolutions, a coming to rest in some place which was always there waiting for one. The "real me" at last!

The fact is "black" has never been just there either. It has always been an unstable identity, psychically, culturally and politically. It, too, is a narrative, a story, a history. Something constructed, told, spoken, not simply found. People now speak of the society I come from in totally unrecognizable ways. Of course Jamaica is a black society, they say. In reality it is a society of black and brown people who lived for three or four hundred years without ever being able to speak of themselves as "black." Black is an identity which had to be learned and could only be learned in a certain moment. In Jamaica that moment is the 1970s. So the notion that identity is a simple—if I can use the metaphor—black or white question, has never been the experience of black people, at least in the diaspora. These are "imaginary communities"—and not a bit the less real because they are also symbolic. Where else could the dialogue of identity between subjectivity and culture take place?

Despite its fragmentations and displacements, then, "the self" does relate to a real set of histories. But what are the "real histories" to which so many at this conference have "owned up"? How new is this new condition? It does seem that more and more people now recognize themselves in the narratives of displacement. But the narratives of displacement have certain conditions of existence, real histories in the contemporary world, which are not only or exclusively psychical, not simply "journeys of the mind." What is that special moment? Is it simply the recognition of a general condition of fragmentation at the end of the twentieth century?

It may be true that the self is always, in a sense, a fiction, just as the kinds of "closures" which are required to create communities of identification—nation, ethnic group, families, sexualities etc.—are arbitrary closures: and the forms of political action, whether movements, or parties, or classes, those too, are temporary, partial, arbitrary. I believe it is an immensely important gain when one recognizes that all identity is constructed across difference and begins to live with the politics of difference. But doesn't the acceptance of the fictional or narrative status of identity in relation to the world also require as a necessity, its opposite—the moment of arbitrary closure? Is it possible for there to be action or identity in the world without arbitrary closure—what one might call the necessity to meaning of the end of the sentence? Potentially, discourse is endless: the infinite semiosis of meaning. But to say anything at all in particular, you do have to stop talking. Of course, every full stop is provisional. The next sentence will take nearly all of it back. So what is this "ending"? It's a kind of stake, a kind of wager. It says, "I need to say something, something . . . just now." It is not forever, not totally universally true. It is not underpinned by infinite guarantees. But just now, this is what I mean; this is who I am. At a certain point, in a certain discourse we call these unfinished closures, "the self," "society," "politics," etc. Full stop. OK. There really (as they say) is no full stop of that kind. Politics, without the arbitrary interposition of power in language, the cut of ideology, the positioning, the crossing of lines, the rupture, is impossible. I don't understand political action without that moment. I don't see where it comes from. I don't see how it is possible. All the social movements which have tried to transform society and have required the constitution of new subjectivities, have had to accept the necessarily fictional, but also the fictional necessity,

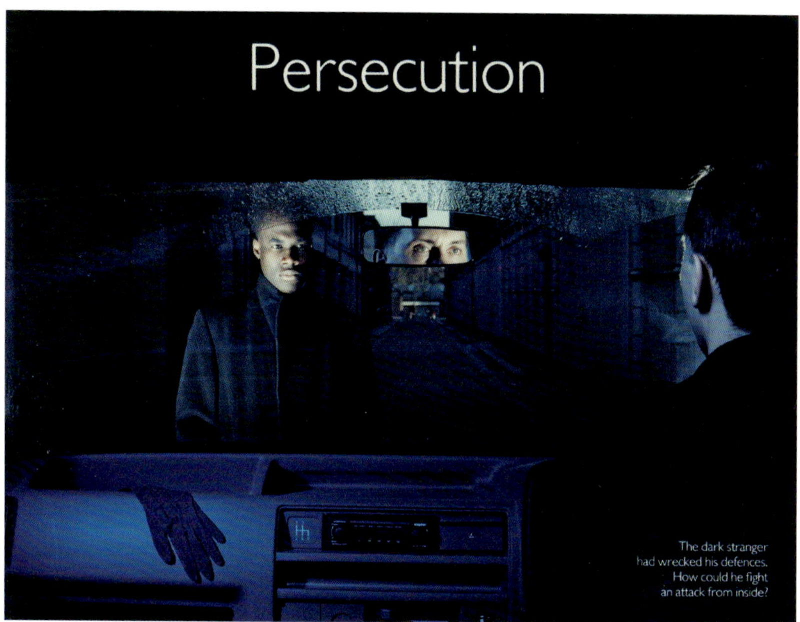

Figure 11.1. Mitra Tabrizian, *The Blues (Persecution)*, 1986–1987, with Andy Golding. Kodak Type C print. 48 × 60 cm. © Mitra Tabrizian. All rights reserved, DACS/Artimage 2022.

of the arbitrary closure which is not the end, but which makes both politics and identity possible.

Now I perfectly recognize that this recognition of difference, of the impossibility of "identity" in its fully unified meaning, does, of course, transform our sense of what politics is about. It transforms the nature of political commitment. Hundred-and-one percent commitment is no longer possible. But the politics of infinitely advancing while looking over the shoulder is a very dangerous exercise. You tend to fall into a hole. Is it possible, acknowledging the discourse of self-reflexivity, to constitute a *politics* in the recognition of the necessarily functional nature of the modern self, and the necessary arbitrariness of the closure around the imaginary communities in relation to which we are constantly in the process of becoming "selves"?

Looking at new conceptions of identity requires us also to look at redefinitions of the forms of politics which follow from that: the politics of difference, the politics of self-reflexivity, a politics that is open to contingency but still able to act (fig. 11.1). The politics of infinite dispersal is the politics of no action at all: and one can get into that from the best of all possible motives (i.e.: from the highest of all possible intellectual abstractions). So one has to reckon with the consequences of where that absolutist discourse of postmodernism is pushing one. Now, it seems to me that it is possible to think about the nature of new political identities, which isn't founded on the notion of some absolute, integral self and which clearly can't arise from some fully closed narrative of the self. A politics which accepts the "no necessary or essential correspondence" of anything with anything, and there has to be *a politics of articulation*—politics as a hegemonic project.

I also believe that out there other identities *do* matter. They're not the same as my inner space, but I'm in some relationship, some dialogue with them. They are points of resistance to the solipsism of much postmodernist discourse. I have to deal with them, somehow. And all of that constitutes, yes, a politics, in the general sense, a politics of constituting "unities"-in-difference. I think that is a new conception of politics, rooted in a new conception of the self, of identity. But I do think, theoretically and intellectually, it requires us to begin, not only to speak the language of dispersal, but also the language of, as it were, contingent closures of articulation.

You see, I don't think it's true that we've been driven back to a definition of identity as the "minimal self." Yes, it's true that the "grand narratives" which constituted the language of the self as an integral entity don't hold. But actually, you know, it isn't just the "minimal selves" stalking out there with absolutely no relation to one another. Let's think about the question of nation and nationalism. One is aware of the degree to which nationalism was/is constituted as one of those major poles or terrains of articulation of the self. I think it is very important the way in which some people now (and I think particularly of the colonized subject) begin to reach for a new conception of ethnicity as a kind of counter to the old discourses of nationalism or national identity.

Now one knows these are dangerously overlapping terrains. All the same they are not identical. Ethnicity *can* be a constitutive element in the most viciously regressive kind of nationalism or national identity. But in our times, as an imaginary community, it is also beginning to carry some other meanings, and to define a new space for identity. It insists on difference—on the fact that every identity is placed, positioned, in a culture, a language, a history. Every statement comes from somewhere, from somebody in particular. It insists on specificity, on conjuncture. But it is not necessarily armour-plated against other identities. It is not tied to fixed, permanent, unalterable oppositions. It is not wholly defined by exclusion.

I don't want to present this new ethnicity as a powerless, perfect universe. Like all terrains of identification, it has dimensions of power in it. But it isn't quite so framed by those extremities of power and aggression, violence and mobilization, as the older forms of nationalism. The slow contradictory movement from "nationalism" to "ethnicity" as a source of identities is part of a new politics. It is also part of the "decline of the west"—that immense process of historical relativization which is just beginning to make the British, at least, feel just marginally "marginal."

NOTE

This essay first appeared in *Identity: The Real Me*, ICA Document 6, ed. Lisa Appignanesi (London: ICA, 1988), 44–46.

CHAPTER 12

Assembling the 1980s:
The Deluge—and After

This paper tries to frame a provisional answer to the question: How might we begin to "assemble" the 1980s as an object of critical knowledge? It does not aspire to a definitive interpretation of the period. Not being a practicing artist, art critic, historian, or curator, mine is a strictly amateur view. What I try to do, instead, is to "map" the black arts in Britain in the 1980s as part of a wider cultural/political moment, tracking some of the impulses that went into its making and suggesting some interconnections between them. I "assemble" these elements, not as a unity, but in all their contradictory dispersion. In adopting this genealogical approach, the artwork itself appears, not in its fullness as an aesthetic object, but as a constitutive element in the fabric of the wider world of ideas, movements, and events, while at the same time offering us a privileged vantage point on that world.

In *Different: Contemporary Photographers and Black Identity*, Mark Sealy and I make the argument that contemporary black photography continues, in many ways, to operate on a problematic first defined by the practitioners who emerged in the 1980s.[1] We may think of this as the first, genuinely "postcolonial" moment in black artistic practice. It witnessed an explosion of creative work by artists from places historically marginalized from the centers of power and authority. It opened up certain possibilities in art practice and defined an "economy" of themes and images with which contemporary practitioners are still reckoning. Though not a unified, coherent, or organized phenomenon, this "movement" (if something so loose can be called such) must be tracked, not only in the visual arts, film, and photography, but across music, literature, and the performing arts, popular culture and fashion. Broadly speaking, it is driven by the struggles of peoples, marginalized in relation to the world system, to resist exclusion, reverse the historical gaze, come into visibility, and open up a "third space" (between the weight of an unreconstructed tradition and the impetus of a mindless modernism) in cultural representation. It therefore belongs to that uneven, contradictory, and bitterly contested transformation of cultural life now in progress across the globe, which attempts to de-center Western models and open a broader, more transcultural and "translative" perspective on cultural practice and production. It challenges the institutional spaces, established circuits, and validated canons of critical achievement of the metropolitan mainstream.

This "movement" has global significance. It refuses to be constrained by national boundaries, emphasizing instead a lateral, diasporic, transnational perspective. The project persists, despite being confronted on all sides by deepening inequalities of power and material resources and marked by a persistent racism. Unable as yet to stem frontally the tide of Western-driven, neoliberal globalization and its cultural agendas, this is globalization's Other, transnational face—its subversive reverse side. As we argued, "Refusing, simultaneously, either to disappear into the global bazaar of the international art market or to be holed up forever in some 'local' ethnic ghetto, this movement is 'located' in, without being rendered motionless by, places of origin, skin colour, so-called racial group, ethnic tradition or national belongingness and is part of a new, emergent kind of 'vernacular cosmopolitanism.'"[2]

The 1980s, then, saw the onset of a "deluge" of creative activity. However, the "Shades of Black" conference also constituted the 1980s as a puzzle, an enigma. In the history of the post-war black visual arts in Britain, the 1980s remain a vigorously contested space. This may be because they have become an object of desire, weighed down by the projection of powerful but unrequited psychic and political investments. Thus, some see the 1980s as the moment when the dream that artists from the former colonial empires could enter the mainstream of modern art and claim their rightful place there was abandoned. Some see the 1980s as the moment when art as an essential weapon in the armory of antiracist politics surfaced—and was derailed. Some see the decade as the moment when the arts were harnessed to the expression of excluded cultural, national, ethnic, and racial identities—and became mired in the multicultural trap of "cultural difference." Some see the 1980s as the moment when what was progressive in modernism was subverted by the vagaries of postmodernism and betrayed by cultural theory's so-called collusive relationship with global capitalism. The protagonists of these various positions are unlikely to agree—or even to agree to differ! Indeed, the old antagonisms are still pursued, sometimes with a venomous intensity. We are still in the post-1980s, living its turbulent afterlife, with all the heated controversy of an unsettled history in which everything is still urgently at stake.

We need to bear in mind the transatlantic nature of the dialogue that "Shades of Black" initiated. Here, comparisons are useful, but closeness can also be a source of misunderstanding. The Black Arts Movement in the United States, which emerged during the post-civil rights period, was enormously influential for black British artists like Eddie Chambers and Keith Piper and the formation of the Pan-Afrikan Connection in 1982. However, the term "black" in the British context (and, incidentally, in this essay) always also references migrants from the Asian subcontinent as well as the African diaspora, a fact that makes the politics of antiracism significantly different on the two sides of the Atlantic. There are deeper historical differences. For African-Americans, the key factor has always been slavery, whose consequences continue to shape daily domestic American life. In the Caribbean case, in the 1950s and 1960s, the central issue seemed to be, not slavery per se, but colonialism. Certainly, the post-war generation of Caribbean and Asian artists who migrated to Britain were primarily motivated by anticolonialism and the struggle for national independence. Further, because Britain—unlike the United States—managed slavery and colonization at a safe distance, the migrations of the 1950s were the first time a black working population in any significant numbers had come to live, work, and settle in the white domestic space. These and other facts should make us wary of easy US/UK comparisons. The powerful impact of black American popular culture on black British culture in the 1990s and after has tended to obscure these historical distinctions.

I attempt to treat the 1980s as a conjuncture, as Gramsci understood it: a fusion of contradictory forces that nevertheless cohere enough to constitute a definite configuration.[3] Althusser called it "a condensation of dissimilar currents," the "ruptural fusion of an accumulation of contradictions."[4] The forces operative in a conjuncture have no single origin, time scale, or determination. Like a symptom, conjunctures are always *overdetermined*. They have different time scales—"How long," Gramsci asked, "is a crisis?"—and are defined by their articulation, not their chronology. Decades seems a convenient way of getting a handle on conjunctures but can be misleading because they tend to fetishize them, condensing them into easily assimilable blocks of time, giving them a sequential form and an imaginary unity they never possessed. Much the same can be true of "generations," which, as David Scott argues, should be defined, not by simple chronology but by the fact that their members frame the same sorts of questions and try to work through them within the same epistemological, political, or aesthetic horizon, or as he calls it, "problem-space."[5] For example, did the highly politicized artwork of the late 1970s and early 1980s and the more figural and neoconceptual work of the late 1980s and 1990s belong to the same problematic because they were produced by the same generation? Did both belong to the same conjuncture? Perhaps, indeed, the differences between them constitute something more like a profound rupture. If so, we need to know why this break occurs within what on the surface appears to be the same conjuncture.

My argument is indeed that the problematic that frames this work did fracture decisively *in* the 1980s, leading to a profound "conjunctural shift." Framing the discussion as "the 1980s" may therefore serve to conceal how deep and extensive these seismic shifts turned out to be. I therefore tend to see the decade as a period of breaks, as well as of continuities, setting in play a number of impulses whose directions do not necessarily, in the end, add up. Instead, I try to map them as a series of overlapping, interlocking, but noncorresponding histories, and the shifts and fissures they opened up.

Bearing in mind the caveats above, we can still usefully divide the British post-war black art scene into two distinct waves. The first generation were born as colonial subjects in their countries of origin before World War II and, with one or two exceptions, came to Britain as practicing artists, with a body of work already behind them. They arrived on the crest of the wave of post-war decolonization in the 1950s and 1960s. Between 1949 and 1966, Francis Newton Souza, Frank Bowling (fig. 12.1), Aubrey Williams, Donald Locke, Ahmed Parvez, Anwar Shemza, Avinash Chandra, David Medalla, Balraj Khanna, Iqbal Geoffrey, Uzo Egonu, Saleem Arif, Ivan Peries, Li Yuan-chia, and Rasheed Araeen, among others, arrived in Britain. Incidentally, the only member of that generation who was a contributor to this symposium was Rasheed Araeen—painter, sculptor, curator, editor of *Third Text*—the last of that group to arrive and manifestly a transitional figure who spans both generations. The leading figures of the second wave, who surfaced in the late 1970s and early 1980s—including Eddie Chambers, Keith Piper, Lubaina Himid, Sonia Boyce, Claudette Johnson, Mona Hatoum, Maud Sulter, Donald Rodney (fig. 12.2), Gavin Jantjes, as well as many later contributors—were all born in the 1950s or 1960s and did not exhibit work until two decades later.

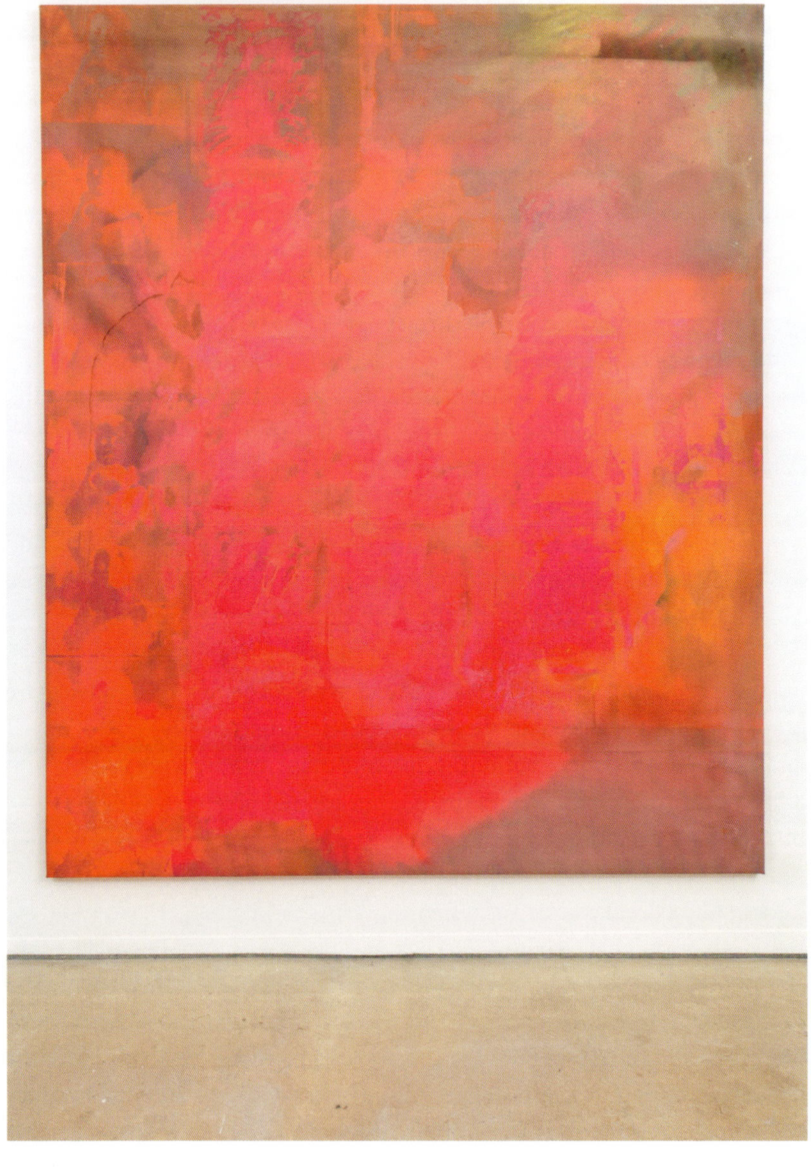

Figure 12.1. Frank Bowling, *Dan & Them*, 1972. Acrylic on canvas. 282 × 240 cm. © Frank Bowling. All rights reserved, DACS/Artimage 2022. Photo: Damian Griffiths.

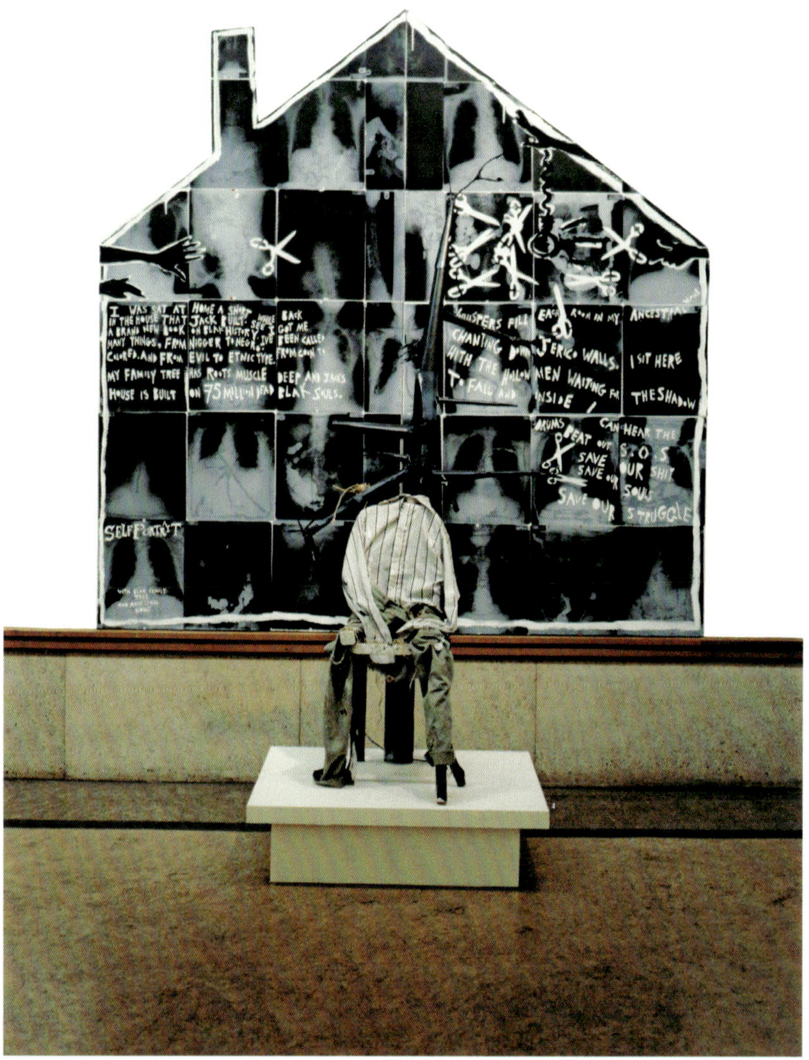

Figure 12.2. Donald Rodney, *The House That Jack Built*, 1987. Mixed media. © Estate of Donald Rodney. Courtesy of the Estate of Donald Rodney.

One immediate contrast is between the attitudes to modernism of these two waves. Broadly speaking, the artists of the first wave came to London in a spirit not altogether different from that in which early European modernists went to Paris: to fulfil their artistic ambitions and to participate in what they saw as the heady atmosphere of artistic innovation in the most advanced center of art at that time. The visual artists were not alone in this. In the 1950s and 1960s, London was a mecca for a whole generation of Caribbean writers, intellectuals, and artists who felt at that moment that they had to migrate to fulfil their artistic ambitions. The West Indian novel—of Sam Selvon, George Lamming, V. S. Naipaul, Wilson Harris—was in many ways the product of this migratory movement.

They came, of course, to claim their place as artists in a movement from which, as colonials, they had been marginalized but to which in every other sense they felt they naturally belonged and that, in a way, belonged to them. The promise of decolonization liberated them from any lingering sense of inferiority. Their aim was to engage the art world as equals on its own terrain. In that sense, they shared much with, and were clearly part of, the rising optimism of the *Windrush* generation of Caribbean migrants, who came in the 1950s and 1960s to make a better life for themselves and their families, and whose jaunty self-confidence is so palpable in the images of their arrival published in the press and magazines at the time. They came because of the colonial connection, however deep their anticolonialism; because it was to many "the mother country," as well as the "mother" of all their troubles. They came to see for themselves, to look it in the eye—and to conquer.

The distinctiveness of this world and its anticolonial mentality may be difficult for younger contemporaries to imagine or inhabit. It may also be difficult now to understand the degree to which modern art was seen by these artists as an international creed, fully consistent with anticolonialism and its profound resistance to the imposition on colonial peoples of false European values. Contemporary art was regarded as essential to a modern consciousness. These artists shared with other colonial intellectuals of their generation an aspiration to destroy the feudal structures of the traditional world they inhabited as well as the foreign institutions associated with colonialism. But their dream was not to restore the ancient past so much as to issue in a new era of progress, change, modernity, and freedom. Critical of the mindless imitation of Western artistic models, they nevertheless saw, as Rasheed Araeen has argued, an engagement with "modern art" as "the only way to deal with the aspirations of our time."[6] They regarded the artistic vocation as a universal calling capable of transcending narrow cultural or historical conditions. They claimed art in the name of "humanity" in general.

Many were already familiar with developments in contemporary Western art and already practicing what they saw as "modern art." Some, no doubt, as Araeen remarked in his *Black Manifesto*, accepted "the 'supremacy' of Western developments in the contemporary field by following whatever styles [were] developed or produced in the major art centres of the West."[7] But others, certainly, in the spirit of those indigenous "modernisms" that had taken authentic root in the "periphery," subscribed to the views of Herbert Read, one of British modernism's leading apostles, who saw modern art as the attempt "to create forms more appropriate to the sense and sensibility of a new age."[8] These artists were, in that sense, "moderns" in spirit, if not specifically "modernists." They had internalized the spirit of restless innovation, the impulse to "make it new," which defined the modern attitude. Frank Bowling, who left London for the United States in 1966 and who has had an unswerving loyalty to abstraction throughout his career, said, "I believe the Black soul, if there can be such a thing, belongs in Modernism."[9]

Rasheed Araeen put it clearly in *The Black Manifesto*, albeit with perhaps a stronger "Third World" emphasis than many of the first generation would have adopted. He argued that some

> Third World artists have taken an entirely different direction, by accepting the challenge of this modern age. While conscious of their own indigenous cultural backgrounds (which they sometimes reflect in their work), they recognize the technological nature of various developments in the West. They consider it their legitimate right to make use of *contemporary* knowledge in their work . . . just as Western artists were able to benefit, and are still benefitting from their knowledge of Afro/Asian traditions. . . . What is singular about these artists is that they are innovators. Thus they contribute to contemporary developments in their own right, by their own original ideas, concepts and synthesis/antithesis; and more importantly they offer a challenge to Western domination by defying the hegemony of art styles perpetrated and promoted internationally by the *transatlantic* gallery circuit of the Western world.[10]

There are many parallels with this complex attitude to "the idea of the modern." The Harlem Renaissance aspired to combine the formal mastery of European modernism with what Houston Baker calls "the deformation of mastery" through which the black vernacular could be expressed.[11] There is that vibrant, heady, syncretic, urban culture that surfaces in the 1950s in the mixed areas in some South African cities, providing the matrix out of which the anti-apartheid struggle emerged, including that astonishing company of black journalists and photographers grouped around the magazine *Drum*: Peter Magubane, Bob Gosani, Alf Kumalo, and others.[12] More personally, I remember the young black intellectuals I knew in Kingston, Jamaica, in the late 1940s and early 1950s, dreaming of freedom to the subtle, haunting, but forbiddingly complex and uncompromisingly "modern" tonalities of Charlie Parker and Miles Davis. The attitude today—that modernism somehow belonged intrinsically and exclusively to the West, was in effect part of a wider conspiracy to entangle artists in the Western "grand narrative," and that salvation lay in the return to neglected indigenous cultural traditions— is quite alien to this perspective.

This is a question not just of different attitudes but of a different structure of consciousness, different conjunctures. The loss of confidence in the first approach was the cumulative result of a devastating critique which has proved historically decisive. Its complex history would have to include, inter alia, the critique of cultural imperialism developed by the intellectuals and leaders of the anticolonial and national liberation movements, the growing awareness of "the dark side" of the Enlightenment and the ways its universalistic promise has been particularistically appropriated by the West, the searching exposures of Eurocentrism and Orientalism, and the critique of modernism's celebration of "primitivism" which simultaneously opened Western art to non-Western knowledge and appropriated the latter as an exoticized, subordinate support.

The difference in attitude between the generations, then, registers on the one hand as a profound epistemological shift from what we might call the anticolonial to the postcolonial, and on the other as a transformation in what Raymond Williams called "the structure of feeling."[13] This shift was inevitably reflected in the work of artistic production. The outlook of the first generation (like that of the Western political left of the time) was cosmopolitan and universalist. Think of the range, in content and style, of Aubrey Williams's work, combining as it does the Mayan-inspired figures and natural forms of his Guyanese and Latin American "continental" work, the swirling modernist abstraction of his "cosmologies," and his struggle to find a visual correlative to the symphonies of the Russian composer Shostakovich. That of the second generation tended to be more relativist and particularistic. One way of posing the question about the 1980s, then, is: "How, when, and why did this shift from universalism to relativism come about?" This involves our thinking through the connections and transitions between a series of overlapping histories, all of which come together around the shifting genealogies and topographies of race.

Of special relevance was the actual experience of the first wave, which turned out to be a patchy and dispiriting affair. Many participated alongside British artists in the movements of the period, exhibiting and attracting favorable critical attention. They were perceived for a time as central to the British avant-garde, operating at what Guy Brett calls the heady interface between artistic innovation and transnationalism. But many had a difficult time, found the doors of recognition barred, and became progressively disenchanted. Some experienced isolation and lived in virtual self-imposed exile. At one point, Ahmed Parvez tore up his canvases and in 1967 left England for good. Anwar Shemza experienced a kind of artistic trauma at ignorant and patronizing attitudes to non-European art and totally changed artistic direction. Many followed the shifting index of significance in the international art world and emigrated to the United States. Even the best found their work increasingly side-lined, their place in modern British art progressively written out of the story (hence the title of Rasheed Araeen's epic exhibition, "The Other Story"). Araeen himself remarked:

> In the early Seventies, after I had been in Britain for almost ten years, I went through a personal crisis losing all hopes of becoming a successful artist. What really bothered me was not that I had not yet become a successful artist but the institutional indifference towards a work that was central to the development of modernist sculpture in the mid-60s. I could not rationalise this indifference, particularly when my understanding of the art institution was that of an enlightened institution keen to recognise and celebrate any historically important work—as it was doing in other cases. My first response to this crisis was to abandon making art for a while in favour of political activity, with a hope that it would help me understand this institutional anomaly.[14]

Hostile accounts of this shift attribute it to the movement from the anticolonial/antiracist political critique of the 1960s and 1970s and its replacement by the cultural politics of the postcolonial 1980s and after—a shift for which so-called cultural theory is held largely responsible. This is, to put it mildly, a simplification. What it ignores or ruthlessly foreshortens is the fact that, in this period, the whole fulcrum of the political world as we knew it shifted fundamentally. To speak metaphorically, between the work of Souza or Williams and that of Eddie Chambers or Keith Piper falls the shadow. We can mark the transition by way of a series of iconic critical events: the Notting Hill race riots of 1958; the Smethwick election of 1964; the visits of Martin Luther King and Malcolm X; the formation of the Campaign Against Racial Discrimination in 1965; the immigration acts restricting entry, with their second-class citizens and "partial" categories; the appearance of Stokely Carmichael at the "Dialects of Liberation" conference; the sound of Bob Marley and the sight of locksmen on the streets of Handsworth; the new "sport" of Paki bashing; Enoch Powell's 1968 "rivers of blood" speech. Rage and anger at the speed and depth of this racializing process "at home" explode across and literally scar the surfaces of work like Gavin Jantjes's *Freedom Hunters* (1977), Eddie Chambers's *Destruction of the National Front* (1980) and *I Was Taught to Believe* (1984), and Keith Piper's *Reactionary Suicide: Black Boys Keep Singing* or *Another Nigger Died Today* (1982).

By the mid-1970s, race and racism had finally "come home." There was a fully formed, popular black consciousness, a full-blown, indigenous antiracist British politics and a powerful grassroots mobilization against racism and racialized disadvantage, as well as a growth in visibility of racist grassroots organizations and police harassment using the "sus" laws in the streets.[15] The "subjects" of this antiracist politics were identified by the single, collective signifier *black*—a generic term, a composite political identity, which deliberately eschewed any distinctions between Afro-Caribbeans, Asians, and Africans. When, in his *Black Manifesto*, Rasheed Araeen speaks in the name of a black "we," he means, as he says, people of the Third World, from "Asia, Africa, Latin America and the Caribbean." But, he adds, "we *must* also include in it all those non-European peoples (whom we shall collectively call 'blacks' or 'black people') who now live in various Western countries and find themselves in a similar predicament to that of the actual Third World."[16] This was actually part of the work of constructing a new collective black subject, though this identitarian language was not available or in use at the time.

The implications of all this for cultural production and for the Black Arts Movement in the 1980s is beautifully captured in the struggle to connect, as well as the failures of connection between, two different generationally inflected conceptions of "a black arts movement" in two significant texts, loci classici for the British debate, which help us to ground the transition I am attempting to document. The first is the lecture by Aubrey Williams on "A Black Aesthetic" given at a "Race Today" seminar in 1987, followed by discussion. This document is interesting for at least three reasons. First, here is a distinguished member of the first wave addressing a problem in terms defined by the second. Second, it reveals Williams's (and, I think, his generation's) complex *ambivalences* toward the question of "a black aesthetic." On the one hand, he affirms, "My work is dominated by my black roots. And I don't have to express that verbally." But he enjoins his audience to move away from the mere surface of the issue and "turn a little bit more inside and really face what we have inside." It is not clear exactly what he means by this, but it is not hard to see that the idea of art harnessed to a militant, public, black politics is not endorsed by Williams, either in content or tone. Third, there is the gap of incomprehension between him and his younger black audience. The latter are not at all happy when he answers a question about "roots" by quoting the example of pre-Columbian influences in his Olmec-Mayan work. And when challenged directly about a new black British creative period, his response is: "I see it, but it's very squeaky."

Even more revealing is the Rasheed Araeen/Eddie Chambers exchange in *Third Text*. "I would define Black art," Chambers told Araeen, "as art produced by black people largely and specially for black audiences, and which, in terms of its content, addresses black experience."[17] As he put it in 1986, "It is black artists alone who determine the form, functioning and future of black art";[18] his artist's statement to the Black Art An' Done exhibition at Wolverhampton Art Gallery in 1981 describes it as "a tool to assist us in our struggle for liberation, both at home and abroad."

One problem with this formulation concerns the question of "separatism": black art defined by black artists for black audiences about black experience. How, Araeen asks, does this relate to the Asian experience? Chambers acknowledges that his perspective has shifted since the early 1980s and that he has had to "take on board other people's realities . . . working with all artists of both Asian and Afro-Caribbean origin." But elsewhere he returns to "the cultural specificity of . . . contemporary [black] experiences." Araeen expresses fears about "being separated from the main body of this society." Shouldn't black art address the whole society and fight to enter the mainstream?

Then there is the issue of essentialism. Does the category "black art" include whatever a black artist produces, or is there something historically or aesthetically specific about it? Are paintings like Shanti Thomas's *The Roti Maker* (1985) and Errol Lloyd's *The Domino Players* (1986–88) black because the artists are black? Or because they are about a black experience? Or because they deploy a black aesthetic language? And, if so, of what does this black aesthetic consist? Eddie Chambers says it involves the visual arts using easily recognizably black languages and forms, as music does with jazz, reggae, and calypso. Araeen emphasizes the syncretic roots of jazz and the specificity of the black American experience from which historically it emerged.

Two visions or pathways for the black arts seem to be in contention here. They are not diametrically opposed. Both are informed by a political critique; both want an art practice that is engaged with these larger political questions. But they register deep differences of experience and political perspective, which plays through into the aesthetics. Araeen's perspective remains embedded in a radical third worldist position, by which the black experience is itself framed. Chambers's perspective is more rooted directly in the experience of being black and its practices derive from the cultures of the black world.

From my point of view, understanding the 1980s involves explaining how *both* these perspectives differ from what we have been calling the anti-colonial consciousness of the immediate post-war artists; how these two variants of a more politicized perspective on the black arts come to be on offer at the end of the 1970s; and why, in the event, the work that follows later in the 1980s, while maintaining significant continuities with both positions (Keith Piper is a good example here), charts, on the whole, a third, distinctive and different path.

The new experience of racialized exclusion bore directly on the second-generation born and schooled in Britain. Those separated by migration from their original homes but profoundly alienated by racism from any sense of belonging to, or recognition by, British society were haunted by questions of identity and belonging: Who are we? Where do we come from? Where do we belong? Questions of identity were particularly pertinent for postcolonials whose connections with their pre-colonial and ancestral cultures had been brutally interrupted by transportation, slavery, and colonization. West Indians were said to have a special problem with identity because of this fractured history.[19]

The question of identity, which surfaces in the work of black artists in the 1980s, far from being some apolitical subjective indulgence, related to what we would now call "the production of a new, black subject." Rediscovering a language within which these fractured linkages could be understood and redeemed was essential to that "decolonization of the mind" for which writers like Frantz Fanon and Amilcar Cabral had called, without which political independence would be an empty shell. Distinctive to the postcolonial moment, then, were issues of culture and identity—affirming an alternative to the degraded experience of colonization—and these gradually took their place not as secondary to but as *constitutive* of the politics of anti-racism and social justice. Identity acquired a political meaning. Political struggle acquired a cultural dimension. This generated a new racial consciousness, which reshaped the critical debates, the political activism, the arguments—and inevitably the artistic work and cultural production—of the late 1970s and early 1980s.

Here, we need to slot a set of histories into place. The identity question was overdetermined from at least three different directions. First, there was the way this question surfaced among second-generation blacks in Britain, where it tended to be answered, in the 1970s, in terms of a symbolic restoration of the African connection, for so long submerged and disavowed in the Caribbean itself. This is better described as the rediscovery of an African identity *through* its diasporic translation and dissemination. This is that Africa that is "alive and well in the diaspora," as much a "country of the mind," "an imagined community," as a real, historical space: a sign of blackness, which connects with Africa through its New World displacements. This Africa began to be spoken at this time by young black British people primarily through the languages of Rastafarianism, resistance, and the symbolism of dreadlocks, which provided that symbolic identity they could not find elsewhere. Its iconography was evident everywhere in the black culture of the period—in the visual arts, perhaps, most splendidly, as celebrated in the photography of Vanley Burke, Horace Ové, and Armet Francis, and given erotic value in the images of Rotimi Fani-Kayode and Robert Taylor. They testify to the way a new Pan-African diasporic imaginary surfaced at the center of the black community, redeeming through image and sound the breaches and terrors of a broken history.

This is the performative identity we find in the rhythms of Bob Marley and "roots" reggae: a syncretic, contemporary music masquerading as a traditional music of memory, transmitting ancient pulses by the most modern of technologies, and speaking as much of Kingston and London as of Nigeria or Angola. This whole formation that made black, hitherto a negative and degraded object, into a positive point of identification was grounded in the double and triple inscriptions of a richly metaphorical syntax. It condensed into one narrative or visual trope the dissimilar currents of the search for identity; the displacements of migration; the loss of Africa; the terrors of the Middle Passage; the trauma of enslavement and indenture; the suffering still in place, despite independence, in Kingston's Trench Town; *and* the new kinds of suffering that had emerged in the "Babylons" of Handsworth, Brixton, Bradford, Toxteth, and Moss Side.

Second, there was the impact of the civil rights struggle, especially the path the movement took from the integrated "black-and-white-unite-and-fight" civil rights desegregation struggles of the mid-1960s to the Black Power, Black Consciousness, "black is beautiful" phase, with its much greater emphasis on race as a positive identity category and its separatist, cultural, nationalist, Afrocentric, and essentialist emphases. This, too, was a seismic shift. It was from this that Eddie Chambers, Keith Piper, and others picked up the idea of a black arts movement grounded in an Afro-centered black identity and a black aesthetic. Exhibitions like Black Art An' Done (Wolverhampton Art Gallery, 1981) and Five Black Women (Africa Centre Gallery, London, 1983), organized by Sonia Boyce, Lubaina Himid, Claudette Johnson, Houria Niati, and Veronica Ryan, translated these vibrations to the British scene, opening the floodgates to the deluge of independent shows and exhibitions that staked out the terrain of the autonomous Black Arts Movement of the 1980s.

The third set of histories has to do with the sea change that transformed the political field in the 1970s. This, too, is an extremely complex story, whose detail cannot be encompassed here. However, it is important to register it at this point, if only to dispel the illusion that the history of black politics can somehow be written and understood exclusively from within its own parameters and frame of reference. Here, we must include such general factors as the changing composition of social class in the post-industrial economies of advanced societies; the collapse of class as the single, master category of political change, into which all other contradictions (of race, gender, etc.) could be condensed; and the greater awareness of the specificity and "relative autonomy" of social divisions like race as a cross-cutting dimension in social conflict. With the rise of the so-called single-issue social movements, each with its own relative autonomy and "subject" defined in terms of the authenticity of those in whose name political demands were being made, we can trace the fragmentation of the political field, the complexity of building political alliances and new conceptions of the political subject. There was a loss of confidence in "objective" class interests to determine fully political involvement and a greater attention to "subjective" factors. Overarching all this was the "crisis" of Marxism (especially its economic variants during the 1970s) as the general theoretical horizon within which all serious political struggles (including antiracism) had to be organized, and the lack of any alternative comprehensive framework of analysis or action.

Thatcherism and free market neoliberalism were the forces that successfully hegemonized this crisis in the post-war settlement. This historic watershed in world history not only reshaped in its wake the New Right and New Labour but redrew the whole political landscape. The destruction of the social fabric, the assault on the welfare state and punishment of the poor and disadvantaged at home, globalization, and the deregulated market economy abroad together unbent the springs of social and political action, including antiracist politics. The racial upheavals of 1980–81 and 1985, though undoubtedly a response to the brutal impact of these developments on black and Asian communities, were in fact the last of their kind for fifteen years, until the racially motivated riots in northern industrial towns in 2001. Of course, racism and racial violence—casual, deliberate, and institutional—did not abate. But nor were black and Asian populations immune from either the effects of the privatization of "the public good" or the seductions of the enterprise culture.

The new political conjuncture affected black politics very directly. But it also had a much broader impact on the thematic concerns of the Black Arts Movement. For example, the rise of gender and sexual politics, loosened from the iron grip of economic determinism by the same process that made race more visible and autonomous, was just as decisive for black consciousness. Gender and feminist politics and the sexual liberation movements were the revolution within the revolution—movements that exposed the structures of oppression and exclusion and the habits of "secondariness" *within* the ranks of the oppressed, exposing the unconscious practices of "male mastery," which passed unremarked in the daily and sexual life of the subordinate, while never entirely supplanting the struggles against other forms of oppression. This introduced a necessary complexity into the political field: the complexity of a double inscription, because black women had to negotiate solidarity with their sisters (or gay people with their partners) against the heterosexual norm prevailing within their own side, while simultaneously finding ways of affirming solidarity in the common struggle against racial oppression and economic exploitation. And men had to bring to consciousness the unconscious habits and expectations of their privileged position within a wider subordination. The same problem emerged in the post–civil rights struggle in the United States, and African American women have written with great depth of feeling about the issue. This struggle on two fronts introduced the radical principle of *difference* into a political field hitherto constructed primarily in terms of a unifying, undifferentiated solidarity.

It is difficult to underestimate the rupture that flowed from all this. For example, a whole continent of themes, issues, figures, and experiences, hitherto excluded from the political field proper because they were considered too personal, too emotional, too subjective, or too domestic, was opened up to the visual gaze in the work of the 1980s women artists. Until then, the black family album had remained, so to speak, a firmly closed book. It is not an exaggeration to say that, without this conjuncture of feminism and black politics, the outstanding work of the period by Sonia Boyce, Claudette Holmes, Lubaina Himid, Maud Sulter, Mona Hatoum, Sutapa Biswas, and others would simply never have appeared. The fact that black women artists were often organizing and exhibiting separately from men, the tensions that were obvious at the time between them, the powerful eruption of this unfinished question in an unexpected reprise at the time of "The Other Story," and its continuing presence as an underground rumble in the debates around the "Shades of Black" conference are enough to suggest that its reverberations remain resonant.

There were also significant theoretical issues at stake. Here we must map into place the theoretical deluge that swept, in a series of waves, across the 1970s and 1980s and that is often too polemically and simplistically corralled into the convenient term of abuse: cultural theory. In fact, the issues include often different, and mutually contesting, developments: new theories of language and discourse; the post-Bakhtinian attention to the way that polysemic nature of language and the "slippage of the signifier" had sparked struggles over meaning, constituting the cultural field as a key site of political struggle; the growing importance of psychoanalytic and other theories of subjectivity, bringing into the visual field the inner landscapes of the racialized experience; feminist theorizations of gender, sexuality, and desire and their articulations with racial and other kinds of difference; and the rise of postcolonial theorizing and the philosophy of the Other. In this space of renewed theoretical debate—registering a fateful (some would argue, fatal) historic, epistemological half-turn—there emerged what would have come to be called the "posts": poststructuralism, post-Marxism, post-feminism, the postcolonial. The prefix signalled not the passing of time but the waning of old paradigms: passage without supersession, dialogic movement without dialectical sublation, the condition of the postmodern as a stage of permanent transition.[20]

The details of these debates matter less than their cumulative consequences for the politics of representation and their impact on the artistic practices of the 1980s. Broadly speaking, the main effect was to undermine confidence in the ability of aesthetic languages to represent sociopolitical reality in a direct or literal way. Realism and naturalism in the visual arts and the documentary mode in photography were radically undermined in terms of their direct capacity to capture the political realities of racialized exclusion, exploitation, or otherness. These were not simple facts, whose complexity of meaning and experience was manifest immediately on the surface of things, or accessible—without mediation—to the naked eye. This is why the strategy of simply replacing negative racial imagery with "positive images" was quickly abandoned. In fact, the stereotypes and tropes of racism could not be subverted or overturned by a strong dose of unmasking reality—in part because it is not possible to live outside representation. A damaging system of representation can only be dismantled, not by a sudden dose of "the real," but by another, alternative system of representation, whose form better approximates the complexity of the real relations it seeks to explore and contest.

These developments radically problematized the question of race itself and what Fanon identified as "the fact of blackness." Race offered too simple and banal a surface to this analysis. Like gender, it was a difference whose complexity did not immediately reveal itself to the naked eye. The racial gaze was itself a constructed one. Was black identity, then, to be defined historically or biologically? The historical product of living in a racialized world, or a genetic inheritance? If blackness was transmitted biologically, how did the antiracist case differ from the racist one, apart from the question of how positively or negatively this racial inheritance was evaluated? Did race transcend time and place? Such issues connected directly with the shift in practice in the 1980s from the binary of pure abstraction or pure documentary realism to the more mixed or hybrid mode of the constructed image and the return to the figural. These questions about the distinction between an essentialist and a historical definition of race and the foregrounding of the racial signifier underpinned the growing preoccupation, in the work of black artists and photographers in the 1980s, with representations of the black body, with putting the abjected black body "in the field of vision." The body became a space or horizon on or within which to explore the complexities of the black subject, the inner landscapes of black subjectivity, and the intersecting planes of difference around which its social space is constructed. With this questioning of the black body, we come face to face with what elsewhere I called "the end of the essential black subject," triggering that kaleidoscopic proliferation of meanings around blackness and the hidden connections between the racialized, the gendered, and the sexualized body—a site of convergence that for so long had been the privileged operational zone of racist discourse.[21]

The issues posed here are complex and profound and, in my view, remain unresolved. They have to do with how to think, in a non-reductive way, about the relationship between the work and the world, form and content, signifier and signified. They ask the question of whether identity has a full positivity of its own, self-present to itself, or whether it can only be thought through its "lack," its *différance* (neither its absolute difference nor its pure sameness) from all the other terms with which it is articulated. And what are the political and aesthetic and cultural implications of the answers we give to that question?

Subsequently, these questions have been represented as falsely and illegitimately forced on artistic practices by so-called cultural theory, with the implication that it was part of some deliberate conspiracy to deflect the Black Arts Movement from its true objective. It would be hard to deny the heady theoretical climate that prevailed in the 1970s and 1980s, as one French theorist after another took his or her place on the rapidly rotating conceptual stage. However, I hope I have said enough to show that, in my view, it was the different currents of ideas and events flowing into the 1980s, the seismic movements of the time, the profound political and other shifts they registered, in whose aftermath we continue to live, that were transmuted into the problematic of the work. With artists such as Sonia Boyce, Rotimi Fani-Kayode, Sutapa Biswas, Joy Gregory, Sunil Gupta, Roshini Kempadoo, Ingrid Pollard, Dave Lewis, Ajamu, Zarina Bhimji, Mitra Tabrizian, and Chila Kumari Burman, these issues were not so much blindly repeated as "worked on," using the image as a kind of "problem-space" for conducting an investigation. These real political, economic, and cultural shifts are, in my view, what really defined what we might think of as the agendas of artistic practice in the 1980s. To represent them as the result of intellectual bad faith or artistic naïveté, or to suggest that black art practice could or should somehow have ignored them, is to trivialize history, because it requires us to simplify the connections between politics and cultural production. It misses the significance of conjunctural change and encourages us to indulge in a form of idealism, in a strategy that is ultimately unlocated in the materiality of historical circumstances. Such an approach to the question of "assembling the 1980s" no doubt feeds the spirit of sectarian animosity that too often animates critical discourse but falls woefully short on analytic or explanatory power.

Despite the sophistication of our scholarly and critical apparatus in art criticism, history, and theory, we are still not that far advanced in finding ways of thinking about the relationship between the work and the world. We either make the connection too brutal and abrupt, destroying that necessary displacement in which *the work* of making art takes place. Or we protect the work from what Edward Said calls its necessary "worldliness," projecting it into either a pure political space where conviction—political will—is all, or into an inviolate aesthetic space, where only critics, curators, dealers, and connoisseurs are permitted to play. The problem is rather like that of thinking the relationship between the dream and its materials in waking life. We know there *is* a connection there. But we also know that the two continents cannot be lined up and their correspondences read off directly against one another. Between the work and the world, as between the psychic and the social, the bar of the historical unconscious has fallen. The effect of the unseen "work" that takes place out of consciousness in relationship to deep currents of change whose long-term effects on what can be produced are, literally, tidal, is thereafter always a delicate matter of *re-presentation* and *translation*, with all the lapses, elisions, incompleteness of meaning, and incommensurability of political goals that these terms imply. What Freud called "the dream-work"— in his lexicon, the tropes of displacement, substitution, and condensation—is what enables the materials of the one to be reworked or translated into the forms of the other, and is what enables the latter to "say more" or "go beyond" the willed consciousness of the individual artist. For those who work in the displaced zone of the cultural, the world has somehow to become a text, an image, before it can be "read."

I have tried to present some of the tumultuous currents flowing into the 1980s. But what happened to them—in terms of the work—as they fed into the visual imaginary? We certainly cannot say that the work *resolved* them. They are as yet unresolved in any final sense, which is why the period is so contentious, and why we keep returning to it. We know that, somewhere during the 1980s, the world—*our* world—changed dramatically and decisively. How, remains to be specified, in all the rich conjunctural detail we can assemble. The very intensity of the deluge produced an extraordinary creativity from the most marginal spaces. What it did not produce was *answers*. Instead, the work itself became a kind of "problem-space," in which, literally, our "troubles" were given form.

NOTES

This essay first appeared in *Shades of Black: Assembling Black Arts in 1980s Britain*, ed. David A. Bailey, Ian Baucom, and Sonia Boyce (Durham, NC: Duke University Press; London: Institute of International Visual Arts, 2005), 1–20.

1 Stuart Hall and Mark Sealy, *Different: Contemporary Photographers and Black Identity* (London: Phaidon, 2001).

2 Hall and Sealy, *Different*, 34.

3 Antonio Gramsci, *Selections from the Prison Notebooks* (London: Lawrence and Wishart, 1971).

4 Louis Althusser, "Contradiction and Over-determination," in *For Marx* (Harmondsworth: Penguin, 1969), 99.

5 David Scott, "Conscripts of Political Modernity: C. L. R. James, Toussaint Louverture and the Making of the Caribbean," unpublished paper.

6 Rasheed Araeen, *The Other Story*, exhibition catalogue (London: Hayward Gallery, 1989), 60.

7 Rasheed Araeen, "The Black Manifesto," in *Making Myself Visible* (London: Kalas, 1984), 1.

8 Herbert Read, *A Concise History of Modern Sculpture* (London: Thames and Hudson, 1964), 11, quoted in Araeen, *Other Story*, 16.

9 Frank Bowling, "Frank Bowling and Bill Thompson: A Conversation between Two Painters," *Art International* 20, no. 10 (December 1976): 61–67.

10 Araeen, "Black Manifesto," 10.

11 Houston A. Baker, *Modernism and the Harlem Renaissance* (Chicago: University of Chicago Press), 56.

12 Hall and Sealy, *Different*.

13 Raymond Williams, *The Long Revolution* (Harmondsworth: Penguin, 1961), chapter 2.

14 Rasheed Araeen, "Re-thinking History and Some Other Things," *Third Text* 15, no. 54 (Spring 2001): 95.

15 The "sus" laws were laws of suspicion that permitted the police to arrest individuals not only for crimes that had been committed but for crimes the police believed a "suspect" was about to commit. They further permitted the police to designate entire areas as "criminal" and so to arrest anyone in those spaces.

16 Araeen, "Black Manifesto," 1.

17 Rasheed Araeen and Eddie Chambers, "Black Art: A Discussion," *Third Text* 2, no. 5 (Winter 1988): 52.

18 Eddie Chambers, "The Marginalisation of Black Art," *Race Today Review* (1986): 33.

19 On a personal note, it was to explore this issue that, in 1956, I turned from my doctoral research on a literary topic to pursue the question, raised in the anthropological debates of the time, about Africa survivals and syncretism in the New World, a deviation that led me into cultural studies and the much abused "cultural theory."

20 Stuart Hall, "When Was the Post-colonial?," in *The Post-colonial Question*, ed. Lidia Curti and Iain Chambers (London: Routledge, 1996).

21 Hall and Sealy, *Different*, 101–3.

PART V

PHOTOGRAPHY, REPRESENTATION, AND BLACK IDENTITY

The Vertigo of Displacement:
Shifts within Black Documentary Practices

Once we have recognised that there are many forms of black representations—all of which have their weaknesses, ideological limits and strengths—then we can also recognize that there can't be any one right moment, genre or discourse. The notion of one correct perspective suggests that there is a form of black representation which is permanently secure from being ideologically recuperated, and that, clearly, is not so. The history of blacks in the media is one where we see a selection of images move from the margins to the mainstream fashion magazines overnight: what shocked people the day before yesterday becomes the most effective way of selling commodities today. The Benetton campaigns are an obvious example.

It is perfectly possible that what is politically progressive and opens up new discursive opportunities in the 1970s and 1980s can become a form of closure—and have a repressive value—by the time it is installed as the dominant genre. There is, therefore, no value in saying that any one black discourse carries forever the sort of guarantee and security of being the right way to represent things. It will run out of steam; it will become a style; people will use it not because it opens up anything, but because they are being spoken by it, and at that point you need another shift.

A major shift took place in the 1980s when a significant body of work from black photographers challenged, explored and pushed back the parameters of photographic practices. A range of influences, many derived from film, performing and visual arts came into play. But perhaps the most crucial shifts occurred within documentary genres. The development of theories which called into question documentary photography's claims to some form of objective truth, the growing critique of the classic realist text, and the reappropriation of the avant-garde and surrealism were important. At the same time, the development of poststructuralist theory introduced new concepts of identification, plural identities, and encouraged the move away from the essential subject towards the development of the de-centered subject. There were also campaigns orchestrated by a range of constituencies within the black communities to create and circulate positive images. All of these had a significant influence on the content and form of black photographic practices in the 1980s. This article explores these shifts and influences in order to map out how a particular moment in black photography developed.

Documentary Truth and Guaranteed Knowledge

The history of black photographic image-making has been obsessed with opening up the apparently fixed meanings of images. One of the key sites for this struggle is documentary. Documentary photography carries a claim to truth, with the meta message of *this is how it really was*. This stems from its close relationship with classical realism and the classic realist text— exemplified most powerfully by the nineteenth-century novel—which places the spectator in a position of absolute knowledge and truth. In a similar way, documentary claims to reveal the truth, because realism as a narrative form places the spectator in the position of guaranteed knowledge.

The use of documentary form by many black photographers in the 1970s and early 1980s has, therefore, to be seen within a wider political framework— as part of the attempt to reposition the guaranteed centres of knowledge of realism and the classic realist text, and the struggle to contest negative images with positive ones. For example, both Armet Francis in *The Black Triangle* and Vanley Burke (fig. 13.1) in his portraits of Handsworth used the documentary form to articulate a political statement about making visible black images and black image-makers. Linked to this was the issue of access for black people to the discourse of photography so that they could represent and reflect on their own experience—which has been a major theme throughout the 1980s. There was a general campaign to give black photographers the opportunity to do work that would be seen, gain some kind of credibility, and work against the negative or Eurocentric representations of the dominant regime.

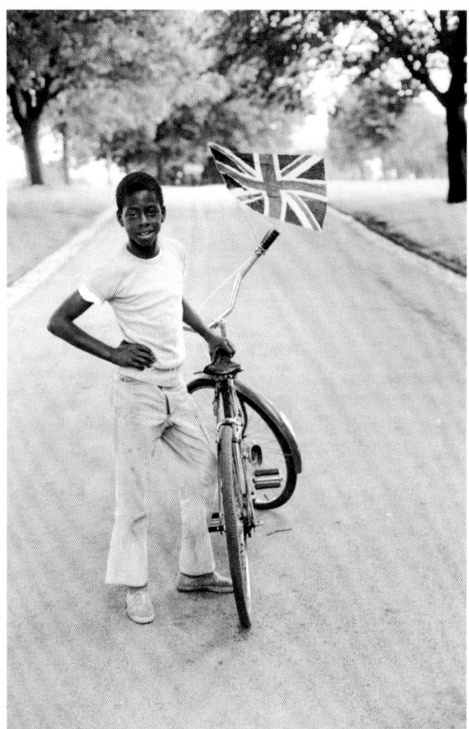

Figure 13.1. Vanley Burke, *Boy with Flag, Winford in Handsworth Park*, 1970. © Vanley Burke. All rights reserved, DACS/Artimage 2022.

This contestation by black photographers was not done in isolation, but was linked to a larger campaign, which had support from institutions, academic bodies and a wide range of black individuals and organizations. Within the GLC (the Greater London Council), for example, there was a campaign against negative imagery and the way in which certain communities were disenfranchised, discriminated against and marginalized. A key element in the campaign was to give access to these groups by way of finance, infrastructure, lobbying and distribution. At the same time, the GLC created a platform for debate through conferences, seminars, workshops and publications.

Cultural Studies and the Shift to Avant-Gardism

A further key element in the development of this debate came from the body of writing and teaching known as cultural studies, which developed ideas from Gramsci as well as from black and feminist movements, and addressed the notion of hegemony. It was argued that the question of power has important cultural and ideological aspects. In *The Empire Strikes Back* and *Policing the Crisis*—both published in the early 1980s—the notion of popular cultural resistance is explored as a form of political resistance. Cultural studies work on race opened up what was going on at the base of English society around race and authoritarian populism, locating new forms of racism articulated around forms of national identification, a sense of Englishness, and the crisis facing a society going through post-imperial trauma.

Against this background, a number of black photographers began to explore questions of identification, the issue of how best to contest dominant regimes of representation and their institutionalization, and the question of opening up fixed positions of spectatorship. This was a move away from documentary, away from the image as something which referred beyond itself to an objective truth, to a concern with representation as such. This mode of contestation goes against the grain of realism: indeed, it opens up realism and exposes it as a particular genre and privileges instead non-realist modes such as formalism, modernism and surrealism, which can be grouped together under the rubric of avant-gardism (figs. 13.2 and 13.3).

This anti-realism was developed at a theoretical level in *Screen* magazine, which argued that the way in which the realist text places the reader/spectator in the position of guaranteed knowledge serves to conceal and naturalize ideology. In order to disrupt this naturalistic ideology of truth it becomes necessary to disrupt the very thing which positions the spectator so securely—the form of realism. Hence, the importance of avant-gardism which breaks up the realist relationship between work and spectator, thereby preventing the spectator from settling back into an empiricist and secure relationship to knowledge.

It would be misleading, however, to view the shift from documentary to avant-gardism in black photographic practice as simply one visual discourse replacing another. The shift needs to be contextualized within a wider field where a variety of questions—both new and old—were being addressed around black imagery. We need to look again at the early documentary forms which were supposedly being superseded in the mid-1980s and recognize that they continue to offer something of value. It would be as absurd to consider documentary a reactionary form *per se* as it would be to assume that a deconstructive avant-garde practice must be progressive. Clearly, there is a need for a more refined critical apparatus for seeing what someone who is practicing in the documentary genre can and can't do, how the genre

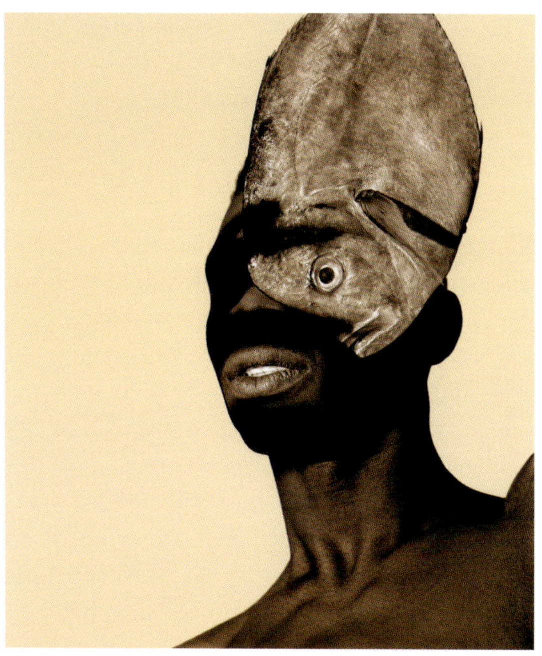

Figure 13.2. Franklyn Rodgers, *Monolith One*, 1991. © Franklyn Rodgers. Courtesy of the Artist.

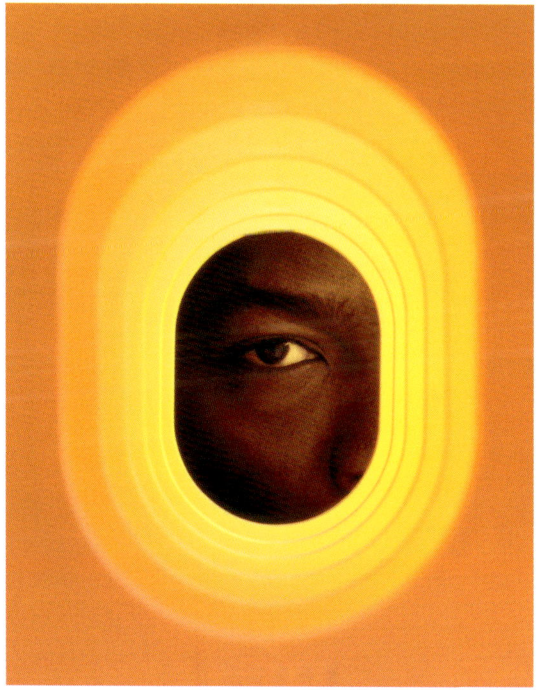

Figure 13.3. Dave Lewis, *Untitled 1*, 1992. From the series "Black Youth and Mental Health." Digital color print. 20 × 24 in. © Dave Lewis. Courtesy of the artist.

limits them and how the genre allows them to refer to certain things which those who are working in the avant-garde genres cannot, as well as how avant-garde genres open up connections which realism blocks out.

Exploring the Kaleidoscopic Conditions of Blackness

By the mid-1980s, the campaign to contest negative images with positive ones had moved on to an enquiry into the politics of the image itself. It was here that the black photography movement produced its most innovative and exciting work in a range of work that explores complex debates on fine art practices, gender, sexuality, and being black and British.

It was at this stage also that many black practitioners began to articulate the view that black is something which is only partly represented by skin colour—a conceptual shift which owed much to poststructuralist discourses on identity and de-centering the subject. Poststructuralist thinking opposes the notion that a person is born with a fixed identity—that all black people, for example, have an essential, underlying black identity which is the same and unchanging. It suggests instead that identities are floating, that meaning is not fixed and universally true at all times for all people, and that the subject is constructed through the unconscious in desire, fantasy and memory. This theory helps explain why, for example, an individual might shift from feeling black in one way when they are young, to black in another way when they are older—and not only black but male/female, and not only black but gay/ heterosexual, and so on.

The notion that there is no essential blackness—that black is a cultural term, a political term, that it is a choice of identity—also forced the recognition that the fact of a photographer being black did not guarantee an anti-racist image, any more than the fact of being black guarantees right-on politics.

Black photography therefore moved towards the need to represent plural identities which are never fixed and never settle into a fixed pattern—which, in a nutshell, is what de-centering the subject means. Instead of concentrating on representing an essential black (as opposed to white) identity, the emphasis shifted to the process of identification. A black male, for example, might in some situations identify with being black and in other situations identify with being male—and sometimes these two forces do not pull in the same way. Identities can, therefore, be contradictory and are always situational. Being black does not override the fact that along another axis such as class, gender or sexuality a person may come out in a different position. Identities are then permanently de-centered, and there is no master identity such as class or nationality that can gather all these strands into a single weave. In short, we are all involved in a series of political games around fractured or de-centered identities.

This means that there is no one thing that is black—black is connected to all these different categories—some blacks are sexist, some blacks are not, some blacks are heterosexuals, some blacks are gay and some blacks are middle-class. Identities are positional in relation to the discourses around us. That is why the notion of representation is so important—identity can only be articulated as a set of representations. And, perhaps more importantly, since black signifies a range of experiences, the act of representation becomes not just about de-centering the subject but actually exploring the kaleidoscopic conditions of blackness.

In such a situation, it became clear that the individual black artist could not represent the whole of the black experience. How could all of those experiences be spoken of through one photograph, one voice? An aspect of the black experience can be represented, but this representation has to be seen as more tentative and partial.

The 1980s therefore signalled the end of the essential black subject and the kind of essentialism which assumes that the progressive, creative character of black representation is guaranteed by the fact that it is made by a black subject.

This in turn demanded a climate where it was possible to say: "Black this may be, black you may be, well-intentioned the work may be, but it doesn't come off." And, by implication, it also required the acknowledgement that it is equally possible that a white photographer, with only limited understanding of the black experience, might be able to say something of significance to a black audience. Unquestionably, this is a much harder form of political practice to take on because the sides are not neatly drawn up: the goodies and baddies aren't given for you neatly nor are they any longer inscribed as to who they are and what their position is. So, the struggle ceased to be simply a binary opposition, replacing one bad photographic practice with an oppositional good photographic practice. It shifted into the arenas of criticism: the politics and the ethics of criticism.

This was highlighted, for example, in critical responses to the work of Robert Mapplethorpe and Rotimi Fani-Kayode.

Black and White: Towards a New Critical Response

The essentialist position was effectively saying that as a white photographer photographing a black body, Mapplethorpe could by definition only appropriate and fetishize it. This body of criticism is underpinned by the belief that a white photographer photographing a black subject is photographing across the line of domination and subordination and that this determines the nature of the image.

Against this, the 1980s produced a fresh body of criticism which said: Yes, Mapplethorpe does fetishize, abstract, formalize, and appropriate the black body. But, on the other hand, we can see that Mapplethorpe is contesting the dominant representation of black masculinity in much black photography—he lets loose his desire for the black male form which many black male photographers suppress. So, on the one hand Mapplethorpe is contesting a one-dimensional representation of black masculinity, while on the other expropriating the black male form in a fetishistic way. Both things are true.

If you say only the first thing, you feel uncomfortable: but you haven't yet given yourself up to that extraordinary play of desire which is why black photographers can't leave Mapplethorpe's work alone.

In Rotimi Fani-Kayode's work we can see many of the same forms of desire and contestation about black masculinity that we find in Mapplethorpe's work. Rotimi Fani-Kayode's work operates alongside Mapplethorpe's critique of dominant representational regimes of black masculinity, and it does not really contest Mapplethorpe's fetishism of the body. So, you have to say both things about Mapplethorpe and both things about Rotimi Fani-Kayode.

However, one of the ways in which Rotimi's work does differ is in the way that Mapplethorpe artificially constructs the forms of the body—black and white, male and female—in an iconographic way, turning them into icons but suppressing the real forms of ritualism in which the construction of iconography forms part of a social practice. Mapplethorpe's ritualization is tied only to an aesthetic, whereas Rotimi Fani-Kayode's ritualization seems to reach back to a longer tradition. When he uses a mask it connotes generations of masks used in different spiritual, social, figurative traditions. We don't feel that kind of tradition in Mapplethorpe. The only thing behind Mapplethorpe's work is fashion, the ritualization of fashion, the iconography of fashion.

It is also important to recognize that there are many things in Rotimi's work which are not in Mapplethorpe's—in other words, we have to get to the stage of refusing to talk about Mapplethorpe as only a fetishistic, gay, white, male photographer, and Rotimi's work as either limited and restricted because it is influenced by Mapplethorpe or entirely encapsulated and appropriated by Mapplethorpe. Rotimi has both learned from him, fought him off and brought another tradition of representation into his own work.

To get some kind of genuine comparative assessment you have to get inside the contradictory modes and forms and practices of representation operating across both these photographers' work.

Black Photography in the 1990s: A Struggle on Two Fronts

The blurring of the old oppositions of black/white, good/bad, documentary/ avant-garde does not remove us from earlier struggles to open up more space for black photographers. Simply because the game has got more complicated it does not mean that you lose sight of the struggle. Although a second front has been opened the first front must not be neglected. Questions of access to the means of representation, the relationship of black photographers to the institutions, visibility and exclusion are still as important.

If you don't have the means of representation at your disposal then you do not have the access to the places where photographic work can be exhibited, discussed and criticized. You are not even in the game, and you are not part of the photographic discourse. The struggle for entry is a struggle for all black photographers, but once the door has been opened then the name of the game changes. It is then necessary to ask what these photographers are doing with the space that has opened, and what are they doing in relation to discursive practices to which they now have access. Both have to go on. It is very dangerous to talk about the second and not talk about the first because that would be a way of closing the door after a small elite has gone through.

Ultimately, there has to be a wide, active dialogic community which is interrogating, evaluating, reconstructing histories, putting back in place the invisible discursive conditions which make new texts possible. All that scholarship, criticism and political and cultural interrogation is part and parcel of the development of a well-articulated theory and practice of black representation—doing it, writing about it, arguing about it, theorising it, writing its history and so on—it is all crucial work.

NOTE

This essay first appeared in "Critical Decade: Black British Photography in the 80s," ed. Stuart Hall and David A. Bailey, special issue, *Ten.8* 2, no. 3 (1992): 14–23.

CHAPTER 14

Preface to *Different*

This book—*Different*—represents a sample of the striking photographic images produced, in an explosion of creative work since the mid-1980s, by artists culturally or geographically marginalized from the centres of power and authority. Following an introduction which sets the work in a historical context, the book's main focus is the work of a selection of contemporary photographers who have used the image to explore and subvert the idea of "black identity." It charts their struggles to make the invisible visible, to open a "third space" in cultural representation, and to "write" their experiences, their bodies and their subjectivities back into the frame from which they were excluded—a new kind of photographic "writing-of-the-self" or *auto-graphy*.

The book includes the work of African, African American, Black British, Asian, Afro-Vietnamese, Aboriginal and other diaspora artists. The term "black photography" is used in its broadest, most inclusive sense. Black is considered to be a political and cultural, not a genetic or biological, category. It is a contested idea, whose ultimate destination remains unsettled. And "identity" is understood as always, in part, an invention; about "becoming" as well as "being"; and subject to the continuous play of history, culture and power. What makes it possible to compare the work of these photographers across their significant differences is their common historical experience of living in a racialized world. The many ways in which this fact inflects their practice is the "difference" which generates the title: *Different*.

Since the 1980s there has been an explosion of creative work from artists and places historically marginalized from the traditional centres of power and authority. This cultural movement can be traced not only in photography, film and the visual arts, popular culture and fashion. It is part of a wider, dynamic drive for cultural expression by those historically excluded from the institutions, circuits and canons of artistic achievement in the metropolitan mainstream. This must be seen in the context of the slow, uneven, contradictory, often bitterly contested transformation of cultural life across the globe, driven by the struggles of the marginalized to enter "History," come into visibility, write themselves into the frame and open up a "third space" in cultural representation. Unable, frontally, to stem the tide of Western-driven globalization, this movement nevertheless signifies the slow but inevitable de-centering of Western-based cultural models. Refusing, simultaneously, either to disappear into the global bazaar of the international art market or to be holed up forever in some "local" ethnic ghetto, this movement is "located" in, without being rendered motionless by, places of origin, skin-colour, so-called racial group, ethnic tradition or national belongingness and is part of a new, emergent kind of "vernacular cosmopolitanism."

The avant-garde and "modernist" traditions have, for years, effectively defined the sort of work in photography that was exposed in galleries, collected in books of contemporary photography and won critical acclaim. In fact, there were many modernisms. However, the term has retrospectively acquired an exclusively "Western" referent. This Western-centric definition of excellence effectively denied photographers who, on whatever grounds, did not intrinsically "belong," access and audiences, markets and sponsors, visibility and critical dialogue—all conditions essential for their artistic development. In recent years, agencies like Autograph: The Association of Black Photographers in Britain have emerged, designed to encourage and represent these artists, create centres of critical activity, exhibit and exchange work, inform and educate audiences world-wide. The images selected here emerge from such centres of work. Necessarily, the selection cannot be fully representative of its true breadth. It focuses on contemporary artists who, through their work or in exhibitions, commissions, publications, studio residencies, visits or conferences organized by these agencies, have helped to influence and shape photographic practice and critical dialogue in the artistic diasporas.

In this context, the term "black" must be understood in a broad and inclusive way—as it was used, for example, in Britain in the 1970s and 1980s to refer to *all* those communities, of whatever ethnic or "racial" origin, who were regarded as "other"—*different*—and thus racially excluded. As used in this text, "black" does not reference a particular racial group, with fixed characteristics, whose social being or artistic imagination is determined by skin colour, genetic make-up or biological inheritance. It does not invoke an essentialized cultural identity, frozen in time, which is automatically transmitted into the work, and can thus be held to "represent" collectively all those who belong to a particular "race," ethnic community or tradition. "Black," as deployed here, is a politically, historically and culturally constructed category; a contested idea, whose ultimate destination remains unsettled. Indeed, the work itself is part of its ongoing redefinition. What these practitioners, with their diverse backgrounds and projects, share is not the same biogenetic make-up, but the historical experience of living in a "racialized" world—on whatever grounds this exclusionary violence is accomplished. Even when the work does not directly or explicitly engage with this theme, it cannot evade or escape its accompanying shadow. This is the "difference" signalled in our title.

As artists, they have "travelled," literally or imaginatively, and are still subjectively "on the move." They have travelled by different routes, drawing on different cultural repertoires (fig. 14.1). Instinctively, they work across cultural boundaries and vocabularies. They work with and on "difference." But they do not have a binary, either/or, conception of it. Rather, they seem to subscribe to what the French philosopher Jacques Derrida calls *différance*: "the playing movement that produces these effects of difference, a weave of similarities and differences that refuse to separate into fixed binary oppositions." They know that everyone comes from somewhere, speaks from some place, is multiply positioned. But they don't see cultures as autonomous, self-sufficient entities that bind people forever into common scripts or seal them off from a wider dialogic conversation. As Kobena Mercer argues, they are committed to abandon the hierarchies of binary thinking "so as to enter the over-determined spaces in between, in which relations of identity and difference are actually lived."

None is satisfied with being labelled an "ethnic artist," or having their work corralled into some racial or ethnic ghetto. Though profoundly aware

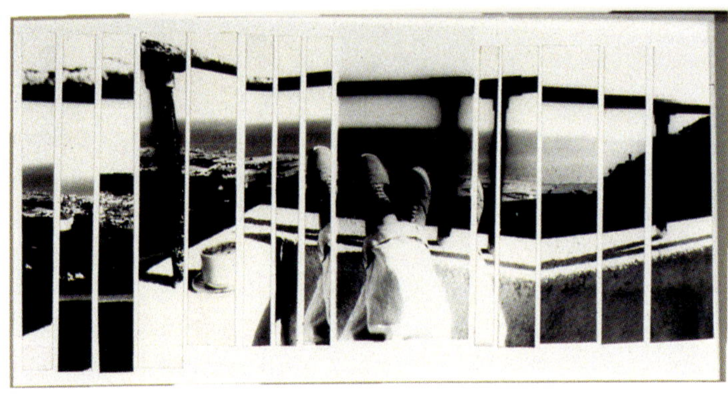

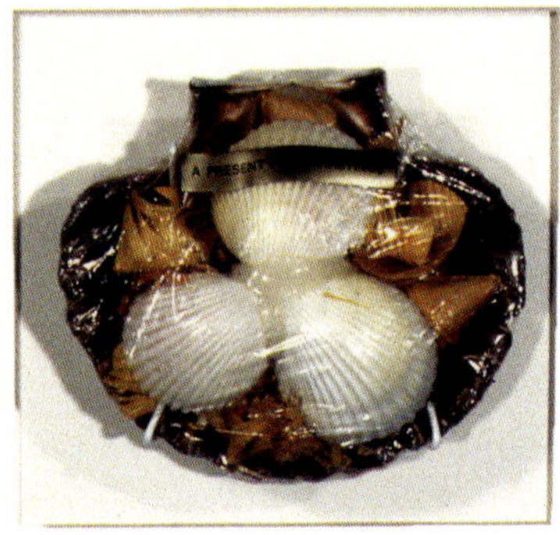

See England under my rule

Figure 14.1. Ingrid Pollard, *Seaside Series*, 1989. © Ingrid Pollard. All rights reserved, DACS/Artimage 2022.

of the way they have been constructed as "different," theirs is not strictly speaking a *multicultural* practice, if by that one invokes the fixed hierarchies of cultural belonging. They work in symbolic spaces, and with image economies which have been culturally translated. Since "race" and ethnicity are historical and cultural, not genetic or biological facts, these influences cannot in any final sense determine meaning, aesthetic form or political value. On the other hand, few practitioners seem to be satisfied with just claiming to be free-standing "artists"—privileged nomads within some unspecified international "art world" space. They are practicing *after* what has been called "the end of the essential black subject." They neither take up nor refuse "identity." Instead, they use the image as a symbolic space in which to put identity in question. The process of "identification"—the struggle to take positions which may not be final, rather than the fixed positions of "identity politics"— is what concerns them. Identification is not a more polite name for identity: it is, in some ways, its opposite. As Ernesto Laclau remarked, "If I need to identify with something, it is because I don't have a full identity in the first place." These artists are "post-identity," without being beyond the reach of its effects.

Traditionally, peoples and societies peripheral to the West have been represented as modernity's "Other": immured forever in an unchanging tradition. This is another binary—modern/traditional—that these practitioners seem to reject. Living in a globalizing world, they are obliged—for good or ill—to engage "modern conditions of life" as modern subjects, without forgetting their pasts nor falling for Western modernity's "grand narrative." Today, the margins are at the very cutting edge of modern experience, which is no longer the property of the West: marginalized people are as much the agents and subjects of many possible "futures" as those who tried to colonize the idea of the modern for themselves. For the world's majorities, "modernity" in this radically de-centered sense is only just beginning: it involves the struggle not only to recover and "speak from" past silences, but to produce ourselves again as subjects for the future.

These images did not arise out of thin air. As we suggested in the Introduction, outstanding work in photography has been produced by African, Asian, African-American, Caribbean, Latin-American and other practitioners from marginalized communities and societies since photography began. Overwhelmingly, those photographers worked in the genres of portraiture, social reportage, documentary and photo-journalism. Major work of great originality continues to be produced in these genres. However, with some significant exceptions, the images in this book are *constructed* ones: deliberately composed, staged or in some significant way manipulated, both before the lens and in the production process.

How do we account for this shift away from the documentary? There is, of course, no one, correct genre, any more than there is one "true" photographic moment. No style is capable of securing a critical practice against ideological recuperation. However, at a significant moment in the mid-1980s, the majority of practitioners—following one of those deep, tidal currents which ebb and flow without clear origin in the arts—lost confidence, not so much in documentary photography as such, as in the *idea* that "the documentary" somehow embodied the essential truth of photography. Many things contributed to this change of perspective. Developments in critical cultural theory—the critique of the realist text in film studies, post-structuralist theories of language and meaning, the so-called de-centering of the subject—played their part. Following post-war migration, many second-generation diasporic artists were trained for the first time in metropolitan art schools and encountered dominant modernist and avant-garde theories and practices. Modernism acquired a powerful Western inflection early in the century. However, as we suggested, it also crossed boundaries. There were strong, indigenous "modernisms" in Africa, the Indian subcontinent, Latin America; and artists from the four corners of the globe—now written out of the official story—travelled to its metropolitan centers and came to regard it as a *lingua franca*, ripe for translation and reappropriation.

Whatever the precise causes, this produced a conviction among many younger practitioners that the documentary's claim to represent objective truth—a claim it tried to ground in the material nature of the photographic image itself—had to be extensively critiqued. They began to explore the image's other regions, concerned less with capturing objective circumstances than with exploring subjective experience. Many came to the conclusion that, despite the force of Roland Barthes's startling formulation, the photographic image is *not* a "message without a code." Reality cannot speak for itself, through the image, in an unmediated way. Its "truth" is not to be measured in terms of its correspondence to some objective "reality" out there, beyond the frame. Rather, representation in its wider meaning modifies, augments or displaces the circumstantial or evidential order of "the real," in order to bring other kinds of order, meaning or "truth" to visibility. Artistic production is thus always a labour of transformation—as we say, *the work*. Of course, it is difficult for photography completely to eradicate the *trace* of the referent. But the image is always implicated in a "politics of truth" as well as a "politics of

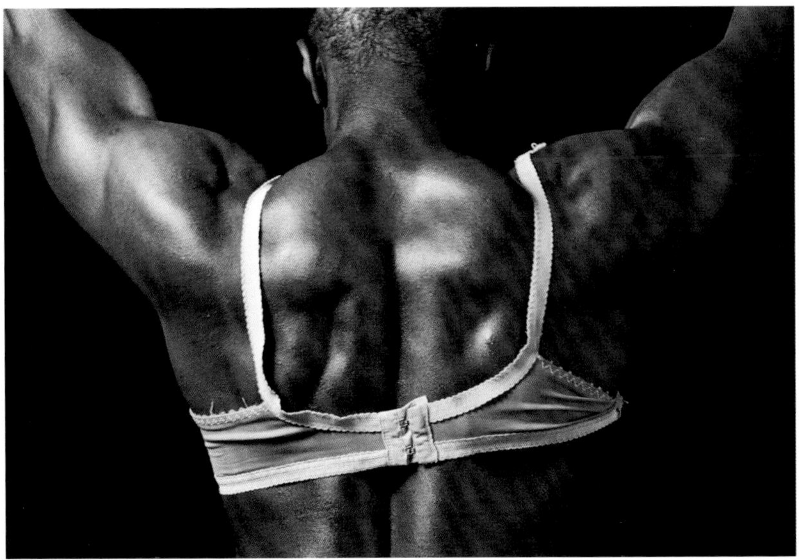

Figure 14.2. Ajamu, *Bodybuilder in Bra*, 1990. Photograph. © Ajamu. Courtesy of the artist.

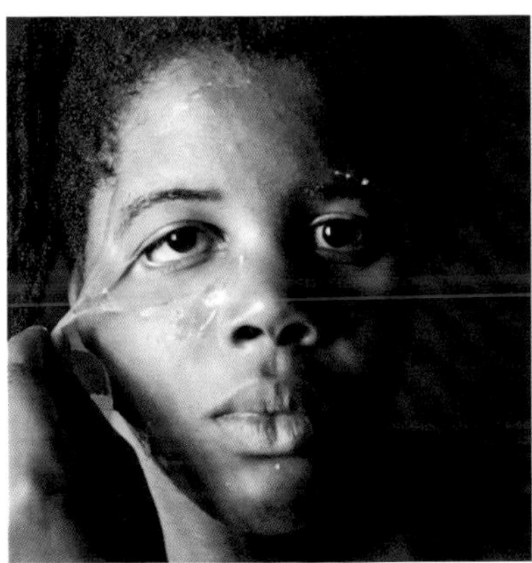

Figure 14.3. Maxine Walker, *Untitled*, 1997. Courtesy of Autograph, London.

desire." Paradoxically, its apparent transparency to "reality" is when it is at its most ideological—for example, when photography disavows its status as a cultural practice, passing itself off instead simply as "Nature's paintbrush."

One of the most critical sites in this work is the intersection of racial, ethnic, gender and sexual difference; and in particular that of *the body* itself (figs. 14.2 and 14.3). The body is at one and the same time the "container" of identity and subjectivity, the overdetermined point where differences

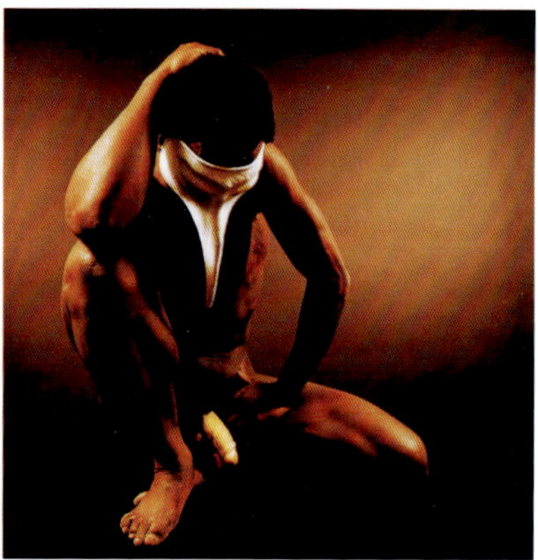

Figure 14.4. Rotimi Fani-Kayode, *The Golden Phallus*, 1989. © Rotimi Fani-Kayode. Courtesy of Autograph, London.

collide, the epidermal surface on which racism etches its mark, and a ground of resistance from which alternative counter-narratives can be produced. On the site of the body, racial discourses had long undertaken the work of systematically reducing history to biology, culture to nature: here, in the ritual exchange of stereotypes of the body between "race," gender and sexuality, racism and cultural differentialism had deployed their most violent and destructive fantasies. How could this be contested and undone? Simply reversing the terms, so that such terms as "black" ceased to be abjected and became "beautiful"—the strategy of "positive images"— proved inadequate. Reversal did not subvert the system of representation itself, but left it in place—only, now, standing on its head! Consider how biological conceptions of "race" are—bizarrely—*confirmed* by the way the black body is currently repositioned in sport, fashion, advertizing and the music industries. It was necessary not just to vary the stereotypes but to *go inside* the image itself, to deconstruct it from within: in short, to undertake a dangerous "politics of representation." Far from producing an essential counter-narrative, this politics of the image led to an astonishing prolif-eration of positions—the so-called "kaleidoscopic experience of blackness." This deconstructive work was conducted not only by putting the black sub-ject centre-stage within the frame, but by re-mapping the abjected body, disrupting and reinventing it in new ways.

Classical accounts of the nude body suggest that it is "nude" because it is not "naked"—because the body has been subsumed into some "higher," purer, realm of disinterested aesthetic value. However, the photographers in this selection negotiate this figure in a wholly transformed way. They engage

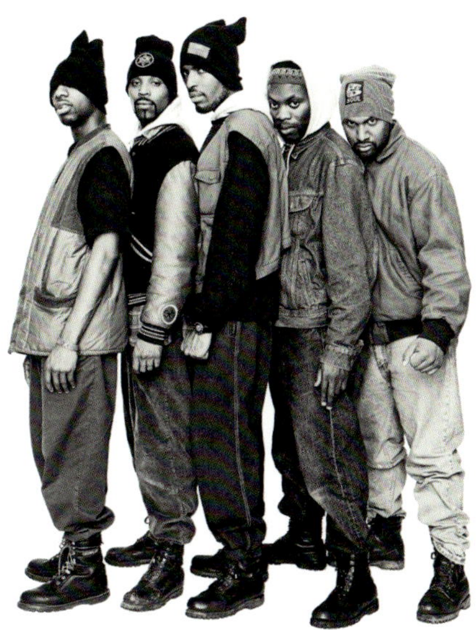

Figure 14.5. Faisal Abdu'allah, *I Wanna Kill Sam Cause He Ain't My Motherfuckin' Uncle*, 1993. © Faisal Abdu'allah. All rights reserved, DACS/Artimage 2022.

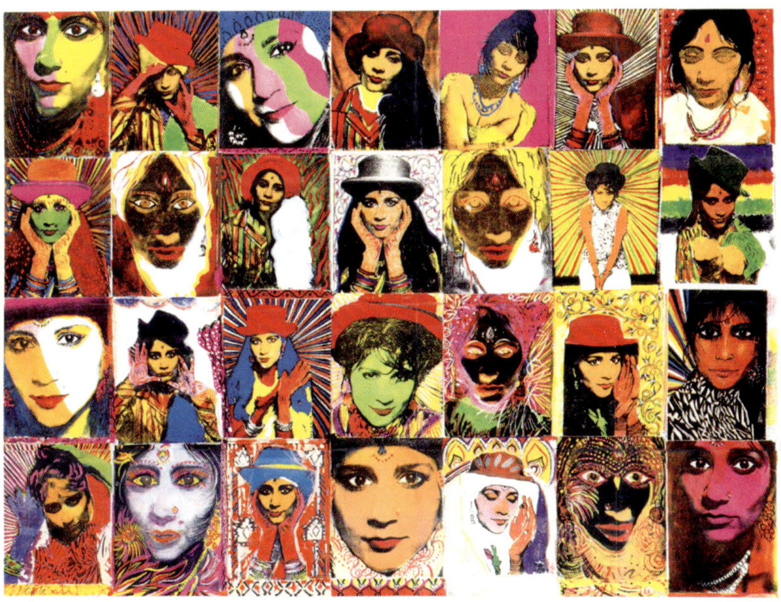

Figure 14.6. Chila Kumari Burman, *28 Positions in 34 Years*, 1992. Laser print and painting. 47 × 62 in. © Chila Kumari Burman. All rights reserved, DACS/Artimage 2022. Photo: Nick Morris.

the body precisely within, not outside, the domains of pleasure and desire, and in its profound implication with "race" and sexuality (figs. 14.4–14.6).

NOTE

This essay first appeared in Stuart Hall and Mark Sealy, *Different* (London: Phaidon, 2001), 34–39.

CHAPTER 15

"Speak Easy":
Black in the 1970s

Over a lifetime of professional work, Dennis Morris has used cameras—to which he was first introduced at the age of eight—to produce a stunning archive of images of life in the black diaspora. His work is well recognized, professionally, and he has been widely exhibited internationally. But, paradoxically, his name is best known for its fortuitous association with music. As a result of a chance encounter outside the Speak Easy Club when he was only seventeen, followed by a long and fruitful collaboration, he produced some memorable images of that most iconic popular black musician of our times: Bob Marley.

These images are typically associated with Marley's global reputation and instant recognizability. However, they are in fact expressive, intimate, penetrating studies, far removed from the publicity still. *A Rebel Life* (1999), for example, offers us a serious, sober, purposeful Marley: his formidable intensity, brow furrowed in concentration; the unswerving directness of address to the viewer; the eyes looking straight at you, demanding attention; the mouth parted, as if about to speak; the trademark goatee beard, and locks, growing electrically stiff and straight out from his head, framing the face. On the other hand, *Legends* (2007) catches him in lighter, more exuberant mood: playful, cocky, both hands proudly showing off two bunches of locks, and laughing with and at us about it, his face split by the great gash of an irrepressible grin.

The work here draws on a very different strand in Morris's archive. It turns aside from the legendary stage of world music (including his work

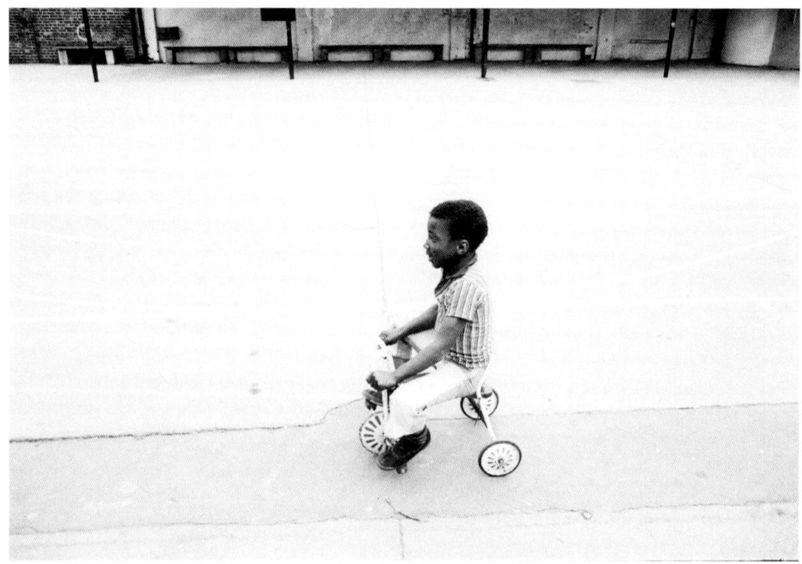

Figure 15.1. Dennis Morris, *Riding into the World, Hackney, 1976*, 1976. Gelatin silver print on paper. © Dennis Morris, 2021. Courtesy of the artist.

with The Wailers, the Sex Pistols and various punk bands) to personal, domestic and familial life in the black community. It "documents" from the inside the experience of living through and growing up black in the 1970s (figs. 15.1–15.4). Very little of this in its more intimate mode seems to have been captured by the camera or properly archived outside the family photo-album (Autograph's Heritage Lottery Fund Archive project will make an enormous difference here). The material of everyday life seems to have been regarded as too humdrum and insignificant to record. Consequently, this aspect of the migrant experience is beginning to slip out of the record, giving way to a more simplistic account.

However, this is what Morris spent much of his personal and professional life photographing. Without working consciously to a plan, he seems to have used every opportunity—studio work, special occasions, photo-shoots, in the street, around the "hood," indoors, the big moments, the incidental—to capture another dimension of this experience. The results constitute a thoughtful, beautifully observed, richly expressive, quietly eloquent collection of images of everyday black diaspora life, as well as making a major contribution to an archive of tremendous social, historical and visual significance.

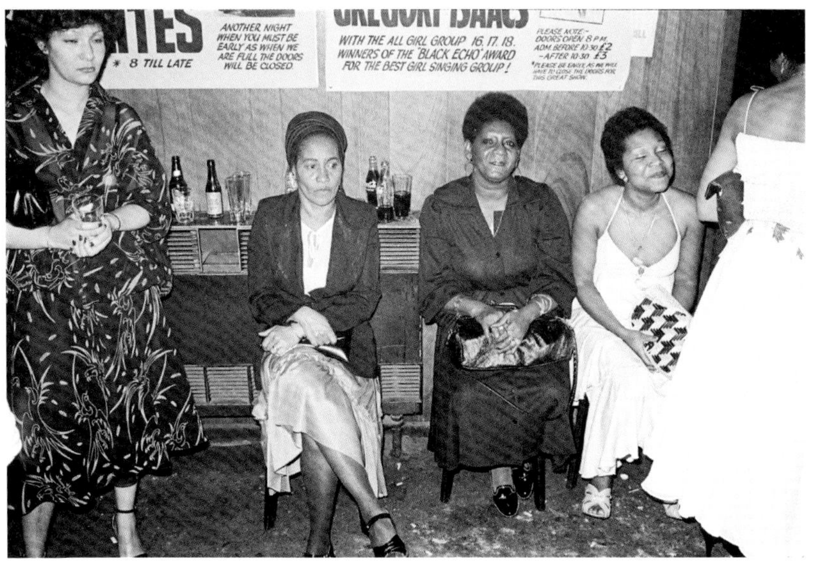

Figure 15.2. Dennis Morris, *Blue Dance Queens, Hackney, 1973*, 1973. Gelatin silver print on paper. © Dennis Morris, 2021. Courtesy of the artist.

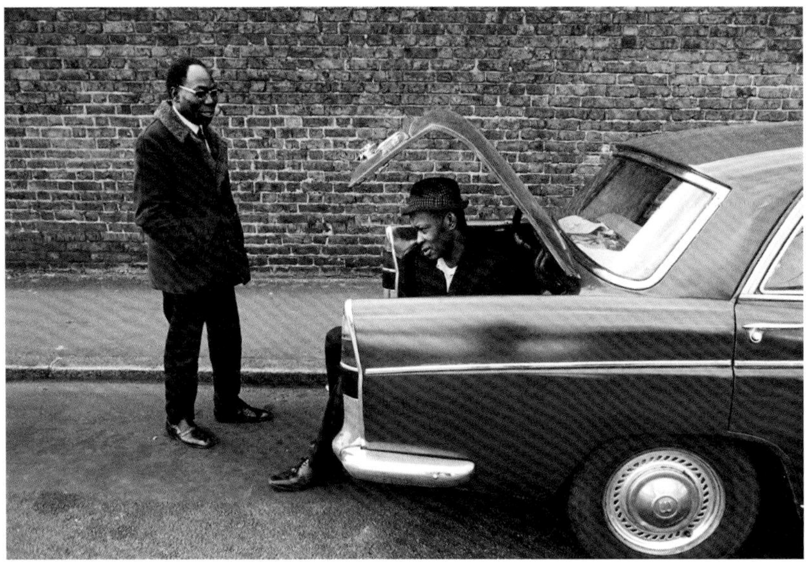

Figure 15.3. Dennis Morris, *Car Boot Conversation, Hackney, 1976*, 1976. Gelatin silver print on paper. © Dennis Morris, 2021. Courtesy of the artist.

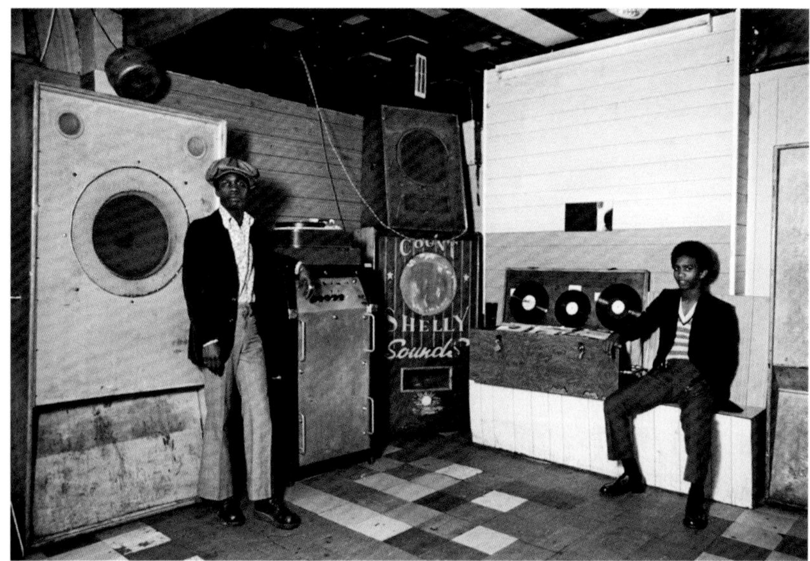

Figure 15.4. Dennis Morris, *Count Shelley Sounds, Hackney, 1973*, 1973. Gelatin silver print on paper. © Dennis Morris, 2021. Courtesy of the artist.

"Documenting black life" is, of course, a tricky concept. In the "high days" of creative photography, the photographic image was thought to rely exclusively on the camera's intrinsic realism, its capacity to literally transcribe the world as it is. Its referent was "the real." Its test was "truth," a warrant of what had happened, and what French cultural critic Roland Barthes called its "having been there."[1] For this reason, it was judged to lack the aesthetic qualities appropriate to a work of art, and thus to be of historical interest only.

This counterposing of the social/political/historical and the aesthetic turns out to be a misleading binary. The image does indeed testify and witness to what happened, though it cannot tell the whole truth. It locates an event, not just in time but also in historical context and its social conditions of existence. It helps us remember, though its memory is not transparent. Its evidence remains ambiguous and open-ended—it can be used to support very different, counter-readings. It harnesses events, in this form, to popular historical memory, and puts them on record, even when it cannot guarantee the interpretation it offers. It gives the event not only date, time, detail and specificity, but also shape and meaning. Nevertheless, the accuracy, veracity, certainty, fixity and authenticity that it appears to offer may be, in the end, illusory.

Photography does not in fact capture reality; it *punctuates* the real and brings real time, space, action and movement to a halt. In the suspended space/time or chronotope, which that opens up, it expands the image laterally, allowing the viewer to "see" another kind of space, time and movement emerging beyond or inside what is literally there. This amplifies the range of expressive meanings, feelings, attitudes and emotions that the image can express or awaken; the spectrum of meanings it can signify; the unexpected connections it can make; the contexts it can suggestively connote. It defines a position and a mode of "looking" for the spectator, from which these latent meanings become legible. The photographer's look is fixed on the subject in the frame, harvesting every detail, but the governing visual logic is associative. The chosen split second of the shutter's arrest is itself an almost instinctive exercise—at one and the same moment—of aesthetic judgement and social intelligence.

So photographic representation is never simply a mimetic exercise, "holding up a mirror to Nature"; and what it represents (re-presents) can never be "purely" factual. It is always a matter of *the practices* of representation, which is what we really mean by calling what is produced "the work": choice of an angle, framing, focus, manipulating spatial relationships, centring, foregrounding side-lining; manipulating light to redirect attention; drawing incidental features into the overall composition. It is, also, always a matter of *form*—the photographer's signature way of looking, of giving what seems random "significant form." These practices transform "the real." Without the introduction of a single extraneous or "fictional" element, they profoundly recompose and reconfigure the meaning of so-called "reality."

To see this at work one need look no further than the image of the toddler on his little three-wheeler, caught in concentrated and purposeful self-propulsion. He is the center of the image, but not *in* the center, because what the still image most suggests is movement forwards across the frame. He is utterly oblivious of the camera: the fixed look, the concentration; the little body tensed with the effort of mastering the task; the eyes fastened, unswervingly, on the objective ahead. This young man is not to be put off or deflected from where he is going. The incidental white lines on the wall behind him are pulled into the picture's overall effect—they underwrite his direction of travel, his forward thrust. (They remind me of the flaky dashes that I used to pencil in behind figures like Superman to indicate speed when I was trying to imitate American comics in my childhood.) However, in the still image taken only a few moments later, when he comes to a stop, he notices the camera at last and now, at rest (the lines are gone), gives a great grin of achievement: mission accomplished. I have seen these qualities before, transposed to a different setting and occasion: my first sight in 1951 of migrants from the boat train streaming out of Paddington Station. This image is a sort of résumé, on a micro-scale, of some of the qualities that sustained the early phases of migration to an unknown destination. However, this lad is now in full occupation of the place to which those early migrants were heading.

The images of childhood are particularly resonant in the ways that they "speak" of beginnings. The boy in the warm woolly jumper sitting on the stool is waiting for something and hugs himself in pleasurable anticipation. The eyes of the little girl speaking on the telephone, whose ribbons make her plaits look like wings, are round, sharp, bright as buttons, wide open, seeing everything, unclouded by what is to come. Those of the young man dressed up to the nines in his suit, laced-up shoes and tie, are more wary, but he is holding on for reassurance to a great brocaded chair. Even more arresting is the frank, unguarded openness and vulnerability of the look of the beautiful lad in the patterned sweater, with lips parted in sheer, undisguised wonder. The older boys playing tag or the four sitting in a row, fully engaged in active, mischievous play, are untroubled by what is around them. The silhouette image of the boy with the lollipop, tongue poised for another glorious lick, distils a moment of pure pleasure. But parenting in these conditions has its costs too: for example, the darker, more sombre, smoky image of the young woman on the bed holding the child protectively. He has been distracted by something happening on the other side of the room; but she looks at us, reflectively, with poignant, sad eyes that speak volumes.

The work of the image, then, is not simply to pin down and illustrate, but to bring into the field of vision the ways the things it shows are lived—experienced, responded to, resisted, made sense of—from the inside. The image is resonant with other meanings and experiences, which are summoned up by the frame but are not contained within it. It works metonymically, that is, further along the signifying chain. These images show the inner, domestic landscapes of public events, so that each becomes the "subject" of—is made a subject by, as well as subjected to—the other. They are each other's reverse image. It is Morris's great gift to be able—without fuss or excessive self-consciousness—to use images like windows to open up these rich interior spaces.

What dominates the visual record, popular memory and public narrative of the early 1970s are the landmark political events that shattered the mood of suspended animation that accompanied the early stages of post-war black migration in the years leading up to and following Enoch Powell's 1968 "Rivers of Blood" speech. Paul Gilroy's *Black Britain* (2007) has a memorable image of the fixed, implacable backs of the assembled white citizens at the "Keep Britain White," "Stop the Coloured Invasion," demo. Race exploded into the center of British politics after the Smethwick election and the 1958 Notting Hill riots—with Oswald Mosley as parliamentary candidate, racist talk at the hustings, fascists on the street for the first time since the war, white kids in front of the pubs, harassing black people on their way home from the tube station, back to the terraces and peeling, multi-occupation town houses of North Kensington. On the night of 17 May 1959, in the wake of the riots, a young Trinidadian, Kelso Cochrane, was stabbed to death in the Golborne Road by a gang of white youths. The *Daily Mail* observed the following day, "the first fatality in the 'war' that flares intermittently in the seamy side of the Royal Borough of Kensington."[2] No one was charged and Mark Olden's meticulously researched book which unravels what really went on that night was only published over fifty years later.

The 1960s and 1970s were indeed tumultuous times for these newly forming black diaspora communities. The immediate post-*Windrush* shock of separation and arrival was tapering off, and the slow-burn trauma of racial discrimination, and the trials of settlement and accommodation, had begun; and with them a new stage in the racialization of both British and black life. In their book, *Windrush* (1998), Trevor and Mike Phillips characterized the period in terms of "the energy and determination which Caribbeans across different generations [brought] to the task of coming to terms with their own new racialized identity, and with the problems of establishing footholds within the environment."[3]

More pointedly, the period witnessed the birth, at the very heart of "the old country," of "colony society," with its typical inner-city, bombed-out or abandoned wasteland locations and scenarios, its physical and social deprivations in housing and living conditions, its indignities, casual violence and degrading humiliations. Paradoxically, "colony society" facilitated the articulation of these discordant elements into a distinctively different way of life. The young man walking across a desolate urban scene, with his palm held out to the camera in an ironic gesture as if soliciting a handout—Morris entitles it *Sandringham Road, Hackney 1976*—wears his coat over his head, anticipating the "hoodie" whom David Cameron once, in an ill-advised moment, loved to hug. The teenage boy looks as if he is hurrying to avoid being swallowed up again by the dust and smoke-filled wasteland from which he has just mysteriously emerged. But—looked at more closely—he is purposefully on his way, at top speed, to somewhere else (as well as being, you might think, in transition to becoming a new kind of black subject).

It was hard to make a decent life, let alone keep your spirits up, in the conditions of racial hostility and social deprivation that the migrants discovered in England, which they had exchanged for the conditions that they had left behind. Viewers today may be shocked to see Morris's image of the temporarily assembled line of washing, which artificially divides a family's single room into two habitable living spaces. However, he is right to draw our attention to the way that deprivation brought out self-respect, pride and a stubborn perseverance in unpropitious circumstances. The man who fills the frame, despite everything, exudes a commanding confidence. Though indoors, he is keeping up appearances—dark shirt, contrasting tie, buttoned-up jacket, fountain pen clip displayed in his top left pocket—and wearing, in the fashion of the day, an indomitable trilby. In a subsequent image, the washing line is gone, the curtains are drawn back, and the man is solidly "in place," with his razor-pressed trousers and polished black shoes, sitting on the sofa with his daughter. This genteel squalor, he seems to be saying, will pass: we are here to stay.

When the family can afford to rent a bigger flat or a small, terrace house, or get lucky and move into council housing, the sheer ingenuity of adaptation and "indigenization" is everywhere to be seen, especially in the "creolized" interior design. Vivid, vibrant, contrasting tropical colours have been introduced at will into this drab London scene, evident in the wallpaper, sofa covers, curtains and mats. Things, necessarily bought as available and whenever they can be afforded, do not match, but they fit the busy life, the domestic comings and goings, show what distances have been travelled, and catch the affirmative spirit of the times.

The family circle is assembled, dressed up for visitors. The young people come together for a formal photo in front of the splendidly gathered curtains. The ubiquitous—and sometimes lethal—paraffin stove keeps the room at an unseasonal but comfortingly high temperature.

The table bristles with (sometimes incongruously English-looking) celebratory cards and an iced birthday-cake. Everyone takes the opportunity to pose before the glass-door cabinet, without which, as Michael McMillan's book *The Front Room* demonstrates, no "West Indian front room" was thought to be properly furnished. The cabinet shows off the family treasure, such as a few, much-prized, seldom-used, wedding presents, some decorated crockery, one or two long-stemmed wine glasses, a cake stand and old (Coronation?) mugs.[4]

These images reveal, from the heart of the poverty, racial oppression and social deprivation, a rich, improvizational, creative syncretism that has been rightly described as "diasporic." Kobena Mercer argues that the diasporic is a "subversive" tendency, which "creatively explores and exploits the creative conditions of the clash of cultures . . . a 'syncretic' dynamic, which critically appropriates elements from the master codes of the dominant culture and 'creolises' them, disarticulating given signs and re-articulating their symbolic meaning otherwise."[5] In *There Ain't No Black in the Union Jack*, Paul Gilroy argues that the diasporic framework, reflecting the "contingent and partial belonging to Britain" that blacks enjoy alongside "their ambiguous assimilation and specific forms of exclusion," best explains the cultural syncretism and "the complex combination of resistances and negotiations" that framed the black British experience. It provides an "alternative to the different varieties of absolutism that would confine culture in 'racial,' ethnic or national essences."[6]

The black communities remained small and scattered—there were few exclusive, classic, black ghettos. However, wherever there was a concentration of migrant families, something like a black "colony" way of life began to emerge, with its own shops and market stalls selling Caribbean produce, its hairdresser and barbershops, its local churches, associations and networks, the pubs that it "colonized," the record shops with their pulsating sounds selling bootleg 45s available only from Kingston, its venues, cafés and clubs, its all-weekend blues parties and dances, its dress-codes and fashions, and even a few large, but often clapped-out American-style limos with their suspiciously springy shock absorbers and fraying upholstery.

Morris evokes this emerging world in a few memorable visual vignettes. One of my favourites is the two black men by the caff, engaged in earnest conversation but very relaxed and oblivious to everything happening around them—for all the world as if this were Kingston not Dalston. The boot of the car is open, the door raised high—and *one of the men is actually sitting inside* it! Another reminder of the kaleidoscopic nature of the many varieties of black life that surfaced at this time can be found in two contrasting images. The first can be found in the wonderful photograph of the black St Marks choirboys, with their out-sized white collars and black surplices, looking like chattering birds. The second is of the assembled all-black congregation of Shiloh Pentecostal Church and takes us into a quite different religious universe. The women in the choir are finely dressed and shod for church—as they always were for parties and for travelling—but the singing is enthusiastic and the organ has disappeared, replaced by the syncopated rhythm of the guitar. Dramatic, intense, revivalist events, unknown at St Marks morning service, are unfolding at the front of the church. However, the young boys are easily distracted and turn around in their pews to stare with unashamed curiosity at what is happening at the back of the church. (They discover that Dennis Morris, a black photographer, who was one of those original angelic Anglican choirboys, is taking a photograph of the congregation of the first, fully black-owned Pentecostal church.)

Local clubs and dance halls run by West Indians provided regular entertainment for grown-ups. The women sitting expectantly in a row, holding their handbags, beneath a Russell Club poster advertising a dance and addressed to "You black beauties," are dressed up for a night out in a mature but fashionable West Indian style. The black couple on the dance floor hold each other close and look into one another's eyes with a casual familiarity, their bodies attuned to some romantic, slow-rhythm lovers' rock. They are locked into a murmured, flirtatious conversation and dance with that casual, unstudied eroticism that is a classic Caribbean dance style for older folk.

In the early days, when black migrant men outnumbered women, they often dated white women, and many clubs, both local and in the West End, catered for mixed-race couples. There is such a couple in the shadows behind the dancing couple described above. In another image, the young man with a beard, looking somewhat the worse for wear, and very relaxed, leaning familiarly against his attentive white companion, has partaken a bit too liberally of the drinks arrayed on the table in front of them. But life around here has clearly begun to have its little pleasures . . .

Of course, the encounter with the Brits at home "on native ground" could be spectacularly unnerving. Black people found themselves identified as a distinctive ethnic community. South Asians who began to arrive in the 1970s fitted neatly into this categorization. At the same time, they were all "sharing space"—high streets, housing, school, playgrounds, churches, jobs, places of work, public transport, hospitals, clubs and pubs—with the white, English working class, who had very different interests, prejudices, notions, habits and customs from them, knew little about them, and found it hard to imagine what black people were doing here; but alongside whom, however reluctantly, they were obliged to live in the deprived conditions of the inner city. This was, and has continued to be, an explosive mix.

It would be too simplistic to tell this story without acknowledging the grudging accommodations, the partial adaptations, the awkward silences, the occasional breakthroughs, the hesitant negotiations, the unexpected moments of intimacy beneath the carapace of difference, coupled with the taunts and racial insults, the sneers and the hostility, which, in reality, constituted the unsettled "settling in" process out of which new black identities and, even later, contradictory, hybrid identifications such as "black British," with all its ambivalences and differences of emphasis, emerged. Many of those who grew up in the 1970s acknowledge that this "mixed," unresolved, experience was an important aspect of what it was really like to "grow up black" for them.

There is a reminder of this in the images of the mixed marriage that Morris includes in his portfolio. This is a "normal," full-on, proper wedding: black bride in white organza wedding dress and veil; white bridegroom in dark suit and tie. There is a bevy of bridesmaids, the couple are supported on either side by her black relatives, some wearing carnations, and there is a three-layer wedding cake. Mixed-marriages this way around—white man, black woman—were not common and the breaking of taboos took some courage. The groom, however, looks quietly resolute. He gives his mother a kiss. Can we detect a shadow of apprehension passing across her face? One wonders how the couple got on, and where they are now.

What was it *really* like to be born, to spend one's childhood in, to be drawn into, an extended West Indian family network; to participate in the daily cycle of domestic activities; to feel at home or threatened in the spaces you inhabited; to live or be schooled locally; to survive the vicissitudes and sample the pleasures of youth, and become an adult, in the interstices of this emerging, urban, postcolonial world? For young black people, with their multiple loyalties and belongings, it was contradictory, unsettling, dangerous and uncharted—but at the same time, exciting and potentially creative—territory.

Above all, the colony areas became the fulcrum of the new expressive cultures that transformed black life in the 1970s: a point of intersection, on diasporic ground, between different parts of the world and historical traditions of struggle. These elements came together as a "culture of resistance," resonating with the pervasive experience of racialized intolerance to which black people were subjected in daily life, and reflecting the ambiguous position and inevitable "double consciousness" of, especially, a second generation, with its sense of being cast adrift in dangerous waters from all points of attachment or belonging. It was nourished and sustained by a fusion of the most varied cultural sources and influences, tossed into the cultural "cook pot" of black Britain. These included the cultures of resistance developed during and after plantation slavery in the Americas, the Pan-African, anti-colonial, decolonizing and independence movements of the early twentieth century, the dream of freedom and emancipation from bondage, which inspired the enslaved with its Old Testament echoes, and the hope of a return to the Promised Land (Africa) translated to the modern world by black visionaries like Marcus Garvey.

It was energized by the way migration and direct experience of "the mother country" broke the silences about slavery and race that had characterized colonial societies; by the rediscovery of African roots, and the political and expressive forms which that consciousness took in the anti-apartheid and civil rights struggles; and the Black Power, black pride and "black is beautiful" movements of the 1960s. It was stimulated by the political trouble, social unrest and increasing crime arising from the deep sense of disillusionment of poor and unemployed black people in the Caribbean, at how little independence had changed their fortunes. This was echoed in the diaspora, not least by the parallels, real and metaphorical, that were drawn between there and here.

Its political forms were to be found in an intensifying range of ways, from anti-racist and anti-fascist demonstrations and opposition to racist legislation, to local community action to defend black places of association like the Mangrove restaurant, and confrontations between black people in "the colony" and those who policed them. It took expressive form above all culturally: in the succession of black music that captured the scene, from blue-beat, ska, rock-steady to reggae; in musical forms like the sound systems and DJ toasting, which mediated between an expanding recording market and live performance; in language, including the rise of a distinctly British-inflected American-influenced patois; the widespread adoption of Afro styles; the rich metaphorical structures of Afro-Christianity; the apocalyptic religio-political metaphors and prophetic symbolism of Rastafari; and the "dreadlocks" and "rude-boy" self-styling. The coming together of these elements, as we said, "provided a new vocabulary and syntax of rebellion . . . closely attuned to the material existence as well as to the emergent consciousness of those condemned to the drifting life of the streets."[7]

One way or another, music was at the heart of it. Morris (whose territory, as a youth, this was and who started his own drum-and-bass band) reminds us that blues parties could last the whole weekend. Some Sunday afternoon sessions were alcohol free. Some venues were regular haunts in well-mapped terrain. Others, farther afield, were less familiar. A few were positively dangerous.

The visual coming-of-age story that Morris constructed is beautifully sequenced. The handsome, self-contained young man with the Afro-style haircut stands on the cusp. He is a study in the "new black": roll-neck black sweater, silver watchband bisecting his forearm, and the out-sized, round and impenetrably black shades. The self-possessed young woman in a sheepskin jacket, with her even bigger Afro-combed hairstyle and elegant fingers, wears not one but *two* pairs of dark glasses, with contrasting black and white rims. In general, the young women are astonishingly stylish: striped miniskirts, smart shoes, slim sleeveless or halter-neck shifts, flared skirts. Sometimes they are more deliberately posed, one gloved hand on the hip, the other holding a slender cigarette holder. The opposite sexes have entered each other's social scene with a purposeful intensity. An altogether new generation is growing up. Putting on the style, fashioning the black self, to pulsating soundtracks and the new fashions, has become a serious pastime.

The young men engaged in the serious business of delivering the sound system from the back of a truck—or casually propping themselves up on one—are simulating a "harder," more grown-up front. They too are impeccably styled: well-tailored dark jackets; smart trousers cut to *exactly* the right length (in contrast to the baggy tracksuits and waists cut down to the buttocks to come); boots or platforms; flat caps or the requisite thin-brimmed pork-pie hats. They could be mistaken for black Mods. The black teenagers playing table football are still young enough to enjoy larking about, but the members of the cricket team—a study in black and white—with their strong, well-honed bodies and mature faces, are really fully-formed, resolute, young black men. They present a gallery of facial expressions, each deep, serious, different. Their eyes are ready to look the world straight in the face.

In this selection from his archive, Dennis Morris gives us a beautifully well-judged and eloquent portrait of the black diaspora, frozen at a particular moment in time. It is pregnant with anticipations of what is still to come, infused with future possibilities. We are invited to read these images backwards and forwards. Growing up black in the 1970s, they suggest, was not so much a state of being as a process of becoming.

This essay first appeared as the introduction to Dennis Morris, *Growing Up Black in the 1970s* (London: Autograph, 2012), 4–7.

1 Roland Barthes, "Rhetoric of the Image," in *Image—Music—Text* (London: Fontana, 1987), 44.

2 Cited in Mark Olden, *Murder in Notting Hill* (Winchester: Zero Books, 2011), 4.

3 Mike Phillips and Trevor Philipps, *Windrush: The Irresistible Rise of Multi-racial Britain* (London: HarperCollins, 1998), 352.

4 Michael McMillan, *The Front Room: Migrant Aesthetics in the Home* (London: Black Dog, 2009).

5 Kobena Mercer, "Diaspora Culture and the Dialogic Imagination," in *Black Frames: Critical Perspectives on Black Independent Cinema*, ed. Mbye Cham and Claire Andrade-Watkins (Cambridge, MA: MIT Press, 1988), 50–61 and 57.

6 Paul Gilroy, *There Ain't No Black in the Union Jack: The Cultural Politics of Race and Nation* (London: Hutchinson, 1987), 155.

7 Stuart Hall, Chas Critcher, Tony Jefferson, John Clarke, and Brian Roberts, *Policing the Crisis: Mugging, the State and Law and Order* (Basingstoke: Macmillan, 1978), 357.

PART VI

RECONSTRUCTION WORK

Histories, Archives, and Diaspora

CHAPTER 16

Reconstruction Work:
Images of Post-war Black Settlement

The history of black settlement in Britain in the post-war years is only just beginning to be written. One of the essential preconditions of such an account is the collection, preservation and interpretation of "documents," public and private, formal and informal, as well as the oral testimonies of those who actually went through the experience in the early days. The past cannot speak, except through its "archive."

When such histories do come to be written, the photographic evidence is likely to play an extremely important role in their construction. One hopes that by then the historians will have gained some experience in "how to read" it. This contribution examines some of the difficulties inherent in reconstructing those histories from existing photographic texts, which are themselves extremely diverse.

There is no such unitary thing as "photography." Photography is a convenient way of referencing the diversity of practices, institutions and historical conjunctures in which the photographic text is produced, circulated and deployed. Many of the photographs relevant to the history of post-war migration will already have made a public appearance in the field of representation (in the press, magazines, etc.)—and are therefore already inscribed or "placed" by that earlier positioning. Their meanings will already have been inflected by the discourses of photographic studio, high-street shop, news-photo agency, book publishing, newspaper or magazine, colour supplement or gallery. The vast majority will already have been organised within certain systems of classification which transfer to them the supplementary imprint of their own generic meanings, etc.: family portrait, news shot, agency scrapbook, photo exposé, etc. Each practice, each placing, each discourse thus slides another layer of meaning across the frame.

It is difficult, if not by now impossible, to recapture the earlier meanings of these photographs. In any event, the search for their "essential Truth"—an original, founding moment of meaning—is an illusion. The photographs are essentially multiaccentual in meaning. No such previously natural moment of true meaning, untouched by the codes and social relations of production and reading, and transcending historical time, exists.

The exercise in interpretation thus calls for considerable caution, historical judgement—in essence, a politics of reading. The evidence which the photographic text may be assumed to represent is already overendowed, overdetermined by other, further, often contradictory meanings, which arise within the intertextuality of all photographic representation as a social practice. It is unclear which constitutes the greater danger: the confusions caused by the relays of meanings in which the photographs are already overinscribed; or the riot of deconstruction to which they are certain to be exposed, not least from some of the new orthodoxies of the "cultural left," caught as they sometimes are in the spirals of the post-Marxist, post-structuralist, postmodernist deluge. Black historians, especially, handling these explosive little "documents," will have to steer their way through the increasingly narrow passage which separates the old Scylla of "documentary realism as Truth" from the new Charybdis of a too-simplistic "avant-gardism."

Take, for example, the news agency photographs of the arrival of black people from the Caribbean on the boat-trains. These shots were taken at the big London rail-stations, where the steamers spewed out their human cargo at the end of their long journeys—Kingston via Southampton, Avonmouth-Bristol and Liverpool docks; then by steam-train through the English rural and urban-industrial heartland, to Paddington, Victoria and Waterloo. Here are the crowded stations; people sitting on their luggage or standing about, hands clasped, waiting: waiting to be met, or to recognise a friend or an unexpected relative or even just for an acknowledgement from a friendly face amongst the crowds with their bulging suitcases and straw baskets. Men, women and children, already battened down against the freezing weather by the ubiquitous wearing of hats. People "dressed up to the nines," formally, for "travelling" and even more for "arrival." Wearing that expectant look—facing the camera, open and outward, into something they cannot yet see . . . the new life.

These people are in the liminal—the in-between—state: in suspended animation. This, for better or worse—their faces seem to say—is the dead end of one thing and the uncertain beginning of another. It is a scene of transition which occurred any day of the week in the immigration "high season" throughout the 1950s and early 1960s, until the barriers closed. Trickling out from these focal points into the grey light of Paddington, Notting Hill, Brixton, Handsworth, Moss Side . . . A graphic record. But what do these pictures mean? Can they fix and prescribe their own reading, decipherment? What do we make of these images *now*?

For one thing, they contradict our expectations. Why are the men and women so formally got up? Why does everybody wear a hat? Why are they carrying their clothes in straw baskets? Why do they look so respectable? Where are the street fighters, the rude boys, the Rastas, the reggae? How are we to read what these photographs most powerfully construct: a certain form of innocence?

Innocence is a dangerous, ambiguous, ambivalent construction for black people. White discourses so often represent us as simpletons, simple-minded primitives, smiling country people, not quite keeping up in the fast lanes of the advanced world. It is a reading to be refused. These are not country bumpkins, or indigent cousins "from the Tropics," or primitives just swinging down from the coconut trees, or anybody's *Smile Orange* folks. These people have just survived the longest, hardest journey in their lives: the journey to another identity. They are people "in transition" to a new state of mind and body: migranthood. They are probably from a city, like Kingston, as big and swinging in its poverty and style as any small colonial capital. They have torn themselves up by their roots, saved up what for them (considering the annual average wage) is a colossal sum, paid it over to a steamship company travelling incognito under some assumed Panamanian flag. Half the family is left behind and nobody knows when or whether they will ever be united again. These men and women have just burnt their boats in the determination to carve out a better life.

All this may be "beyond the frame"; but it registers inside the frame—precisely as a kind of "innocence." This is another way of referring to that moment of "waiting" just before you step off the end of the earth into . . . another life, in a Britain the ingrained, embattled nature of whose racism you do not yet know (that is, of which you are still, in a way, "innocent") because it hasn't yet hit you hard between the eyes . . . A liminal movement, caught between two worlds, hesitating on the brink.

We can find this trace of innocence too, if you know where to look, else-where inside the frame. The people are "dressed up" because they are on the longest one-way journey of their lives, literally and figuratively. Jamaicans trav-elled as they went to church, or visited their relatives—in their "Sunday best"; the best thing you had in your wardrobe, for special occasions. The suits and dresses are the clothes of someone who is determined to make a mark, make a favourable impression. The formality is a signifier for self-respect. These are not the victims of migration, like the Jews and East Europeans photographed by Thomas Hine arriving at Ellis Island in New York. These folks are in good spirits. They mean to survive. The angle of the hats is universally jaunty, cocky. Already, there is *style*. "Face the music, darling, and let's make a move."

There is a similar problem of interpretation about the vast, uncatalogued collection of formal "high-street" photo-portraits which are certain to be brought to light by a systematic search, crumbling away in files or shoved under the beds in boxes. For example, the young woman with the gloves and handbag, holding up or being held up by the basket of artificial flowers. (There is a wonderful re-presentation of the same idea in the self-portrait by the black painter Sonia Boyce, of herself, surmounted by her parents and sisters, entitled *She Ain't Holding Them Up, She's Holding On (Some English Rose)*.) The well-dressed young man held together by the clip-on fountain pen is talking on a phone which is not connected to anything, but sits incon-gruously on top of a mock-Greek column, straight from the disused basement of the British Museum.

Yet despite these ambiguities and disavowals of meaning, these high-street portraits also contain a sort of alternative history of black people in Britain—alternative to the documentary or the "social problem" traditions, their codes and meanings, which now construct the dominant reading of that history (and to which we will come in a moment). Every photograph is a structure of "presences" (what is represented, in a definite way) and "ab-sences" (what is unsaid, or unsayable, against which what is there "repre-sents"). We will have to struggle to bring out what these formal portraits, so powerfully inscribed by the practices of the high-street photographer, so much under subjection to the codes of late-Edwardian portraiture, have to "say"—as well as their silences.

They signify a certain democratisation of representation. They are poor-person's "portraits." The camera did, for the poor, what painting could not do. The formality and sense of occasion of these photographs are inscribed in the ways in which the figures are formally posed, frozen, in the way they have been suspended in formal space and time. They are certainly not "at home." They are not at work either. In fact, they are not represented as being in any human or social environment. They exist only in and for studio time, studio space. They are the bearers of the professional, small-time photographer's aspiration to "art." They have been transferred directly under his rules of construction. They exist for him. (I use the male pronoun advisedly, since overwhelmingly—but not exclusively—these professional photographers were, until recently, men.) You can see what has been "constructed out" by the very positive functions of the composition only by contrast with, say, the same figures, but this time "caught" in time, in place—for example, a photo of a roadsweeper at work.

And yet, before we think we have a complete grasp of these archaic representations, it is worth recalling that these formal portraits were also, in their own time, "documentary." They documented where people were at a certain stage of life, and how they imagined themselves, how they became "persons" to themselves and to others, through the ways in which they were represented. The photos were what you sent home as "evidence" that you had arrived safely, landed on your feet, were getting somewhere, surviving, doing all right. It would therefore be wrong to read these portraits as exclusively the result of the imposition of the codes of formal (white) portrait photography on an alien (black) subject, for that simplification would be precisely to collude, however unconsciously, with the construction of West Indians as objects, always "outside time," outside history. The photographed subjects also had a real investment in these representations. In fact, Edwardian portraiture and the formal photograph—icons in the domestic gallery of memories—were as common in my childhood in poor but respectable homes in Kingston as they were in Kingston upon Thames. The round centre-table in my grandmother's living-room in a tiny country village in Old Harbour in rural Jamaica was crammed with them; one formal pose (my grandfather, resplendent in his gold watch-chain and three-piece suit) jostling for a place behind another (my wistful fading great-grandmother, grey hair in a bun, with a Victorian tortoiseshell comb resolutely stuck through it).

Our family history was constructed through these representations. The codes of respectability and of respect were every bit as powerful, and as complex, amongst black people in post-Victorian colonial Jamaica as they were in post-Victorian colonising Britain. Slavery, colonisation and colonialism locked us all—them (you) and us (them)—into a common but unequal, uneven, history, into the same symbolic and representational frames.

Afro-Caribbean culture is precisely the result of the contradictory ways these symbolic histories were irrevocably bound together. Those who doubt the complexities of positioning which this history of uneven development contains should read C. L. R. James, the English-speaking Caribbean's most outstanding Marxist historian and intellectual, on the subject of cricket in *Beyond a Boundary*—and think again. Jamaicans may have been placed in the subordinate position by the codes of the formal family portrait, but they were never *outside* those codes.

This is one aspect of the history of black migration that is going to be all too tempting to forget or disavow, since it does not fit easily with current expectations. It does not fit with either "Jamaica," the Black Nation, or "Jamaica," the sign of the Tropical-Exotic. That is why I am pleased this informal evidence exists. Its ambiguities *resist* simplification and disrupt our reading. That is also why I admire the corrective provided by Val Wilmer's photographs of "everyday Jamaican life" in Britain in the 1960s—and why I refuse to be absolutist either about the fact that she is a white photographer photographing blacks or about the so-called "documentary-realist tradition" in which her images are often constructed. I find an astonishing plenitude in the constructed complexities of some of those photographs: the pastor and his wife at his front gate; the church-going family—everyone (again) in a hat, including the babe in arms. These images are part of the frequently unrecorded, unrecognised, unspoken history of everyday life and practice in the black communities in Britain. The cultural historian who sets out to interpret this record without an understanding of the complex position which religion has played in the *life* of the black communities in the Black Diaspora will undoubtedly see something, but will not have learnt to read the cultural signposts and multiaccented traces which history has left behind—traces, as Gramsci says, "without an inventory."

And yet, of course—to repeat an earlier point—what "signifies" is not the photographic text in isolation but the text, caught in the network of the chains of signification which overprint it, its inscription into the currency of other discourses, its intertextuality. The photograph of boat-loads of West Indians at the Customs actually appeared, already in place with others, in a *Picture Post* article of 1956. It was part of a very distinctive way of constructing its subject: black migrants as *a problem*: "Thirty Thousand Colour Problems." Three thousand, the article tells us, is the rate of arrivals per month. Thirty thousand are expected in 1956. And every last one of them "a problem." The written text anchors—as the preferred, the *dominant*, meaning—one of the many potential meanings which the multireferentiality of the photographic texts supports. This is how a problem is produced within representation. Black people come in such large numbers. Surprisingly, they all want to work and to live in homes. They don't understand how to dress for the uncertainties of the English climate. They don't have an accurate picture of life "over here." The problem they pose for "us" is universal, ubiquitous. It is overdetermined from every conceivable direction. It is outside the norm, beyond the pale. It is—they are—the Other.

I have written elsewhere about the particular strengths and weaknesses of *Picture Post*'s social documentary style of "realism." In many ways, the critique of social documentary is strengthened and reinforced by the discourses of social exposure which are in play in this example. *Picture Post* turned an observant, socially enquiring eye on many corners of English life and society, before and after the war, which were excluded or invisible to the media of social communication. It became part of a significant ideological formation—what I once called the "eye" or "gaze" of social democracy.

This way of looking at England was capable of representing hitherto invisible social issues; but, characteristically, it always constructed them as *social problems*. It represented the subjects of its "look" as the intensely interesting, intensely human, intensely ordinary, objects of forces they could not control or comprehend. It summoned up a concern which made powerful claims on our humanism; but it could not penetrate more deeply because it had no language for social contradiction, no way of breaking the surfaces of "naturalism" in which the problem presented itself, or of "speaking" the oppositional forces out of which radical social transformation might be generated. I have argued that both the strengths and the limitations of this particular "way of seeing" were bound up with its actual codes and practices of representation: the observing eye, the external, objective character of reality, the documenter in a position of knowledge, the confinement of meaning to the rich surface of things: its particular variant of what I have called (for I believe it to be articulated as a political formation as well as an ideological and discursive field) "social democratic realism."

This "look," inscribed through a particular set of codes and discourses, is all too plainly to be seen again in some of the "best" documentary photojournalism about "the problem of blacks" in the early decades of migration. How much this is the product of the practices of representation, how little the outcome of "natural," inevitable, or in any simple way "true" ways of seeing and believing is shown, I think, by an intriguing paradox. In the issue of *Picture Post* for 30 October 1954, "the problem" is constructed as the black presence. However, in the news-photo of the first major race riots—Notting Hill, 1958—which shows young people charging through the streets of North Kensington in ways which might be thought to be part of "the problem," there is not a black face to be seen. Absences sometimes speak louder than words.

However, it must also be said that the current critical orthodoxy has somewhat trivialised the argument about documentary realism by assimilating all "realisms" (which one ought to be at pains to discriminate and differentiate) into one great, essential so-called "realist discourse." This, in turn, has been assimilated, not as a negotiation of the dominant discursive codes (which *Picture Post* clearly was) but as a mere repetition of *the* dominant code, *tout court*; and this in turn, via a further echoing of Foucault, has been identified, without qualification, with the univocal, scrutinising "gaze" or the surveillance of the populace by the ruling class. Of course, all regimes of representation are inscribed in the "play" between power and knowledge, and Foucault's work is wonderfully insightful on this score. But the kind of account outlined above is built on a sliding series of reductions, of an astonishing—and in the end unacceptable—kind. There is no *one* system of realist representation, always and forever fixed in position, from which one type of political practice, one empiricist reading of history, emanates; any more than there is one deconstructionist avantgardism, always–forever already inscribed in its progressive modes of seeing. Yesterday's deconstructions are often tomorrow's clichés. It depends, as always, on the way concrete practices are implemented in concrete historical conditions, the effectivity with which certain codes are constituted as "in dominance," the struggle within the social relations of representation, at a particular conjuncture, as to whether a tendency can be articulated towards or away from the politically progressive pole. The fact is, there is no universally transhistorical "progressive style" and the search for it is itself deeply essentialist, even when constructed under the sign of theoretical anti-essentialism. We are always and for ever in the terrain of *articulation*: linkages which can be reversed, meanings which change their sign from negative to positive as they are repositioned in the field of interdiscursivity in which ideology constantly intervenes, with its reordering, recomposing power. Hegemony is a hard taskmaster, but it really is different from the idea of the permanent and fixed ascription of an eternal dominance within any one discourse across the entire face of history.

Take, for example, the now overtypical and overtypified so-called "documentary" shot of the man looking at the sign which reads: "Rooms to Let. No Coloured Men." It is in the classic documentary, re-creating-the-lived-experience, style. It constructs the black man as "barred" and names the bar as "discrimination": in the language of the time, the "Colour Bar." This representation cannot be fixed in its Truth by any Real, since it stops short before the deeper realities of "Racism"—a phenomenon which this "way of seeing" finds impossible to name or identify. All the same, *in its time*, this situation, which was part of the experience black migrants faced everywhere, was also systematically denied everywhere—unspoken and unspeakable. It required to be, as one might say, represented—"documented": *of course*, within the "social exposé" discourses of the period (how else do you represent except discursively?).

But anyone with a proper historical sense, not reading back everything with hindsight into "pure" theoretical time (i.e., reading in a historical, not historicist, way), will know that, in this conjuncture, "documenting it"—in the sense of putting one's finger on it, giving it an image, naming it, representing it, bringing it into the sightline (including that of other blacks who may have expected things to be different)—mattered. It registered. It was part of the politics of representation. It disturbed the "field of vision" of its time. If it had been left unseen, unsaid, the black politics of resistance of a *later* period would have had only an empty void to build on. So there is no point in giving an account or reading of that photograph which *suppresses* time, disavows the contradiction. Things which really are contradictory are not made more "revolutionary" by being translated into comforting theoretical simplifications . . .

Sartre once said that a "lazy Marxism" was that which tells us only what we already know. Looking again at some of these early images, I saw something which I had not been aware of before. We have already seen how black migration was constructed in many of the news-photos as a problem. But I had forgotten how persistently in these early days, at the centre of the problem—the problem of the problem, so to speak—was the core issue of sexuality: specifically, sexual relations between different ethnic or racial groups—or, to give it its proper name, the traumatic fantasy of miscegenation. It is as if, at the centre of this whole regime of representation, there was one unrepresentable image, which nevertheless cast a silent shadow across the visual field, driving those who sensed its absent-presence crazy: the image of black sexuality figured transgressively across the boundaries of race and ethnicity. In the mirror of the imaginary—screaming to be spoken—we find figured this "unspeakable": the traumatic inscription of black and white people, together, making love—and having children, as the proof that, against God and Nature, *something worked.* How often since, in the syntax of white racism, coiling through the Enoch Powell "Rivers of Blood" speech, or in fantasies that drive young bullet-headed fascists or Thatcherite skinheads into an unspeakable frenzy, or in the obscene scrawls that trail their slime across the face of black people's houses and shops, or carved into the walls of public lavatories and on the sides of apartment blocks, has one "read," hiding behind what is actually written, this great unsaid?

The *Picture Post* of 1954 had a word for it, a way of putting (representing) it: "Would you let your daughter marry a Negro?" Typically, it is the "sympathetic," winsome portrait of a white mother and a black child which is used to construct this representation. If we look at the contact sheets from which this particular image was selected, we find a much wider range of shots, with alternative ways of representing the white mother and black father: close, not distanced; together, or together with the child; doing things, in context—shopping, playing, walking about. The choice of a static mother-and-child image as the principal signifier of the white-family-norm-in-trouble is certainly not fortuitous, however fragile or contingent the meaning seems to be. Indeed, even through its oblique treatment here (we are once again in the negotiated discourses of *Picture Post*) we are reminded that English racism is not so much a single discourse as the interdiscursive space when several discourses are articulated together: the discourses of race, and colour, and sexuality, and patriarchy and "Englishness" itself. "If she was my kid," muttered the man in overalls, "I'd tan the backside off her." Against this vivid, idiomatic, common-sense English "truth" is counterposed the silent "appeal," the sentimental eyes—playing straight to the heartstrings: "Sometimes they say it loud enough for her to hear."

The pull is irresistibly towards the sense of fairness, the common humanity. The *humanist* inflection is central to the *liberalism* of this whole rhetoric. The more consciously posed, formally contrasting, white couple/black couple from another Keystone agency photograph is inflected in the same direction. "The look of the couple in front is full of scepticism. He is black—she is white," the caption in *Picture Post* reads, in case we are in any doubt. "The other couple—bound to current traditions. Their world has to be safe, their desires are security and prosperity." The two representations have been set up as binary opposites, mirror-images. Then comes the mediation: "But there is one thing that they have in common: they are equivalent people with their sorrows and desires—with their hope and anxiety." Here again, the neatly composed construction of oppositions, the "surface" hostility, resolved by a deep, underlying, essential, oneness. The photograph as Universal Humanism. A likely story.

Each period lays its own inflections on the image. Each photograph already has a context, a set of histories within which alone it signifies. Since the photographs discussed here were taken—many now more than thirty years ago—black people in Britain have been constructed, and begun to construct themselves, as new kinds of subjects—visually, in new, different, often more challenging ways. Of course, a "sense of history" is never confined to the past: it is always a seizure by history of the present, as Benjamin said. But it does require a delicate excavation, an archaeology, a tracing of the contradictory imprints which previous discourses have stamped, through those old images, on the iconography of popular memory.

NOTE

This essay first appeared in *Ten.8*, no. 16 (1984): 2–9.

Picture research for this article, in its original form, was undertaken by the photographers Derek Bishton and John Reardon, editors of the Birmingham-based quarterly photographic magazine, *Ten.8*, for which it was commissioned and first published in the special issue "Black Image," *Ten.8*, no. 16 (1984): 2–9. It is republished here without images; these can be viewed in earlier reprints. See Jo Spence and Patricia Holland, eds., *Family Snaps: The Meaning of Domestic Photography* (London: Virago, 1991), 152–64 (with fewer photographs); James Procter, ed., *Writing Black Britain 1948–1998* (Manchester: Manchester University Press, 2000), 82–93 (with many of the original photographs); and Stuart Hall, *Writings on Media: History of the Present*, edited by Charlotte Brunsdon (Durham, NC: Duke University Press, 2021), 78–94 (with images of the original spreads in *Ten.8*). The article was first titled "Reconstruction Work" but has subsequently often included the subtitle "Images of Post-war Black Settlement." Ellipses within the text come from the original and do not indicate editing.

CHAPTER 17

The "West Indian" Front Room

Class (of which race/colour was an important component) made a significant difference to the aesthetics of the front room in the Caribbean. The front room of my parents' home in Kingston was clearly that of a middle-class Jamaican family house: full of rather heavy wooden furniture, disposed over a wide space. Compared with the lower-middle or respectable working-class front room, the relationship between objects and people in the space had already been "straightened out" by a more directly English or European influence. However, it retained many of the classic features of the front room found across the Caribbean. It was much more crowded with objects and things than an English middle-class parlour. It had a big cabinet with glassware and china that, like elsewhere, were never used unless on special occasions. In our house, there was also a piano, which I played, and an ancient phonograph. But we didn't sit in the front room for everyday pleasure and relaxation. It had been reserved, by some unwritten rule, for public social occasions, not for informal ones.

Whereas my grandmother and her extended family lived in Old Harbour, a dusty country town near Spanish Town, on a small plot of land full of fruit trees, in a small, wooden "Gingerbread"-style family house with wooden porches and balustrades on all three sides of the "front room." It was a typical lower-middle-class rural Jamaican home, over which my grandmother presided (my grandfather was long dead); and I would often visit with my family on special occasions such as Christmas and Easter. The dining room opened into the front room. The former was in some ways the focus of social life in the home, especially when we visited from Kingston (we were close to but not treated as part of the immediate family); and all pathways between the back and front of the house—the two main "regions"—passed through it. (The sociologist Erving Goffman spoke of a "back" and a "front" region in houses of this kind with clear distinctions between the type of behaviour appropriate to each: and Pierre Bourdieu confirmed this in his analysis of how space was socially demarcated in the Berber house in North Africa.)

Most of the everyday family activities took place in the dining room and the outside kitchen attached to the back of the house where cooking for visitors and friends was a major familial activity; or in the bedrooms of my aunts surrounding it; or on the verandas, with the cool breeze blowing in through the windows from the Bay. But the moment a visitor who was not "family" appeared, he/she was invited to sit in the front room.

Front rooms in the Caribbean would belong to houses, which had been occupied for several generations by the same family and were therefore a repository of shared life across generations. Everything there had echoes of another generation: two or three generations were present in the room; and one of the things I liked about my grandmother's front room was that it gave me an excuse to interrogate her about the past of the family, simply by saying "Who is that a picture of?" or "Where did that come from?" or "What is that object on the wall?" or "Who gave you that glass dish" etc. It was a storehouse of memories and connections across time.

The Old Harbour house was a much more convivial place than our family home in Kingston, which I always thought of as rather cold, restricted to our nuclear family and connected to a much narrower middle-class social world. But despite its conviviality, the staging of respectability was a matter governed by many unwritten rules. One of the things I loved about going to Old Harbour was talking to my aunts who were discreet but well-informed gossips and who told the most wonderful stories about life and the "goings-on" in the town, while I pretended not to listen. But they never gossiped in the front room, only in the bedrooms where I lay on the bed with the doors and windows flung wide open as my Aunt Iris, the best of the *raconteurs*, told the most hilarious stories about the locals. And when we went to the front room, one of the locals who had been the subject of her story might well call in to see my grandmother as they passed the front gate, which had a special piquancy for me; but someone would always tell me to sit up and insist that I put on some decent clothes: "make yourself respectable," as they would say.

This has to do with the commitment of the family, not only to be, but also to present itself in a morally—and socially—respectable and respected way.

Every corner of my grandmother's front room was loaded with photographs of family, friends and relations. I remember a centre table covered with lace crochet that she had made, but you couldn't put a glass down on the table because it was crammed with these photographs, frame after frame, of formal self-representations of older relatives, of young people getting married and first-born babies.

There was something very "Victorian" about all this, which is mainly about packing out a space with objects. That in turn had probably been influenced by Britain's role as the marketplace of the world, connected by trade to the far flung corners of its colonial world, the centre of this cornucopia of commodities and goods which somehow also circulated from one colony to another; and with the Victorian period as the high water-mark of the practice of collecting things and cramming them together in a display space—the aesthetics of *bric-à-brac*. As that giant imperial firm, Unilever's, said in one of its advertisements designed to persuade the colonies to purchase the means to achieve standards of cleanliness appropriate to the metropolitan world: "Soap Is Civilization."

Somehow everything seemed to find its way into, and to find a place in, the front room: for instance, the antimacassars embroidered by my grandmother and passed on to her daughters which decorated the backs of chairs were designed to produce, visually, an image (and a physical feeling) of respectability which was itself a very Victorian phenomenon. In the colonial setting, respectability was a highly prized family value. It was produced by the desire to distinguish yourself from—and never to be confused with—the "rough" masses you had only recently left behind. But it also connoted moral approval, the right moral conduct and the right way for a family to belong together and to keep up standards. The culture of respectability was partly inherited from the coloniser, and the strong dissenting religious traditions they brought with them. But it also had its roots in the degraded circumstances of plantation life and the efforts after abolition to struggle out of it and to make another kind of life—one which enhanced rather than destroyed self-respect. We're talking, then, about an authentic West Indian tradition of respectability—one both forged indigenously *and* borrowed from elsewhere—which therefore, strictly speaking, had no "authenticity" about it. To what could it be "authentic" when so much of Caribbean culture is precisely this amalgam of traditions, modifications, borrowings, adaptations, resistances, transcriptions, translations and appropriations, locked in an unequal relationship? The front room represents precisely a creative cultural act or form of that doubly-inscribed, hybrid or creolized kind.

West Indian Migrants

Many lower-middle-class people from the Caribbean, once they came to England, became working people, so there was a kind of class shift as you moved from the Caribbean. In the Caribbean, the front room was closer to a Victorian parlour tradition and in England the front room was closer to a respectable working-class tradition. This is how the West Indian migrant front room in the black British context intersects and overlaps with the respectable working-class front room because they both had a Victorian ancestry though differently interpreted in the colonial context and in the migrant context, they are nevertheless variations of the same tradition.

To find a space in which to recreate a sense of the home that they had in the Caribbean took a long while in Britain, but once that took place, the front room was recreated as the spiritual, moral and social centre of the public presentation of the family towards the outside world. As you can imagine, the houses that West Indian families could afford at this stage were very small and the front room was a more confined space: but people still found a way to designate a space which is not packed out with people, where the family don't slouch about and relax and where there are distinct rules as to when the whole family went in there and when they did not. The "West Indian" or Caribbean front room in England is a cumulative migrant space, the result of movement between two places, two cultures. As a migrant you have to start again: there are no native materials from "back home" except English and Western furniture which, if you can afford it, you source by looking for something that reminds you of the front rooms or of the homes that you had left behind. Reconstructing the front room out of these materials is trying to deal with the rupture of migration.

How did the West Indian front room in Britain become so uniform? Well, partly people visited one another and monitored what the next-door neighbour had: "they have a new paraffin heater, they've got a new radiogram and a china closet" etc. The question is not simply having the money to establish a home, but what you do when you do have it—which is where the aesthetic comes in. So there are lots of reasons why these spaces should be very similar; but what I think is really riveting is that everybody thinks they are making a huge effort to make an individual space of their own. Much the same pieces of furniture may be involved, but every arrangement is a bit different from everybody else's. The ornaments signify something special and different because they are individual to this family and grounded in its history and memory, which the objects somehow preserve and translate to another life. Most of the walls in the homes were wallpapered—this was particular to the time, and considered a cut above paint. But the colours of the wallpaper in the West Indian front room were very different: vividly-colored, in colors drawn from a tropical palette, and intricately patterned; each wall in a different—but, as it were, matching—color. The carpets were similarly *sort of, but never perfectly,* "matched" to others in the room. Everyone had wallpaper and carpets; but no-one had this particular wallpaper. The family expressed its aesthetic sensibility in terms of the way these elements were combined. So within this very common pattern, which testifies to our collective social and cultural identity, everybody was making an individual imprint on it by changing the arrangement. This is the play of difference and commonality that is so important and can be found throughout cultural life amongst black people and also in how they express this in terms of the arrangement of objects in space.

Whilst there may be neighbours and close relatives coming for a chat in the kitchen, rituals in the front room are partly about entertaining people who don't belong to the family. Ritual in the front room is therefore strongly inscribed in the difference between the inner domestic family and public world. It also marks the difference between when the family is "being itself"—such as relaxing, listening to music, lounging, or even larking about—and special occasions such as a christening, wedding or funeral etc., when everybody sat up straight and the children were on "best behaviour." There are no rules written down because it is just understood that you inspect your behaviour carefully, monitor how you speak and what you say in the front room, because it is the place where the external world has an eye on and into what the family is like. There is no informal slackness and no swearing in there because, for one thing, your mother won't let you. The mother of the house was the keeper of the rules.

Respectability and Respect

There are really three layers: first, there's the outside world that has no real conception of black people other than as invading a typically British world; then secondly, there's the world black people are actually living in; and then thirdly, there's the front room. The front room is a conservative element of black domestic life, which is more complex and richer than the generality of the society ever understands. Why does it remain such a relatively conservative space? What is being conserved? This takes us back to the Caribbean because it plays a similar function there and this is the function of respectability and respect. Respectability—that is to say, the family must respect itself, it must maintain a certain code of behaviour between young people and older people; and it must win and maintain respect from your elders, your friends and other families from the outside. Respectability is what you achieve in the eyes of the outside world. And behind it is the ever-present threat represented by the real poor, the urban and rural poor who are living in one shack with no front room, back room or side room, just trying to have a space where the rain doesn't come in all the time. So it's always a question of lifting yourself in your own eyes and in the eyes of the external world out of that pit, that possibility of urban and rural poverty, which is still the reality of most people in the Caribbean. Therefore, respectability is about people raising themselves in ways which are validated by the outside world. So that when people come into the house the family knows it is regarded with respect. Visitors don't slouch into the house and take a seat in the front room but must be invited to do so, and always go to the kitchen and see grandma and "respect" her first. There's a code which must be respected and that validates their own sense that they are worthy of respect and not so battered down by the circumstances of the material world that they can't even afford to have a decent front room. These are critically important values in the culture, and to give them the casual name of "keeping up with the Joneses" is to fundamentally misread them.

Are there African precedents to this? I'm sure there are. We know that even in the simplest societies there are spaces designated differently with different functions and codes of behaviour appropriate to them. In other societies, you may not have a front room as such but there is a designation of space. How this impacts on the Caribbean is very complicated because things are borrowed and remembered. Remember, too, that the whole function of slavery was to cut the connection to Africa, to dis-remember Africa, in order to "re-cultivate" slaves to their new plantation life. When they do acquire the capacity to build their own homes in villages after abolition, what do they do? How do they live? Is there space for such a thing as a bedroom? Is there a front room? Obviously two important cultures are being played out here; there is the Victorian culture of the white dominant ex-slaving colonialist and, in the West Indian front room, you can see the imprint of an indigenous version of Victorian respectability, no question about it.

One of the contributing factors to this value of respectability is religion. There is the long tradition of practices and beliefs in the Caribbean, which are African in origin and overlaid by a powerful missionary and Christianising influence. And the notions of respect and respectability are underpinned by the way native life became infused with Christian religious values. These are deeply religious societies—even politicians speak in Biblical phrases and rhythms. Religion in the Caribbean is always more important than you think; it is always there shaping and giving meaning to other practices. It is always the neglected element; and the front room would not be a "front room" without that religious connection. But religion is not the sole key that unlocks the front room, which is not to deny that the front room most often resembles a series of domestic "altars": but the influence is as much social and moral as religious in the strict sense.

Respectability is a social, but also a moral and religious question: It depends on codes of behaviour which are inscribed by a sense of what is right and what is good. In the front room we see a partly remembered African past impacted by the disruption of slavery and then by the colonial world. The front room in the Caribbean is a translated space; and then you move all of that through migration to Manchester, or Birmingham, or Liverpool or Brixton, with all those new urban influences impacting as well. Not surprisingly, the front room is a very conservative space. It moves slowly, it resists change; but it is also a culturally translated space because it is always borrowing from the "outside" while expressing something of what is intrinsically "inside."

This came to me powerfully when I went to see "The West Indian Front Room" exhibition at the Geffrye Museum curated by Michael McMillan (figs. 17.1 and 17.2). I have never seen so many people animated by an exhibition, pointing out this and that to each other, "remember that!" and "we had one of them!," etc. But also, going around the exhibition with me was a white Jewish working-class couple. The husband had been a lorry driver and had a good West Indian mate. I don't know if he had ever been invited into his friend's home. But the couple did not regard the attempt to recreate the West Indian front room as such a foreign idea. They were enlivened, they said, because the exhibition was a revelation for them. The revelation was that it was just like their Jewish mother's front room in London's East End!

Here you can see another migrant culture moving into England and borrowing from an English notion of respectability and it is the same process coming from the Caribbean. Both migrant cultures recognize each other's aesthetic tastes coming from two opposite ends of the earth but ending up in the

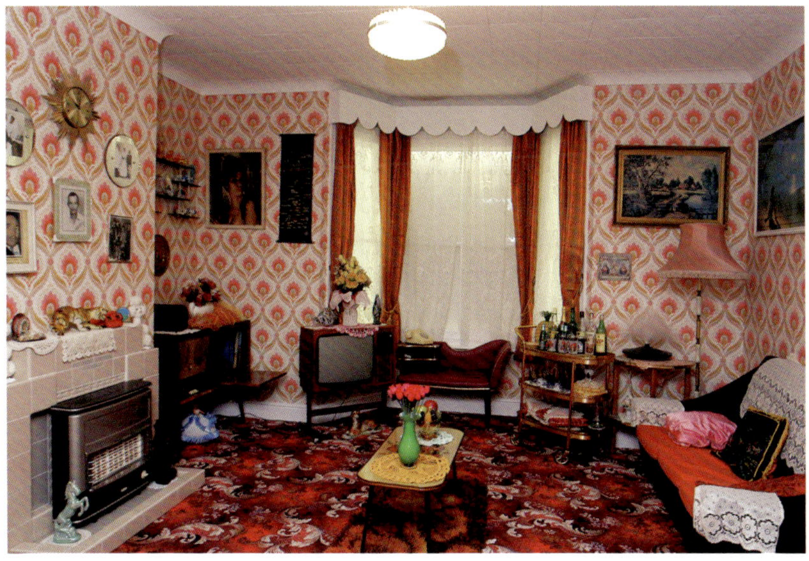

Figure 17.1. Michael McMillan, *The West Indian Front Room*, Geffrye Museum, London, 2005–2006. Installation comprising found objects, home furnishings, and wood. Dimensions variable. © Michael McMillan. Photograph, courtesy of John Nelligan, 2005.

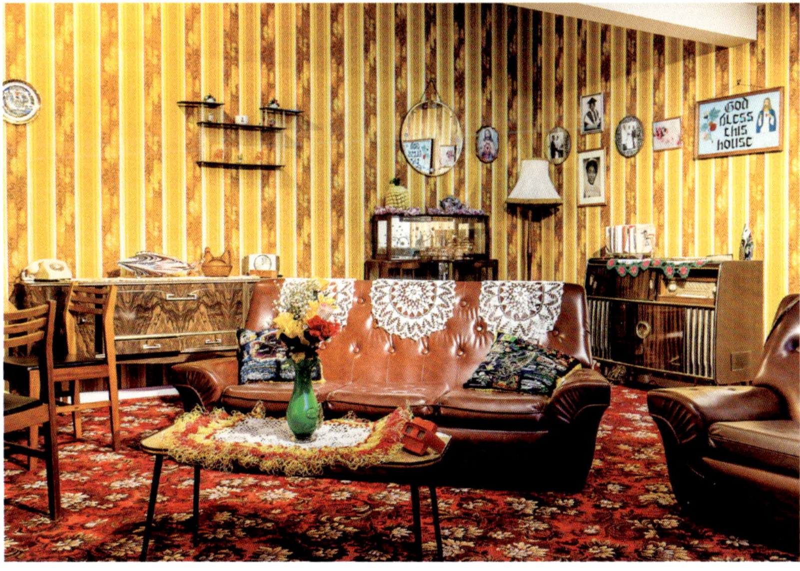

Figure 17.2. Michael McMillan, *The Front Room*, Museum of the Home (formerly Geffrye Museum), London, 2021–. Installation comprising found objects, home furnishings, and wood. Dimensions variable. © Michael McMillan. Photograph, courtesy of Em Fitzgerald and the artist, 2022.

one migrant space where there is a similar process of translation for both of them. The front room is not a pure African space unchanged over centuries, but it isn't a purely British space either. It is a hybrid space, constantly changing, constantly borrowing but adapting to a ground that is internally validated by its past history, which is itself very complicated. It's not just about "keeping up with the Jones'" although that may have happened in later stages in the West Indian front room with the arrival of the television, because if you didn't have one of those you weren't respected and like the radiogram and player and the glass cupboard and the green Chinese lady on the wall, it occupied a space almost like a sacred object. In a more consumer-orientated society, the West Indian front room took on consumerism; but it goes beyond that because, there, objects are revalorized by a way of being, a way of looking at life.

Second Generation

The 1970s and 1980s was an explosive moment in black British society. It's the moment of Pan-African consciousness, of roots music and Rastafarianism, and it's the moment of black resistance and of anti-racism. It's the moment of the sus laws and trouble with police. So this is the generation that is demonized publicly, this is the trouble generation throbbing to a kind of music and a language that its elders found difficult to understand. When West Indians first came to England they were perfectly intelligible when they spoke to one another. But no-one could understand the second generation. "Where did they get that way of talking from?" their parents inquired of one another. "They haven't even been to Kingston, Jamaica!" Partly, of course, they got it via the transistor and locally pressed tracks. The pulse had reached them across the Atlantic, and so had the language; the transistor brought the message and the whole place changed. A new black urban insurgent culture arose. It was also a moment of transformation for the front room.

How do the representatives of this new culture negotiate the front room? I don't know of any studies, but my impression is that these boys, who are the main carriers of this shift during the 1970s (this was not to last: the girls soon got into the act!), are *tamed* by the front room. You couldn't do such a study now because you would have to include girls, but even today the boys either don't go home or "straighten up" when they do, with no swearing or bringing any "bad boy" attitude from the street when they enter the front room. Not in here! I think they learned how to negotiate these two worlds: the street and the front room. They were the sons and they showed their mothers respect, whoever else they disrespected. And I speak of mothers because they are keepers of the ethos of the front room. Even though the father may be present, reading the evening paper or supping on Red Stripe, it is the mother who generates what the social order of this room is about. Men may occupy the front room but it is women who are the guardians of that sacred space. So "the youth" show their mothers respect, otherwise they don't come home; and that speaks to the power of this room as a cultural and social institution in shaping behaviour. Is any space symbolically more powerful than that?

The Sacred

The objects in the West Indian front room are invested with an element of the sacred. The sociologist Emile Durkheim once said that everything in life is social. But the social is either everywhere and everyday or specially marked off from the everyday, which means it is regarded as sacred. His use of the word "sacred" did not necessarily mean religion but that everything was marked out as belonging to either routine or special. The front room is a space marked out in this way and there are ways of investing the objects in it with the special attention associated with quasi-religious practices, where perfectly ordinary objects are lifted out of an everyday context and placed in a special context of worship and thereby take on a "sacred" dimension.

What I still have is a passionate attachment to the whole assembly—all of those objects in the same cramped space. I now live in a different sort of space, but the influence of the West Indian front room is not absent from it. The object that most reminds me of this is my piano, the top of which is packed out with photos of my grandchildren and other family members and occasions and events. I change them all the time but I can't get out of the habit, just like my grandmother who, if there was space on a table would always say, "Send me a photo!" I have an umbilical connection with constructing the space in that way and I understand what it means in terms of the absolute centrality of the family as an extended and expanded social unit to Caribbean life, whether there or here. I'm attached to the ways in which this space speaks of the capacity of West Indian people to make a distinctive life and style for themselves, wherever they are, often out of practically nothing.

NOTE

> This essay first appeared in *The Front Room: Migrant Aesthetics in the Home*, ed. Michael McMillan (London: Black Dog, 2009), 16–23.

CHAPTER 18

Constituting an Archive

To articulate the past historically does not mean to recognise it "the way it really was." It means to seize hold of a memory as it flashes up at a moment of danger. . . .
—Walter Benjamin

No archive arises out of thin air. Each archive has a "pre-history," in the sense of prior conditions of existence. We need to pay particular tribute to all those who have been involved over the years, often in very informal, personally taxing and under-funded ways, to secure in one place selections of the works, catalogues, exhibition notices, reviews and other texts relating to the artistic production of the black and Asian diaspora, without whom this moment of archival retrieval would not exist. Above all, we must acknowledge the role which Eddie Chambers has played in that long history, since without his patience and fierce commitment, against all odds, over several decades, no African and Asian Visual Artists' Archive (the AAVAA) would now exist.

Constituting an archive represents a significant moment, on which we need to reflect with care. It occurs at that moment when a relatively random collection of works, whose movement appears simply to be propelled from one creative production to the next, is at the point of becoming something more ordered and considered: an object of reflection and debate. The moment of the archive represents the end of a certain kind of creative innocence, and the beginning of a new stage of self-consciousness, of self-reflexivity in an artistic movement. Here the whole apparatus of "a history"—periods, key figures and works, tendencies, shifts, breaks, ruptures—slips silently into place. It was an especially bold move to bring together at that point a number of key figures, who had both contributed to the body of work and were willing to help secure, nourish, extend and contest the terms of its "archiving"; for this helped to underline the intention that this should be, not an inert museum of dead works, but a "living archive," whose construction must be seen as an on-going, never-completed project. Here, the task begins of bringing to the surface for critical attention what has existed, hitherto, only "in solution"—as it were, within the flow of the work itself. "The Living Archive" conference is thus both a kind of ending for one phase of work, and a kind of beginning for another. It was planned as one of a series of events—a continuous sort of "event"—designed to identify certain key questions and issues which will help us to identify what this archive can be said to represent and how we are to begin to think of and debate the post-war moment out of which it emerged, in a more concerted way.

In the idea of a "living archive of diaspora" all three terms need to be considered for the hidden implications they carry. "Living" means present, on-going, continuing, unfinished, open-ended. The new work which will come to constitute significant additions to the archive will not be the same as that which was produced earlier, but it will be related to that body of work, if only in terms of how it inflects or departs from it. This notion of "living" is strongly counterposed to the common meaning accorded to "tradition," which is seen to function like the prison-house of the past. As the Jamaican critic and anthropologist David Scott reminds us: "A tradition . . . is a special sort of discursive concept in the sense that it performs a distinctive labour; it seeks to connect, authoritatively, within the structure of its narrative, a relation among past, community and identity. A tradition therefore, is never neutral with respect to the values it embodies. Rather [it] operates in and through the stakes it constructs." Scott adds that everything hangs on "an embodied argument within—and especially between—the generations over . . . the meaning in the present of our past. . . . Everything hangs on that moment when a new reading of this signifier offers a doubt and a disagreement about those readings that have gone before, offers a respectful if agonistic challenge, and offers another interpretation. It is this ongoing dispute that is the stuff of discursive tradition."[1]

"Diaspora" is equally complex in its field of reference: and since, like so many similar terms, it is operating "under erasure," it too cannot be deployed without a certain deconstructive operation being performed. Of course, "diaspora" recognizes the specific place and subject matter involved, but it must also acknowledge the peculiar status of an archive situation, as C. L. R. James once put it, "in but not of Europe": located in that disjunctive, unsettled space between metropolis and periphery, "colonizer" and "colonized." The closed conception of diaspora rests on a binary conception of difference and identity. It stands in the relation of "copy" to that "original" culture from which it is endlessly doomed to be separated. "It is founded on the construction of an exclusionary frontier and depends on the construction of an 'Other' and a fixed opposition between inside and outside. But the syncretised configurations of [diasporas] require Derrida's notion of *différance*—differences that do not work through binaries, veiled boundaries that do not finally separate but double up as *places de passage*, and meanings that are positional and relational, always on the slide along a spectrum without end or beginning. Difference . . . is essential to meaning. But in a profoundly counter-intuitive move, [post-Saussurean] linguistics insists that meaning cannot be finally fixed. There is always the inevitable slippage in the open semiosis of culture, as that which seems fixed continues to be dialogically re-appropriated. The fantasy of a final meaning remains haunted by 'lack' or 'excess' but is never graspable in the plenitude of its presence to itself."[2] How much more true is this of the visual signifier, whose numinous reverberations are broad and deep, but whose power of reference is less precise than the linguistic sign?

Of course, "diasporic" does not prescribe the form of the work. Many different styles can shelter beneath the canopy of the diasporic. The modernisms of the inter-war and immediate post-war years, the documentary impulse, the politicized signifier of the Black Art Movement, the highly constructed image of the 1980s and after—all share in their different ways in the diasporic attitude. What I mean by "diasporic" is perhaps most succinctly captured by Kobena Mercer in his essay on "Diaspora Culture and the Dialogic Imagination."[3] He remarks that "Across a whole range of cultural forms, there is a 'syncretic' dynamic which critically appropriates elements from the master code of the dominant culture and 'creolizes' them, dis-articulating given signs and re-articulating their symbolic meaning otherwise." He describes this diasporic attitude in terms of an "interruption," which "seeks not to impose a language of its own . . . but to enter critically into existing configurations to re-open the closed structures into which they have ossified."[4]

Then there is "archive." Foucault, who uses "archive" in a distinctive way, makes a distinction between the "language" in which artists practice—its *langue*—and what he calls "the corpus," which he defines as the relatively inert body of works which happen to be produced and survived. The "archive" he thinks of as something which is between the two. An "archive" does have something specific in terms of its boundaries—though what has been said about location and "diaspora" means that what constitutes its boundaries in any specific case is not a natural "given" but remains to be critically specified. It is neither unified as a single collection from a single source, nor so amorphous as an inert corpus of work. An archive is a discursive formation; however, since the materials of an archive consist of a heterogeneity of topics and texts, of subjects and themes, what governs it as a "formation" is not easy to define. The temptation would be to group together only those things which seemed to be "the same." And Foucault does succumb for a moment to the idea of, perhaps, some unity of "style"—"a certain constant manner of statement." But he quickly rejects it. The fields he examined were not tightly-packed, continuous fields, but instead, "a series full of gaps, intertwined with one another, interplays of differences, distances, substitutions, transformations." The emphasis there is on how what we might call the field of an archive is marked by rupture, significant breaks, transformations, new and unpredicted departures. The trick seems to be not to try to describe it as if it were the *oeuvre* of a mythical collective subject, but in terms of what sense or regularity we can discover in its very *dispersion*. The critical effort is to discern the regularity in its heterogeneity—"an order in their successive appearances, correlations in their simultaneity, assignable positions in a common space, a reciprocal functioning, linked and hierarchised transformations."[5]

The application of this perspective of regularity-in-dissemination to a visual archive is hardly begun. But the emphasis on transformations is exemplary. To begin its application here may be one way of avoiding the futile struggle by any one position to hegemonize the whole field in perpetuity.

It is worth remembering how heterogeneous a practice collecting and archiving is. It is partly public, partly private. It includes those inert collections which have emerged, fortuitously, when odd individuals record or purchase works over time—works which may not be exhibited or accessible to anyone who is trying to do an archaeology of a practice. That is the most buried, most inaccessible, most unrecoverable end of the archive. At the other end are the public spaces which have conscious policies of collection and selection, of display and access, where complex, often hidden, criteria of value operate in a closed community of taste and authority beyond the reach of ordinary mortals. The nature of AAVAA's archive must take its place somewhere along this complicated spectrum.

The activity of archiving touches a range of professional skills and expertises. This includes those who produce the work and those curators who selectively display and situate the work, as well as critics and historians who create the informed climate in which the work is situated and who are involved in discussions and debates which embed the work itself in a network of associative meanings and interpretations. This reminds us of the complex ways in which artistic practice and historical conditions interpenetrate in any archival activity. This is especially the case in relation to work from the Afro-Caribbean and Asian diasporas since, in the absence of any sustained attention or critical dialogue within the dominant institutions of the art world, and given a systematic marginalization over the years (see, *inter alia*, Rasheed Araeen's *The Other Story*), practitioners themselves have been obliged to act first as curators, and now as archivists. Eddie Chambers, David A. Bailey and Rasheed Araeen are three obvious names which, among many others, spring to mind in this context.

This question has been transformed, qualitatively, in recent years by the new technological developments which are transforming the practice of archival collection, in ways which have an impact, not only on what and how much can be preserved, but on how widely it can be disseminated and circulated—on how a wider access to an archive can be instituted. There are brilliant archives which are closed to a wide-ranging critical discourse or to students wishing to familiarize themselves with the productions of former times, and which have, therefore, cut themselves off from the vitality of argument, debate and reinterpretation which make an archive live and change. The question of technology, of access and therefore inevitably of funding are as central to a "living archive" as the aesthetic, artistic and interpretative practices.

Foucault does suggest that an archive is inevitably heterogeneous; but it cannot simply be open-ended. It does not consist of simply opening the floodgates to any kind of production in any context, without any ordering or internal regularity of principle. He does, however, argue that it is not possible wholly to define an archive from within its rules. Partly because—especially in AAVAA's case—the very practice of putting the collection together is informed by practitioners who are themselves active participants in defining the archive. They may have contributed to it. They may have collected some of it. They have appreciated and helped to interpret it. They have learned from the work in their own practice: and this new work will, in turn, become candidates for inclusion. An archive of this kind is a continuous production. The archivist cannot bring to it principles from some abstract and disinterested aesthetic out there, from which a template of universal practice can be winnowed out and against which some criteria of inclusion and exclusion can be confidently applied. As David Scott reminded us, a tradition is an embodied discourse, which operates in and through the stakes—the investments—which it creates. Archiving in this context is a practice which both has its limits and its disciplines yet has no definitive sense of origin, boundary or termination.

It is impossible to describe an archive in its totality. The very idea of a "living archive" contradicts this fantasy of completeness. As work is produced, one is, as it were, contributing to and extending the limits of that to which one is contributing. It cannot be complete because our present practice immediately adds to it, and our new interpretations inflect it differently. An archive may be largely about "the past" but it is always "re-read" in the light of the present and the future: and in that reprise, as Walter Benjamin reminds us, it always flashes up before us as *a moment of danger*. Thus it is extremely important that archives are committed to inclusiveness, since it is impossible to foretell what future practitioners, critics and historians will want to make of it. The archive has to insist on a certain *heterodoxy*. It cannot afford to become the prisoner of a single "line," aesthetic principle or style, no matter how powerful and apparently universally valid. To do that is immediately to exclude, to cut out, to cut off the possibility of returning to the archive in the spirit of the genealogist who will map the relation of past configurations as part of "the history of the present" in radically different, unpredictable ways. Archives are not inert historical collections. They always stand in an active, dialogic, relation to the questions which the present puts to the past; and the present always puts its questions differently from one generation to another. The archive has to be rich, varied and in a sense "eclectic" enough to bear the weight of different contested interpretations and to allow them to battle out their differences in relation to the different texts and inter-texts which the archive itself makes available.

Consequently, heterogeneity, the multiplicity of discourses, not only of practice but of criticism, history and theory, of personal story, anecdote and biography, are the "texts" which make the archive live. Of course, as critic, practitioner, artist, historian, it is imperative to drive through the particular line of interpretation which animates one's work. But as *archivist*, it requires a certain withdrawal of investment, a certain disinterestedness, a certain respect for the work itself, for the practice of artists who have worked in contexts and paradigms different from one's own. It requires attention—even, humility—for the real discontinuities and contingency of history, since each archive must produce not only the continuities, the discursive links, between the practices of different artists operating at any one time, but also chart the paradigm shifts, the moments when the pattern or "periodic" breaks, when there is rupture, and new paradigms very different from earlier prescriptions come into place. The most important thing an archive can do is to ask or allow us to interrogate those moments of transition, because they are often also the moments of high creativity and we cannot see from our privileged position where those ruptures are most likely to occur or in what direction they are likely to lead. There is a major rupture of this kind in photography, painting and the visual arts, between the "modernist" and "difference" protagonists, between the embattled and politicized 1970s and early 1980s and what followed, or between "the black arts movement" and the "cultural politics" of succeeding decades. Perhaps it is time some of these fortified barricades were dismantled or at least lowered and the "struggle" conducted more profitably "in the light of the archive."

"The Living Archive" conference was hosted by the Tate Gallery (we must now say "Tate Britain," which contains its own bleak ironies); and its success owed much to the hospitality which Tate Britain offered. The Tate, in that sense, related in a supportive way to AAVAA's rebirth in a new form: but it is not churlish to remember that it also belongs to, indeed, was (until recently) *the* jewel in the crown of a British visual archival tradition of its own, which has never been conspicuously hospitable or open to diasporic work. Inevitably, the AAVAA archive must have an interrogatory relation to those dominant lines of continuity that the existing archival institutions put in place and sustain despite repeated challenge. The activity of "archiving" is thus always a critical one, always a historically located one, always a contestatory one, since archives are in part constituted within the lines of force of cultural power and authority; always one open to the futurity and contingency—the relative autonomy—of artistic practice; always, as we tried to define it earlier, an engagement, *an interruption* in a settled field, which is to enter critically into existing configurations to re-open the closed structures into which they have ossified.

NOTES

This essay first appeared in *Third Text* 15, no. 54 (2001): 89–92. It is based on a paper delivered at "The Living Archive" conference organized by the African and Asian Visual Artists' Archive (AAVAA) and held at the Tate Gallery (now Tate Britain) in London in March 1997.

1 David Scott, *Refashioning Futures: Criticism after Postcoloniality* (Princeton, NJ: Princeton University Press, 1999), 125, 123.

2 Stuart Hall, "Thinking the Diaspora: Home-Thoughts from Abroad," *Small Axe* 3, no. 6 (September, 1999): 1–18.

3 Kobena Mercer, "Diaspora Culture and the Dialogic Imagination," in *Black Frames: Critical Perspectives on Black Independent Cinema*, ed. Mbye Cham and Claire Andrade-Watkins (Cambridge, MA: MIT Press, 1988).

4 Mercer, "Diaspora Culture," citing David Silverman and Brian Torode, *The Material Word* (London: Routledge, 1980).

5 Michel Foucault, *The Archaeology of Knowledge* (London: Tavistock, 1972).

CHAPTER 19

Whose Heritage?
Unsettling "The Heritage," Reimagining the Post-Nation

This conference on "Whose Heritage?" provides an opportunity to look critically at the whole concept of "British Heritage" from the perspective of the multicultural Britain which has been emerging since the end of World War II. How is it being—and how should it be—transformed by the "Black British" presence and the explosion of cultural diversity and difference which is everywhere our lived daily reality?

In preparing to say something useful on this topic, I was struck again—as many of you may have been—by the quaintness of the very term, "Heritage." It has slipped so innocently into everyday speech! I take it to refer to the whole complex of organizations, institutions and practices devoted to the preservation and presentation of culture and the arts—art galleries, specialist collections, public and private, museums of all kinds (general, survey or themed, historical or scientific, national or local) and sites of special historical interest.

What is curious in the British usage is the emphasis given to preservation and conservation: to keeping what already exists—as opposed to the production and circulations of new work in different media, which takes a very definite second place. The British have always seen "culture" as a vaguely disquieting idea as if to name it is to make self-conscious what well-bred folk absorb unconsciously with their mother's milk. Ministries of Culture are what those old, now discredited, eastern European regimes used to have, which is altogether the wrong associations. Culture has entered the nomenclature of modern British government only when sandwiched alongside the more acceptably populist terms, "Media" and "Sport."

This gives the British idea of "Heritage" a peculiar inflection. The works and artefacts so conserved appear to be "of value" primarily in relation to the past. To be validated, they must take their place alongside what has been authorized as "valuable" on already established grounds in relation to the unfolding of a "national story" whose terms we already know. Heritage thus becomes the material embodiment of the spirit of the nation, a collective representation of the British version of *tradition*, a concept pivotal to the lexicon of English virtues.

This retrospective, nation-alized and tradition-alized conception of culture will return to haunt our subsequent thoughts at different points. However, it may also serve as a warning that *my* emphasis does include the active production of culture and the arts as a living activity, alongside the conservation of the past.

We spend an increasing proportion of the national wealth—especially since the National Lottery—on "Heritage." But what is it *for*? Obviously, to preserve for posterity things of value, whether on aesthetic or historical criteria. But that is only a start. From its earliest history in Western societies—in the heterogeneous assemblages of the "cabinets of curiosity and wonder"—collections have adorned the position of people of power and influence—kings, princes, popes, landowners and merchants—whose wealth and status they amplified. They have always been related to the exercise of "power" in another sense—the symbolic power to order knowledge, to rank, classify and arrange, and thus to give meaning to objects and things through the imposition of interpretative schemas, scholarship and the authority of connoisseurship. As Foucault observed, "there is no power relation without the relative constitution of a field of knowledge nor any knowledge that does not presuppose and constitute . . . power relations."[1]

Since the eighteenth century, collections of cultural artefacts and works of art have also been closely associated with informal public education. They have become part, not simply of "governing," but of the broader practices of "governmentality"—how the state indirectly and at a distance induces and solicits appropriate attitudes and forms of conduct from its citizens. The state is always, as Antonio Gramsci argued, "educative." Through its power to preserve and represent culture, the state has assumed some responsibility for educating the citizenry in those forms of "really useful knowledge," as the Victorians put it, which would refine the sensibilities of the vulgar and enhance the capacities of the masses. This was the true test of their "belong-ingness": culture as social incorporation.

It is important to remember that the nation-state is both a political and territorial entity, *and* what Benedict Anderson has called "an imagined community."[2] Though we are often strangers to one another, we form an "imagined community" because we share an *idea* of the nation and what it stands for, which we can "imagine" in our mind's eye. A shared national identity thus depends on the cultural meanings which bind each member individually into the larger national story. Even so-called "civic" states, like Britain, are deeply embedded in specific "ethnic" or cultural meanings which give the abstract idea of the nation its lived "content."

The national Heritage is a powerful source of such meanings. It follows that those who cannot see themselves reflected in its mirror cannot properly "belong." Even the museums and collections apparently devoted to surveying the universal, rather than the national, achievements of culture—like the British Museum, the Louvre, or the Metropolitan Museum in New York—are harnessed into the national story. Carol Duncan and Alan Wallach have argued that these institutions "claim the heritage of the classical tradition for contemporary society and equate that tradition with the very notion of civilization itself."[3] Much the same could be said about the museums of Modern or Contemporary Art in terms of the way they have colonized the very idea of "the modern," "modernity" and "modernism" as exclusively "Western" inventions.

Heritage is bound into the meaning of the nation through a double inscription. What the nation means is essentialized: "the English seem unaware that anything fundamental has changed since 1066."[4] Its essential meaning appears to have emerged at the very moment of its origin—a moment always lost in the myths, as well as the mists, of time—and then successively embodied as a distilled essence in the various arts and artefacts of the nation for which the Heritage provides the archive. In fact, what the nation "means" is an on-going project, under constant reconstruction. We come to know its meaning partly *through* the objects and artefacts which have been made to stand for and symbolize its essential values. Its meaning is constructed *within*, not above or outside, representation. It is through identifying with these representations that come to be its "subjects"—by "subjecting" ourselves to its dominant meanings. What would "England" *mean* without its cathedrals, churches, castles and country houses, its gardens, thatched cottages and hedge-rowed landscapes, its Trafalgars, Dunkirks and Mafekings, its Nelsons and its Churchills, its Elgars and its Benjamin Brittens?

We should think of Heritage as a discursive practice. It is one of the ways in which the nation slowly constructs for itself a sort of collective social memory. Just as individuals and families construct their identities in part by "storying" the various random incidents and contingent turning points of their lives into a single, coherent, narrative, so nations construct identities by selectively binding their chosen high points and memorable achievements into an unfolding "national story." This story is what is called "Tradition." As the Jamaican anthropologist David Scott recently observed, "A tradition . . . seeks to connect authoritatively, within the structure of its narrative, a relation among past, community, an identity." He goes on to argue that,

> A tradition therefore is never neutral with respect to the values it embodies. Rather a tradition operates in and through the stakes it constructs—what is to count and what is not to count among its satisfactions, what the goods and excellences and virtues are that ought to be valued. . . . On this view . . . if tradition presupposes "a common possession" it does not presuppose uniformity or plain consensus. Rather it depends upon a play of conflict and contention. It is a space of dispute as much as of consensus, of discord as much as accord.[5]

Heritage is also a classic example of the operation of what Raymond Williams called the "selective tradition":

> Theoretically a period is recorded; in practice, this record is absorbed into a selective tradition; and both are different from the culture as lived. . . . To some extent the selection begins within the period itself . . . though that does not mean that the values and emphases will later be confirmed.[6]

Like personal memory, social memory is also highly selective, it highlights and foregrounds, imposes beginnings, middles and ends on the random and contingent. Equally, it foreshortens, silences, disavows, forgets and elides many episodes which—from another perspective—could be the start of a different narrative. This process of selective "canonization" confers authority and a material and institutional facticity on the selective tradition, making it extremely difficult to shift or revise. The institutions responsible for making the "selective tradition" work develop a deep investment in their own "truth."

Heritage inevitably reflects the governing assumptions of its time and context. It is always inflected by the power and authority of those who have colonized the past, whose versions of history matter. These assumptions and co-ordinates of power are inhabited as natural—given, timeless, true and inevitable. But it takes only the passage of time, the shift of circumstances, or the reversals of history, to reveal those assumptions as time- and context-bound, historically specific, and thus open to contestation, renegotiation and revision.

This is therefore an appropriate moment to ask, then, who is Heritage *for*? It is intended for those who "belong"—a society which is imagined as, in broad terms, culturally homogeneous and unified.

It is long past time to radically question this foundational assumption.

It is, of course, undeniable that Britain has been in recent times a relatively settled society and "culture." But as something approaching a nation-state, the United Kingdom of Great Britain and Ireland (subsequently "and Northern Ireland") is in fact a relatively recent historical construct, a product of the eighteenth, nineteenth and twentieth centuries. Britain itself was formed out of a series of earlier invasions, conquests and settlements—Celts, Romans, Saxons, Vikings, Normans, Angevins—whose "traces" are evident in the palimpsest of the national language. The Act of Union linked Scotland, England and Wales into a united kingdom, but never on terms of cultural equality—a fact constantly obscured by the covert oscillations and surreptitious substitutions between the terms "Britishness" and "Englishness."[7]

The Act of Settlement (1701) secured a Protestant ascendancy, drawing the critical symbolic boundary between the Celtic/Catholic and the Anglo-Saxon/Protestant traditions. Between 1801 (the date of the Act of Union which brokered Ireland into the Union) and Partition in 1922, the national story proved incapable of incorporating "Irishness" into "Britishness" or of integrating Irish Catholic migrants into an imagined "Englishness." Their culture and presence remain marginalized today.

Though relatively stable, English society has always contained within it profound differences. There were always different ways of being "English." It was always fissured along class, gender and regional lines. What came to be known, misleadingly, as "*the* British way of life" is really another name for a particular settlement of structured social inequalities. Many of the great achievements which have been retrospectively written into the national lexicon as primordial English virtues—the rule of law, free speech, a fully-representative franchise, the rights of combination, the National Health Service, the welfare state itself—were struggled for by some of the English and bitterly resisted by others. Where, one asks, is this deeply ruptured and fractured history, with its interweaving of stability and conflict, in Heritage's version of the dominant national narrative?

The British empire was the largest *imperium* of the modern world. The very notion of "greatness" in Great Britain is inextricably bound up with its imperial destiny. For centuries, its wealth was underpinned, its urban development driven, its agriculture and industry revolutionized, its fortunes as a nation settled, its maritime and commercial hegemony secured, its thirst quenched, its teeth sweetened, its cloth spun, its food spiced, its carriages rubber-wheeled, its bodies adorned, through the imperial connection. Anyone who has been watching the Channel 4 series on *The Slave Trade*, or the "hidden history" of the West India Regiment, or the bbc's *The Boer War* will not need reminding how deeply intertwined were the facts of colonization, slavery and empire with the everyday life of all classes and conditions of English men and women. The emblems of empire do, of course, fitfully appear in the Heritage. However, in general, "empire" is increasingly subject to a widespread selective amnesia and disavowal. And when it does appear, it is largely narrated from the viewpoint of the colonizers. Its master narrative is sustained in the scenes, images and the artefacts which testify to Britain's success in imposing its will, culture and institutions, and inscribing its civilizing mission across the world. This formative strand in the national culture is now re-presented as an external appendage, extrinsic and inorganic to the domestic history and culture of the English social formation.

Despite all this, the idea of Heritage *has* had to respond to at least two major challenges. The first we may call the democratization process. Increasingly, the lives, artefacts, houses, work-places, tools, customs and oral memories of ordinary everyday British folk have slowly taken their subordinate place alongside the hegemonic presence of the great and the good. The inclusion of domestic vernacular architecture and the agrarian and industrial revolutions, together with the explosion of interest in "history from below," the spread of local and family history, of personal memorabilia and the collection of oral histories—activities witnessed to in, for example, Raphael Samuel's memorable celebration of the "popular heritage," *Theatres of Memory*—have shifted and democratized our conception of value, of what is and is not worth preserving.[8] A few courageous if controversial steps have been taken in our direction—the Liverpool Museum on the Slave Trade, the Maritime Museum's re-hang. However, by and large, this process has so far stopped short at the frontier defined by that great unspoken British value—"whiteness."

The second "revolution" arises from the critique of the Enlightenment ideal of dispassionate universal knowledge, which drove and inspired so much of Heritage activity in the past. This has to be coupled with a rising cultural relativism which is part of the growing de-centring of the West and Western-oriented or Eurocentric grand-narratives. From the "*Magiciens de la Terre*" exhibition at the Pompidou Centre in Paris in 1989, on through the "*Te Maori*" exhibition from New Zealand at the Metropolitan Museum of New York, the "Paradise" exhibition from New Guinea at the Museum of Mankind, "The Spirit Sings" exhibition of Canada's "first peoples" at Calgary, the "Perspectives: Angles on African Art" at the Centre for African Art in New York, and on and on, the exhibiting of "other cultures"—often performed with the best of liberal intentions, has proved controversial. The questions—"Who should control the power to represent?" "Who has the authority to re-present the culture of others?"—have resounded through the museum corridors of the world, provoking a crisis of authority.

These two developments mark a major transformation in our relation to the activity of constructing a "Heritage." They in turn reflect a number of conceptual shifts in what we might loosely call the intellectual culture. A list of these shifts would have to include—a radical awareness by the marginalized of the symbolic power involved in the activity of representation; a growing sense of the centrality of culture and its relation to *identity*; the rise amongst the excluded of a "politics of recognition" alongside the older politics of equality; a growing reflexivity about the constructed and thus contestable nature of the authority which some people acquire to "write the culture" of others; a decline in the acceptance of the traditional authorities in authenticating the interpretative and analytic frameworks which classify, place, compare and evaluate culture; and the concomitant rise in the demand to reappropriate control over the "writing of one's own story" as part of a wider process of cultural liberation, or—as Frantz Fanon and Amilcar Cabral once put it—"the decolonization of the mind." In short, a general relativization of "truth," "reason" and other abstract Enlightenment values, and an increasingly perspectival and context-related conception of truth-as-interpretation—of "truth" as an aspect of what Michel Foucault calls the "will to power."

Each of these developments would take a whole lecture on their own to elaborate. But I take them here as together marking an unsettling and subversion of the foundational ground on which the process of Heritage-construction has until very recently proceeded. We see it reflected in different ways: in how the texts supporting art works and framing exhibits are written by museums; in the attempts to make explicit the "perspective" which has governed the selection and the interpretative contextualization, so as to make it more open to challenge and reinterpretation; in the exposing of underlying assumptions of value, meaning and connection as part of a more dialogic relationship between the cultural institutions and their audiences; and in the tentative efforts to involve the "subjects" themselves in the exhibiting process which objectifies them. These are only some of the manifest signs of a deep slow-motion revolution in progress in the practices of cultural representation.

They have taken hold, but are certainly not yet extensively or ubiquitously deployed in the institutional complex of the British Heritage "industry" as a whole. Their appearance is at best patchy, more honoured in the breach—in profession of good intentions—than actual practice. Nevertheless, the question "Whose Heritage?," posed in the context of the current "drift" towards a more multicultural Britain, has to be mounted on the back of this emerging "turn." I take the appearance of "cultural diversity" as a key policy priority of the newly restructured Arts Council, its greater visibility in statements of intent by the government and the Ministry of Culture, Media and Sport, the recent efforts by the British Council to project a more "diverse" image of British culture abroad, and even the much-delayed declaration of a "Year of cultural diversity"—two years after Amsterdam, but much to be welcomed nevertheless—as potential but uncertain harbingers of change.

Suppose this *were* to turn out to be a propitious moment. What would those new constituencies who feel themselves woefully inadequately represented in the mirror of culture which Heritage holds up to British society want out of it?

It goes without saying that we would need more money specifically targeted at this objective. The corners of the government's mouth tend to drop significantly when the money and material resources required to meet objectives are mentioned, and the weary muttering about "not simply throwing money at the problem" rises to a quiet crescendo. However, the idea that a major culture-change—nothing short of a cultural revolution—could take place in the way the nation represents the diversity of itself and its "subject-citizens" without a major redirection of resources is to reveal oneself as vacantly trivial about the whole question.

In fact, however, money really *is* not enough. For if my arguments are correct, then an equally powerful obstacle to change is the deep institutional investment which the key organizations have in going and doing things in the ways in which they have always been done; and the operational inertia militating against key professionals re-examining their criteria of judgement and their gate-keeping practices from scratch and trying to shift the habits of a professional lifetime. It will require a substantially enhanced programme of training and recruitment for curators, professionals and artists from the "minority" communities, so that they can bring their knowledge and expertise to bear on transforming dominant curatorial and exhibitory habits. It also will take the massive leverage of a state and government committed to producing, *in reality rather than in name*, a more culturally diverse, socially just, equal and inclusive society and culture, and *holding its cultural institutions to account*. There are some straws in the wind and a lot of wordage, but so far no consistent sign of this.

Nevertheless, it seems to me that *we* have here an opportunity to clarify our own minds and to refine our agendas so that we can seize every opportunity to challenge institutions, shift resources, change priorities, move practices strategically in the right direction. The rest of my talk is devoted to this task of clarification.

We need a better idea of who the "we" are in whose name these changes are being articulated. Principally, we have in mind the so-called "ethnic minority communities" from the Caribbean and Indian sub-continent, whose presence in large numbers since the 1950s has transformed Britain into a multicultural society, together with the smaller groups of non-European minorities from Africa, the Middle East, China and the Far East and Latin America. Their impact on diversifying British society and culture has been immediate and significant. It may therefore surprise you to hear me say that it is really very complex to understand how appropriately these communities should now be culturally represented in mainstream British cultural and artistic institutions. Our picture of them is defined primarily by their "otherness"—their *minority* relationship to something vaguely identified as "the majority," their cultural difference from European norms, their non-whiteness, their "marking" by ethnicity, religion and "race." This is a negative figuration, reductive and simplistic.

These are people who have formed communities in Britain which are both distinctively marked, culturally, and yet have never been separatist or exclusive. Some traditional cultural practices are maintained—in varied ways—and carry respect. At the same time, the degrees and forms of attachment are fluid and changing—constantly negotiated, especially between men and women, within and across groups, and above all, across the generations. Traditions coexist with the emergence of new, hybrid and crossover cultural forms of tremendous vitality and innovation. These communities are in touch with their differences, without being saturated by tradition.

They are actively involved with every aspect of life around them, without the illusion of assimilation and identity. This is a new kind of difference—the difference which is not binary (either-or) but whose *"différances"* (as Jacques Derrida has put it) will not be erased, or traded.[9]

Their lives and experiences have been shaped by traditions of thought, religious and moral values, very different from the Judeo-Christian and classical traditions whose "traces" still shape "Western" culture; and by the historical experience of oppression and marginalization. Many are in touch with cultures and languages which pre-date those of the "West." Nevertheless, colonization long ago convened these cultural differences under the "canopy" of a sort of imperial empty "global" time, without ever effectively erasing the disjunctures and dislocations of time, place and culture by its ruptural intrusion into their "worlds." This is the palimpsest of the postcolonial world. These communities are, as C. L. R. James once put it, "in but not of Europe."[10] Nevertheless, they have known "Europe" for three or four centuries as what Ashis Nandy, in his unforgettable phrase, calls "intimate enemies."[11] They are what David Scott has called "conscripts of modernity." They have dwelled for many years, and long before migration, in the double or triple times of colonization, and now occupy the multiple frames, the in-between or "third" spaces—the homes-away-from-homes—of the postcolonial metropolis.

No single programme or agenda could adequately represent this cultural complexity—especially their "impossible" desire to be treated and represented with justice (that is, as "the same") simultaneously with the demand for the recognition of "difference." The agenda will itself have to be open and diverse, representing a situation which is already crosscut by new and old lateral connections and reciprocal global influences and which refuses to stand still or stabilize. We ourselves should recognize that there will be many complementary but different ways of being represented, just as there are many different ways of "being black."

Without becoming too specific, what would be the basic elements or building blocks of such an agenda?

First, there is the demand that the majority, mainstream versions of Heritage should revise their own self-conceptions and rewrite the margins into the center, the outside into the inside. This is not so much a matter of representing "us" as of representing more adequately the degree to which "their" history entails and has always implicated "us," across the centuries, and vice versa. The African presence in Britain since the sixteenth century, the Asian since the seventeenth and the Chinese, Jewish and Irish in the nineteenth have long required to be made the subjects of their own dedicated heritage spaces as well as integrated into a much more "global" version of "our island story." Across the great cities and ports, in the making of fortunes, in the construction of great houses and estates, across the lineages of families, across the plunder and display of the wealth of the world as an adjunct to the imperial enterprise, across the hidden histories of statued heroes, in the secrecy of private diaries, even at the center of the great master-narratives of "Englishness" like the two world wars, falls the unscripted shadow of the forgotten "Other." The first task, then, is redefining the nation, reimagining "Britishness" or "Englishness" itself in a more profoundly inclusive manner. The Brits owe this, not to only us, but to themselves: for to prepare their own people for success in a global and de-centred world by continuing to misrepresent Britain as a closed, embattled, self-sufficient, defensive, "tight little island" would be fatally to disable them.

This is not only a matter of history. London and other major cities have been, throughout this century, "world cities," drawing to themselves the creative talents of nations far and wide, and standing at the centre of tremendously varied cross-cultural flows and lateral artistic influences. Many distinguished practitioners who chose to live and work in Britain—Ronald Moody, Aubrey Williams, Francis Souza, Avinash Chandra, Anwar Jalal Shemza, David Medalla, Li Yuan Chia, Frank Bowling, and many others—have been quietly written out of the record. Not British enough for the Tate, not international enough for Bankside, I guess. The ways in which the "modernist" impulse in Western art drew inspiration from what it defined as "primitive" is now an art-historical cliché. But the numbers of non-European artists who played a central part in European, and especially British, modernism is far less widely acknowledged—what Rasheed Araeen called, in his historic retrospective in 1989, "The (Largely Untold) Other Story." The existence of major "other modernisms," with their own indigenous roots elsewhere, passes without serious attention. The incontestable truth of the observation that "The search for a new identity expressed in modern forms has been the common denominator of most contemporary art movements in Africa" is, for Western curators and art-historians, still a well-kept secret.[12]

Then, secondly, there is the enormous, unprecedented, creative explosion by contemporary practitioners from the so-called "minority" communities in all the arts (painting, visual arts, photography, film, theatre, literature, dance, music, multi-media) which has marked the last three decades. Unless this work is funded and exhibited, young talent and promise will simply dribble away. And it needs to be said loud and clear that this is not work which is likely immediately to appeal to the new culture-heroes of the art world—the corporate sponsors—who are already in search of their next Monet outing at some prestigious venue. For a time, the work of contemporary artists from the minority communities was patronisingly secured within an "ethnic" enclave, as if only non-European work reflected the cultural idioms in which they were composed—as if only "we" had "ethnicities." However, the movement has long ago breached its boundaries and flooded—but only when permitted by the cultural gate-keepers—into the mainstream. Its visibility has depended largely on a few pioneering figures and the efforts of a whole fleet of small, local and community-based galleries.

Like the rainbow, this work comes and goes. Major practitioners surface and pass quietly from view into an early and undeserved obscurity. Their work occasionally surfaces in mainstream venues—and has an innovative vitality which much "indigenous" work lacks. But they cannot be properly "heritaged." The critical records, catalogues and memorabilia of this great tide of creative work in the visual arts since the 1980s, for example—from which, one day the histories and critical studies of black diaspora visual culture will be written—existed for many years in boxes in a filing cabinet in Eddie Chambers's bedroom in Bristol, before they found a resting place in AAVAA, the Asian and African Visual Arts Archive, courtesy of the University of East London. No proper archive, no regular exhibitions, no critical apparatus (apart from a few key journals like *Third Text* and the now-defunct *Ten-8*), no definitive histories, no reference books, no comparative materials, no developing scholarship, no passing-on of a tradition of work to younger practitioners and curators, no recognition of achievement amongst the relevant communities . . . Heritage-less.

Thirdly, there is the record of the migrant experience itself. This is a precious record of the historical formation of a black diaspora in the heart of Europe—probably a once-in-a-life-time event—still *just* within living memory of its participants. Anyone who watched the *Windrush* programmes and listened to their moving and articulate interviews; or saw the images which Autograph (The Association of Black Photographers) helped to research and mount at the Pitzhanger Gallery in Ealing; or read the first-hand evidence of the political struggles of the period 1940–90 being put together by the unfunded George Padmore series edited by a veteran figure—John LaRose— whose autobiography we await; will know the rich evidence in visual imagery and oral testimonies which is waiting to be consolidated into a major archive.

It needs, of course, to be, supplemented by extensive oral histories, personal accounts, documents and artefacts, from which, alone, "the black experience" in Britain since the 1950s could be recreated. We know, from a few bold efforts to build the everyday concerns of migrant people into "daily life" local exhibitions (for example by the adventurous Walsall Museum and Art Gallery) of the rich and complex details—customs, cuisine, daily habits, family photographs and records, household and religious objects—which remain to be documented in these domestic settings, poised as they are on the edge of and constantly negotiating between different "worlds." There is no such systematic work in progress though the Black Cultural Archives with its recent Lottery grant *may* at last be able to make a small start on oral histories. Some selective attempts have been made to do this for some Afro-Caribbean communities. So far as I know, there is very little comparable work as yet on the Asian experience(s). Heritage? *Which Heritage?*

Fourthly, there is the question of those "traditions of origin," so often deployed to represent minority communities as immured in their "ethnicity" or differentiated into another species altogether by their "racialised difference." These "traditions" are occasionally on view in performances by visiting companies, framed as an exotic entertainment. But in general terms, the public is deeply uninformed about them. The complexities of practice, interpretation and belief of Hinduism or Islam as world systems of religious belief are virtually a closed book, even to the intelligentsia. The long, highly complex and refined traditions of Indian music or dance, the key texts, poets and novelists, of these great civilizations, the extraordinarily varied cultural history of the Indian subcontinent itself, are beyond the reach of even the well-educated. Equally obscure are the complexities of tribe, language and ethnicity in sub-Saharan Africa.

These basic building blocks of the new global universe we inhabit confront a blank and uncomprehending provincial "Englishness" as if fitfully glimpsed from outer space. Beyond sea, sun, sand, reggae and ganja, the fantastic intricacies of the "transculturation" of European, African and Indian elements over centuries, which have produced the variety and vibrancy of Caribbean "creole" cultures, is another Great Unknown. Latin America with its highly evolved Hispanic and Amerindian cultures may well be less familiar than the surface of Mars. The "peculiarity" of Afro-Caribbeans— that they are simultaneously deeply familiar because they have lived with the British for so long, and ineradicably different because they are black—is regarded by most of the British (who have never been asked by their "Heritage" to spare it a thought) as culturally inexplicable. Here, the National Curriculum and the truncated remnant of history as a discipline which remains, with only its most simplistic relationship to notions of "Heritage" intact, has done irreparable damage.

And yet many of the creative talents of these communities are still "framed" within a familiarity with the practices of these richly-traditional arts, so deeply are they interwoven with the textures of a lived culture itself; and even new and experimental work draws on their repertoires, idioms and languages of representation. Unless the younger generation has access to these cultural repertoires and can understand and practice them, to some extent at least, from the inside, they will lack the resources—the cultural capital—of their own "heritage," as a base from which to engage other traditions. They will in effect be culturally "monolingual" if not silenced—literally, deprived of the capacity to speak—in a world which requires us all to be or become culturally bi- if not multi-lingual.

There is no intrinsic contradiction between the preservation and presentation of "other cultures" and my fifth point—the engagement with the production of new diasporic forms. The popular culture of our society especially has been transformed by the rich profusion of contemporary hybrid or "crossover" cultural forms—in music, dance, street-style, fashion, film, multi-media—which mark the production of "the new" and the transgressive alongside the traditional and the "preservation of the past." Here, "modernity" (or postmodernity) is not waiting on some authority to "permit" or sanction this exploration of creativity in contemporary media and form. This is the leading-edge cultural phenomenon of our time—the "multi" in multicultural, the "Cool" in "Cool Britannia." For a time, black Afro-Caribbeans were in the vanguard of these avant-garde cultural practices, like cultural navigators crossing without passports between ragga, jungle, scratch, rap and electro-funk. In recent years, they have been decisively joined by the "disorienting rhythms" of Asian youth. Perhaps this aspect of cultural production needs to "archive" or "heritage." But it is proceeding unrecorded and unanalyzed, consigned to the ephemera of its day—expendable. Yet it represents one of the most important cultural developments of our time: the stakes which "the margins" have in modernity, the local-in-the-global, the pioneering of a new cosmopolitan, vernacular, post-national, global sensibility.

What I have offered is a wholly inadequate sketch—leaving out whole tracts of activity and countless examples aside. The account is inevitably skewed by my own interests and preoccupations. The detail does not matter.

What matters is some greater clarity about "the big picture." I have tried to suggest not only *what* but *why* the question of "Heritage" is of such timely and critical importance for our folks at this time. "British" most of us were, at one time, but that was long ago and, besides, as Shakespeare said, "the wench is dead." "English" we cannot be. But tied in our fates and fortunes with "the others"—while steadfastly refusing to have to *become* "other" to belong—we do, after all, have a stake, an investment, in this phase of globalization, in what I might call "the post-nation." But only if it can be reimagined—reinvented— to include us. That is the bet, the wager, the gamble we are here to discuss.

NOTES

This essay first appeared in *Third Text* 13, no. 49 (Winter 1999–2000): 3–13. It is the text of Stuart Hall's keynote speech given on November 1, 1999, at the national conference "Whose Heritage? The Impact of Cultural Diversity on Britain's Living Heritage," which took place at G-Mex, Manchester, England.

1 Michel Foucault, *Discipline and Punish* (London: Tavistock, 1977).

2 Benedict Anderson, *Imagined Communities* (London: Verso, 1983).

3 Carol Duncan and Alan Wallach, "The Universal Survey Museum," *Art History* 3, no. 4 (December 1980): 451.

4 Norman Davies, "But We Never Stand Quite Alone," *Guardian*, 13 November 1999.

5 David Scott, *Refashioning Futures: Criticism after Post-coloniality* (Princeton, NJ: Princeton University Press, 1999).

6 Raymond Williams, *The Long Revolution* (Harmondsworth: Penguin, 1961).

7 On this whole question, see Norman Davies, *The Isles, a History* (Basingstoke: Macmillan, 1999).

8 Raphael Samuel, *Theatres of Memory* (London: Verso, 1997).

9 Jacques Derrida, *Margins of Philosophy* (Brighton: Harvester, 1982).

10 C. L. R. James, "Popular Art and the Cultural Tradition," *Third Text* 4, no. 10 (Spring 1990): 3–10.

11 Ashis Nandy, *The Intimate Enemy* (New Delhi: Oxford University Press, 1983).

12 Salah Hassan, "The Modernist Experience in African Art: Visual Expressions of the Self and Cross-Cultural Aesthetics," in *Reading the Contemporary: African Art from Theory to Market Place*, ed. Olu Oguibe and Okwui Enwezor (London: Institute of International Visual Arts).

CHAPTER 20

Modernity and Its Others: Three "Moments" in the Post-war History of the Black Diaspora Arts

How are we to write the histories of non-Western societies in relation to modernity? Modernity is, as we know, an extremely slippery signifier, and appears here with as many quote marks as I can muster: and "the modern" in its many derivatives—early modern, late modern, postmodern, modernity, modernism—has long been effectively appropriated to the story of the West, monopolizing for Western civilization the privilege of living to the full the potentialities of the present "from the inside." It is therefore difficult to imagine this story in any way other than as a binary polarity: modernity and its "Others." Only two narrative alternatives then seem possible. Either the story is told from within the perspective of modernity itself: in which case it is difficult to prevent it becoming a triumphalist narrative in which the "others" are permanently marginalized. Or one reorients the story within its margins, seeking by this move to reverse and disrupt the normalized order of things by bringing into visibility all that cannot be seen from, or is structurally obscured by, the usual vantage point.

This "turning-the-world-upside-down" move has generated many of the critical histories of our time—histories from below; histories of subordinated peoples, genders, classes, races; subaltern histories; the histories of the conquered and the colonized, the exploited and the oppressed; of "peoples without a history." This has constituted an astonishing revolution in thought and learning, in knowledge, scholarship and research, in political narrative and popular memory. Perhaps, in a more conservative time, the tide is beginning to turn against this critical current, as education and learning become more instrumentalized. But where would the contemporary humanities be now without it?

Yet this reversal strategy has its limitations too. Since the inaugural moment of the colonial encounter between the West and the rest at roughly the end of the fifteenth century—the moment of the first of many globalizations—it has been increasingly difficult to encompass the relationship of modernity to its others within this binary structure. This is the achievement of the postcolonial and post-imperial historians and critics, who have insisted on trying to narrate these different times and places together: not as "the same"—for they are not the same—but as connected; connected, not despite, but *through* their differences. Since then, it has been impossible, within the narrative of modernity, to keep separate and inviolable "in here" from "out there." "There" was "here," materially and symbolically: in the raw materials and finished goods, the resources and commodities, the revenues and profits, the products of forced labour, and free; in the imported tastes and delicacies, in the refinement of sensibilities and the marking of distinctions, which made possible, and constituted, modernity; above all, in the modern imaginary, forming the subjects and constituting the "outside" in relation to which, alone, modern subjectivities are constituted. "There" was "here"—in the cups of tea that soothed a savage breast and eased a troubled heart, the silks that adorned the bodies and houses, even in the sugar and sweetmeats that rotted a million civilized teeth. "Here" was "there"—in the trading ports, the plantations, mines and markets, the conquering armies and naval fortifications, the systems of colonial administration, of governance and education, the churches and schoolrooms: sustained by the ceaseless tides of migration, to and fro, the formation of the "world" as potentially one market, in short, the relations of capitalist modernity as a global enterprise and the sinews of empire, which drew these different worlds together and ineradicably implicated their pasts and futures with one another.

Modernity and its "Others": interconnected—but were they, therefore, the same? Certainly not. Much of the history of the world remains "outside," or at least moving to a different rhythm, though not untouched by these modern forces. But the way difference was lived after the violent rupture of colonization was and had to be different from how these cultures would have developed had they done so in isolation from one another. Thereafter, they were coupled—conscripted—to modernity. There is, of course—even now, in the latest phase of globalization—no "empty, homogenous (Western or global) time." There are only "the condensations and ellipses," the endless discrepancies and displacements, the syncretisms, mimicries, resistances and translations, which arise when all the different temporalities, while remaining "present" to each other and "real" in their differential effects, are also over-written—rupturally convened—in relation to a disjunctive time, a "combined and uneven development." They must mark their differences, their disjunctive rhythms, within the framework of the overdetermining effects of Western temporalities, systems of representation and power. This is the overdetermined, sutured, and supplementary character of "modern times," the dislocated and over-centered character of "the global," which follows from re-phrasing colonization as a world event with pertinent and continuing effects within the framework of globalization.

The Caribbean was always a paradigmatic instance of this larger pattern. The indigenous peoples having by and large failed to survive the conquest, the region was thoroughly remade by drawing elements from across the globe into plantation slavery, and constructing a system and social order, subaltern and subordinated in relation to the metropolitan "elsewhere"; and which, in its subsequent development, was shaped in its very differences and inequalities, and its subjects formed, by modern power in its colonial form. C. L. R. James, the great Caribbean Marxist historian of the Haitian Revolution, the only successful slave revolution of modern times, among others, has always argued that the Caribbean, as David Scott recently put it, "begins in the ordering structure of power and reason that constitutes colonial modernity." This was, as Scott remarks, to be conscripted to a process at one and the same time "civilizing" and "demoralizing."[1] Writing later about the formation of the black diaspora in Britain in the 1950s, James observed that "Those people who are in western civilization, who have grown up in it but yet are not completely a part (made to feel and themselves feeling that they are outside) have a unique insight into their society. . . . What such persons have to say will give a new vision, a deeper and stronger insight into both western civilization and the black people in it."[2]

I.

In what follows, I try to explore these preliminary thoughts on the relation between modernity and its "Others" through the example of the work in the visual arts produced by artists from the black and colonial diasporas. The purpose of the paper is to identify and roughly characterise three "moments" in this history of the black diaspora visual arts in post-war Britain. My aim is not only to continue the project of inserting this "constitutive outside" into the center of "our island story," but—in choosing the visual arts as my point of departure—to do so from an unexpected angle. But first, some words of clarification. "Black" is a highly contested term—a slippery signifier—whose referent, since the emergence of a sizable black diaspora in Britain the 1950s, has been under almost constant reconstruction. It is used here with a deliberate imprecision; deriving from the 1970s, when the term "black" encompassed all the minority migrant communities, without the careful discrimination of ethnic, racial, regional, national and religious distinctions which has since become *de rigeur*. I hope it goes without saying that it is used here, not as the marker of an ineradicable genetic racial imprint but as a signifier of *différance*: a set of differences which, being social and historical, are therefore always changing, always located, always articulated with other signifying and material elements: but which, though never absolute, nevertheless, continue—persistently—to register their disturbing and differentiating effects.

As to "the arts": since I am neither an artist, art critic nor art historian, I will not attempt to discuss individual works of art or individual artists in the aesthetic and critical depth they deserve. The images are contrapuntal to, rather than illustrative of, the theme. My hope is thereby to encourage those of you who don't know this work to become better acquainted with its astonishingly rich diversity. My focus in this paper, then, is on historical or cultural moments and their periodization. I discuss the art work principally as part of a wider cultural/political formation. Works of art appear here as a constitutive element in a wider discursive field of ideas, practices, social movements and political events: though I do also want to insist that they offer us a certain privileged vantage point on that world.

The approach, then, is, broadly, "historical." Or rather, since I am not a historian either, I had better settle for the term "genealogical." I want to begin to construct an outline "genealogy" of the post-war Black British diaspora arts. Genealogy here means marking out periods into distinct "moments"; noting certain striking convergences between very different kinds of work within any one "moment" and many significant continuities between them; but, more significantly, identifying the breaks and ruptures, the diverging pathways, as "moments" unravel and disseminate, their elements evolving in radically different directions. (Or sometimes, paradoxically, refusing to evolve.) Frank Bowling, whose work you are looking at at the moment, continued to produce, in the 1980s, challengingly original and beautifully conceptualized "maps" of abstract colour and geometric form, long after the art historians declare their moment to have passed. I am, of course, concerned with shifts in thematic concerns; with changes in "ways of seeing," with the construction of different "fields of vision," and what they tell us, symptomatically, about changes in what Raymond Williams called "structures of feeling."[3]

This is to think of such moments, as *conjunctures*. Thinking conjuncturally inevitably involves the necessarily interpretive act of "clustering" or assembling elements into a formation. However, such formations, though they do exhibit a distinctive shape, have no simple unity. There is, for example, no single "black arts movement" here, evolving, teleologically, in step with wider social and political movements, to which all these artists could be said to belong. Rather, I try to assemble these three "moments" in what I want to call their fused but contradictory dispersion. As I will try to show, the 1980s was a moment of explosive creativity in the black-diaspora visual arts in Britain. But it was characterized by deep fissures, which set in play currents, directions and trajectories which diverged rather than "adding up." Often, they diverge *within* the work of a single artist. That is why the 1980s remain so contested, open to such different interpretations, representing such an object of unfulfilled desire. They can be "mapped" only as the "condensation" of a series of overlapping, interlocking but non-corresponding "histories."

Does this undermine the genealogical enterprise? Not necessarily. It depends on how a "moment" is defined. Neither membership of the same decade, accident of shared date of birth or location will do. Artists of the same generation do different kinds of work. Or they go on working, across different moments, often in radically different ways from how they began. Or they continue to follow a trajectory long after its "moment" seems to have passed. Artists therefore appear here, not in their radically-creative individuality, but as the "bearers"—the "subjects," in a displaced, Foucauldean sense—of their artistic practices. By "moment" then, I mean the coming together or convergence of certain elements—practices and events—so as to constitute, for a time, a distinct discursive formation, a "conjuncture," as Gramsci has it. This is always "a fusion of contradictory forces"; or as Louis Althusser once put it, a "condensation of dissimilar currents, the ruptural fusion of an accumulation of contradictions" whose so-called "unity" is necessarily always over-determined.[4]

Here I think of a "moment" as what the Caribbean anthropologist David Scott, in his challenging new book *Conscripts of Modernity*, calls a *problem space*. A "problem space," Scott argues, "is a historically constituted discursive space." It is constituted by the coming-together of historical and discursive elements. Epistemologically, a "problem space" may be thought of as posing a set of cognitive, political, artistic questions which provide a sort of "horizon" of possible futures, within which we "think the present," and to which our practices constitute a sort of answer or reply. Following Quentin Skinner and R. G. Collingwood, Scott argues that a problem space is defined as much by the implicit questions we are posed at different moments, as by the "answers" we seem, from different positions, constrained or "conscripted" to give. When the historical conjuncture changes—as it does significantly between the 1960s and the 1980s and again between the 1990s and the present—the problem space—and thus the questions demanding answers, and so our practices, which always constitute a sort of reply to them—also change; since, as David Scott vividly puts it, what was a "horizon of the future" for *them* has become for the next generation, for *us*, our "futures past": a horizon which we can "no longer imagine, seek after, inhabit," or indeed create in, *see* or *represent*, in the same way.[5]

II.

We can usefully divide the post-war Black British diaspora arts into three distinct "waves." The first generation of artists was born in the 1920s and 1930s, in the far-flung corners of the British empire. They came to Britain, as the last "colonials," in the 1950s and 1960s, immediately after World War II, on the eve of decolonization: following—in the Caribbean case—the political upheavals of the 1930s out of which the Caribbean labor movement emerged and, everywhere across the colonial world, the birth of independence movements and the rise of the anti-colonial struggles. They came to Britain to fulfil their ambitions to become practicing artists. A pioneer figure was Ronald Moody, a major sculptor of the black body and a leading figure in the international movement around "Negro sculpture," whose work sadly awaits a major retrospective. Moody was born in Jamaica in 1900. He lived and worked in London and Paris before the Second World War and returned to London in 1941. Between the mid-1940s and the mid-1960s, an outstanding company of colonial artists, including Moody himself, F. N. Souza, Avinash Chandra, Frank Bowling, Aubrey Williams, Donald Locke, Ahmed Parvez, Anwar Shemza, Balraj Khanna, Iqbal Geoffrey, Ivan Peries, Uzo Egonu, Li Yuan Chia, and David Medalla, among others, arrived in Britain. Rasheed Araeen, who was born in Karachi in 1935, came to London in the 1960s, already an accomplished painter and sculptor. He subsequently became an influential activist and cul-

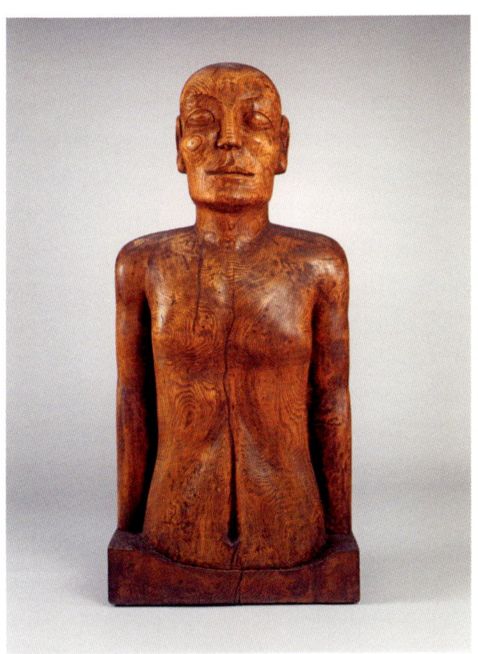

Figure 20.1. Ronald Moody, *Johanaan*, 1936. Elm. 155 × 72.5 × 38.8 cm. © Estate of Ronald Moody. Courtesy of the Estate of Ronald Moody. Photo: Tate.

tural animator, curator in 1989 of the famous *The Other Story* Hayward exhibition, which traced the neglected story of the "black arts" in Britain; founder-editor of *Third Text*; and tireless champion of what he described as "the unique story . . . of those men and women who defied their 'otherness' and entered the modern space that was forbidden to them, not only to declare their historic claim on it but also to challenge the framework which defined and protected its boundaries."[6] Araeen and Avtarjeet Dhanjal, a sculptor in the modern idiom from India who arrived in 1974, via East Africa, are manifestly transitional figures between the first and second waves, spanning the two moments. Whereas the majority of the leading early figures of the second wave—people like Eddie Chambers, Keith Piper, Donald Rodney, Sonia Boyce, Lubaina Himid, Claudette Johnson, Mona Hatoum, Maud Sulter, Gavin Jantjes and others—were born after the war and did not exhibit work until two decades later. These two "waves" constitute the main focus of my talk. I will discuss the relations between the second and the third moment—which seems to emerge in the 1990s and after—more briefly at the end.

One immediate contrast between the first two waves lies in their respective attitudes to modernism. Broadly speaking, the artists of the first wave came to London in a spirit not altogether different from that in which Picasso and others went to Paris: to fulfil their artistic ambitions and to participate in the heady atmosphere of artistic innovation in the most advanced centres of art at that time. This may come as a surprise, since modernism has become so exclusively a property of advanced "Western" art, and colonials are still thought of as either by definition marginalized from such developments or instinctively hostile to it. In fact, these artists came to Britain feeling that they naturally belonged to the modern movement, and, in a way, it belonged to them. The promise of decolonization not only fired their ambition; it also—in ways which seem to have been forgotten—deeply enhanced their sense of themselves as "modern persons." Their commitment to the anti-colonial struggle had liberated them from any lingering sense of inferiority. Their aim was to engage the modern world as equals on its own terrain. In that sense, they shared, and were clearly part of, the rising optimism of the first *Windrush* generation of West Indian migrants, who also came to Britain in the 1950s and 1960s in search of a better life, and whose unquenchable determination and jaunty self-confidence is so palpable in the images of their arrival produced at the time—for instance, in magazines like *Picture Post* and in the photographic archive of the Hulton Picture Library.[7]

They—we (for of course this is my generation too)—came, of course, *because* of the colonial connection: re-tracking well-trodden pathways, following linkages forged by imperialism; completing processes—triangular trade; forced migration; the unequal reciprocities of cheap labor; natural resources and modern manufacture; systems of colonial education and governance—which for more than three centuries had harnessed the margins of empire to its imperial centre and "conscripted" its peripheries into a dependent "modernity." An ambiguous journey towards "modernity," then, since they/we knew "Britain" both intimately and from afar, and as both "the mother country" and "the mother of all our troubles." They—we—came to see for themselves/ ourselves, to look it in the eye—and, if possible, to conquer it.

Artists were not alone in this aspiration. In the 1950s and 1960s, London became the mecca for a group of Caribbean writers and intellectuals, who seemed to feel almost intuitively, at the same moment, that they had to migrate to fulfil their ambitions. The novelist George Lamming, a pioneering figure in this fraught adventure, has written poignantly in *The Pleasures of Exile* about how a whole generation of West Indian writers—Lamming himself, Edgar Mittelholzer, Vic Reid, Roger Mais, Sam Selvon, John Hearne, Jan Carew, V. S. Naipaul, Andrew Salkey, Neville Dawes—all "felt the need to get out." A necessary, and necessarily ambivalent, journey. Only a young writer steeped in the English literary tradition would conceive of framing a book—as *Pleasures of Exile* is framed—with a reading of *The Tempest*. Only one already liberated from any subservience to that tradition would feel free to re-read *The Tempest* radically from its colonial margins. As Lamming says, referring to the very colonial education which shaped and freed him, "How in the name of Heavens could a colonial native taught by an English native within a strict curriculum diligently guarded over by yet another English native . . . ever get out from under the ancient mausoleum of this historic achievement?" One way was to travel, not away from but *towards*, this contested center. The West Indian novel is the product of this migratory movement because, as Lamming observed, "most West Indians of my generation were 'born' in England"—meaning that only there did so many dispersed colonial subjects, from different islands first see themselves in terms of this common identity.[8] The intellectual and artistic ferment amongst West Indian writers and artists in London in these years of exile is finely documented in Anne Walmsley's history of *The Caribbean Artists Movement* (1992), an organization to which they all belonged.

The distinctiveness of this anti-colonial attitude to modernism is a difficult "horizon of the future" for younger contemporaries to imagine or inhabit. As a result of what Edward Said has called the "dynamic of dependency" in colonial societies, the writers and artists were already knowledgeable about new developments in Western writing and painting long before they set out. However, "modern art" was seen by them, not as it would be now—as a potential Eurocentric trap—but as an international creed, fully consistent with anti-colonialism and the latter's resistance to the imposition of European institutions and values on colonial societies: consistent with anti-colonialism *because* it was regarded as essential to a modern consciousness. These writers and artists were, of course, deeply critical of the colonial imposition of Western cultural models. Nevertheless, as Rasheed Araeen—a fierce critic of institutional Eurocentrism in the arts—himself has argued, they saw an engagement with modern art as "the only way of dealing with the aspirations of our time," though he adds that it "radically re-defined that tradition through an experience that was not only socially unique but also historically important."[9] They seemed to agree even with so "English" a figure as Herbert Read, a leading apostle of English modernism, that modern art was an attempt "to create forms more appropriate to the sense and sensibility of the new age." They were, in that sense, "moderns" in spirit, if not specifically "modernists" in artistic practice: internalizing the spirit of restless innovation, the impulse to "make it new," which defined the modern attitude. As Frank Bowling, who left London for the US in 1966 and who has maintained an unswerving loyalty to abstraction throughout his later career, said "I believe the Black soul, if there is such a thing, belongs in modernism."[10] They regarded the artistic vocation as a universal calling. They claimed art in the name of humanity in general. They were universalist and cosmopolitan in outlook.

There are many parallels elsewhere with this complex attitude from the margins to the idea of "the modern." There were, of course, the vigorous indigenous modern art movements in India, Africa and Latin America—one thinks, for example, of the Mexican muralists or the astonishingly bold and, formally, revolutionary space opened up by Brazilian artists like Hélio Oiticica and Lygia Clark. These movements have since been largely written out of the history of "Modernism" with a capital "M." Between the wars, the Harlem Renaissance had, in the words of the African-American critic Houston Baker, aspired, in literature, poetry and painting, to combine the formal mastery of European modernism with "the deformation of mastery" through which the black vernacular found expression.[11] There was that vibrant, heady, syncretic, urban culture which surfaced in the 1950s in the mixed-race areas of some South African cities, the matrix out of which the anti-apartheid struggle emerged: including that astonishing company of black journalists and photographers like Peter Magubane, Bob Gosani and Alf Kumalo, grouped around the magazine *Drum*. There was the way jazz was translated into the explosive, syncopated world of West African urban music. More personally, I remember the young black intellectuals I knew in Kingston in the late 1940s, before I too set off in pursuit of "the pleasures of exile," dreaming of freedom to the haunting but forbiddingly complex and uncompromisingly "modern" tonalities of Charlie Parker, Miles Davis and Thelonius Monk.

Of course, many artists from the colonial world shared the anti-colonial objective to destroy the feudal structures they inhabited and to replace or indigenize the foreign institutions imposed by colonialism. Side by side with the tendency we have been describing, there was also a powerful "nativist" current in anti-colonial nationalism, especially where anti-colonial movements were grounded in strong, indigenous, traditional cultures which colonialism had overlaid and transformed but not destroyed; sustaining the hope that a culture of the new nation could emerge from a redemptive revival of, or "return" to, these older values.

This "cultural nationalist" position was to become the dominant one, as the critique of colonialism deepened and the difficulties of building genuinely independent nation states and national cultures in neo-imperial and postcolonial circumstances gradually emerged. But it was by no means absent, as a tension, in the first wave since, after all, whatever their commitment to the modern movement in art, these artists were also consciously creating modern work and developing modern artistic practices out of native and indigenous experiences, materials, traditions and resources. Anwar Jalal Shemza, for example, one of those migrating artists who came to modernism steeped in the formal traditions of Islamic art, never resolved the contradictory pulls between these currents. As we know, these tensions between the "nativist" and the modernizing impulses in anti-colonial nationalism have never been resolved—it is the theme of that wonderfully-rich chapter on "Resistance and Opposition" in Edward Said's *Culture and Imperialism*, published in 1994. They continue to haunt the cultural debate today.

However, as far as we can judge, the dream of the "first wave" was not to restore the past so much as to look forward, expecting independence to issue in a new era of progress, change, modernity and freedom, which would provide the basis for a new, postcolonial culture as well as enhance the individual capacity for creative innovation. Certainly, the artists continued to paint and create with varying degrees of memory of, and reference to, the sights and sounds, cultures and traditions, histories and natural worlds of their places of origin. However, increasingly, they seem to *see* these things within a modern vision-field, via the modern consciousness of a certain "deterritorialization" of colour and form.

Aubrey Williams's career is exemplary here. There are his early figurative and naturalistic paintings, including the astonishing birds and other natural forms of his Guyanese and Latin-American "continental" work; there is work like *Kaituk* (1970)—a painting of the Kaieteur waterfalls in Guyana, which is a landscape literally in the process of becoming an abstract; then, the explosive move into abstraction; there is the exploration of "lost traditions" combined with the formal experimentation of his Arawak and Carib compositions and his Olmec and Mayan-inspired canvases (fig. 20.2); the swirling colours and shapes of his "cosmologies"; and his struggle to find visual correlatives for the symphonies and quartets of the Russian composer Shostakovich.

As the critic Guy Brett observed of Williams,

> He arrived in London as a young artist with a unique combination of experiences: an agronomist's knowledge of the fauna and flora of his country, political experience of a moment of profound historical change, a

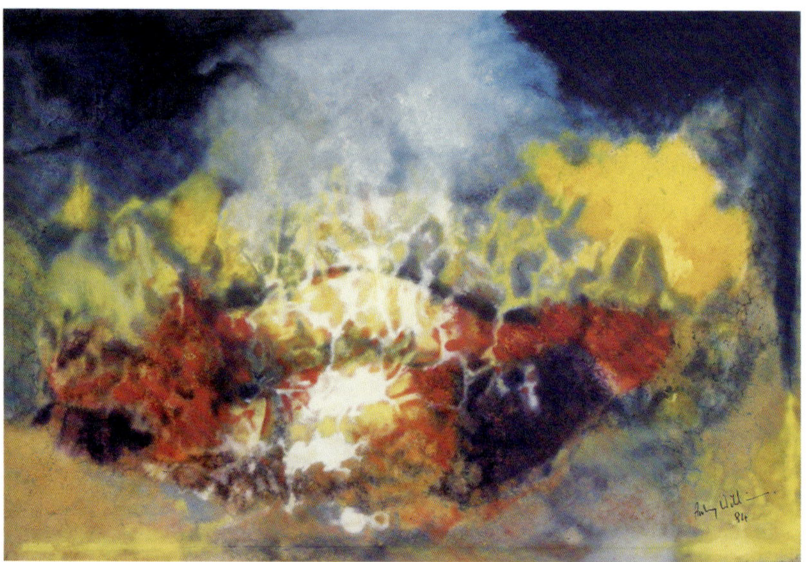

Figure 20.2. Aubrey Williams, *Hymn to the Sun IV (Olmec-Maya)*, 1984. Oil on canvas. 119.9 × 184.8 cm. © Estate of Aubrey Williams. All rights reserved, DACS/Artimage 2022.

deep curiosity about the pre-Columbian culture of Central and South America, and memories—human, affective ones—of a people for whom "life" and "art" were interconnected. With these memories, he began working in the "mainstream of modern art" influenced by Pollock, Kline and especially Gorky, as well as Rivera, Orozco, Tamayo and Matta (the North and South American vanguards had a connection, especially in the thirties and forties, which they have never had before and since).[12]

III.

What happened to this "structure of feeling"? The disintegration of this "moment" is a complicated affair—overdetermined from several directions. There was the actual experience of the first "wave," which turned out to be a patchy and dispiriting affair. For a time they were central to the *avant-garde* of the day, exhibiting in the leading galleries in solo and group shows, in the UK and internationally, alongside names which have since become "household"; attracting critical acclaim, and operating at what Guy Brett calls "the heady interface between artistic innovation and trans-nationalism."[13] But some found the doors of recognition barred, and became progressively disenchanted. The Western appropriation of the modern movement and the crisis of institutional visibility surfaced. A few retreated into self-imposed exile. At one point, Ahmed Parvez tore up his canvases and left England for good. Anwar Shemza experienced an artistic trauma and totally changed direction. Frank Bowling emigrated to the US. Rasheed Araeen describes the onset of a "personal crisis" in the early 1970s, "losing all hope of becoming a successful artist" as a consequence of "institutional indifference."[14]

Another factor was the shift in attitudes towards modernism itself, which ceased to be an all-encompassing name for, and became just one more phase in, the long, unwinding story of, contemporary art. Some questioned modernism's ambivalent celebration of "primitivism"—which seemed to have opened up the Western world to non-Western art, rejuvenating the former's jaded spirits, whilst appropriating the latter as an exoticized, "support" to the West's inventiveness. There was a loss of confidence in its universalist and cosmopolitan claims—the result of a devastating critique of "the dark side of the Enlightenment" which has proved historically decisive. There emerged the new critiques of "cultural imperialism," growing out of a fuller understanding of the *cultural* dimensions of imperial power; of Eurocentrism and Orientalism, arising from a growing awareness of how the universalistic promise of the Enlightenment had been appropriated in a particularistic manner by the West; and a deepening cultural relativism.

More significantly, the whole fulcrum of the political world shifted fundamentally. To speak, metaphorically, between the work of Souza or Aubrey Williams and that of Eddie Chambers, Keith Piper and the Pan-Afrikan Connection falls the shadow of *race*. We can mark the transition by way of a series of iconic critical events. The Notting Hill Race riots of 1958 followed by the murder of Kelso Cochrane; the Smethwick election; the visits of Martin Luther King and Malcolm X; the formation of the Campaign Against Racial Discrimination; the passing of the immigration Acts, with their "second-class" and "patrial" categories; the appearance of Stokeley Carmichael at the Dialectics of Liberation Conference; the sound of Bob Marley and the sight of locksmen on the streets; the new sport of "Paki-bashing"; the campaign against the "sus" laws, and Enoch Powell's "Rivers of Blood" speech. Horace Ové's photographic and film work, recently revived in an important retrospective, is a dynamic visual testimony to this moment. The result was a full blown, indigenous, anti-racist politics, a powerful grass roots and community mobilization against racism and racial disadvantage

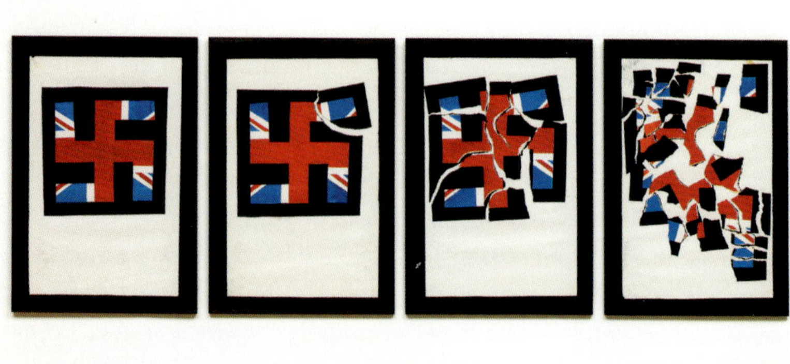

Figure 20.3. Eddie Chambers, *Destruction of the National Front*, 1979–80. Four screen-prints on paper on card. 82.7 × 57.2 cm each. © Eddie Chambers. Photo: Tate.

and a fully-formed black consciousness, fed by Civil Rights, anti-apartheid and other global struggles. By the mid-1970s race had finally "come home" to Britain. It had been fully indigenized.

This is the world into which the second "wave" emerged. In the place of anti-colonialism, *race* had become the determining category. This changed conjuncture reshaped the experience, the political outlook and the visual imaginary of the first black generation to be born *in* the diaspora. There was nothing in the experience of the first "wave"—who had certainly experienced racial discrimination—to match the speed and depth of this racializing process. The anger it provoked exploded across Britain's black communities, and literally scars, fractures, invades, scribbles and squiggles, graffiti-like, across, and batters the surfaces of, works like Eddie Chambers's *Destruction of the National Front* (1979–80) (fig. 20.3) and *I Was Taught to Believe* (1982–3); Keith Piper's *Reactionary Suicide: Black Boys Keep Swinging (Another Nigger Died Today)* (1982) and *Arm in Arm They Enter the Gallery (This Nigger Is Sure as Hell Stretching My Liberalistic Tendencies)* (1982/3); or Donald Rodney's *The Lexicon of Liberation* (1984).

This new "horizon" produced a polemical and politicized art: a highly graphic, iconographic art of line and montage, cut-out and collage, image and slogan: the "message" often appearing too pressing, too immediate, too literal, to brook formal delay and, instead, breaking insistently into "writing." The black body—stretched, threatened, distorted, degraded, imprisoned, beaten, and resisting—became an iconic recurring motif. Keith Piper's and Donald Rodney's work of this period is exemplary—a magisterial rebuttal of the cliche that art and politics cannot creatively co-exist. It was of a piece with Eddie Chambers's statement in *Black Art an' Done* (1981) that Black Art "is a tool to assist us in our struggle for liberation both at home and abroad."

The moment of the late-1970s/early 1980s was, however, divided at its heart. Right alongside this politicized work, we can identify a second set of impulses, less overtly political, though no less "engaged" with wider issues: concerned with exploring the experience of and resistance to racism, but in a more subjective idiom. At first these tendencies overlapped. A critical factor here was the Civil Rights struggle. It was here that Eddie Chambers, Keith Piper, Marlene Smith and others picked up the idea of a Black Arts movement grounded in an anti-racist politics, an Afro-centered black identity and a "Black Aesthetic." Perhaps more significant in the long run was the path which the civil rights movement took, from the integrated "black-and-white-unite-and-fight" desegregation struggles of the mid-1960s to the Black Power, black consciousness, "black-is-beautiful" phase, with its greater focus on "race" as a positive, but exclusive, identity category, and its more separatist, cultural-nationalist, Afro-centric and essentialist emphases. Exhibitions like the *Black Art an' Done* show (1981), organized by Chambers, Piper, Dominic Dawes and others at the Wolverhampton Art Gallery; and the *Black Woman Time Now* show organized by Brenda Agard, Lubaina Himid, Claudette Johnson, Sonia Boyce, Houria Niati, Ingrid Pollard, Chila Kumari Burman, Veronica Ryan and others at the Battersea Arts Centre (1983), translated those vibrations to the British scene—though the decision of black women artists to exhibit separately may have been a harbinger of trouble to come. These and similar initiatives opened the floodgates to a veritable deluge of independent shows and exhibitions in film, photography and the visual arts, the prelude to that extraordinary explosion of creative production which staked out the terrain of the autonomous "Black Arts" movement of the 1980s and 1990s.[15]

In what follows, I can only track one theme from the array of new questions and answers—the new problem space—which this creative upsurge posed. The experience of racialized exclusion bore down in a particular way, subjectively as well as politically, on this second generation. Overwhelmingly, they were born into and schooled in the black diaspora. Separated from their homes of origin, marginalized from society's mainstream, excluded and stereotyped, discriminated against in the public sphere, pushed around by the police, abused in the streets, and profoundly alienated from recognition or acceptance by British society at large, they were haunted by diasporic questions of identity and belonging. "Who are we?" "Where do we come from?" "Where do we really belong?"

Of course, the identity question had already surfaced in the 1970s, regarded at the time as not alternative to but integrally a part of the politics of black resistance. A language within which the fractured linkages of colonial history could be redeemed was essential to that "decolonization of the mind" for which writers like Frantz Fanon and Amilcar Cabral had called, and without which political independence would be an empty shell. It first surfaced amongst Afro-Caribbeans (the largest ethnic minority community at the time) as a symbolic restoration in collective memory of slavery and the African connection, so long disavowed in the Caribbean itself. This took the form of the rediscovery of an African identity *through* its diasporic translation and dissemination. "Africa" is "alive and well in the diaspora," representing a "country of the mind," an imagined community, as much as a real, historical space, which connects with Africa through its New World displacements. This "Africa" begins to be spoken at this time by young Black British people, in part through the languages and iconography of Rastafarianism and "dreadlocks" and is evident everywhere in street life, in the styling of dress and the body, in music and black popular culture. In the visual arts, it is, perhaps, most splendidly first celebrated in the photographic work of Armet Francis, Vanley Burke and Franklyn Rodgers, later as the problematic of the 1980s takes over, given an erotic re-reading by Rotimi Fani-Kayode, Robert Taylor and others. A new Pan-African diasporic imaginary surfaces for a time, redeeming through image and sound the breaches and terrors of a broken history.

This is the performative identity we find in the rhythms of Bob Marley and "roots" reggae—a syncretic, contemporary music masquerading as a traditional music of memory, transmitting "ancient" pulses by the most "modern" of technologies, and "speaking" as much of Kingston and London as of Guinea or Angola: grounded, in the double inscriptions of a richly metaphorical syntax, which condensed into one narrative or visual trope such dissimilar currents as the "loss" of Africa, the terrors of the Middle Passage, the trauma of slavery and indenture, the humiliations of colonialism, the displacements of migration, the search for identity, the "suffering" still in place, despite independence, in Kingston's Trench Town *and* the new kinds of "suffering" emerging in the "Babylons" of Handsworth, Brixton, Bradford, Toxteth and Moss Side.

In this moment, long before the quarrels between the different tendencies of the second conjuncture surface, identity had acquired a political meaning and political struggle acquired a cultural dimension. By the 1980s, the question of identity surfaced decisively, opening up in effect a new thematic, a new imaginary, a new problem space. Identity-politics has, perhaps deservedly, since acquired a bad name. However, I want to argue that in this moment the emergence of the identity question constituted a compelling and productive "horizon" for artists: not so much for the celebration of an essential identity fixed in time and "true" to its origins, but rather—as the Rastafarian case, despite appearances, actually demonstrates—what we would now call "the production of a new, black subject." And since that is a conception of identity and subjectivity which can only be constituted within, rather than outside, representation, the "answers" which music and the visual arts provided in practice were absolutely critical.

As I argued at the time, "Cultural identities come from somewhere, have histories. Like everything which is historical, they undergo constant transformation. Far from being eternally fixed in some essentialised past, they are subject to the continuous 'play,' of history, culture and power. Far from being grounded in a mere 'recovery' of the past, which is waiting to be found, and which, when found, would secure our sense of ourselves into eternity, identities are the names wc give to the different ways we are positioned and position ourselves within the narratives of the past."

Such issues connected directly with the shifts in artistic practice between the 1960s and the 1980s—from the binary of "pure abstraction" versus "predocumentary realism" to a more mixed or hybrid mode: in photography—the constructed image—and in the visual arts more broadly—the "return to the figural," best located in the foregrounding of the black body as the key racial signifier. This is especially striking in photography, which for a time dispenses with the documentary mode altogether and turns to the consciously-staged image, the photograph aspiring to the condition of the work of art.[16] We find this preoccupation with body and self in artists and photographers as diverse as Sonia Boyce, Keith Piper, Mona Hatoum, Rotimi Fani-Kayode, Joy Gregory, Maxine Walker, Ingrid Pollard, Sunil Gupta, Franklyn Rodgers, Clement Cooper, Dave Lewis, David A. Bailey, Ajamu, Roshini Kempadoo, Chila Burman and many others. This deliberate "staging" of the black body is the only motif I have time to consider in any depth.

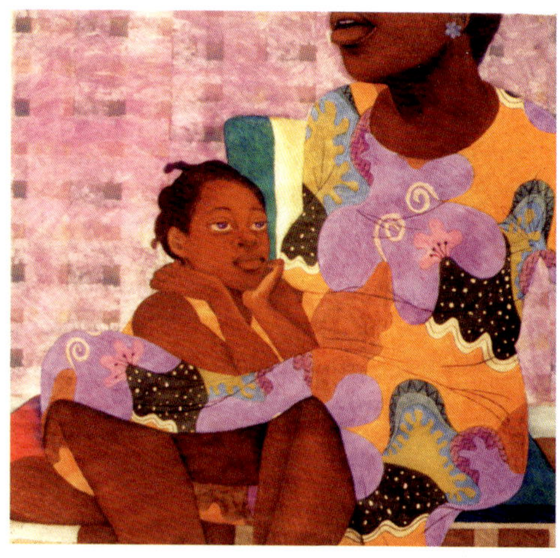

Figure 20.4. Sonia Boyce, *Big Women's Talk*, 1984. Pastel on paper. 122 × 122 cm. © Sonia Boyce. All rights reserved, DACS/Artimage 2022.

It includes the preoccupation with portraiture, and particularly, self-portraiture; with "putting the self in the frame"; with relocating the stereo-typed, abjected, black body of racialized discourse "in the field of vision." "Black self-portraiture," I argued, "broke its links with the western humanist celebration of self and became more positional—the staking of a claim, a wager. The black self-image was in a double sense, an exposure, a 'coming out.' The self is caught in its very emergence." These selves are contextu-alized, but, as it were, on the inside. The experience of historical rupture and break, of loss and resistance, of migration and upheaval, of the strug-gle to live within multiple locations and to sustain multiple versions of the self, multiple strategies of resistance, "are allowed to invade and disrupt the mythical inner wholeness of the self-image"[17] (fig. 20.4).

This was the black body, resurrected as a moving signifier—first, as an object of visibility, which can at last be "seen"; then as a "foreign body," tres-passing into unexpected and tabooed locations; then as the site of an excava-tion. This is the body as a space or canvas, on which to conduct an exploration into the inner landscapes of black subjectivity; the body, also, as a point of convergence for the materialization of intersecting planes of difference— the gendered body, the sexual body; the body as subject, rather than simply the object, of looking and desire. The gaze, the "look" from the place of the other—Fanon's "Look, Mama! A Negro!"—came to be understood as both constitutive of the subject and inscribed by power.

With this putting of the black body into question we come face-to-face, not with some essential "truth" about blackness, but with what elsewhere I called "the end of the essential black subject"—triggering that kaleidoscopic proliferation of meanings around blackness and bringing into the light the hidden connections between the racialized, the gendered and the sexualized body—a space of condensation which for so long had been the privileged operational zone of racial discourse.[18]

I argued in *Different* (2001) that "This body is at one and the same time the 'container' of identity and subjectivity, the over-determined point where differences collide, what Fanon called 'the epidermal schema' or surface on which racism etches its indelible mark, and a ground of resistance from which alternative counter-narratives can be produced. On the site of the body, racial discourse had long undertaken the work of systematically reducing history to biology, culture to nature."[19] In the ritual exchange of stereotypes around the body between "race," gender and sexuality, racism had deployed its most violent and destructive fantasies. This could not be undone by simply reversing the terms, whereby in a single move "black" became "beautiful"—a strategy of positive imagery by substitution which was briefly tried but proved inadequate. Reversal does not subvert a system of representation. It leaves it intact, only standing on its head! Indeed, as we know, *nothing* can protect the black body—a signifier caught in the endless play of power and meaning—against reappropriation: witness the way the black body in representation has subsequently transmogrified, apparently seamlessly, from a reduced, abjected stereotype into the well-honed, "designer" bodies found everywhere in the contemporary iconographies of sport, fashion, the music business, street "chic" and advertising. In culture, there are no guarantees. It was therefore necessary not just to vary the stereotype, or to challenge it head-on, but to *deconstruct* it from within: entering the terrain of a dangerous, unguaranteed "politics of representation" which, in Rotimi Fani-Kayode's work, for example, involved undoing from inside the very fetishism which had been deployed to try to fix it irreversibly.

If we ask what were the wider conjunctural elements which fused together sufficiently to make this "turn" into a new problem space possible, one can only indicatively map into place a number of different histories. There is the fragmentation of the landscapes of social class, the collapse of "class" as the master, analytic category, into which all other contradictions—race, gender and so on—could be subsumed. This led to the rise of the so-called "new social movements," each with its own authentic constituency, in whose name political claims had to be made, producing a further fragmentation of the political field.

There was the rise of gender and sexual politics, loosened from the grip of economic determinism by the same process that made "race" more visible and relatively autonomous. Feminine, personal, familial and domestic themes, hitherto excluded from the political field, were exposed to view. Black women did not slot easily into a feminism led largely by white women. However, without this conjuncture of feminism and black politics, the work of the period by people like Sonia Boyce, Claudette Holmes, Lubaina Himid, Maud Sulter, Mona Hatoum, Sutapa Biswas and many others, would never have taken the form it did. Equally significant was the impact of feminism and sexual politics in opening up the question of masculinity, the homo-erotic gaze, and gay desire. The early work by Rotimi Fani-Kayode, Sunil Gupta, Ajamu, and in film, Isaac Julien and others, broke the tabooed silence around black male desire and exposed how, through an aggressive black masculinity, some black men continue to live out and reproduce, in inverted form, their own historic subordination and infantilization.

Thatcherism and free-market neo-liberalism were the forces which successfully hegemonized the crisis in the post-war settlement. The destruction of the social fabric, the assault on the welfare state, the punishment of the poor and disadvantaged at home, the exposure to the unregulated laws of the free market, and the resumption of the unrequited search for lost imperial glory abroad, unbent the springs of political action, including anti-racist politics. The race uprisings of 1980, 1981 and 1985, undoubtedly a response to its brutal impact, provided the context for the rise of the Black Arts movement. They appeared to be the culmination of the anti-racist tumult of the 1970s. In fact, they turned out to be the last of their kind for fifteen years, until the riots in northern industrial towns in 2001, with their very different motivation and ethnic composition. Of course, racism and racial violence persisted, right alongside multiculturalism. But black and Asian people were also not immune to the seductions of "the enterprise culture."[20]

Finally there was the theoretical deluge which swept across the 1970s and 1980s, and is sometimes held responsible for the loss of political momentum. In this category we must include new theories of language and discourse; the post-Bakhtinian attention to the polysemic nature of language and the poststructuralist themes of "the slippage of the signifier," constituting the struggle over meaning and the relations of representation as key sites of political struggle; Foucauldean, psychoanalytic and other theories of "the subject" and "subjectivity"; theorizations of "difference"; the rise of postcolonial theory and the "philosophy of the Other." In this space of renewed theoretical debate, there emerged what have come to be called the "posts"—poststructuralism, postcolonialism, postmodernism, post-feminism, post-Marxism etc.: "post" signalling, not the passing of chronological time, but the waning of old paradigms: the passage without supercession, the dialogic movement without dialectical overcoming.

Hostile accounts of this shift attribute it to the movement from the anti-racist political mobilization of the late 1970s to the cultural politics of the 1980s, a shift for which cultural theory, and especially that flavour-of-the-month whipping-boy, cultural studies, is held largely responsible. This is, to put it mildly, a gross simplification. It is an idealist view of politics—as a matter of will and intention alone—and reflects the pessimism of thwarted political hopes: whereas what seems to be required is the more difficult combination of "pessimism of the intellect and optimism of the will." What it ignored or ruthlessly foreshortened is the fact that, in that conjuncture, the whole ful-crum of the political world, and an epochal shift in the global relations of power, was taking place from whose impact art could not be insulated.

The second "moment," then, is really two moments condensed into one, or one moment of fusion from which two very different trajectories, in terms of artistic practice and visual imaginaries, flow. It was followed by a sustained wave of new work in the 1990s which I have no space to discuss at length. I have had my say about much of it in photography in *Different*. The 1990s were a period of novelty, innovation, of cutting-edge achievement—but not, in my terms, of conjunctural change. This seems to me to have oper-ated, by and large, on a "problem space" which the 1980s defined. If there is a third moment, then it is the one emerging now, before our eyes, and it is probably too soon to attempt to configure it. What we can say is that, in the age of refugees, asylum seekers and global dispersal, "black" by itself will no longer do. Not because biological [*sic*] racism has disappeared or the experi-ence of "being black" has lost either its purchase or its specificity, but because racialized difference has become radically pluralized, requiring new terms to capture its disseminating specificities. "Race" has become just one of the disseminating axes of difference which provide intersecting lines of identi-fication, exclusion and contestation, and which have—as usual—proved to be both sharply divisive, socially, and highly productive, artistically. Only a "civilizational discourse"—the dominant discourse of the new imperial world order—is broad enough to capture its globally-shifting contours. In culture, the polarizing tendencies—present everywhere in that highly contradictory formation called "globalization"—between the pull towards fundamentalism, ethnic and religious particularism, on the one hand, and a homogenizing, evangelizing Western assimilationism, on the other—has left the ground in between, the ground of a pluri-centered world and of many, competing modernities, more threatened and embattled.

Yet the diaspora arts, for which "black" remains a fading signifier, stand in a more engaged position in relation to contemporary art practice and mainstream arts organizations: simultaneously, in and against. In part this is because the art world itself, like everything else, has been obliged to become more "global," even while some parts of the globe remain, in this respect, radically more "global" than others. We can call upon here the thematics of what Zeigam Azizov calls "the migration paradigm," drawing our attention to the boundaries and border crossings, the liminal and disrupted places, the voyaging and displacements, the fault-lines and states of emergency. Or, from different angles, the "changing states," which was a theme of the volume marking the tenth anniversary of the Institute of International Visual Arts (INIVA), or the "between camps" approach, which Paul Gilroy suggests is surfacing and intruding "within the work" everywhere, as the costs of living in one, deeply uneven, interdependent but dangerously unequal world make themselves felt.[21] Difference—or rather, the trace of *différance*—refuses to be disappeared. There is also the collapse of the different domains of practice and a synergy across the various visual artistic fields which seems unstoppable. In terms of artistic practice, we are now unequivocally in the terrain of the installation, of multi-imaging, the digital arts and, above all, neo-conceptualism; though, fortunately, the concepts which the diaspora arts deploy are actually *about* something. They have a content, and are not floating about in a passionless, self-referential void, entertaining themselves.

IV.

I end with two, somewhat disconnected, reflections. First, I have been trying, as it were, to contribute to the "writing" of modernity and its others through the post-war history of the black diaspora and the optic of its visual arts. In doing so, I have been insisting that it should be properly "historical"—that is, with proper attention to determination, formation and conditions of existence, to questions of periodization and conjuncture—and not just a celebration of a general and undifferentiated "black presence." I have been concerned to give it specificity; but also to read it *both* in its connectiveness with, *and* its difference from, other surrounding histories. In doing so I have tried to follow Edward Said's injunction to "think contrapuntally." "By looking at different experiences . . . as making up a set of . . . intertwined and overlapping histories . . . think[ing] through and interpret[ing] together experiences that are discrepant, each with its particular agenda and pace of development, its own internal formations, its internal coherence and system of external relationships, all of them co-existing and interacting with others."[22]

The second reflection concerns the perennial difficulty of trying—as I have—to make connections between works of art and wider social histories without collapsing the former or displacing the latter. Despite the sophistication of our scholarly and critical apparatus, we are still not very far advanced—especially when the language concerned is the visual—in finding ways of thinking about the relationship between the work and the world. We either make the connection too brutal and abrupt, destroying that necessary displacement in which *the work* of making art takes place. Or we protect the work from what Edward Said calls its necessary "worldliness": projecting it into either a pure political space where conviction—political will—is all, or into an inviolate aesthetic space, where only critics, curators, dealers, collectors and connoisseurs are permitted to play.

The problem is rather like that of thinking the relationship between the dream and its materials in waking life. We know there *is* a connection there. But we also know that the two "continents" cannot be lined up and their correspondences read off directly against one another. Between the work and the world, as between psychic and the social, the bar of the historical unconscious, as it were, has fallen; and the effect of the unseen "work" which takes place out of consciousness in the relationship between creative practice and deep currents of historical change whose long-term effects on what can be produced are, literally, *tidal*, is thereafter always a delicate matter of *re-presentation* and *translation*, with all the lapses, elisions, incompleteness of meaning and incommensurability of political goals these terms imply. What Freud called "the dream-work"—in his lexicon, the tropes of displacement, substitution and condensation—is what enables the materials of the one to be "re-worked" or translated into the forms of the other; and for the latter to be enabled to "say more" or "go beyond" the willed consciousness of the individual work or artist.[23] For those who work in the displaced zone of "the cultural," the world has somehow to become a text, an image, before it can be "read." But the "purely textual" is never enough.

This essay first appeared in *History Workshop Journal* 61, no. 1 (Spring 2006): 1–24.

1   David Scott, *Conscripts of Modernity: The Tragedy of Colonial Enlightenment* (Durham, NC: Duke University Press, 2004), 125.

2   C. L. R. James, "Africans and Afro-Caribbeans: A Personal View," *Ten.8*, November 1984, 55.

3   Raymond Williams, *The Long Revolution* (Harmondsworth: Penguin, 1961).

4   Louis Althusser, "Contradiction and Overdetermination," in *For Marx* (London: Penguin, 1966).

5   Scott, *Conscripts of Modernity.*

6   Rasheed Araeen, "Introduction: When the Chickens Come Home," in *The Other Story: Afro-Asian Artists in Post-war Britain* (London: Hayward Gallery, 1989), 9.

7   Stuart Hall, "Reconstruction Work: Images of Post-war Black Settlement," chapter 16, this volume.

8   George Lamming, *The Pleasures of Exile* (London: Pluto, 2005 [1960]), 41, 27, 14.

9   David A. Bailey, Ian Baucom, and Sonia Boyce, eds., *Shades of Black: Assembling Black Arts in Britain in the 1980s* (Durham, NC: Duke University Press; London: Institute of International Visual Arts, 2005), 28–29.

10   Frank Bowling, "Frank Bowling and Bill Thompson: A Conversation between Two Painters," *Art International* (1976), quoted in Araeen, *Other Story.*

11   Houston A. Baker, *Modernism and the Harlem Renaissance* (Chicago: University of Chicago Press, 1987).

12   Guy Brett, *Aubrey Williams* (London: Institute of International Visual Arts, 1998), 25.

13   Brett, *Aubrey Williams,*

14   Rasheed Araeen, "Rethinking History and Some Other Things, *Third Text* 54 (Spring 2001), 95.

15   David A. Bailey and Stuart Hall, eds., "Critical Decade: Black British Photography in the 1980s," special issue, *Ten.8* 2, no. 3 (1992).

16   Stuart Hall and Mark Sealy, *Different: Contemporary Photographers and Black Identity* (London: Phaidon, 2001).

17   Stuart Hall, "Black Narcissus," *Autograph Newsletter*, 1991.

18   Stuart Hall, "New Ethnicities," chapter 4, this volume.

19   Hall and Sealy, *Different*, 9.

20   Stuart Hall, "Aspiration and Attitude: Reflections on Black Britain in the 90s," *New Formations* 33 (1998): 38–46.

21   Gilane Tawadros, *Changing States: Contemporary Arts and Ideas in an Era of Globalisation* (London: Institute of International Visual Arts, 2004).

22   Edward Said, *Culture and Imperialism* (London: Chatto and Windus, 1993), 19, 36.

23   Sigmund Freud, *The Interpretation of Dreams* (London: Penguin, 1991).

MUSEUMS, MODERNITY, AND DIFFERENCE

CHAPTER 21

Museums of Modern Art and the End of History

I have no authority to address this occasion either as an art critic or as a historian—a lack which I find curiously liberating in this distinguished company. I am very involved in some areas of the practice of visual arts in Britain at the moment, as I have the honour to chair the boards of both the Institute of International Visual Arts (INIVA) and Autograph, the Association of Black Photographers. I therefore know something about the area of contemporary artistic practice, which I regard as one of the liveliest, most vigorous and most creative sectors of the contemporary arts anywhere. It might therefore be useful to say something from this non-specialist point of view about what I would call the cultural "conditions of existence" for the exhibition and production of contemporary art.

I put "exhibition," out of sequence, first because the question of the museum is foregrounded in the conference title; and I use the expression "cultural conditions of existence" in the specific sense that all important practices, art practices included, always have prior conditions of existence. "Conditions of existence" are different from the notion of a determining force, in the strong sense of determinacy. Conditions do not determine either the form or the content or, indeed, the tendency and direction of a practice, but nevertheless without conditions of existence, a practice could not exist. A practice is always a labor—a "work"—on pre-existing materials and traces. Conditions therefore have a bearing on how those practices are actually executed in the world. Those who in a professional capacity are specifically related to judging, assessing and exhibiting the results of a practice come high in the pecking order and those who are actually producing the work come highest of all—though they are not always accorded the status and rewards they deserve—which leaves me as a lowly handmaiden in this operation. But I want to pick out certain aspects of these conditions of existence for contemporary art and, in a simple way, relate them to the themes and questions signaled in the title.

Rather than "Museums of Modern Art and the End of History," I am tempted to suggest that the title of this conference should be "The End of Museums of Modern Art and the Beginning of History." We could learn a great deal simply by reversing all the terms. What I want to talk about is exactly the sort of "ending" signaled by that kind of reversal. Of course, it would be too easy to think that simply turning all the terms of a dominant paradigm upside down will help us to understand what is going on. In that sense, I am not interested in endings; instead, I am going to talk about "turns." The idea of museums in general, but also museums of modern art, is in trouble as a result of certain deep historical shifts or "turns": transformations of theory and consciousness, but also shifts in the actual cultural landscape itself.

This "crisis," if we may call it that, is the cumulative effects of a rather dispersed set of developments—what I refer to as a series of turns—which constitute the end of certain ideas of the museum, of the modernity of modern art and, indeed, of history. That notion of a turn is important for me. A turn is neither an ending nor a reversal; the process continues in the direction in which it was traveling before, but with a critical break, a deflection. After the turn, all of the terms of a paradigm are not destroyed; instead, the deflection shifts the paradigm in a direction which is different from that which one might have presupposed from the previous moment. It is not an ending, but a break, and the notion of breaks—of ruptures and of turns—begins to provide us with certain broad handles with which to grasp the current crisis of modernity, and thus of the museums of the modern.

This is clearly related to the much-abused notion of the "post," which has already been referred to, so I must spend a moment dogmatically reiterating what "post" means to me. I do not use the term to mean "after" in a sequential or chronological sense, as though one phase or epoch or set of practices has ended and an absolutely new one is beginning. Post, for me, always refers to the aftermath or the after-flow of a particular configuration. The impetus which constituted one particular historical or aesthetic moment disintegrates in the form in which we know it. Many of those impulses are resumed or reconvened in a new terrain or context, eroding some of the boundaries which made our occupation of an earlier moment seem relatively clear, well bounded and easy to inhabit, and opening in their place new gaps, new interstices.

Let us look at three examples. The postcolonial is not the ending of colonialism but is what happens after the end of the national independence movement. All those contradictions and problems which constituted the dependency of colonial societies are reconvened, partly now within the old colonized societies, but also inside the metropolis, which was previously regarded as standing outside of this process. Similarly, poststructuralism spends all its time and energies saying how it is an advance on structuralism, and yet the first thing to recognize is that, without structuralism, poststructuralism could not exist. It continues in its bloodstream, but in a disseminated or deconstructed form, which allows the original structuralist impulse, transformed, to take on new directions. I think the term postmodern is exactly the same.

I do not want to evoke any of the enormous rubbish that has been talked about under the title of post-modernism, but instead want to focus on the kernel of significance in the term once it has been stripped of some of its many accretions. It seems to me that "the modern" has ceased to be an ever-increasing present form or state of existence and is becoming a moment in history. When that happens, our understanding shifts from an awareness of the ground on which a practice stands to seeing where it came from, how it evolved, and this enables us to ask the question: "What might come after it, 'post' it?"

There has always been something contradictory about the relationship between modernity and history, which is bound to problematize the notion of art history itself. Art history has given the museum its principles of organization, providing the practices of curating, exhibiting, collecting and classification with a scholarly ground. The historicization, therefore, of what was previously perceived as an entirely new historical moment inevitably leads to a sense of operating in a gap between a past which is not quite over and a future which has not yet started (and may never happen in the totalized form in which we imagine it). Writing the history of a phenomenon or of a movement or of an epoch does, in a very complex way, suggest that one can trace its genealogy—what its evolution has been, define the principal forces which will drive it forward and ask the question of whether it has a conclusion. But this historizing tendency is seen as contradictory in the context of modernity, since modernity was precisely a fundamental rupture with "the past" in that sense. It was a break into contingency and, by contingency, I do not mean complete absence of pattern, but a break from the established continuities and connections which made artistic practice intelligible in a historical review. It focused as much on the blankness of the spaces between things as on the things itself and on the excessive refusal of continuities. It was always caught between the attempt, on the one hand, to turn the sign back to a kind of direct engagement with material reality and, on the other, to set the sign free of history in a proliferating utopia of pure forms. Writing histories of modernity is not impossible, but I think they have always been extremely difficult to suture back into the more confident historical organization of the history of Western art, which extends roughly from the Renaissance until the modern itself. I think we have reached the death of that idea of the modern, the logic of whose architecture, T. J. Clark (*Farewell to an Idea: Episodes from a History of Modernism*, 1999) argues, we can no longer intuitively grasp.

I want to talk instead about the turn from modernism, but using "turn" in the sense I have already established. Let me return to that version of postmodernism, which cites modernism as if the entire modern movement can be condensed forwards to the point of its elaboration under the aegis of American art and architecture—the "American" moment. The notion of modernism which reads as if it came to its apotheosis only at its very end seems to me to misunderstand, misread and grossly oversimplify the radical, aesthetic, social and cultural impulses which made modernism the dynamic movement that it was. American cultural critics have a great deal to answer for by trying to subsume the many modernisms under the aegis of what we might call the age of the American empire.

It seems that something significant has to be taken on board about the persistence of the impulse of modernity itself within postmodernism. I cite three examples. The first is what I would call modernism in the streets. I think postmodernism is best described as precisely that; it is the end of modernism *in the museum* and the penetration of the modernist ruptures into everyday life, which is closely related to my second example, the aestheticization of daily life. This might puzzle people in this room who think of contemporary life as the very antithesis of the aesthetic, but personally I think the symbolic has never had such a wide significance as it does in contemporary life. In earlier theories, the symbolic was corralled into a narrow terrain, but it has now entirely imploded in terms of late-modern experience and we find the languages of the aesthetic as appropriate within popular culture or public television, as they are within the most *recherché* rooms of the Museum of Modern Art. There are aesthetic practices distributed by a massive cultural industry on a global scale and the aesthetic is, indeed, the bearer of some of the most powerful impulses in modern culture as a whole, including what we used to think of as its antithesis, the "new economy" which is, par excellence, a *cultural* economy. This notion of a modernism that is to be found inscribed on the face of everyday life, in everyday fashion, in popular culture and in the popular media, in consumer culture and the visual revolution, does obviously jeopardize the whole concept of gathering together the best of all this in one place and calling it "a museum."

Alongside all of this is my third example, the proliferation of media or, in other words, the means of signification. I read recently that it is completely ridiculous to define modern contemporary visual art practices in terms of the media in which they are executed; instead, we must consider the pro-liferation of sites and places in which the modern artistic impulse is taking place, in which it is encountered and seen. This is not just a reservation about the white cube gallery space. This is an explosion of the boundaries—the symbolic as well as physical and material limits—within which the notion of art and aesthetic practices have been organized. Young intellectuals—barely able to spell intellectual, let alone call themselves that—who are working somewhere within the cultural industries, with visual languages, are as deeply and profoundly implicated in the breaking point of modern artistic practices as the most fully paid-up members of the most academic, scholarly schools of art. That they came in through the back door and went out into industry is not important. What is relevant, however, is the proliferation of these practices and the degree to which this proliferation sits most uncom-fortably with the prestige attached to the process which attempts to sift, on some universal criteria of historical value, the best that is being produced and gets it displayed inside some well-patrolled set of walls. Modernism in the streets, the aestheticization of everyday life and the proliferation of sites and means of signification are some ways of re-reading postmodernism, or the postmodern "turn," as the aftermath of modernism.

Postmodernism is not a new movement that kicked modernism into touch, but, instead, by building on and breaking from modernism, it trans-formed it by taking it out into the world. Similarly, we might talk about the post-museum—not in the sense of the necessary end of all museums, but in terms of the radical transformation of the museum as a concept. I would call it the *relativization* of the museum, which can now be perceived as only one site among many in the circulation of aesthetic practices. It is certainly true that the museum remains a very privileged, well-funded site, which is still closely tied to the accumulation of cultural capital, of power and prestige, but in terms of the real understanding of how artistic practices proliferate in our society, it is only one site and no longer enjoys the privileged position that it had historically.

Now I want to look at what one might call "post-history." In exactly the same way that I have been talking about the postmodern, post-history is not the end of history. In fact, some of the most important critical and theoretical developments have arisen from the greater historicization of aesthetic practices, which we have tended to talk of as if they were universal. The historicizing function has not therefore gone away; but History, with a capital "H," which is now increasingly understood as one grand narrative among many narratives, has managed to situate itself, or substitute itself, in the place of the Universal. The history around which the practices of the arts have organized and ordered themselves is the lifeblood of the museum's self-understanding and opens connections which I find so delicate and impossible to understand that I only cite them. There is an almost impossibly refined and elaborated exchange between history and value, which you might think are antithetical terms—after all, if something was important in a particular period, it is highly unlikely that it will be important in all other periods—and yet value reaches for a universal horizon from within a deeper and more profound sense of historical understanding.

In what sense then, do we have a post-history? Firstly we should be aware that histories *are* narratives and that accordingly we have histories rather than a singular history. These narratives are a discursive imposition of beginnings, middles and, indeed, endings onto which histories which do not naturally produce themselves in this convenient form. Therefore, we are not talking about the history of art, but about how we have chosen to narrate the identity of the histories of art to ourselves; the notion of narrative has interrupted and deflected the purity of the historical impulse.

There has been a similar deflection from what I would call history to culture—the "cultural turn." If you think of the historical as having always provided the context within which art historians and critics sought to embed particular practices and texts, then I think we have seen an increase in the use of the notion of cultural context, which of course has historical overtones. At the same time, it seems that there has been an important shift from being interested simply in the historical context of a text or an artist or a practice to embracing its cultural conditions of existence. This destroys or subverts the traditional work and its context approach, which has underwritten art historical understanding for so long. It has to do with what one might call the spatialization of time, which is a prominent feature or phenomenon of a contemporary sensibility.

In terms of post-histories, it is the cogency and compulsiveness of evolutionary explanations which have been broken down, that is to say explanations which trace continuities and look at traditions as unbroken, as unfolding webs of influence, trailing from one moment to another. We have been alerted, not to the absence of traditions (plural), but to the inhabitation of traditions—particularly for where they break and for where they turn back on or away from themselves and on to something else. Tradition must be understood as a discursive field. There is always something of *the present* at stake in how it is inhabited. We are more aware of constituting the discursive ground which enables us to connect this to that or this particular text to that particular work. Talking about the history of a practice, of an artist, of a body of work or of a text, as it is read and re-read from one moment to another simply does not support that organic evolutionary conception of the historical or indeed of tradition, genre or convention—the staples of the museum's self-understanding. I am not suggesting that this approach has not had profound pay-offs for art history and for critical understanding, but I am talking about it more as a space which the modern sensibility can no longer inhabit with confidence in the old way. It can no longer rest there in the knowledge of having found a scholarly and evaluative foundational ground from which to organize and classify the objects of a particular collection.

The next "post" that I wanted to talk about is what I want to call post-culture. You will say there is nothing post about culture; it is the ever-present, ever-evolving signifier of our times. Everybody is interested in it, the prime minister most of all; whenever you offer him an institution which seems resilient to reform, he says we need a "culture change." So culture is the ground on which everybody is somehow now said to be operating. But what is entailed in this conception of culture? We can no longer inhabit a notion of culture in the old anthropological sense, as something which is clearly bounded, internally self-sufficient and relatively homogenous across its members, which sustains and regulates individual conduct within the framework that it offers. Cultures, in that anthropological sense of specifically defined ways of life, have been broken into and interrupted by cosmopolitan dispersals, by migration and displacement. I think that the collapse of that anthropological definition—

culture as a way of life—has to do with the point at which the West began to universalize itself. It is connected with the attempt to construct the world as a single place, with the world market, with globalization and with that moment when Western Europe tried to convert the rest of the world into a province of its own forms of life. From that moment onwards—the moment of modernity—we could no longer think in terms of cultures which are integral, organic, whole, which are well bounded spatially, which support us and which write the scripts of our lives from start to finish. The ending of this moment of Eurocentric closure and its panoptic project has been a long and protracted one, but it has been increasingly prized open.

The movement from an anthropological to a signifying conception of cultures does not mean that cultures become less important. Instead, we are now talking more than ever before about the domain, the importance and the proliferation of meanings by which people live their lives, understand and contest where they are and develop aesthetic and artistic forms of expression. What has disappeared is the ability to carve those forms of expressions into strictly classificatory boxes, so that the primitive and the ancient fit like two rooms inside the modern, with the modern itself boxed inside the ancient. The modern has been inside the primitive and the ancient since 1492 roughly speaking, so what is this "new" discovery that all of a sudden there are more than one set of modernities? They have been proliferating ever since the world began, only ever tentatively, unevenly, contradictorily, to be convened under the rubric of Western times. This does not mean that we are merely moving everywhere towards a cloning of the West. Instead, those sharp distinctions which underpin our classification—that fixed notion of primordial cultural difference—between tradition and modernity simply do not explain any longer the way in which individuals and their practices are both embedded in certain cultural languages or repertoires and at the same time reach across any frontiers which they construct to those which lie beyond—the phenomenon of vernacular cosmopolitanism which is globalization's accompanying shadow. This is nothing other than the shift from the notion of difference as an either/or concept to Derrida's notion of *différance*, in which you cannot make an absolute distinction between a here and a there, inside and outside.

The history of the relationship between the West and its others is a history of the transformations which have changed both out there and here. It is true that these changes are more dramatic under the conditions of modern globalization, in which, undeniably, a lot of out there is actually in here now and vice versa. They are in here, trying to become like you, but also making you different, more like them in their *différance*.

The idea that we live in a well-bounded, well-policed, well-frontiered set of spaces, in which you can move from this room to that, tracing how that became this and how the practices governed by a particular culture evolved to become something different, simply misses the degree to which cultures can no longer be clearly categorized. With the modern and even the postmodern condition, the process of *cultural translation* means that cultural languages are not closed; they are constantly transformed from both within and outside, continuously learning from other languages and traditions, drawing them in and producing something which is irreducible to either of the cultural elements which constituted it in the first place. The most dramatic example of how the notion of cultural translation is the only way in which the cultural process today can be properly grasped is found in the history of modernism itself. The latter has been written precisely as if modernism was a set of triumphal artistic practices, located in what you might think of as the West. However, a small number of deracinated artists "out there" were drawn to this pole of attraction and did relate to it, but of course, in the dominant way the history is read, they cannot be considered to have contributed in any central way to the history and evolution of modernist art practices. In reality, the world is absolutely littered by modernities and by practicing artists, who never regarded modernism as the secure possession of the West, but perceived it as a language which was both open to them but which they would have to transform (figs. 21.1 and 21.2). The history therefore should now be rewritten as a set of cultural translations rather than as a universal movement which can be located securely within a culture, within a history, within a space, within a chronology and within a set of political and cultural relations.

The final "post" I would like to talk about has to do with the question of the post-West. In the light of what I said earlier, we are aware that modern museums of art and other kinds of museums now function in the context of a widening and expanding process of globalization, which is often seen from within the West as a kind of inevitable homogenization; it is as if unfortunately everybody in the world is determined, predetermined, to end up looking like "us." In that sense, the process is sometimes referred to as the "end of history," but I do not believe it is. If you think about contemporary forms of globalization—which are of course driven by Western technology, by Western capital on a global scale and by the flows of international finance which have the capacity to undermine societies far removed from ours by the proliferation of the cultural

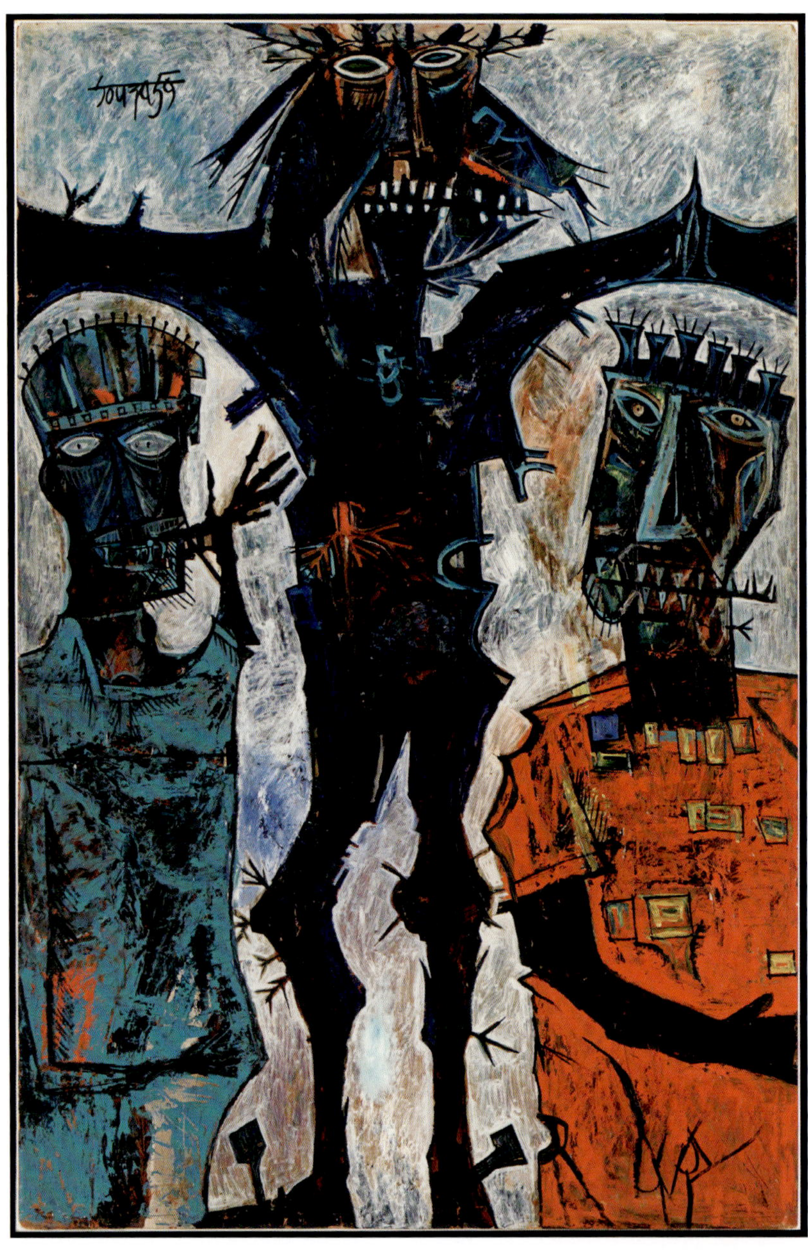

Figure 21.1. F. N. Souza, *Crucifixion*, 1961. Oil on board. 183.1 × 122 cm. © The Estate of F. N. Souza/DACS, London 2022. Photo: Tate.

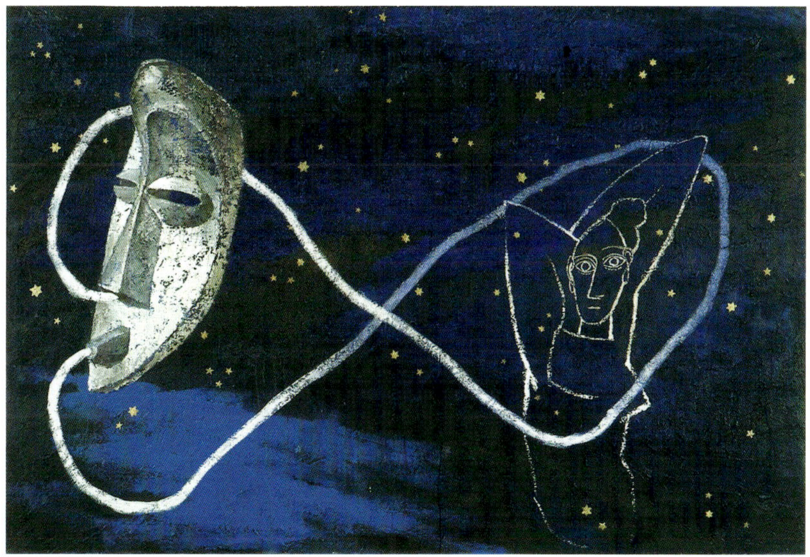

Figure 21.2. Gavin Jantjes, *Untitled*, 1989. Sand, tissue paper, and acrylic on canvas. 200 × 300 × 3 cm. © Gavin Jantjes, 2001. Image courtesy of Arts Council Collection, Southbank Centre, London.

industry—then I quite understand that a dynamic exists, which is grounded and rooted in the development and over-development of the West. However, I think that its actual impact on the rest of the world has not been simply to homogenize it, but also to expose it to differentiation. The impulse of "difference" operating in and across the world is, to me, as powerful and as unintended a consequence of capitalist globalization and modernity as the impulse towards the McDonaldization of the world. I do not believe any law of history exists which will guarantee that the one must prevail over the other, although I recognize the grim unevenness and contradictoriness of what we may call the "global balance of social forces."

If we look at the way in which contemporary art practices locate themselves with an awareness of the slow decentering of the West, we see the constitution of lateral relations in which the West is an absolutely pivotal, powerful, hegemonic force, but is no longer the only force within which creative energies, cultural flows and new ideas can be concerted. The world is moving outwards and can no longer be structured in terms of the center/periphery relation. It has to be defined in terms of a set of interesting centers, which are both different from and related to one another. Inhabiting this uneven language of a more common planetary or cosmopolitan consciousness—and I know that this process of globalization is one which has enormous inequalities built into it—is a deeply and profoundly unequal process. This does not necessarily mean that the game is already so wrapped up that we can designate it with the term "the end of history." Any museum which thinks it can incorporate or grasp the best texts and productions of modern artistic practice, believing the world is still organized in a center/periphery model, simply does not understand the contradictory tensions which are in play. On the one hand are all those lines of force which continue to draw energy, resources, exhibitions and circulation to a very narrow metropolitan center and, on the other, is the disseminating force of what is happening laterally. On the edge of our consciousness, we are aware that some of the most "modern" artists are practicing in the most "underdeveloped" places. The account of what matters in the artistic world, from the point of view of the declining, diminishing cultural authority of the West, is expanding in its potential to gobble up everything and yet this is not happening.

If you think about where important movements are being made, sometimes they happen in the center, but the most exciting artists are those who live simultaneously in the center and at the periphery. In terms of the conditions of consciousness within which these people start to make artistic practices, they inhabit a world which is torn, on the one hand, by the centralizing force of Western modernity, with all the goodies it entails, and, on the other, by the dissemination and proliferation of notions of what it would be like to be vernacular and modern. We are embarking on a hundred different ideas of "the modern," not one, and therefore, of a thousand practicing modern artists, who require recognition within the terms of the criteria that we have stitched into our museum space. Is that the end of the museum? I do not believe it is.

Museums have to understand their collections and their practices as what I can only call "temporary stabilizations." What they are—and they must be specific things or they have no interest—is as much defined by what they are not. Their identities are determined by their constitutive outside; they are defined by what they lack and by their other. The relation to the other no longer operates as a dialogue of paternalistic apologetic disposition. It has to be aware that it is a narrative, a selection, whose purpose is not just to disturb the viewer but to itself be disturbed by what it cannot be, by its necessary exclusions. It must make its own disturbance evident so that the viewer is not entrapped into the universalized logic of thinking whereby because something has been there for a long period of time and is well-funded, it must be "true" and of value in some aesthetic sense. Its purpose is to destabilize its own stabilities. Of course, it has to risk saying, "This is what I think is worth seeing and preserving," but it has to turn its criteria of selectivity inside out so that the viewer becomes aware of both the frame and what is framed.

The viewer should be able to read a particular narrative in the context of other narratives and understand that its identity is always positional. The museum of modern art has a history, a space, a funding, a tradition; it speaks a language but knows that it is no longer the only language in the world. This is a difficult exercise because museums, in spite of what we would like to think, are deeply enmeshed in systems of power and privilege. They are locked into the narrowest circulation of art in its diminishing terms and are consequently locked into mindsets which have been institutionalized in those circuits. The process of breaking free is likely to be a long and nasty business. But it cannot be long before museums of modern art come to look more and more like what the architect Cedric Price in the recent show at INIVA described as "cultural centers," characterized by "calculated uncertainty and conscious incompleteness."

NOTE

> This essay first appeared in *Stuart Hall and Sarat Maharaj: Modernity and Difference*, Annotations 6, ed. Gilane Tawadros and Sarah Campbell (London: Institute of International Visual Arts, 2001), 8–25. The keynote address was given at the Museums of Modern Art and the End of History conference at the Tate Gallery, London, May 1999.

CHAPTER 22

Modernity and Difference:
A Conversation between Stuart Hall and Sarat Maharaj

STUART HALL: As I think is true of all important terms in this kind of debate, it is best to deconstruct a term before you use it, or at least explain what you do not intend it to mean. There is one sense of the term "translation" that I do not want to awaken, which is the notion that there is an original text and that all translations are then necessarily partial renderings of that original. However, I'm really not interested in the notion of origin in that sense, because my position is that most original texts, when looked at closely, turn out to be translations themselves.

I regard translation as an unending process, a process without a beginning. Except in myth, there is no moment when cultures and identities emerge from nowhere, whole within themselves, perfectly self-sufficient, unrelated to anything outside of themselves and with boundaries which secure their space from outside intrusion. I do not think that either historically or conceptually we should think of cultures or identities or indeed texts in that way. Every text has a "before-text," every identity has its pre-identities. I am not interested in the notion of translation in terms of rendering what has already been authentically and authoritatively fixed; what I want to do instead is to think of cultural practices as always involved in the process of translating.

Cultural processes do not have a pure beginning, they always begin with some irritant, some dirty or "worldly" starting point, if I can call it that. When I say "dirty," I mean that there is no pure moment of beginning; they are always already in flow and translation, therefore, is always from one idiom, language or idiolect into another. All languages have their own internal character, their own kind of ethos, their own space, and so it is therefore impossible to think of a perfect translation; no such thing exists. One has always to think of cultural production of any kind as a reworking, as inadequate to its foundations, as always lacking something. There is always something which is left out. There is always mistranslation because a translation can never be a perfect rendering from one space or one language to another. It is bound to be somewhat misunderstood, as we are all always misunderstood in every dialogue we undertake. There is no moment of dialogic relationship with another which is perfectly understood by them in exactly the way intended by us, because translation is a mediation between two already constituting worlds. There is no perfect transparency.

So the notion of a perfect translation does not help us at all. What we usually think of as polarized between copying or mimicking on the one hand and the moment of pure creativity on the other are really two moments that are mutually constituting—they do not exist in a pure form. Pure creativity draws on something which is already there; it moves from one space to another and the creative act is that movement. It is not that I have thought of something or said something or produced something which has never been produced before—it is not the romantic notion of a pure start. Nor is it the notion of a pure finish, because every translation generates another. No-one reads a translation without thinking, "I bet that's what the original really means. I bet I could express it better."

One has to think of meaning as constituted by an infinite, incomplete series of translations. I think cultures are like that too, and so are identities. I think cultural production is like that and I am sure that texts are like that. In fact, the notion of "cultural translation" is absolutely central to an understanding of this whole field. There are many people who have contributed to this particular notion of translation which I am trying to invoke, but I shall mention just three names as a way of orienting my argument: Walter Benjamin, Jacques Derrida and Mikhail Bakhtin.

SARAT MAHARAJ: Stuart has put the ideas across clearly with regard to cultural translation—I feel there is little more I could add, except simply to expand on what he has said and refer back to my essay on the untranslatable, since for me the search for translatability involves constantly bumping into and tussling with what is untranslatable. The names Stuart concluded with—Benjamin, Derrida and Bakhtin—are crucial from the point of view of a theoretical understanding of translation and of analyzing what happens in the process: translation of identities, translation of cultures, translation of ethnicities. Whatever might be the case in hand, the point is that we are always in the process of translation—translation is not so much an exceptional moment in our lives but a condition of being and becoming.

Against the three discursive and analytical commentators who have helped us so powerfully to comprehend the mechanisms of translations in the twentieth century, I would like to say that my own involvement begins in a much less grand, less theoretical way. It started quite simply through living in the apartheid state which assumed to translate one and all "ethnic and native" groups in the way it saw fit for modernity. We would be translated—our primordial, archaic features ironed out. We would be cleaned up, dusted down and given a voice in such a way that the apartheid state could then speak to us and make us intelligible to itself. Growing up in such an environment irked all of us needless to say and the issue of translation was immediately both a violating political act and a political process of resistance.

Later on, during years of more solitary reflection on this question, I found two other thinkers helped me to delve deeper into the mechanisms of translation. They were James Joyce and Marcel Duchamp. They remain the figures with whom I have worked and tried to relate what I have understood about translation through that massive, sprawling, unreading, untranslatable work *Finnegans Wake*, and through the great untranslatables of Duchamp's notes and jottings for the *Large Glass—The Bride Stripped Bare by Her Bachelors, Even* (1911–1923). Richard Hamilton translated one batch of notes in 1960 as *The Green Box* and another bundle in 2000 as *The White Box*. These works served as instruments through which I tried to think about the stickiness of translation. While the analytical contributors to this question have largely focused on what can and cannot be translated, I felt the practitioners Duchamp and Joyce also looked at and probed zones of the untranslatable. How do we live it? What does it mean to be in the experience of the untranslatable? Is it nonsense to talk of the untranslatable in these terms? But what kind of non-sense? Counter-signification, anti-meaning, what?

These reflections through Joyce and Duchamp strengthened the idea that although certain things can be translated in the domain of the linguistic, culture is far more than simply language and words. This produced in me a deep sense of the limits of words and language as the exclusive model through which we might think about cultural life and the translation of our everyday experience. With Joyce and Duchamp, there emerged, it seemed to me, a notion of translation which activates both the visual and the sonic. Beyond the *sense* of word and image are sounds which cannot be entirely drawn into the net of signification and cannot entirely be decoded and deciphered as meaning this, that or the other. These larger sonic pools—the penumbra of the untranslatable that shadow and smudge language and for which we have to venture beyond language—became an increasingly important area of interest in my thinking about cultural translation.

STUART HALL: There are a number of points that I would like to pick up on and develop from what Sarat has just said. One is about the notion of the untranslatable, that which escapes representation, or what is always left behind as a kind of resistant remainder. I, of course, accept the notion that everything cannot be translated. I think of the nature of the remainder in a slightly different way, which perhaps remains too confined within the linguistic domain and for that reason is, I think, somewhat limited. It has to do with how we understand meaning; whatever the medium in which it finds itself expressed, the notion of meaning always depends, in part, on what is not said, and on what is not represented, as part of meaning's constitutive outside. This is the notion, derived essentially from Ferdinand de Saussure, that one cannot know what it is that one means unless one also implicitly affirms or states what one does *not* mean—that every marked term or signifier implicates its unmarked "other."

It is a rather sobering thought to realize that this absent presence is true of all identities. I do not know of any identity which, in establishing what it is, does not, at the very same moment, implicitly declare what it is not, what has to be left out, excluded. In that sense, identities are always constructed through power, even though we do not like to think that they are, because no identity can include everyone. What would be the point of an identity which includes everyone? We understand "sameness" only through difference, presence through what it "lacks." The whole point is to define what I and other people like me belong to; consequently an identity establishes itself by virtue of what is not and cannot be said to belong. To say or establish anything—any position, any presence, any meaning—one has to attend to what is outside the field of meaning and what cannot be expressed—its constitutive outside.

We are defined as much by what we are not as by what we are. The "truth" of the Lacanian insight is that the subject is constructed across a "lack," the self by its "others." This for me is an absolutely fundamental point, because it implies that, within ourselves, within the terms of a meaning, we are always inadequate. We cannot complete ourselves. We are always open to that which is other or different from ourselves, which we cannot encapsulate into ourselves, draw into our field or meaning or representation. This notion of a lack has psychoanalytic Lacanian echoes, but I do not want to get into that today. However, I do not think that you could talk about an identity without talking about what an identity lacks—difference. This is very important because it is the point at which one recognizes that one can only be constituted through the other, through what is different. Difference, therefore, is not something that is opposed to identity; instead it is absolutely essential to it. You cannot talk about the identity of a set of terms without talking about how they are different from what that set of terms does not include. So the question of difference then does, for me, emerge from what Sarat said about the untranslatable.

If I want to say something, I have to form a statement of some kind, which is true of whatever medium I am using. There is always a kind of closure to that, because I have not finished saying anything until I stop. In language, that stop or closure is both necessary and arbitrary. It is necessary because the thought cannot be completed until you frame it, but the frame is completely arbitrary because the moment somebody else responds to that statement, the frame is reopened—your previous statement (totalization) is completely detotalized. My perfectly finished thought stops and somebody else, by taking up the thread and elaborating it in a new direction, implicitly says, "Of course that's not quite so." So we move from arbitrary closure to movement to other closures, which is how dialogue—the dialogic—works. I think of any text, sentence or work as a moment of arbitrary closure in what I call the infinite flow of meaning—the infinite semiosis of language. Thus, as Bakhtin argues, no speech is wholly my own, but is sustained in the passage of meaning between speakers (the metaphor here is linguistic but applies also to the visual field).

Any statement which has a meaning for another human being is therefore grounded in more than what it says—its excess—but is also less than what you want it to say; it is the result of arbitrary closure. It is not a completely full, self-present statement of everything, because if it was, history and meaning would end; it would give up the ghost. It would say, in effect,

"OK, that's the sentence we've all been trying to say since the year dot and, now you've said it, there's nowhere else to go."

The supposedly finished statement is instantly overridden by that which it cannot say, that which it has not said, that which it cannot bring into representation. Meaning—not cognitive meaning only, but anything that somebody else will get something out of—is therefore always constituted in the interplay between excess and lack. And that is another way of thinking about what is *not* and can never be inside representation—the untranslatable.

I am interested in asking Sarat whether what he means by the untranslatable, which in a sense gives power to the images and the language he is talking about, is the same as, or different from, or close to what I have just said about what has to be left out of representation. I am strongly aware that my argument is grounded in a conception of language and is using the linguistic as a kind of master model of meaning, which is something that I do not mean to impose.

SARAT MAHARAJ: I think that Stuart has, as usual, lucidly presented how one would think of the untranslatable if one were to proceed with the linguistic model as a master model. Language has served in most of our thinking about cultural translation and I suppose that translation itself seems to be so tied up with words, translating from one language to the other. Those of us who come from areas that also involve image and sound have therefore had to really sit up and think about second-round translation—the translation of image to image, image to sound, or image to word—which is not entirely served by the linguistic model.

I feel what Stuart has presented is absolutely central to an understanding of identity and difference, difference that cannot be stopped and difference that continuously writes itself in the way Duchamp speaks of writing "in the infinitive." Imagine something that could never be written in "stationary verbs" that give a standstiff account of where one is, but is instead written "in the infinitive," forever suggesting potential movement out of itself into a future that is, as yet, not described, nor defined, nor in any way pictured. Even within linguistic terms, if I think of translation as being an act in the infinitive mood, then I get close to Stuart's notion of perpetual translation in which no sooner you feel you have fixed an identity, you have to translate it again and again and again.

This sometimes produces the effect of saying that identity is a series of negotiations, of saying this is not what it is, this is not what I mean, this is not how I see it. In fact, there has been a line of thinking, particularly in twentieth-century music and visual arts, which can be traced back to the famous words uttered by the Buddha. Asked to describe what is the essence of things, what is identity, he simply answered with three words which have reverberated throughout the twentieth-century avant-garde. He replied, in Sanskrit, "*Neti, neti, neti*," meaning, "Not this, not that, not this." Having heard these words, some felt that this was extreme mystification and were exasperated by this kind of answering. Later commentators, particularly in the Indian school of philosophy called the Nyaya-Vaisesika, went on to elaborate thinking in terms of such negatives. They stopped trying to define what we are, as though one could hold one's identity, one's sense of self in the palm of one's hand. When they did try to, they did so in a very knowing way, conscious that what they said would be translated, rephrased, recast again. So those would be my notations to Stuart's clear account of the linguistic model.

I have tried to struggle with the notion of the untranslatable as that area that is simply the leftover—Stuart mentioned the term remainder—the "leftover-dross" in the act of translation. When one language, one experience, one visual or retinal regime gets translated into another, it has to be re-jigged to fit into the system of thinking of the other and something is "left out." This remainder—at least this is what logically appears when you analyze translation—inhabits the space of the untranslatable, a fog that persists no matter how much in everyday life we feel we overcome the untranslatable and manage to thrash out a ground of crystal-clear communication for ourselves. In some instances, artists have gone on to say that translation—even from one set of words to another—demands picturing or somehow seeing what is left. The remainder which cannot be put into words might be something you can visualize or something that can be suggested through sonic stuff, through "sounding of that difference" as a kind of turbulence, as a cloud of disturbance around clear-cut linguistic meaning.

In the more political sense, I understand the untranslatable to mean that which resists translation—in the sense that it refuses the state's ability to translate and slot a person into a set category of difference. When a government attempts to fix a person into a difference-box and then treats him or her according to a policy or program of diversity, I call this pigeonholing *multicultural managerialism*. In the light of my concern about that managerialism and fixing of difference, I have tried to explore beyond the linguistic model to understand the untranslatable not simply as a place of resistance or turbulence or perturbation, but as one of elusive liquidity—in Duchamp's and Bergson's lingo, as a matter of "passages" rather than "stoppages."

STUART HALL: I think we ought to go straight on, as Sarat has done, and take these ideas into the political arena. There is a great deal of turbulence today when two cultures, two identities, two texts meet in the same space. The greater the turbulence that is created, the more likely it is that managerialism steps in, because everybody expects to define how two incommensurable texts should become more like one another, or at any rate occupy discrete spaces which can be identified, regulated and organized. They want them to remain sufficiently stable and fixed, to achieve a kind of closed system, in which you trade a bit of your differences for a bit of mine and so on. And now I suppose we ought to ask what is wrong with this? Is it not a laudable, liberal, tolerant way of managing these difficult situations? Are you really inviting societies—which are increasingly obliged to try to make a life in which these different cultures and texts join together and occupy the same space—to accept two facts: firstly, that the maps of difference will never settle down in a way which can be predictable, administered by policy, or regulated in a rational way; and, secondly, that an element of the disturbance of the untranslatable will always be part of this encounter? I do not think one can duck the fact that these are not just textual questions, but they are also closely interwoven with social questions.

SARAT MAHARAJ: The move away from the linguistic model to some extent was demanded by my anxiety about cultural translation becoming a purely textual issue, becoming purely commentaries upon texts upon texts. There is a risk that we trap ourselves perfecting the system of conceptualization, never breaking out to connect with the streaming practices and processes of everyday life. That *conductivity* is what I have tried to address in speaking of the untranslatable through a series of scenarios of "juxta-linear translation," of "transubstantiation," or of "currency-rate translation"; there are various other models of translation which I have tried to develop around the master notion. I think the question Stuart has posed is an important and difficult one. I do not think I have an absolute answer. Instead I see the paradoxes and the collision courses that one enters into in this sort of analysis—between the political necessity of wrapping up the flow and the need for "stoppages" and for keeping things "in the infinitive," for "passages."

I can only but support and back the liberal democracies in their attempt to want to grapple with difference. I see that as an extremely important, creative advance on the position that existed twenty years ago, or even more recently, when difference was consigned to invisibility. "Difference" was seen as something that was a pre-modern hangover that would have to be ironed out in a process of assimilation, of being rendered part of the modern world. This assumption that difference is simply a problem that will be overcome when the state inducts the other, the different and the diverse into a notion of sameness and modernity is now being challenged by fresh thinking in the liberal democracies. The European Union, in particular, with its concerted state policies of cultural diversity, has had to tackle the presence of difference which cannot be assimilated and treated as though it is simply an archaic, obsolete element that, given time, will modernize and also begin shopping at Safeway. This shift has led to a concern with wanting to order difference and, in the better sense of the term, to "manage" it.

At the same time, I see—involved as a dialectic within this attempt to order, to address, to create space for difference—elements marked by the apartheid state's attempt to regulate difference. This attempt at regulation at the heart of addressing difference worries me. I feel we have to counter it by a sense of a turbulent process vis-à-vis difference, to look at its disturbances and the way it trips up the all-too-settled frame which the state—or government or European Union—policies establish for us and in which we are expected to operate as functions and factors of difference. I see a political procedure—stoppages—and I see a philosophical, experiential analysis—passages—but I do not think these are squareable. In my mind and my work, they do not run together; there is an element of their always being out of synch. Therefore I shall go back to say that I do not have an absolute answer to this.

STUART HALL: I agree with much of what you say, but I want to explore it further. First of all, I acknowledge the advances which have been made by liberal democracies in exploring what would be involved in coming to terms with difference. I am sure, however, that you would want me to raise a warning note that this is so far an extremely uneven and incomplete process; there are plenty of areas of the liberal democratic world which are still perfectly prepared to override or deny difference, or to manage it in a very different way.

In this context, it is worth identifying with one of the most difficult things to comprehend nowadays about this society—the absolute coincidence of multiculturalism and racism. Far from being the opposite ends of a pole so that one can trade the rise of one against the decline of the other, it seems to be absolutely dead central to society that both multiculturalism and racism are increasing at one and the same time. This is partly because the society we are talking about is not in any sense unified around any of these projects. Some people think multiculturalism is wonderful and they cannot imagine life without it. They are usually young and they mainly live in London. Others think they cannot do anything about the creeping multicultural drift, but they hope that it will stay in the urban centers, and, if they move to the country, it will not try to marry their daughters. Yet others cannot stand the sight of it. They are driven completely crazy by the very idea of a multicultural Britain and a minority of those will go so far as to stick knives into it and beat it over the head with a table leg if they come across it. It is a very confused picture. We could hardly have expected anything different from a society like Britain which has been constituted as a closed culturally homogeneous entity (although Britain has never been a mono-cultural entity in its life, despite its official story of itself). The fact that some parts of society are now willing, tentatively, to ask the question of how differences are to be lived is thus a very important step.

Personally, however, I think that the process could easily be reversed; I do not think that it is by any means secure, even in Europe. Improvements seem to have been made on three bases. Firstly, that of greater and greater assimilation—or where the differences become so minor that they no longer matter very much. If they do not trouble you very much, if they are kept in private and only occur behind closed doors, or in those parts of the city which normal folks do not visit, if they are not "in your face," then they are much easier to accept. This is a pacified form of difference and here the untranslatable is absolutely crucial, it seems, because I feel not a conscious, so much as an unconscious resistance to giving in to assimilation in that way. Secondly, there was a very important moment in liberal democracy, in the 1970s I think, when the dream of some perfect assimilation, in which all differences would be obliterated into a color-free universe, died a death. I do not think anybody thinks that dream is going to be revived, which is a kind of acknowledgement that people feel some things so deeply that they are not going to let them be translated out of existence. They are not going to have them commodified or regulated or managed. The third issue is how we begin to think about or deal with the turbulence that you talked about, the unpredictable nature or raw experience of encountering difference that will not go away, because it is too deeply embedded to be wished away.

Politically, we have to begin to think in terms of a democratic project which is an argument, a real battle or struggle—an agonistic form of democratic dialogue—which is the absolute reverse of everybody going to the polling booth every five years and voting for X or Y. A row has to happen, as people trade away the things which do not matter and get down to those irreducible points where you can say, "My route into modernity is different from yours, and that constitutes me as a different kind of person. It constitutes my life as a different project from yours." Is the only response to difference that we must eat one another? Or is there some way of learning to live *with* difference?

I have been involved this week in the aftermath of the commission on the Future of a Multi-Ethnic Britain, during which people have said to me that I should be proud to be British. There is only one question in response to that: which British? There are many things about Britain that I am proud of. And then there are all the bits of Britishness which I absorbed directly and intravenously at about the age of two months. I came to England thinking that every flower was a daffodil, because the Romantic poets had been injected directly into my bloodstream; I could hardly name a Jamaican flower and to discover that all English flowers were not daffodils was really rather surprising. So, yes, of course there are some senses in which I am "British." And yet I cannot relate to the British empire in the same way that a native English person does. I never will, so either that is the end of the conversation or we have to find some way of getting beyond that. It is not going to be an easy dialogue and it has to recognize my own willingness to trade the specificity of what is different about the routes by which I come to the present and to modernity and the routes by which they have come to modernity. This is an ineradicable, an untranslatable kind of difference, which the Home Secretary and the programs for "cultural diversity" do not want to hear about. So, unfortunately, we have got to go on trying to make the translation as effective as possible and yet also be prepared for the thing to explode in our face because of what is not tradable, what is not manageable, what remains stubbornly outside the field of representational translatability.

GILANE TAWADROS: I would like to ask a pragmatic question about how you deal with the two elements of untranslatability. On the one hand there is a resistance to untranslatability and there exists a point at which you have to define what cannot be negotiated, what is the final border? How does that work? How can that operate? How can one imagine that within the space of everyday life, within the political domain, whether that be as a citizen or in terms of governance? On the other hand, there is a desire for completeness which sits opposite or beneath that untranslatability. It is the desire for that perfect translation and to be able to square that inner circle which is constantly being articulated in one way or another.

STUART HALL: The difference which is untranslatable is not a fixed and essential thing; it is itself the product of a translation and is itself, always, in motion. It is not as though it is and will always be there and that nothing will ever break into it. It is not like that. The moment when one is required to enter some common space is the point at which the recognition of difference is absolutely central, because every real negotiation depends on the recognition of its limits. At the same time, the recognition of similarity is also important, because similarity is the horizontal to the vertical of difference. Nothing is pure difference; there is no essentialized difference. Difference remains, but not fixed immutably by its origins, not immured in an unchanging "tradition," because it is open to movement and located within other dimensions which cut across that, which laterally connect you with other people.

I no longer believe in some abstract universal set of values that you can import into the conversation to trump every other particular, such as your Egyptianness, his South Africanness, my Caribbeanness. Nor do I subscribe to a view of human rights or universal human values which have nothing to do with the own particular lives that we have lived. Far from it. I think the only way in which people who are different could come to constitute a common conversation is by recognizing the inadequacy of each of our positions as well as what is not translatable. The moment you take the radical inadequacy, the "lack," of your own position into account, there is a broadening, a widening, an ethical reach for that which is different from you but which also constitutes you—the reach for the other. It is an ethical acknowledgement of our own incompleteness and it is only in that space that people can begin to trade. That is the point where negotiation becomes feasible, but only if the two elements are entering as equal partners to the trade, as equal partners to the dialogue. It cannot be your conversation into which I am fitting or your idiom which I have to learn.

I do not want to talk about the stubbornness and the rawness of what we are calling the untranslatable as if it is some fixed, originary foundational point. That is not the way to think about it. Whatever moment you cut into it, the positions will be in different spaces, located differently in relation to one another. You therefore have to think both about what people will not give up and what might frame that dialogue in such a way that people can participate equally in working out some future which includes them all and which acknowledges the lack which each of us has in our need for recognition from the other. This is what Ernesto Laclau calls the universal, not as something from outer space which trumps every particular, but an incomplete horizon reached for from within each inadequate particular.

SARAT MAHARAJ: I think it is really important that Stuart has emphasized the fact that we are not speaking of difference as though it were always present as a primordial space—as though the untranslatable were the primordial penumbra of the translated. We face this with regard to the relationship between the global and the local too; there is the assumption that somehow the global is bad and then there is this primordial good called the local that we must somehow hold on to as the point of resistance. It is often overlooked that the local is as much produced by the processes of the global and therefore we have a far more complicated, tricky relationship between the local and global to think through.

The same is true with the translatable and the untranslatable, which is a produced effect of the act and process of translation. It is shifting, fugitive, not easy to pinpoint, define and work out how to deal with, which is what I feel the liberal democratic states tries to do. A bunch of untranslatable immigrants arrive and the state says, "What do we do with them? How do we translate them?" Not unlike how the apartheid state reacted to untranslatable archaic natives, immigrants, indentured labourers, whatever the case was, and set about translating them. In that process difference is treated in the banal form that Stuart was referring to, in which everything seems to be "sorted," to use a colloquialism, and organized and given its place. This display of cultural diversity becomes an extension of cultural tourism.

In the West, we see not only terrible waves of xenophobia, but also greater waves of xenophilia at the same time—a baffling thing about the current, contemporary situation. Cultural tourism tends to promote a strong sense of wanting to be with the other—desiring the different, the foreign, the strange in pre-digested terms—to the extent that we can visit Jamaica and yet not visit Jamaica, we can visit India and yet not visit it, South Africa and yet not quite visit it. We consume the country as a series of markers of difference, which are given to us as packets and packages of experience of the other. They are just different enough to make a good holiday without too many moments of turbulence. The turbulence I speak to concerns the sense of freefall and melt-down of ethical engagement with difference, which goes beyond its packaged, manicured version as the experience of curious, titillating difference sifted down to diversity. The production of cultural tourism is precisely the spectacular condition of the contemporary world engendering a kind of xenophilia, which the liberal democratic state tends to orchestrate through programs of diversity. Important as these programs are in grappling with difference, they screen engagement with difference, producing, as Stuart reminds us, those situations in which you are likely to get your head bashed in or remain the object of murder because you represent troubling difference. You are cast as a remainder that cannot be entertained, re-tussled with, and therefore a difference that has to be violated.

How do we deal with difference without fixing it as a version of ourselves? How do we deal with difference without entirely reducing it to the terms and the categories of our own language? I know we have to deal with it in the social domain, in the everyday domain and in political terms. But I question whether language itself can deal with difference in any fundamental sense. Is language not always subject to a self-deception? It is not able to face the fact that it has demolished the other in some way, recomposed it in terms of its own linguistic competency and grammar regime. This act of violation at the heart of language, at the heart of conceiving the other, leads me to look for para-linguistic ways of engaging the other—drawing it into the ethical encounter with difference. I suppose that I am prepared to say that there is a *xenocidal* drive in language; it murders the "foreign" other, it violates the other to such an extent that it brings to the fore only what it can deal with in its terms—in terms of its own epistemic frame. Now this might be a slightly pessimistic, somewhat downbeat view of language, but I feel that it might help us to explore the complicated cultural situation in the liberal democracies, where we see an advance in dealing with difference, accompanied by some of the most atrocious forms of violation of difference and diversity. And I am asking if this knotted complexity is tackled at all times in the forms of language we have?

STUART HALL: My immediate response is that this is not best thought of in terms of language versus other media of expression. Whatever the medium, unless it is used in such a way as not simply to reproduce existing categories and orders, it will have this violating effect of closure on the other and cause rejection. This may have something to do with modernism, because it is only in and after modernism that languages—both visual and verbal languages of representation—have been broken up and fractured in terms of their ability to reproduce the world directly, in some literal way. It is only when language is "in that break" that you can get disturbance into the language itself and, at that point, to put it crudely, Joyce can do as good a job, and is doing rather the same job, as Duchamp. Within their spheres—the linguistic and the visual—they are both operating in such a way that the objects they constitute, whatever the medium, no longer fit perfectly within an already existing system of reference and meaning; the means themselves disturb and unsettle or subvert any attempt to translate things back into their originals in a seamless way.

I would prefer to talk therefore in terms of what is done with *language*, in the broader sense, or the means of representation of whatever one is talking about, rather than speaking of the linguistic versus the visual. I do not deny that the linguistic, in the narrower sense, has been a powerful carrier in Western culture of the cognitive and the conceptual, and so it is a more difficult model to apply to the visual field. However, I do not think that the linguistic and visual are mutually exclusive. Or, to put it the other way, a lot of visual work seems to me thinkable within the model of what we may call "the linguistic" or "the discursive" turn.

SARAT MAHARAJ: That was not quite what I intended—I am not trying to pit visual against verbal. I could not, at any rate, do so given my equal involvement with Joyce and Duchamp. Both, however, do seriously distress the idea that all meaning is discursive. I am keen, however, to press home the difficulties faced with the linguistic-discursive because I do feel other domains, semantic or otherwise—the visual-sonic—tend to be left out of the discussion of the ethical encounter with difference.

Joyce often tips over the verbal into the visual. Duchamp moves away from the retinal, making the optical into the conceptual as much as, in another about-turn, he makes us look at text as image, as "visible gram-

mar." Both play out convoluted verbal-visual-sonic interactions and semantic fissions. My aim, therefore, is not, as suggested by a member of
the audience, to "discredit" the linguistic. "Discredit" is quite off the mark
and, at any rate, it is too strong a word—this is England! The aim is rather
to put pressure on the conceptual-discursive not so much with a counter-
linguistic but with a para-linguistic—not so much with its binary opposite as with a modality that goes with, around, through and beyond the
linguistic. To adapt Duchamp, a 4-D translation "in the infinitive"—a
"circum-hyper-hypo-translation."

NOTE

This conversation first appeared in *Changing States: Contemporary Art and Ideas
in an Era of Globalization*, ed. Gilane Tawadros (London: Institute of International
Visual Arts, 2004), 286–91.

DREAMING IN AFRO

CHAPTER 23

Chris Ofili in Paradise:
Dreaming in Afro

I have had the privilege of spending time with Chris Ofili in his studio, looking at the series of large paintings he is completing as the artist selected for the British pavilion at the 2003 Venice Biennale. These first impressions were written, not so much "about" as "with" the work.

Chris Ofili is on the move. He is completing the huge canvasses he is exhibiting in his *Within Reach* show for the British pavilion at the 2003 Venice Biennale (figs. 23.1–23.3). As we move around his surprisingly dark studio space (the windows were already covered by green and red cloths when he found it!), reflecting now on one, now on another of these spot-lit, vibrant and pulsating visionary scenes, one is made aware again how intense and protracted is the "work" of painting for Ofili. Only he knows how many of these he has on the go at any one time—bringing them out, one after another, working on them for a while, putting them away again to, as it were, coalesce—perhaps even fundamentally to change shape.

The astonishing work exhibited in the lower room of the Victoria Miro gallery in *Freedom One Day*, with its restricted red-green-black palette, its luxuriant, luminous foliage shapes and those enormous, reclining, black Afro-lover figures, can now be seen to be only part of a series, a longer, on-going, more ambitious enterprise: each new painting emerging as yet another "scene" from an episodic and still incomplete narrative journey.

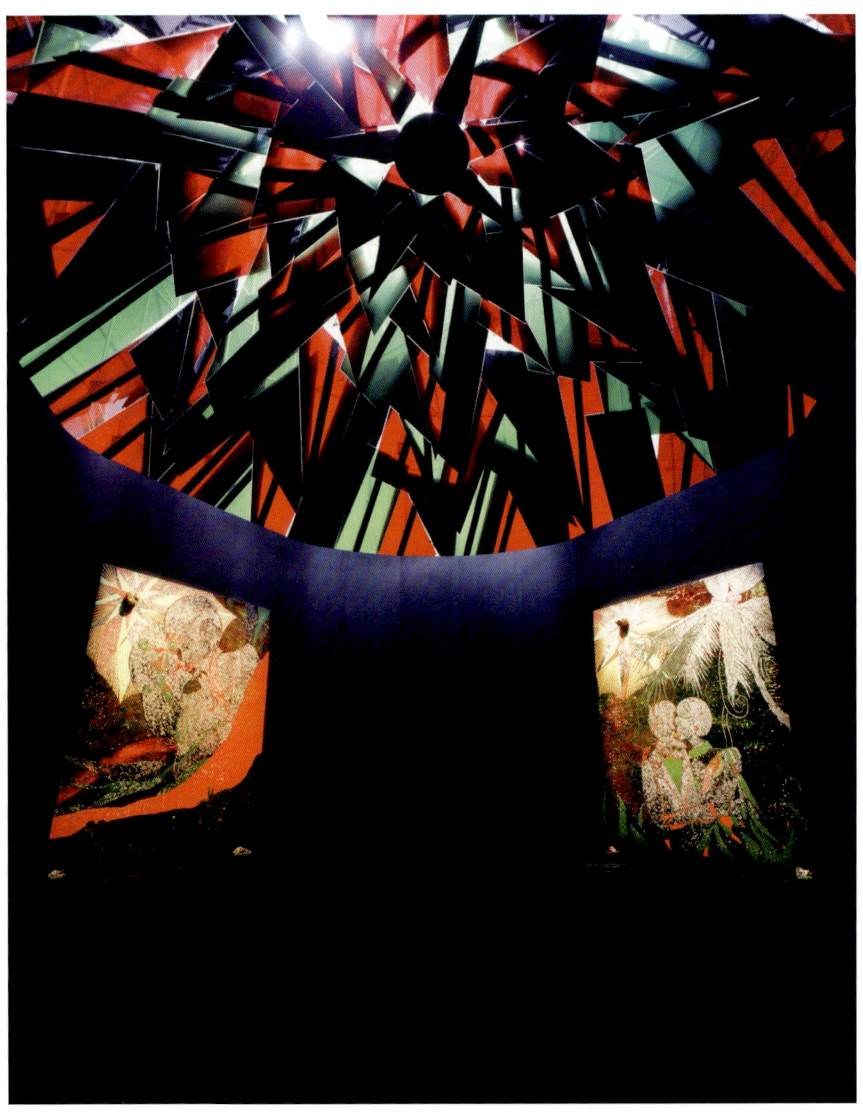

Figure 23.1. Installation view, Chris Ofili, *Within Reach*, British Pavilion, Venice Biennale, June 15–November 2, 2003, with paintings *Afro Apparition* (left) and *Afro Love and Envy* (right). Work above, *Afro Kaleidoscope*. Conceived by Chris Ofili. Designed with David Adjaye/Adjaye Associates. Engineered by Charles Walker, Arup.

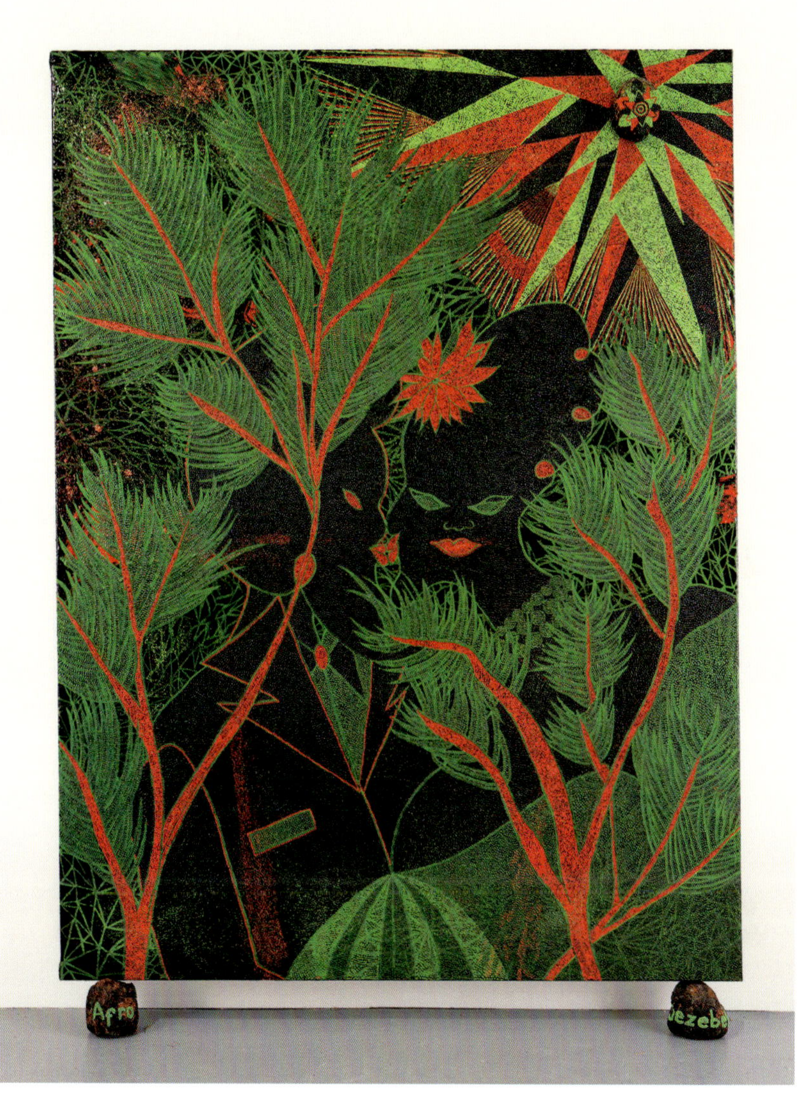

Figure 23.2. Chris Ofili, *Afro Jezebel*, 2002–2003. Oil paint, polyester resin, glitter, map pins, and elephant dung on linen. With two elephant-dung supports. 244×183 cm (96 1/8×72 1/8 in). © Chris Ofili. Courtesy of the artist and Victoria Miro.

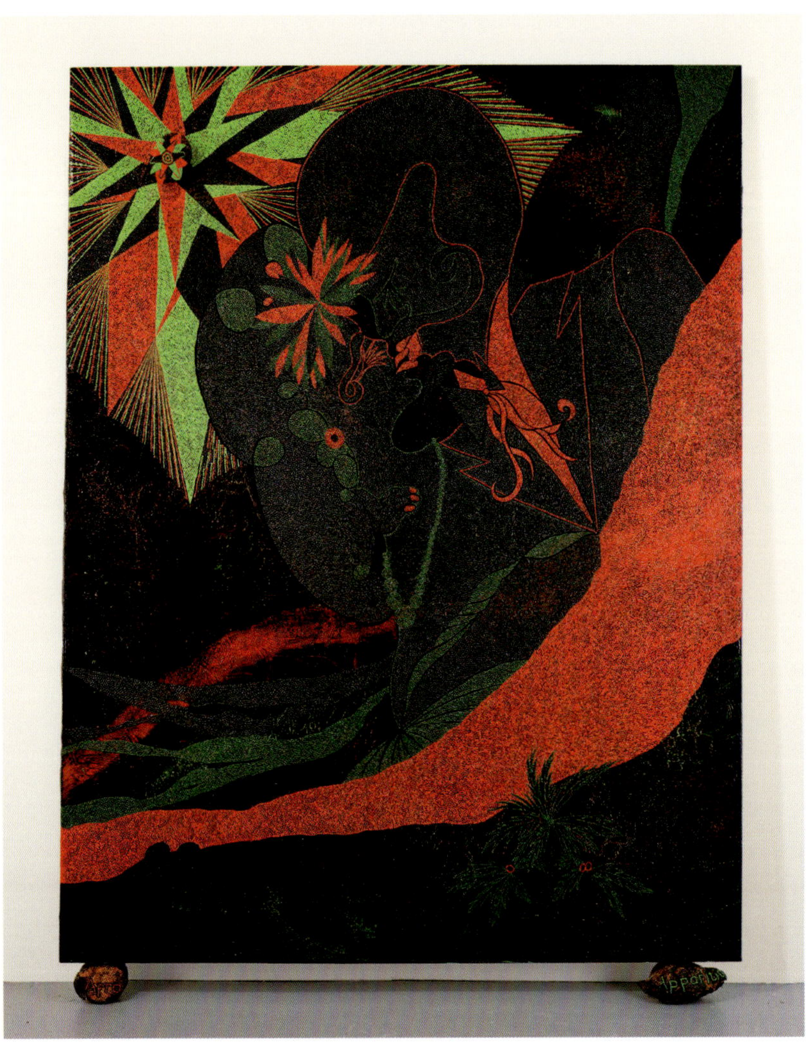

Figure 23.3. *Afro Apparition*, 2002–2003. Acrylic, oil, polyester resin, glitter, map pins, and elephant dung on linen. With two elephant-dung supports. 275 × 214 cm (108 1/4 × 84 1/4 in). © Chris Ofili. Courtesy of the artist and Victoria Miro.

"Halfway along the road we have to go,
I found myself obscured in a great forest . . ."

In one new canvas, a broad, lateral scarlet band running across the lower half of the canvas reminds me of a road, and thus of travelling and a journey. The two outline figures, bottom left, are passing through an enchanted landscape. They are like the illustrations to *The Divine Comedy*, with Beatrice leading Dante towards Paradise. But the couple's vision of themselves transfigured, which is projected upwards in the painting and fills the skies above them, like gigantic changing cloud-forms, assumes the outline shape of the two iconic black "Afromantics"—the sexy hero and heroine of the work we have seen elsewhere, surrounded by the verdant plant-life, encrusted foliage shapes and richly decorative undergrowth of a tropical jungle. What matters for the journey which this series chronicles is not arriving at some final Beatific Vision but the more earthly, carnal dreams and visions to be glimpsed along the way.

Africa, not the Tuscan countryside, is the inspiration here. Not Africa recollected in nostalgia, or site of redemptive return: but "Africa" re-imagined, a landscape of the mind, free for dreaming, visually recalled, as from another place—from *elsewhere*; "Africa," not remembered but dreamt in its translated "Afro" idiom. The themes of Freedom and Unity, with their African/African-American resonances, sustained so powerfully—and obliquely—by the restricted red, green and black colours borrowed from Marcus Garvey's design for the Pan-African flag, which visually organized *Freedom One Day* (and are intended to suffuse the Venice pavilion, with a newly designed red, green and black glass roof), have been pushed forwards, thematically, another half turn—further towards love and romance. This is no vision of perfection ("I think painting, or art, comes from the impure nature of things," he has said) but secular, resolutely "worldly" and—to use Ofili's own word—"pagan." As he said of his monkey masterpiece, *The Upper Room*, "Religion and stuff."

Ofili's vision of Paradise may refer somewhere to the Bible, Heaven and the Promised Land—this would not be the first time these very different visions have been condensed in the African imaginary. The eye may have been partly informed, at some level we can't any longer see, by Botticelli's *Inferno*, or Tintoretto's *Paradise*—Ofili draws on a rich repertoire of multiple, overlapping references and his knowledge of European painting is extraordinarily wide and sophisticatedly unpredictable. However, his Afro "Adam and Eve" have had many, more dazzling, disruptive and "vulgar" antecedents in his work. And, as he told Jonathan Jones about the first *Paradise* series, there is also somewhere in there, "a Caribbean island with aqua-blue water and palm trees and great cocktails and very accommodating natives and then it's back on the charter flight to Leeds." Don't miss the irony, or the last laugh will be on you. Rigorously "of his time and place," Ofili, the master of Afro-kitsch as high art form, has never taken lessons from anyone about who or what he is entitled to "mix."

All the same, don't miss or mistake, either, the commitment—to what painting can do, in the age of conceptualism and the installation; or the engagement—with the vision of exotic/erotic love; or the seriousness—about what it is possible for the Afro-imaginary—as C. L. R. James said, "in but not of Europe"—to see and say now—which the irony only partially disguises. The fact is, no European artist would or could conceivably dream in these forms and colours today. The imaginary at work here is irredeemably "off-shore," postcolonial, diasporic. And it affirms, against the grain, embracing its own creative powers. This Paradise is possible *now*. It is *Within Reach*.

Narratives and themes, however significant for what ultimately we take away, are subordinated in Ofili's work to the painting. Or rather, each element plays into the other, depending on what you are looking at or where you stand in relation to the canvas. The paintings work like palimpsests, built up layer on layer: though this does not create the usual effect of an impacted integument of paint but, instead, makes them seem transparent and translucent: not without depth, but translated into a flatter plane. This may partly be the effect of the layer of resin which covers the surface like glass, or of the glitter, gold leaf and colored glass pins out of which surfaces and lines are built. The paintings, at any rate, glimmer, twinkle and glisten at you. They pulsate with the intense but "cool" interior light of the forest.

As it happens, light is also a recurring theme in the series: like its predecessors, each love scene has a radiating red, green and black orb—sun or moon—in its upper left-hand corner, looking down on, keeping guard over, watching out for the "divine couple," with its signature, decorated, elephant dung centre (how little this petty "scandal" seems to matter anymore). This light, too, is not ethereal but material. Sometimes its rays splinter and shatter like shards of red glass all across the surface. Sometimes it quietly explodes in a geometrically shaped array. Sometimes it is stealthily threaded between and behind the foliage, enfolding the scene in a network of black, felt-tipped light-lines.

The level at which the painting "signifies" moves constantly between foreground and background, depending on where you stand. From a certain distance, the canvas suddenly comes together—falls into place—as a "scene." Central to this are the two red-outlined, black, formalized, cartoon-like figures, smartly dressed-up or luxuriantly nude, locked into an intense, romantic/erotic relationship with each other: their fiery, red lips pursed for the kiss, his eyes glowing white like coals, her necklace aglow. The apocryphal story of their "origin" in the designs Ofili once saw used on a dry-cleaning bag by a Trinidad laundry is intriguing, like a lot of Ofili stories (there is just a hint of a question as to whether he deliberately generates them himself). But the truth is that Ofili has been drawing, in addition to his great decorative portraits of black divas, outline cartoons of a voluptuous black woman with African-coiffured hair and a man with a Rasta beard like a floating phallus, for years—on and on, proliferating across the walls like, at an earlier point, his Michael Jackson Afro heads. Retrospectively, we may say, the "series" rather than the single canvas has always been Ofili's natural *metier*. Nevertheless, in their present form and scale, the blackness of these odalisques gives them an eerie existence, for they are both "modern" and "ancient," somehow "central" to the whole work while often not so much stepping forward from the lush background as forming part of it, absorbed back into nature, in a complex figure/ground reversal.

If you take a step back, they "disappear." Their red outlines become part of the labyrinth of trailing liana-like lines that cover the canvas; or certain parts detach themselves from the figure and take on a visual life of their own. The man's blazing red shirt and tie, for example, float free of his body, and hover like a *memento mori*. At this distance, it is the stylised tropical natural forms—the luxuriant plants, the exotic coconut trees, the bamboo and poinsettia leaf and flower shapes in their swirling, rhythmically repeating patterns—which seem to be "the subject." But move in much closer, and one encounters the dense, richly-worked network of stippled lines, raised dots, ripples and "dribbles" which is where the "brush-work" of the painting— reinforced by the obligatory, but now submerged drawing and blocking out with which it all started—is being done. When Chris Ofili says he has been "working some more on this painting," he means he has been building up the surface some more, and in the process constantly changing the contours of the painting *at this micro-level of operation*.

This Paradise plays with "the primitive" but is ultimately too knowing for that. It *passes through* the primitive without being captured by it. It nods towards Douanier Rousseau, but only as a gesture of recognition between two artists ultimately going in different directions. It is neither pre- nor post-lapsarian: the looks between the lovers are too openly carnal for that. It is, to coin a word, "lapsed." Old Snakey is already inside the picture. Occasionally, we catch a glimpse of some part of his chequered body, coiled contentedly around something. The "simplification" with which everything has been treated is an aspect of a formal complexity, not the fantasy of a return to innocence. Wickedness (evil is too strong a word) has not been banished from Paradise because it is an intrinsic part of the vision. A "wicked," satanic, black devil-figure with blazing red eyes—some conjuror, ju-ju man or Anansi spider figure—occupies the centre of another painting, but he too is the recipient of a kiss on the cheek from that black lady with the lustrous lips, the reclining Madame Triple Beam Dreamer, from his stunning 2001 canvas. The "satanic" figure may be there to remind us of the inevitable limits to joy and happiness; but every "world" has its limits, every "paradise" is incomplete. Besides, Ofili has been drawing and painting Super-Fly and hip-hop "bad boys" for ages. As elsewhere in his work, there are hints of a religious or spiritual motif here and there, but that is not what the paintings are "about." If this motif is anywhere, it is in the exuberant, pan-theistic receptivity to nature and the "way of the world." The dichotomous Christian world of good and evil or the Western binary of barbarism and civility are simply not appropriate here.

Chris Ofili has sometimes been criticized for his irony and evasiveness in not addressing the so-called political questions of "identity" more directly; letting himself off the hook, while allowing the critics to use his work to poke fun at his more seriously-committed, "politically-correct" peers. In the light of his recent work, this criticism now seems misdirected. There is more than one way to skin a tiger. Besides, what matters much more is that one cannot think of a contemporary visual artist whose fecund and excessive visual imagination is more fully saturated with the imagery of the diasporic black imaginary—all of it, African/African-American/Afro-Caribbean/ Black British: with no respect for imposed boundaries of appropriateness or taste. *Within Reach* represents a dazzling new instalment of this evolving story, by a contemporary master. Long may the outrage continue.

NOTE

This essay first appeared in Chris Ofili, *Within Reach: British Pavilion, 50th Venice Biennale: 15 June to 2 November 2003*, vol. 1, *Words* (London: Victoria Miro Gallery, 2003), unpaged.

CHAPTER 24

Maps of Emergency:
Fault Lines and Tectonic Plates

The fifteen African artists presented in *Fault Lines* at the 2003 Venice Biennale follow the global traffic along pathways increasingly tracked by artistic production and the work of art in the age of transnational globalization. Not long ago, this relationship was most conveniently expressed in terms of center and periphery. Differences persist. But they are no longer adequately convened within these fixed spatial poles. Still, one cannot resist the impression that this work has crossed, or migrated even, across a series of invisible frontiers, to one "world"—the space of international exhibitions—from another "world," that of the troubled, unsettled, non-spatialized places of the "South." As such, the *Fault Lines* artists have something unique and challenging to contribute to the discourses that define the so-called international art world which is the Biennale's traditional stamping ground.

The internationalism of that first "world" remains a peculiarly skewed affair. Nevertheless, whatever its structure of inclusions and exclusions, this work from the edge now belongs irrevocably to global circuits. Okwui Enwezor and Olu Oguibe in *Reading the Contemporary* date this "entry [of contemporary African art] into greater circulation in the global network of international exhibitions, museums, galleries, residencies etc" from 1989.[1] Not only because of the key critical responses generated that year in reaction to the (in)famous *Magiciens de la Terre* exhibition in Paris, but also because of the end of the Cold War (which had so constrained Africa in the strait-jacket of global polarization) and because of the accelerating collapse of *apartheid* in South Africa, the date has truly global significance. However, Enwezor and Oguibe also remind us of the deep ambiguities which attach to the incorporation of the margins, and the danger when the very specific differences which continue to separate margin from center are absorbed into the *indifference* of the postmodern celebration of difference.

This work, then, continues to sit awkwardly in the contemporary pantheon. It reminds us of the diversity of visions, artistic practices and forms of life—still largely unknown outside the continent—which are shaping the contemporary African imaginary today. Of course, the forces which are producing these novel effects of similarity and difference are no longer easily distributed between "North" and "South." Given the scale of migration and the transnational character of flows in the globalizing, postcolonial moment, they belong to a shared, deeply intertwined, but highly uneven and unfinished "global" world, from whose impact none is excluded. Considered in their concrete artistic particularity, of course, each work demands to be seen in its own right. Each is the outcome of a conjuncture between a particular artistic vision and an individual practice. Each is in the process of freeing itself from "the burden of representation." There is no one "Africa" here to be positively affirmed. The exhibition radically disrupts that lazy but necessary signifier; disturbing the sight-lines on Africa from within and without, it gives, on this specific occasion, a greater continental centrality in the field of vision to Africa's northern, Islamic and Arab zones and a particularly diasporic inflexion to Africa's unfinished self-definition.

The idea of "an essential African aesthetic"—a totality of works "immersed in a sort of mythological retrospection which seems to issue from the collective unconscious"—has metamorphosed out of existence.[2] Clifford Charles, reflecting on his own practice, argues that his refusal to be frustrated "by the shifting grounds that inform our life . . . the trauma and horror of our incomplete/unresolved past . . . the hoarding and social 'bravado' of the displaced and recently empowered . . ." has drawn his art into "an introspective gaze. This talking to myself becomes a silent self-reflection."[3] However, a few minutes spent with the large, bold, unnervingly black, fluid shapes of his ink-on-paper paintings—clearly still struggling, long after the end of apartheid, with what Frantz Fanon once called "the fact of blackness"—show that this self-reflection has not diverted his work into a false, solipsistic individualism. What we are looking at is more a decisive shift of register, an enhanced freedom of eye, hand and medium in relation to form and project, but not a disconnection. His work remains immersed in what he calls "critically assessing . . . the existing patterns of our thinking."[4]

The work of the *Fault Lines* artists implies a confidence in the individual's subjective aesthetic sensibility and practice—an indulgence long considered the privilege of the Western eye/subject alone. (Individuation, after all, was understood as the gift of the Enlightenment to Western modernity; African art, being "less evolved," was supposed to be, by definition, more anonymously collective.) Each of the artists fully inhabits the range of languages and materials available to contemporary art practice—painting and multimedia, video and film installation, abstraction and neo-figurative, conceptual and collage—though often from within a distinctly non-European, postcolonial paradigm. Each work has its own way of negotiating the tension between tradition and modernity, so critical to Africa's troubled, ongoing dialogue with its Others. Each speaks out of a specific historical conjuncture. Each is engaged in a labor of remapping. Each finds its own way, not so much to address, as to take a new sighting on Africa's present "state(s) of emergency."

We find this, for example, in the earliest work in *Fault Lines*—the remapping that is clearly evident in Frank Bowling's astonishing, postcolonial or diasporic, planetary cartographies. Only here and there do their oceanic swathes of translucent color echo a Mercator projection;[5] only here and there do they reveal, faintly, a replaced outline, a reimagined coastal indentation, the hint of a new continental shelf; and only *very* occasionally do they allow the shape of something more tangible and familiar—a house? a dwelling place?—to half-surface through the thick integument of the paint. Or we see it in Rotimi Fani-Kayode's sensuously erotic re mappings of desire around the transgressive black body, with its triple diasporic displacements, familial, geographic/cultural and sexual.

We find it also in certain effects of *disturbance* in the work: surfaces fractured by a sudden upsurge of violence, rupture or dis-location. Look, for example, at Pitso Chinzima and Veliswa Gwintsa's meditations, out of the heart of the South African experience, on death and the contagion of violence, as it spreads indiscriminately from one location to another, becoming a general global phenomenon. Or look at Zarina Bhimji's light boxes (fig. 24.1), which, like the eerily evacuated Ugandan landscapes of her recent film *Out of Blue* (2002), speak volumes through absence, summoning up the profound sense of emptiness and loss which forced exile produces, and the silent devastation left behind by those who wreak a brutal revenge on difference. Or, in quite a

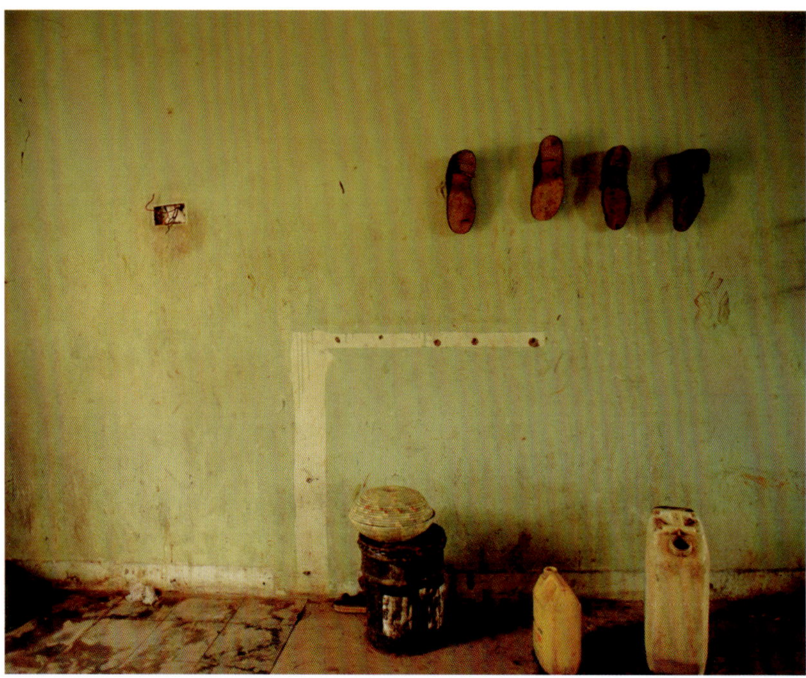

Figure 24.1. Zarina Bhimji, *Memories Were Trapped inside the Asphalt*, 1998–2003. Duratrans mounted on 6mm Diasec with foil. Light box: power-coated mild steel and aluminium, MDF, and LED light panel sheet with dimmer. 130 × 170 × 12.5 cm. © Zarina Bhimji. All rights reserved, DACS/Artimage 2022.

different register, Laylah Ali's disturbingly aggressive and ambiguous cartoon shapes zoom around with their beady, alien eyes fixed on random targets or line up, as victims, waiting passively for the devastating impact.

We see it, in a different measure, in the way the formal arrangement—the "logic of assembly"—of various works mysteriously echoes the way events shatter and disrupt the daily struggle for existence. Wael Shawky's work—reflecting the ambivalent effects of migration and global (so-called) modernization on the life and culture of the Cairo street—requires us to make this connection. As does Salem Mekuria's triptych video installation, in which the regimes of Ethiopian Orthodoxy and Marxism are caught in a repeating circle: systems obliged to echo and confront one another across time and space, made to answer to the breakdown of the "grand narratives" of past and present in that troubled country and to the chaotic lives which they have left behind. In their broken sequences, these works seem to refract the violent displacements which have visited the continent—the fragmentation of time and continuity, the dispersal of innocent and frightened civilians, the forced migrations, the ethnic cleansing, the privatization of war, the rebel gangs, the conscription of children, the "global" trade in arms and gems, the break-up or breakdown of known or settled communities and relationships—of family, group, home, tribe, nation, language, religion, cognitive and epistemological worlds.

In her book *Terra Infirma*, Irit Rogoff interrogates geography as a settled signifying system, placing people and identities in relation to place and territory. This "knowledge map," she argues, is now challenged by the "unhomed geographies" offered by many contemporary artists. Rogoff insists on the links between the experiential and the epistemological effects of this crisis between the "subjects' experiences of disruption and . . . [the] prevailing condition of disrupted knowledge orders . . . [a] crisis of the ability to represent any form of stable geographic knowledge as a set of guidelines regarding identity, belonging and rights."[6] The work of the *Fault Lines* artists is participating in such a "crisis" of representation.

The work is no longer produced out of a settled "geography" of postcolonial Africa any more than it is the product of the optimistic vision of a decolonizing Africa, fired by the dream of cultural revival and national reconstruction. This is the "new world order," the post–Cold War, post-apartheid, postcolonial world of globalization and debt, mass migration and civil war, famine and malnutrition. These landscapes are either shadowed by the threat of impending disaster or already scarred by its aftermath. We glimpse this crisis of representation almost joyously "at play" in the scratched surfaces, montaged interiors and broken compositional planes of Moshekwa Langa's work, with its overwritten, cryptic, often playful, disseminated effects, distributed according to some enigmatic logic of dispersal we cannot exactly fathom. As Gilane Tawadros puts it, the artists seem to be "tracing the fault lines that are shaping contemporary experience locally and globally," whose reverberations "echo through contemporary lived experience."[7]

"In geographical terms," Tawadros argues, "fault lines reveal themselves as fractures in the earth's surface but they also mark a break in the continuity of the strata. Fault lines may be a sign of significant shifts or even of impending disaster, but they also create new landscapes."[8] The metaphor provides a novel and challenging frame through which to interrogate the postcolonial and geopolitical situation of the work of contemporary African artists. When fault lines open up, they disrupt, break up, fragment. They *dis*place and *re*place.

Villages become a war zone. The homed become *unhomed*, and then simply the homeless—the *sans papiers*, the ones on the move, without documents, the multitudes: dispersal without the promise of return, unending exodus.

Of course, fault lines, like other relations of power (as Michel Foucault would remind us) are also *productive*. Those escaping the vertical lines of force forge new lateral connections. New formations appear where older ones disappear beneath the sand. Borders, which divide, become sites of surreptitious crossing. Separate and inviolable worlds meet and collide. Where only the pure, the orthodox, were valorized, a new universe of vernaculars and creole forms comes into existence. Multiple logics of identification and translation operate. Everything becomes what Edward Said calls "contrapuntal"—"this plurality of vision gives rise to an awareness of simultaneous dimensions . . . habits of life, expression, or activity in the new environment inevitably occur against the memory of these things in another environment."[9] Obliged to travel these transcultural circuits, Spinoza's new multitudes of the displaced— economic migrants, refugees, illegal aliens and asylum seekers, the fall-out from extreme situations of displacement and exclusion everywhere—are also, paradoxically, its advance party, its *avant-garde*. Marginality is both unliveable *and* a productive space. The dispossessed disappear from view into the black holes of the migrant metropolis, only to reappear, permanently at risk, but also contingently hybridized, like the transgendered and transsexual migrants from Algeria in Kader Attia's work, who have found an illegal refuge in Paris. More and more, we depend on writers, artists, film-makers, musicians and video-makers to map this emergent cartography, to report on its shifting outlines, and to bring us accounts from its dangerous interior depths: contrapuntal figures "whose writing travels across temporal, cultural and ideological boundaries in unforeseen ways to emerge as part of a new ensemble *along with* later history and subsequent art."[10]

We need to think further about the deeply contradictory effects of the postcolonial maelstrom in Africa, and its global and geoeconomic entanglements, which form the context for this body of work—the shifting tectonic plates, if you like, *below* the surface, which are producing these fracturing effects. Fault lines, Tawadros observes, "have been etched into the physical fabric of our world"—and, we can add, into its mental landscapes, its social and material relationships, its frame of seeing—"through the effects of colonialism and post-colonialism, of migration and globalization."[11] Can we move from this surface topography of implosion, emergence and emergency to the deeper structures of tectonic upheaval without imposing on the work of art some simple message, some "deeper causation," some arbitrary or reductively referential logic?

Colonialism is, in many ways, an old story in Africa, its aftermath long and protracted. The direct colonization of Africa is largely a nineteenth-century affair. Its brutal impact culminates with the "high noon" of European imperialism between the 1870s and the First World War when, in a "scramble for Africa," the imperial powers participated in the massive carve-up of the continent. The pattern laid down then—the opening up and exploitation of the vast, productive land and its natural resources, raw materials, precious minerals, cheap labor and open markets to the advantage of the industrially developed imperial powers—provided the basic template which has shaped much of Africa ever since. Between 1880 and 1914, "about a quarter of the world's land surface was distributed or redistributed as colonies among a half-dozen states. This represented the climax of the creation of a single global economy, progressively reaching into the most remote corners of the world, an increasingly dense web of economic transactions, communications and movements of goods, money and people linking the developed countries with each other and with the undeveloped world."[12]

In this period, the empires continued to expand, even if more often under the banner of indirect rule, protectorates, "spheres of influence," white settlement and the dreaded mandate than by overt colonization.[13] One historian described these intermediary forms of empire as "the crudity of conquest draped in the veil of morality."[14] Many conflict situations which have returned to trouble the world today arise from these later imperial conquests, accretions and settlements—now, of course, largely forgotten. Many recent conflicts in North and sub-Saharan Africa had their origins here.

Africa, then, was shaped from the beginning by a certain kind of globalization. That contemporary catchword needs to be contextualized as a historical process, *à longue durée*. In fact, if the age of European exploration and conquest at the end of the fifteenth century was the first, tentative, movement towards globalization (i.e. what Marx identified as Europe's first steps in the creation of a world market), then naval and trade supremacy was the second, and colonization, in which trading enclaves were consolidated into colonial possessions and a system of colonial governance, was the third such phase. The late nineteenth-century imperial carve-up constitutes the fourth phase; the inter-war (1918–45) period the fifth; and the collapse of empires, decolonization and the new postcolonial nations after the Second World War constitutes the sixth phase of the process. The Cold

War, when conflicts indigenous to Africa were subordinated to the wider geopolitical and military polarization between the two rival models of development, was the seventh. The period we are now in, from the mid-1970s onwards—with its global interdependencies, massive financial investment, technological flows and trans-national production, climaxing with the era of neo-liberal globalization and American superpower hegemony—is at least the eighth phase of globalization, understood as a historical process. A careful periodization could unearth more, although this does not undermine the specific features and distinctions of each phase. The basic point, however, is that, in Africa, and for a very long time, everything has depended on the different ways in which its complex internal histories and regional ecologies have been articulated (one might say, *dis*-articulated) with the changing forms of global capital and imperial rule.

Colonization, then, was driven by the imperatives and conveniences of imperial interests and colonial governance. Effectively, it erased layer after layer of earlier African historical evolution and its complex cultural formations. It superimposed imperial frontiers, territorial boundaries and Western political institutions on countries arbitrarily defined as colonies, with little reference to their mosaic of tribes, groups, languages and religions, to their intricate histories of conflict and alliances, to their ethnic traditions, ecological regions and land tenures. The anti-imperialist movements which came together after the First World War constitute a unifying cause that fed directly off the growing opposition to this process and drew inspiration from the dream of national restitution, often including the nativist revival of precolonial traditions. However, it was *nationalism* which underpinned the different kinds of independence struggle and provided the basis of the postcolonial nations which emerged.

In recent years, many commentators have come to regard nationalism as a negative force. However, as Edward Said has argued, nationalism, "as a mobilized political force, instigated and then advanced the struggle against Western domination everywhere in the non-European world. It is no more useful to oppose than to oppose Newton's discovery of gravity."[15] In a similar vein, Partha Chatterjee observes that "nationalism challenged colonial rule . . . administered a check on a specific form of metropolitan capital dominance. In the process, it dealt a death blow to such blatantly ethnic slogans of dominance as the colonizing mission of the West, the white man's burden, etc."[16]

Nationalism was also a powerfully creative force. It inspired artists, writers, scholars, architects, scientists and critics as well as mobilizing the masses. One thinks here of the work of Hassan Fathy, and his project of "an

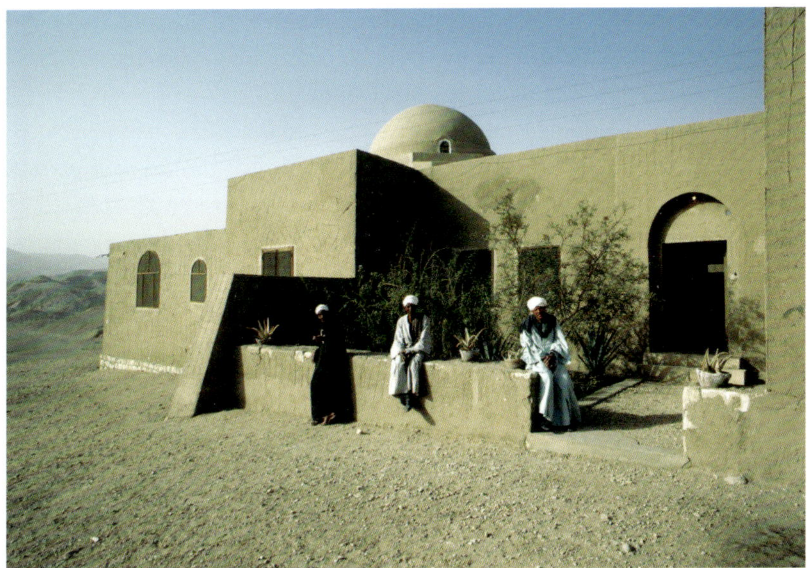

Figure 24.2. Hassan Fathy, Stopplaere House, Luxor, Egypt. © Aga Khan Trust for Culture/Christopher Little (photographer).

architecture for the people," revived in the context of the *Fault Lines* exhibition. Fathy was clearly inspired by the search for some creative synthesis between traditional (especially domestic) Islamic architecture and architectural modernism. His practice and ideas were deeply grounded in Egyptian secular nationalist aspirations and the break with colonial dependency; and, as Nasser Rabbat points out, the evolution of his work "mirrors the trajectory of modern Egypt" from "colonization to independence to development and its aftermath entangled in grand dreams of regional pre-eminence."[17] It is difficult to overestimate the surge of national feeling, for example, which accompanied the emergence of Abdel-Nasser in Egypt.

For the latest instalment of this story, however, we have to progress from the utopia of Fathy's urban vision to the shadowing of the stalled project of contemporary Egypt in the dystopian viscosity of Wael Shawky's asphalt and petroleum metropolis (fig. 24.2). The nationalist project had serious limitations. There was always a tension between its modernizing and nativist impulses which remains unresolved. Chatterjee highlights nationalism's failure to resolve the conflict between the idea of the "people-nation" and metropolitan capital: "by absorbing the political life of the nation into the body of the state . . . the state proceeds to find for 'the nation' a place in the global order of capital, while striving to keep the contradictions between capital and the people in perpetual suspension."[18]

The problem, as Frantz Fanon clearly foresaw, was not nationalism as such; he believed the Algerian liberation struggle demanded a moment of "national consciousness." The danger was that the project would get stuck there and fail to "go beyond nationalism" to the deeper social, cultural and political transformations which were its essential tasks. In such circumstances, Fanon predicted, nationalism could undergo "a process of regression," in which "the nation is passed over for the race, and the tribe is preferred to the state."[19] Early anti-imperial and independence leaderships, like those of Nkrumah, Nyerere, Cabral, Mandela, the ANC (African National Congress) and the FLN (Front de Libération Nationale), had projected a powerful vision for the postcolonial era. However, in "The Pitfalls of National Consciousness," Fanon foresaw post-independence leaderships "colonizing" the nationalist struggle for their own interests. This elite, he suggested, could become "the transmission belt between the nation and . . . capitalism" and the main beneficiaries would be the rising middle classes—the new postcolonial native elites—whom Fanon regarded as a "national bourgeoisie." The result, he prophesied, would be the neglect of the countryside, a yawning gap between leaders and people, "the greatest wealth surrounded by the greatest poverty," where "scandals are numerous, members of parliament feather their own nests," and everyone is invited to join "the great procession of corruption."[20] Moataz Nasr's video installation in *Fault Lines* directly addresses this issue of the gap between politicians and the people in post-nationalist Egypt.

In the degeneration which Fanon predicted, the people would increasingly be regarded "as a blind force . . . held in check either by mystification or by the fear inspired by the police force." The principal agent of this process would be the single political party or "one party state" or a populist figure, dictator or military man, providing "the direction of affairs by a strong authority," which underdeveloped countries were increasingly said to require. Leader, nation, party and people would be absorbed into a single political will, allowing no space for new social forces, real opposition or genuine democratic contestation. Oppositions would be intimidated, critics imprisoned on trumped-up charges, "brought to heel . . . by dint of baton charges . . . condemned first to silence and then to clandestine existence."[21]

This was a grim forecast, which may now seem overdrawn and too pessimistic. It was also not a comprehensive picture; it omitted religion, the

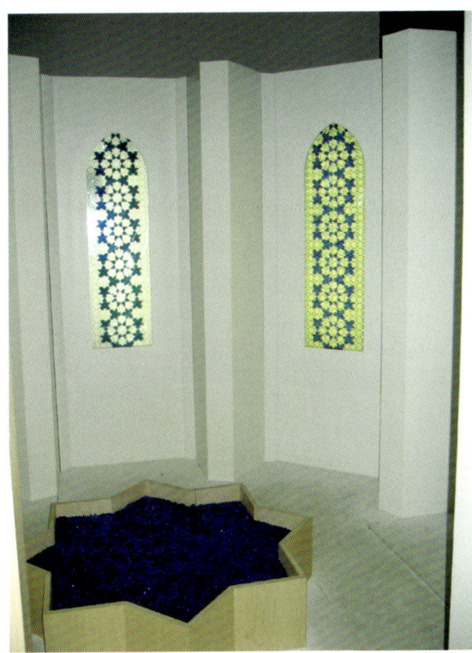

Figure 24.3. Samta Benyahia, *Le Polygone et Le Dédale* (The Polygon and the Maze), 2003. Installation view, Venice Biennale, 2003. © Samta Benyahia. Courtesy of the artist.

radicalization of Islam and religious fundamentalism which were decisive in derailing the nationalist project in Algeria. Samta Benyahia's architectural installation in *Fault Lines* (fig. 24.3), which looks beyond the political violence that has torn Algeria apart, to a utopian space in which past and present do not always destroy one another, was conceived in response to this trauma. However, in other respects, Fanon's dystopic vision has proved disturbingly prescient about many aspects of the "crisis of the postcolonial state" or "post-colony" which has overtaken one African society after another since decolonization. Without significant social or economic reform, many African postcolonial states have failed to redistribute national resources, improve living standards or raise the prospects of the mass of ordinary people. They have been unable to improve subsistence levels, develop sustainable agriculture, or stabilize the price of raw materials on world markets and their populations are regularly exposed to endemic poverty, malnutrition, ill-health and disease. Millions are without food, education or clean water. Their people have little medical protection against the pandemics—malaria, TB, HIV/AIDS etc—that rampage through the continent. A nationalism which cannot deliver to the mass of ordinary people, or project social aspirations and cultural self-images which connect with an indigenous imaginary, has proved incapable of holding the nation together and has increasingly lost its grip on popular hopes and aspirations.

Consequently, in many parts of Africa, internal tensions and conflicts have surfaced, unleashing powerfully fissiparous and disintegrative tendencies in the form of rural/urban, regional, ethnic, tribal, racial and religious conflict. In state after state, the army has become the "unifying" agent of last resort. Dictators have flourished, elections have been rigged, conflict "ethnicized" and social fragmentation "militarized." Torture and imprisonment have become recognized instruments of governance. Weak governments are challenged by military coups, armed rivals for state power, insurgent regional breakaways, lawless militias, invading foreign armies. Increasingly, this crisis of the postcolonial state in Africa has assumed the form of civil unrest, tribal warfare, ethnic cleansing and the killing fields of civil war. The work of Pitso Chinzima and Veliswa Gwintsa, of Salem Mekuria and of Laylah Ali all speak eloquently if obliquely to these developments.

The inevitable effect has been the mass displacement of peoples—the homeless multitudes on the move, the burgeoning temporary "geography" of refugee and transit camps, the flight from impending violence and lawlessness, abandoning homes, families, cattle and land. A host of outside forces have a hand in this crisis—the old colonizing powers, foreign investors and banks, the international arms trade, "development" agencies, NGOs (non-governmental organizations), aid and humanitarian programs.

This is the profoundly contradictory ground of *the postcolonial*, to which the work of the *Fault Lines* artists manifestly belongs. The term "postcolonial" signals, at one and the same time, the continuing hope that real freedom, popular democracy and economic change may one day come to Africa despite its present travail *and* the recognition of the "states of emergency" into which many parts of the continent have been propelled. Certainly it references a temporal process: postcolonial = what followed after colonialism. But, as I have tried to suggest, this cannot mean that colonialism and its effects are *finished*, in the wider sense of "completed and settled." "After" also means "in the aftermath" of colonialism—caught in its wake, exposed to its after-effects, which continue in significantly transformed ways. We must think of the emergence of the postcolonial as a *passage of forms*, rather than the mere passing of time.

The postcolonial therefore marks out, not the successful conclusion of the colonial order, but the opening of a new stage in the relationships of postcolonial dependency. We find "the persistence of many of the effects associated with colonization, but at the same time their *displacement* from the colonizer/colonized axis and their [projection inwards or] *internalization* within de-colonized society itself."[22] External problems of colonial domination are now reworked and lived as internal crises of the postcolonial state. At the same time, the relations of dependency become more global. Conflicts which at an earlier point could be staged as a struggle between the emergent "people-nation" and the external colonizer are replaced by a more complex set of struggles between weak "independent" states, the different forces struggling for ascendancy *within* postcolonial society, and the connections of this whole complex to the neo-liberal global capitalist system and the geopolitical, US-dominated "new world order." An example here is the war of liberation led by the Algerian FLN against the French. After independence, this became a more complex struggle between social, national, secular and Islamist forces within Algeria, further complicated by a shift in Algeria's continuing postcolonial relationships with France (e.g., the problem of North African migrants, the "differential racism" experienced by this diaspora and the rise of an anti-immigrant racist politics). Now also the political crisis of the Algerian state and of the French Algerian metropolitan diaspora is reworked through the new geopolitics dominated by a post–11 September, US-led "global war on terror." In this scenario, "the colonial" is not yet dead, since it lives on in its neo-imperial, postcolonial and globalized forms and after-effects.

This rightly shifts the focus in the crisis of the postcolonial from the shortcomings of the independence movements and the contradictions of nationalism to the larger question of the continuing relations of *dependency* which link postcolonial Africa to the developed world. We can identify at least three stages. First, neo-colonialism, locking dependency to underdevelopment in ways identified by the dependency theorists. Second, the Cold War, when Africa's complex internal crises became subordinated to the East-West struggle, its governments became "clients" of the superpowers and intercontinental rivalries were fought out by proxy on African terrain. Third, in more recent times, the era of neo-liberalism and globalization, which has redefined the relations of subordination between African societies and the global capitalist and geopolitical system as a whole. These articulations set the framework for the so-called failure of the post-colony in Africa.

This most recent phase of globalization is the free market, neo-liberal system of worldwide interdependencies and global flows which began to emerge in the mid-1970s. At its heart are the new multinational corporations, set free from national boundaries and constraints, with their transnational systems of production, directly linking the capital interests of the "North" to the cheap labor reserves and favorable investment regimes of the "South."[23] This is underpinned by the massively enhanced financial and investment flows, powered by the information technology revolution and the spreading net of global consumption sponsored by global media and the cultural industries, promoting the gospel of Western lifestyles among poor and hungry communities. These linkages and space-time condensations rework the profound gaps between rich/developed and poor/developing countries into a highly uneven and unequal but more globally integrated and interdependent "world system."

Some developing societies—the "Tigers" of South-East Asia, for example—have managed to ride the globalization tide with some success. But they had a larger manufacturing and trade base to start from and greater reserves of indigenous capital to partner foreign investment. Besides, their development has depended upon a massive state intervention, often without replicating much of the political infrastructure of democratic elections, rule of law, free speech and human rights conditions which successful free markets are supposed to require. Africa, with its overwhelmingly rural background, has not been so lucky.

The new system does not follow the old lines of colonial connection. The globe has become an open, borderless market. The transnational corporations and their financial supporters can influence the shape of development simply by their power in world markets, their capacity to switch funds globally to wherever the most favorable terms-of-trade conditions prevail, as well as by buying directly into productive enterprises or setting up branches of productive activity locally and integrating them globally. In Africa, their principal effect has been to stimulate large-scale agricultural and cash-crop productions, at the expense of subsistence agriculture which feeds people and sustains incomes and local employment. Also, the large-scale extraction of raw materials for export is at the mercy of world commodity prices, which have been systematically falling as the foreign extraction companies are able to scour world markets for the lowest prices. Western agri-businesses are free to push open aggressively foreign markets at the expense of indigenous production and to dump surpluses which—counter to free trade gospel—are massively subsidized and sold below cost.[24] The transnationals manage rural economies at a distance by supplying high-cost fertilizers and by patenting plant and seed varieties and other genetic sequences which give them effective control over what and when local farmers can plant. They promote free-market criteria, at the expense of ecological sustainability. Famine in East Africa was used to introduce genetically modified food, against local demand. But the pharmaceutical companies continue to keep prices of "priceless" drugs high and tobacco companies dump the most carcinogenic cigarettes cheap on unsuspecting young smokers in urban Africa. The mining and raw material resources are extracted within fortified, high-wage enclaves and integrated into global markets, in whose profitability local elites may participate but from which governments derive little (and much of what they receive leaks away into private bank accounts or to the international illegal traders and arms merchants).

The central feature of this globalized system, however, is the way it has been coupled with or harnessed to the emerging structure of global governance and international "regulation" [*sic*]. The stage was set by the "structural adjustment" programs imposed by the International Monetary Fund (IMF) and the World Bank on one African government after another. The underlying purpose was to "shrink the role of the state and soften markets for private investors."[25] This strategy effectively ruled Africa, a continent in desperate need, out of the whole idea of a "social wage" (the funding of public health-care, education, food and other welfare and development programs out of taxation). It mercilessly promoted market fundamentalism at the expense of the notion of public goods.

Once restructured in this way, postcolonial states were deemed eligible for huge international bank loans, the effect of which, as we know, was to cripple them in massive debt. They were required to open their borders, to encourage foreign investment, to deregulate markets and labor conditions, to let market forces operate freely and to participate in free trade as if on a level playing field with their much wealthier, more powerful and already developed international competitors. Wealth, they were assured, would eventually trickle down. This was the full neo-liberal, free-market, fundamentalist program. The World Trade Organization (WTO), the IMF and the World Bank have been driving the latest phase of deregulation—the privatization of public utilities and services—which has vigorously promoted the sell-off of water, power and electricity, educational and health-care public services to private interests, especially foreign utility corporations, of which the infamous Enron was only one example. They then restrict supplies, raise charges and oblige local authorities to purchase these goods privately.

This is the heart of the new global capitalist system as it bears down on Africa. Its powerful driving centers continue to lie primarily in the developed Western societies. But it is no longer a simple North/South affair, since it includes new kinds of profitable arrangement or "contract" between private foreign capital and the growing business elites of the developing world. In this sense, it is a less "territorialized," more transnational affair, a world without fixed centers in the old spatialized sense because its sites of power and wealth are multiple and ultimately globally disseminated: what Hardt and Negri called a new kind of "empire."[26]

As the Cold War recedes and the US emerges as the single military and economic superpower, its dominant role, though of course globally based, becomes more manifest. A borderless world, in which the conditions of a free market, free trade, corporate-inclined system must be permanently secured, and its fruits unequally delivered, is increasingly a dangerous, restless, envious and fissiparous one, potentially fracturing violently along several fault lines at once. Its frontiers now lie on the banks of the Tigris, in the Bering Straits, on the Red Sea, in the Horn of Africa, at the tourist resorts of the Pacific and along the oil pipelines from Uzbekistan. Although the system ideally works without direct intervention—at a distance, through the hidden hand of the free market—since 11 September, a new interventionism has emerged. Founded on the absolute sanctity of Western interests and values, it is guided by the new doctrine of pre-emptive strikes and organized ideologically along the Manichean lines of "with us—or with the terrorists." Intervention is judged illegitimate, not only to deal with terrorist threats, to police the peripheries and destroy any opposition "by overwhelming force," but also to stabilize, long-term, whole regions of the globe: to precipitate regime-change where necessary; to reconstruct so-called "traditional" societies into Western-style "liberal democracies"; to secure key markets and raw material supplies; and, above all, to ensure the general conditions favorable to "peaceful" investment by international capital and the universal hegemony of Western values. The dream of a multipolar world, which the word "globalization" ambiguously carried, has disappeared. This is "the new world order," neo-liberal globalization's new *civilizational mission*.

What all this means for Africa—and for African art—we have still to see. But the anticipatory shockwaves of the crisis are already registered at some seismic levels in global culture. In Sabah Naim's film installations, for example, she intervenes directly in the image, scratching and scarring it to bring out the violent contemporary disjuncture between the global media and the minutiae of daily existence in the post-colony. In this and other ways, *Fault Lines* invites us not only to read the fractured lines and what they mean, but to read *between them*, for the intimations they offer of our uncertain futures.

This essay first appeared in *Fault Lines: Contemporary African Art and Shifting Landscapes*, ed. Gilane Tawadros and Sarah Campbell (London: Institute of International Visual Arts/Forum for African Arts/Prince Claus Fund, 2003), 31–42.

1 Okwui Enwezor and Olu Oguibe, eds., *Reading the Contemporary: African Art from Theory to the Marketplace* (London: INIVA; Cambridge, MA: MIT Press, 1999), 10.

2 As the introduction to the 1983 exhibition of Senegalese tapestries in New York, quoted in V. Y. Mudimbe, "Rependre," in *Reading the Contemporary: African Art from Theory to the Marketplace*, ed. Okwui Enwezor and Olu Oguibe (London: INIVA; Cambridge, MA: MIT Press, 1999), 37.

3 Clifford Charles, in his personal description of the *Painting on Water* submission.

4 Charles, personal description.

5 A Mercator projection (invented by Flemish cartographer Gerardus Mercator) is the standard Western projection of the globe, offering a very Eurocentric representation of it.

6 Irit Rogoff, *Terra Infirma* (London: Routledge, 2000), 2–3.

7 Gilane Tawadros, "Fault Lines: Contemporary African Art and Shifting Landscapes," press release, Institute of International Visual Arts, London, 2003.

8 Tawadros, "Fault Lines."

9 Edward Said, *Reflections on Exile and Other Essays* (Cambridge, MA: Harvard University Press, 2001), 186.

10 Edward Said, *Culture and Imperialism* (London: Vintage, 1994), 24.

11 Tawadros, "Fault Lines."

12 Eric Hobsbawm, *The Age of Empire* (London: Weidenfeld and Nicholson, 1987), 62.

13 The mandate was the "cover" under which Britain intervened in East Africa and connived with handing over Palestine to the Zionist Commission and sold the Palestinian Arabs down the river.

14 H. A. L. Fisher, *A History of Europe* (London: Fontana, 1960), quoted in Bernard Porter, *The Lion's Share* (London: Longman, 1996), 255.

15 Said, *Culture and Imperialism*, 263.

16 Partha Chatterjee, *Nationalist Thought and the Colonial World* (Minneapolis: University of Minnesota Press, 1993), 168.

17 See Nasser Rabbat, "Hassan Fathy and the Identity Debate," in *Fault Lines: Contemporary African Art and Shifting Landscapes*, ed. Gilane Tawadros and Sarah Campbell (London: Institute of International Visual Arts/Forum for African Arts/Prince Claus Fund, 2003), 196–203.

18 Chatterjee, *Nationalist Thought*, 168.

19 Frantz Fanon, "The Pitfalls of National Consciousness," in *The Wretched of the Earth* (New York: Grove, 1961), 121.

20 Fanon, "Pitfalls," 124.

21 Fanon, "Pitfalls," 121, 139.

22 Stuart Hall, "When Was the Post-colonial?," in *The Post-colonial Question*, ed. Iain Chambers and Lidia Curti (London: Routledge, 1996), 248–49.

23 The ten largest MNCs have a total income larger than that of a hundred of the poorest countries.

24 The 2002 US farm bill subsidized the big American agri-corporations by $248.6 billion.

25 Wayne Ellwood, "The Great Privatization Grab," *New Internationalist*, 1 April 2003, 10.

26 Michael Hardt and Antonio Negri, *Empire* (Cambridge, MA: Harvard University Press, 2000).

modernism (continued)

    liberalism and, 51; museums and, 270; nationalism and, 49; postcolonialism and, 94, 192; postmodernism and, 311, 312–13; primitivism and, 188, 278, 295; universalism and, 51

Monk, Thelonius, 292

Moody, Ronald, 155, 278, 288, *289*

Morris, Dennis, 223–24, *224, 225, 226,* 228, *229*–30, *232, 233, 234*–45

Moss Side, 299

motherhood, 86, 91–92

Mouffe, Chantal, 46

multiculturalism, 26, 51, 70, 275, 276, 331

Mulvey, Laura, 55

museums, 270, 310, 317, 320–21

music, 84, 99, 105, 234, 281. *See also* dancehall; jazz; reggae; soul music

Myrie, Vanessa, 33

Naim, Sabah, 364

Naipaul, V. S., 186, 290

Nandy, Ashis, 277

Nash, Mark, 10, 33

Nasr, Moataz, 358

national identity, 50, 79, 94

nationalism, 26, 44, 49–51, 127, 292, 356–58

nation language, 105, 141–42, *143*

nation-states, 48–49

Negritude, 94, 120, 127–28

neo-colonialism, 361

neoliberalism, 42, 45, 46, 47, 194, 302, 361

New Left Review (NLR) (journal), 2, 3

New Reasoner, The (journal), 2

New World presence. See *présence americaine*

Niati, Houria, 194, 297

NLR. See *New Left Review*

Nonyela, Valentine, *78*

Norris, Christopher, 100

Nyaya-Vaisesika, 328

Oedipus complex, 126

Ofili, Chris, 15, 156, 341–48, *342, 343, 344*

Oguibe, Olu, 349–50

Oiticica, Hélio, 292

Olden, Mark, 229

Orientalism, 188, 295

Orozco, José Clemente, 294

othering, 26, 115–17, 215

Ové, Horace, 193, 295

Padmore, George, 279

painting, pastel, and print-making: 19th century, 151–53, *153*; 1960s, *318*; 1970s, *184*, 266, 293, 296; 1980s, *159*, 266, 293, *294, 300, 319*; 1990s, *221*; 2000s, *156, 342, 343, 344*. *See also* black artists and art

Pan-Africanism, 163, 193, 258, 298

Pan-Afrikan Connection, 156, 182

Parker, Charlie, 292

Parry, Benita, 128

particularism, 51

Partisan (coffeehouse), 3

Parvez, Ahmed, 183, 189, 288, 295

Patterson, Colin, *87, 88*

Peri, Peter, 3

Peries, Ivan, 183, 288

Phillips, Mike, 229

Phillips, Trevor, 229

photography, 7, 213, 214; 1960s, *iii*, 95, *95*, 244; 1970s, 96, 204, *205*, 224, 224–25, 225, 226, 228–35, 266; 1980s, 7, *32, 160, 177*, 203–10, *216*, 220, 266, 299; 1990s, 57–58, *58, 112*, 158, *168, 207*, 211–12, *219, 221, 352*; 2000s, 58–61, *59, 352*; 2010s, *34*; blackness and, 208–9; bodies and, 219–22; cultural studies and, 205–8; documentary photography, 95, 204–05, 218, 223–32, 243–47; history and, 239–40; identity and, 53–54; modernism and, 218; portraits, *iii*, 158, *160*, 242–43, 300; urban dystopia

Prologue: "Subjects in History: Making Diasporic Identities," in *The House That Race Built*, ed. Wahneema Lubiano (New York: Vintage, 1998), 289–300.

Chapter 1: "Isaac Julien's Workshop," in *Isaac Julien: Riot* (New York: Museum of Modern Art, 2013), 222–31.

Chapter 2: "Democracy, Globalization, and Difference," in *Democracy Unrealized: Documenta 11, Platform 1*, ed. Okwui Enwezor et al. (Ostfildern-Ruit: Hatje Cantz, 2001), 21–36.

Chapter 3: "The Way We Live Now," in Mitra Tabrizian, *Beyond the Limits* (Gottingen: Steidl, 2004), 1–6.

Chapter 4: "New Ethnicities," in *Black Film, British Cinema*, ICA Document 7, ed. Kobena Mercer (London: Institute of Contemporary Arts, 1988), 27–31.

Chapter 5: "Threatening Pleasures: A Discussion," in *Sight and Sound*, n.s. 1, no. 4 (August 1991): 17–19.

Chapter 6: "A Rage in Harlesden," in *Sight and Sound*, n.s. 8, no. 9 (September 1998): 24–26.

Chapter 7: "Cultural Identity and Cinematic Representation," in *Exiles: Essays on Caribbean Cinema*, ed. Mbye Cham (London: Africa World Press, 1992), 220–36.

Chapter 8: "The After-Life of Frantz Fanon: Why Fanon? Why Now? Why *Black Skin, White Masks?*," in *The Fact of Blackness: Frantz Fanon and Visual Representation*, ed. Alan Read (London: Institute of Contemporary Arts; Seattle: Bay Press, 1996), 12–37.

Chapter 9: "*Créolité* and the Process of Creolization," in *Créolité and Creolization: Documenta 11, Platform 3*, ed. Okwui Enwezor et al. (Ostfildem-Ruit: Hatje Cantz, 2003), 27–42.

Chapter 10: "Legacies of Anglo-Caribbean Culture: A Diasporic Perspective," in *Art and Emancipation in Jamaica: Isaac Mendes Belisario and His Worlds*, ed. Tim Barringer, Gillian Forrester, and Barbaro Martinez Ruiz (New Haven, CT: Yale University Press, 2007), 179–95.

Chapter 11: "Minimal Selves," *Identity: The Real Me*, ICA Document 6, ed. Lisa Appignanesi (London: ICA, 1988), 44–46.

Chapter 12: "Assembling the 1980s: The Deluge—and After," in *Shades of Black: Assembling Black Arts in 1980s Britain*, ed. David A. Bailey, Ian Baucom, and Sonia Boyce (Durham, NC: Duke University Press; London: Institute of International Visual Arts, 2005), 1–20.

Chapter 13: "The Vertigo of Displacement: Shifts within Black Documentary Practices," "Critical Decade: Black British Photography in the 80s," ed. Stuart Hall and David A. Bailey, special issue, *Ten.8* 2, no. 3 (1992): 14–23.

Chapter 14: "Preface to *Different*," in Stuart Hall and Mark Sealy, *Different* (London: Phaidon, 2001), 34–39.

Chapter 15: "'Speak Easy': Black in the '70s," introduction to Dennis Morris, *Growing Up Black in the 1970s* (London: Autograph, 2012), 4–7.

Chapter 16: "Reconstruction Work: Images of Post-war Black Settlement," *Ten.8*, no. 16 (1984): 2–9.

Chapter 17: "The 'West Indian' Front Room," in *The Front Room: Migrant Aesthetics in the Home*, ed. Michael McMillan (London: Black Dog, 2009), 16–23.

Chapter 18: "Constituting an Archive," *Third Text* 15, no. 54 (2001): 89–92.

Chapter 19: "Whose Heritage? Unsettling 'The Heritage,' Reimagining the Post-Nation, in *Third Text* 13, no. 49 (Winter 1999–2000): 3–13.

Chapter 20: "Modernity and Its Others: Three 'Moments' in the Post-war History of the Black Diaspora Arts," in *History Workshop Journal* 61, no. 1 (Spring 2006): 1–24.

Chapter 21: "Museums of Modern Art and the End of History," in *Stuart Hall and Sarat Maharaj: Modernity and Difference*, Annotations 6, ed. Gilane Tawadros and Sarah Campbell (London: Institute of International Visual Arts, 2001), 8–25.

Chapter 22: "Modernity and Difference: A Conversation between Stuart Hall and Sarat Maharaj," in *Changing States: Contemporary Art and Ideas in an Era of Globalization*, ed. Gilane Tawadros (London: Institute of International Visual Arts, 2004), 286–91.

Chapter 23: "Chris Ofili in Paradise: Dreaming in Afro," in Chris Ofili, *Within Reach: British Pavilion, 50th Venice Biennale: 15 June to 2 November 2003*, vol. 1, *Words* (London: Victoria Miro Gallery, 2003), unpaged.

Chapter 24: "Maps of Emergency: Fault Lines and Tectonic Plates," in *Fault Lines: Contemporary African Art and Shifting Landscapes*, ed. Gilane Tawadros and Sarah Campbell (London: Institute of International Visual Arts/Forum for African Arts/Prince Claus Fund, 2003), 31–42.